MARITIME RYUKYU, 1050–1650

MARITIME RYUKYU, 1050–1650

GREGORY SMITS

University of Hawai'i Press
Honolulu

© 2019 University of Hawai'i Press
All rights reserved
Paperback edition 2020

Printed in the United States of America
25 24 23 22 21 20   6 5 4 3 2 1

Library of Congress Cataloging-in-Publication Data
Names: Smits, Gregory, author.
Title: Maritime Ryukyu, 1050–1650 / Gregory Smits.
Description: Honolulu : University of Hawai'i Press, [2019] | Includes
    bibliographical references and index.
Identifiers: LCCN 2018006251 | ISBN 9780824873370 (cloth : alk. paper)
Subjects: LCSH: Ryukyu Islands—History—To 1879. | Ryukyu Islands—Politics
    and government. | Pirates—East Asia.
Classification: LCC DS895.R97 S65 2019 | DDC 952/.2902—dc23
LC record available at https://lccn.loc.gov/2018006251

ISBN 978-0-8248-8427-7 (pbk.)

University of Hawai'i Press books are printed on acid-free
paper and meet the guidelines for permanence and
durability of the Council on Library Resources.

Cover image: Map showing the East China Sea network (in white) extending in an arc
from the Korean peninsula, through western coastal areas of Japan, and down through
the islands south of Kyushu to the coast of China. Map by Jeff Smits.

Dedicated to Peter Nosco

Contents

Acknowledgments ix
Abbreviations and Conventions xi
Introduction 1

PART I Ryukyu's Network, 1050–1470
    Chapter 1: Ryukyu in the East China Sea Network 15
    Chapter 2: *Wakō* and the Ryukyu Islands 36
    Chapter 3: A State for Trade Purposes 60
    Chapter 4: The Enigma of the Three Principalities 77
    Chapter 5: Geographies of Power 90

PART II Dynastic Turbulence, 1400–1600
    Chapter 6: The First Shō Dynasty 107
    Chapter 7: Seizures, Erasures, and Resurgences 122
    Chapter 8: The Second Shō Dynasty's Challenges 134
    Chapter 9: Assembling a Royal Line 148

PART III *Wakō* to Kings, 1477–1556
    Chapter 10: Centering Shuri and Forging an Empire 161
    Chapter 11: The Ryukyu Empire 178
    Chapter 12: Politics and Religion 193

PART IV The New Order, 1550–1650
    Chapter 13: A Changing World and the Road to War 205
    Chapter 14: The War 224

Chapter 15: Aftermath   235
Chapter 16: Many Ryukyus   245

Notes 255
Bibliography 281
Index 293

Acknowledgments

It is my pleasure to acknowledge those who have made this book possible and those who have made it better. The book would not have been possible without the hard work of the interlibrary loan staff at Penn State University keeping me supplied with sources. No matter how obscure the item, the ILL staff almost always obtained it. Takeishi Kazumi, proprietor of Yōju shorin and extraordinary promoter of Ryukyuan studies, supplied the few items that ILL could not. I also thank Josef Kreiner, Watanabe Miki, Maeda Shūko, Takara Kurayoshi, Tomiyama Kazuyuki, and Takagi Fumi for sending me valuable materials over the years that have contributed to the book. My brother Jeff, proprietor of Cherokee Drafting Specialists, produced all the map figures.

The book has also benefited from the efforts of three dedicated readers. Two anonymous readers for University of Hawai'i Press provided detailed comments and criticism, many of which I was able to implement during the revision process. I truly appreciate the time and effort they contributed to this project. Leon Serafim contributed his vast knowledge of Ryukyuan linguistics, the *Omoro sōshi*, and Ryukyuan culture in general, providing detailed comments and criticism on the entire manuscript. He provided invaluable assistance in interpreting difficult *Omoro* passages, removing weak linguistic evidence, rooting out miscellaneous errors and inconsistencies, and refining several key arguments. Thank you, Leon, for your generous assistance. I have learned much from working with you. Needless to say, any shortcomings that remain are entirely mine.

It has been a pleasure working with acquisitions editor Stephanie Chun of the University of Hawai'i Press and her staff. Likewise, it has been a pleasure working with managing editor Cheryl Loe and copy editor Barbara Folsom.

Behind the scenes, the administration at Penn State has always supported my academic work. In particular, I would like to thank Susan Welch, Michael Kulikowski, Bill Blair, and On-cho Ng for their support while I was writing this book.

This book is dedicated to Peter Nosco, under whose supervision I wrote a long dissertation about early modern Ryukyu more than twenty-five years ago. Thank you, Peter, for your help then and for your support over the years. I would also like to thank phonologist Timothy Vance, my first formal teacher of Japanese.

Finally, I thank my wife, Akiko, for her tireless support of my academic work, even during phases when it occupied most of my waking hours. Thanks, too, to my network of old-time Appalachian music friends for their good music and good company.

Abbreviations and Conventions

Account of East Sea Countries

Sin Sukju's 1471 *Haedong jegukgi* 海東諸国紀, translated by Tanaka Takeo as *Kaitō shokokuki: Chōsenjin no mita chūsei no Nihon to Ryūkyū*. Citations are to page numbers.

Genealogy of Chūzan

The 1725 Sai On version of *Chūzan seifu* 中山世譜 in Yokoyama Shigeru, ed., *Ryūkyū shiryō sōsho*, vol. 4. Citations are to page numbers.

Joseon Veritable Royal Records

Refers to *Joseon wangjo sillok* 朝鮮王朝実録 as compiled and rendered into *yomikudashibun* (the traditional method of transcribing classical Chinese into a type of literary Japanese) by Ikeya Machiko, Uchida Akiko, and Takase Kyōko, *Chōsen ōchō jitsuroku Ryūkyū shiryō shūsei*. 2 vols. Citations take the form: (entry no. [Gregorian year], [vol.] 1: [p. no.]/[vol.] 2: [p. no.]).

Kyūyō

The 1745 official history *Kyūyō* 球陽. Citations are to specific article numbers from Kyūyō kenkyūkai, ed., *Kyūyō, yomikudashi hen*. 2 vols. plus a supplement.

Ming Veritable Records

Míng shílù 明実録 as compiled by Wada Hisanori et al. as *"Min jitsuroku" no Ryūkyū shiryō*. 3 vols. Citations take the form: [vol. no., p. no.] ([entry no./reign year.month.day]).

Omoro sōshi おもろさうし

A collection of Ryukyuan songs totaling 22 volumes and 1553 entries. Citations are to song numbers and take the form: *Omoro sōshi*, no.___. My base text is Hokama and Saigō, *Omoro sōshi*.

Origins of Ryukyu

The 1713 *Ryūkyūkoku yuraiki* 琉球国由来記 as found in Yokoyama Shigeru, ed., *Ryūkyū shiryō sōsho*, vols. 1–2. Citations are to page numbers.

Reflections on Chūzan

Shō Shōken's 1650 *Chūzan seikan* 中山世鑑, in Yokoyama Shigeru, ed., *Ryūkyū shiryō sōsho*, vol. 5. Citations are to page numbers.

Rekidai hōan

Wada Hisanori, *Rekidai hōan yakuchūbon* 歴代宝案訳注本. Citations are to pages in physical volumes. Following the page numbers, I include the traditional citation system of three numbers separated by dashes.

Ryukyu Monument Inscriptions

Volume 1 of Tsukada Seisaku's *Ryūkyūkoku hibunki*. 琉球国碑文記. Citations are to page numbers.

Ryukyu Record

Investiture envoy Chén Kǎn's 1534 *Shǐ Liúqiú lù* 使琉球録, translated by Harada Nobuo as *Shi-Ryūkyū roku*. Citations are to page numbers.

Ryūkyū shintōki

Taichū's 1605 *Ryūkyū Shintōki* 琉球神道記, translated by Ginoza Shigō as *Zenyaku Ryūkyū shintōki*. Citations are to page numbers.

Given the topic of this book, many names have multiple possible pronunciations, and listing even a few of them would quickly become cumbersome. My policy is to use what I regard as the most common or conventional pronunciation, listing one common alternative in parentheses if appropriate. If necessary for clarity, I employ the abbreviations J., C., K., and O., for Japanese, Chinese, Korean, and Okinawan respectively. Except for the commonplace names Beijing, Nanjing, and Fujian, all Chinese names and terms include (modern) tone marks. Korean words appear in the Revised Romanization system.

Dates more specific than the year appear as "[Gregorian year].[lunar month].[day]." Therefore 1609.4.2 means "second day of the fourth lunar month, 1609," not April 2.

The titles of all Chinese government posts and officials follows Charles O. Hucker, *A Dictionary of Official Titles in Imperial China* (Stanford, CA: Stanford University Press, 1985).

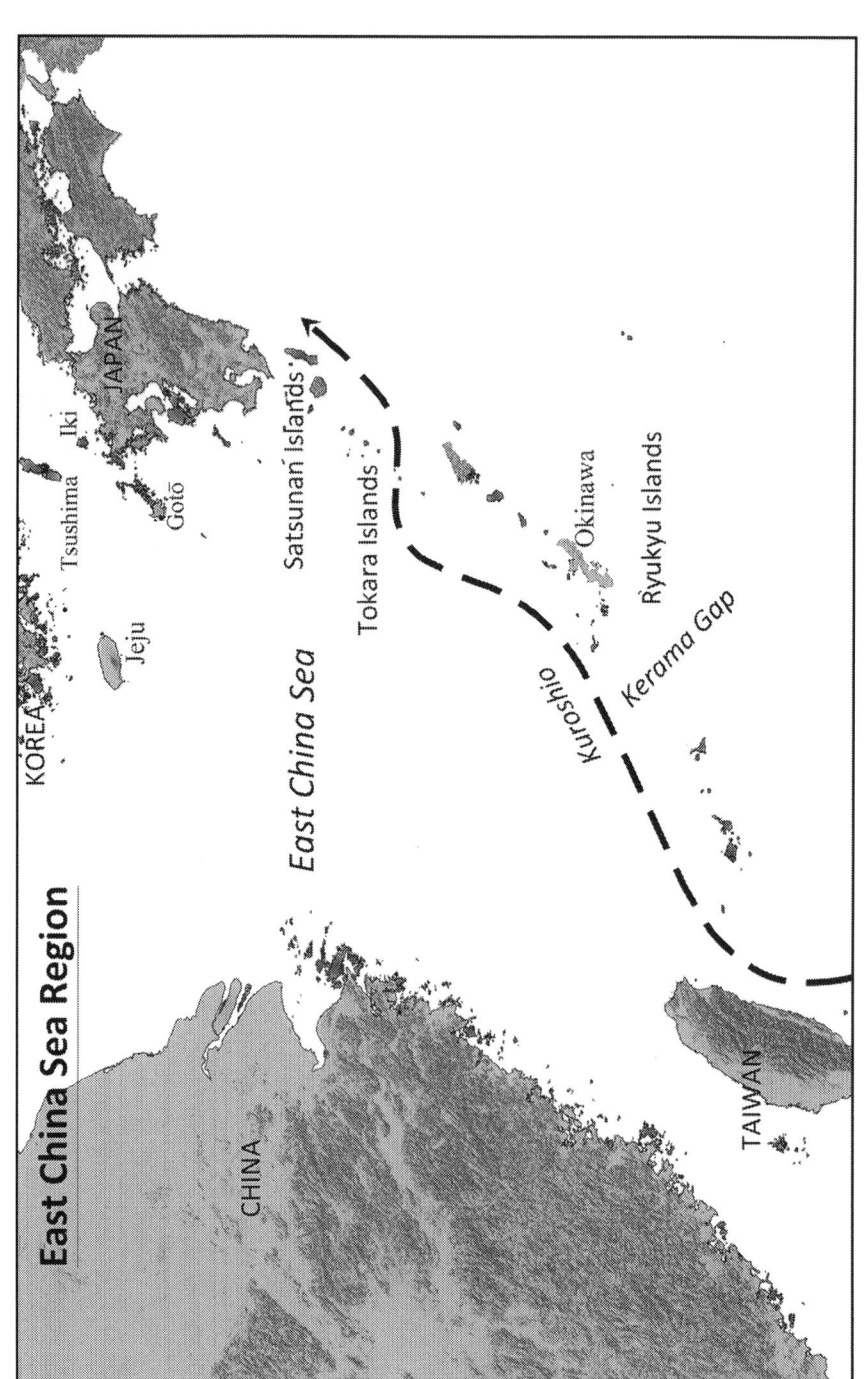

Fig. 1. The East China Sea region

Introduction

This book is an interdisciplinary, revisionist history of the Ryukyu islands between approximately 1050 and 1650 with occasional excursions into later years. The year 1050 marks the approximate beginning of the "Gusuku Period" in the Ryukyu islands, a time when power centers emerged.[1] In 1650, Shō Shōken (1617–1675) published *Reflections on Chūzan* (*Chūzan seikan*), Ryukyu's first official history. For reasons that will become clear, this event is a fitting end point for this study.

RYUKYU'S OFFICIAL HISTORIES

During most of the period covered in this book, Ryukyuans produced few domestic written documents. Chinese residing near the port of Naha handled the documentation connected with tribute trade, and Buddhist priests from Japan were available to assist with diplomatic correspondence. However, there is no evidence of the use of written documents to conduct government administration before the sixteenth century. Even as late as 1606, Xià Zǐyáng, a Chinese investiture envoy residing in Ryukyu, concluded that "literary culture is not widespread" even among the priests of the royal temple of Enkakuji, who were deeply respected as Ryukyu's learned elite.[2] Shō Shōken was among the first generation of Ryukyuan officials who could engage Chinese or Japanese literate society in a sophisticated manner.

What, therefore, were the sources Shō Shōken and later writers of official histories used? According to the introduction in *Reflections*, he interviewed elderly officials.[3] Chinese records and written accounts by

1

Japanese or Korean visitors provided some information, but for the most part, the details of early Ryukyu in the official histories are based on lore of unverifiable provenance. To some extent for sixteenth-century material, and more so from the seventeenth century onward, it is possible to corroborate accounts in the official histories using other sources. For material before the sixteenth century, however, such corroboration is rarely possible.

Ryukyu's official histories share an ideological perspective. Steeped in Confucian historiography, they assume that a morally attuned universe guides the trajectory of human societies. Morally upright rulers bring tranquility, prosperity, dynastic longevity, and other desirable social characteristics. Strife, disorder, succession disputes, and dynastic turnover, by contrast, are evidence of rulers' moral shortcomings. Founders of a ruling line were always virtuous. Conversely, the last ruler of a line could only have been morally deficient, not a victim of forces beyond his control. In addition, the official histories functioned to project an image of Ryukyu for outside consumption. In this context, they exaggerated the antiquity of a unified Okinawan state, positing its origins around 1200, approximately three centuries too early.

The official histories have created the dominant framework for early Ryukyuan history to this day. This book is an attempt to write a history of early Ryukyu from outside that framework. Instead of assuming that the official histories are probably accurate unless proven otherwise, I took the working hypothesis that material in the official histories before the sixteenth century is likely to be unreliable unless corroborated by other sources or evidence. Implicit in distancing myself from the official histories is the argument that it is possible to write a more nuanced and accurate history of early Ryukyu by looking elsewhere.

One important alternative source is *Omoro sōshi,* a collection of songs composed between approximately the twelfth and early seventeenth centuries. Other than diplomatic and trade documents and a few monument inscriptions, it contains the only native Ryukyuan source material predating the sixteenth century. Using *Omoro sōshi* as a historical source is not new. Iha Fuyū (1876–1947) did so, and in 1987 Mitsugu Sakihara published *A Brief History of Early Okinawa Based on the Omoro Sōshi.* Sakihara sought to combine "the traditional official records and histories" with the *Omoro* songs to create "a more accurate and vivid reconstruction."[4] In 2006 Yoshinari Naoki and Fuku Hiromi published a revisionist history of early Ryukyu based on a close reading of *Omoro sōshi* songs.[5] They have expanded this initial effort in subsequent single- and dual-authored books.

To use *Omoro sōshi* effectively it is necessary to map the cultural geography reflected in its songs. While later chapters of this book rely on a mix of sources more typical of historical research, the early chapters are interdisciplinary. In them, I rely on published research in the fields of cultural anthropology and archaeology and supplement this material with conventional historical sources such as official Chinese and Korean records. Throughout the analysis, I engage Ryukyu's official histories when appropriate, but I rarely rely on them. Moreover, I often arrive at different conclusions.

MAJOR SOURCES

The major sources for early Ryukyuan history are little known among nonspecialist readers. Therefore, I summarize them briefly below.

Ryukyu's Official Histories

The title of Shō Shōken's 1650 official history is *Chūzan seikan*. While "Mirror of Chūzan" would suitably translate the title, here I follow Lina Terrell and Robert Huey and translate it as *Reflections on Chūzan*,[6] abbreviated as *Reflections*. Except for the preface and many quoted passages, *Reflections* was written in Japanese. Confucian scholar Sai Taku (1645–1725) wrote *Genealogy of Chūzan* in 1701, ostensibly as a Chinese translation of *Reflections*. Sai Taku's son, Sai On (1682–1761), wrote the 1725 version of *Genealogy of Chūzan* as a substantial revision. Unless otherwise noted, references to *Genealogy of Chūzan* (*Genealogy*) in this book are to the 1725 edition. When necessary to distinguish them, I use the terms "1701 *Genealogy*" and "1725 *Genealogy*." *Kyūyō* is the fourth text I include under the umbrella term "official histories." Its title literally means "beautiful (*yō*) Ryukyu (*kyū*)." It is a series of articles arranged chronologically. Confucian scholars initially composed *Kyūyō* between 1743 and 1745.

Omoro sōshi

Omoro sōshi ("[the] *Omoro*" when referring to the collection as a whole) is a compilation of chants or songs (*omoro* with a lower-case o). The extant *Omoro* consists of twenty-two volumes and 1,553 songs. The song numbering and content of extant editions is the same. The first volume appeared in the early 1530s. By 1623, all the volumes had been produced. Today's *Omoro* comes from a 1710 re-compilation in the wake of a palace fire.

Omoro uses *kana* script to record the songs, with an occasional simple Chinese character appearing here and there. As Ryukyuan songs were transcribed using Japanese script, even in printed form, the original surface text of the *Omoro* would make no sense to most modern readers. The meaning of some parts of some songs is debatable, and some *Omoro* words and phrases are entirely undeciphered. Because a Romanized version of the original *kana* spelling would make no sense to anyone except *Omoro* specialists and would present many technical problems, I omit it in quoted passages. When a particular word or phrase is at issue, I provide the relevant details in the discussion or in the notes.

Omoro songs do not include dates of composition, but sometimes it is possible to place a song within a temporal frame based on its content. As a royal project, the songs reflect political biases. Pioneering *Omoro* scholar Iha Fuyū (1876–1947) posited that during the seventeenth century the text probably came to be regarded as dangerous thought. As such, the government kept it under tight control. Why would anyone have regarded such a text as dangerous? Because the *Omoro* sometimes disagrees sharply with the official histories.[7] Precisely for this reason, it is valuable as an alternative window on Ryukyu's past.

Omoro songs typically praise any person, place, or topic that appears in them. Therefore, if someone, someplace, or something of historical significance is not mentioned in the *Omoro*, that absence may be significant. For example, the *Omoro* and the official histories seem to be in agreement about King Shō Toku (r. 1461–1469). The official histories regard him as evil, and the *Omoro* never mentions him. Conversely, the *Omoro* and the official histories appear to disagree in their assessment of Gosamaru (d. 1458), a powerful local lord. The official histories regard Gosamaru as a tragic hero, but he is absent from *Omoro* songs. Moreover, Amawari (d. 1458), Gosamaru's opponent, is portrayed as a villain in the official histories. However, the *Omoro* praises Amawari, using language that places him on a par with the king.

Gazetteers

Ryukyu's earliest gazetteer is *Origins of Ryukyu* (*Ryūkyūkoku yuraiki*, composed 1703–1713), abbreviated as *Origins*. It is arranged first in terms of geography, starting with Shuri and moving outward, and then topically. Each entry is an independent article. *Origins* was compiled by Ryukyuans from a similar intellectual background to that of those who wrote the official histories. Nevertheless, *Origins* is not always in perfect alignment with the official histories. In some cases, it can provide additional perspectives, information, or clues.

Chinese and Korean Official Records

Reading Ryukyu's official histories in light of official records from China and Korea can both corroborate information and events and reveal meaningful discrepancies. The key sources for our purposes are *Ming Veritable Records* (C. *Míng shílù*, J. *Min jitsuroku*), compiled over the course of China's Ming dynasty (1368–1644), and *Joseon Veritable Records* (K. *Joseon wangjo sillog*, J. *Chōsen ōchō jitsuroku*). Korea's Joseon dynasty began in 1392.

Accounts by Outside Sojourners

In 1605 (published 1648), Taichū, a Jōdo sect priest from Kyoto, wrote an account of Ryukyuan religion, *Ryūkyū shintōki*, based on his three-year sojourn in Okinawa. Koreans sometimes arrived in various Ryukyu islands as a result of trade, shipwreck, or human trafficking. An important collection of their observations is the 1471 *Account of East Sea Countries* (K. *Haedong jegukgi*, J. *Kaitō shokokki*). Several other accounts are included within the *Joseon Veritable Records*.

Starting in 1534, Chinese investiture envoys sent to Ryukyu began producing book-length descriptions of history, customs, important events, and observations made during their stay. We have already encountered Xià Zǐyáng's 1606 observations about literary culture, and we will turn to Xià for more observations. Also of great importance is Chén Kǎn, investiture envoy to Shō Sei (r. 1527–1555). Chén wrote *Ryukyu Record* (C. *Shǐ Liúqiú lù*; J. *Shi Ryūkyū roku*), based on his sojourn in 1534.

Rekidai hōan

Rekidai hōan (C. *Lìdài bǎoàn*) is a large collection in Chinese of the formal diplomatic and trade records between Ryukyu and Korea, China, and Southeast Asia, covering the years 1427–1867. Resident Chinese or their descendants compiled these records.

Household Records

Between the seventeenth and eighteenth centuries, locally prominent households throughout the Ryukyu islands produced formal lineage chronicles. They vary in format, language, degree of detail, and the inclusion (or not) of dates for distant ancestors. Throughout this book, I use the umbrella term "household records" for such sources. These records sometimes include writs of appointment (*jireisho*), central government documents that first appeared during the sixteenth century. Household records often reach further back in time than any other documents, although it is rarely possible to verify specific claims they make about the distant past.

Monument and Temple Bell Inscriptions

Starting in the 1490s under Shō Shin, the capital of Shuri, the structure of government, and the royal court began a major transformation. Writs of appointment produced in the sixteenth century provide some insight into these changes. Another important source is monument inscriptions, some of which date from the fifteenth century. From Shō Shin's time onward, it became common practice for Ryukyuan kings to commission monuments.

Military Chronicles

There are several accounts of the 1609 war between the Shimazu domains (typically called Satsuma) and Ryukyu. Usually presented as eyewitness testimony, some were written as late as a century after the event. Chapter 14 examines these works in greater detail.

The Land, People, and Environment

As we will see, the early Ryukyu islands were a frontier crossroads, the abode of maritime travelers. Such people rarely if ever produced written sources despite possessing a rich culture and significant technical know-how. Fuku Hiromi states the case for taking such people seriously, despite the late appearance of written documents:

> The Southwestern islands (*Nansei shotō*) . . . fashioned a distinct society that was deeply connected with the history of Japan. If we were to place within our purview the possibilities of non-literate worlds and the repeated movements of non-literate people, as well as the cultural items people carried as seafarers, pirates (*kaizoku*), or *wakō*, then we would be able to develop a version of history entirely different from what has hitherto come down to us.[8]

It is reasonable to consider the territory and peoples of the East China Sea region as constituting an archive. Scholars of archaeology, anthropology, folklore, literature, and religion have produced a vast literature about the region, some of which has contributed to this book.

DEFINITIONS OF RYUKYU

Because the name has entered English, Ryukyu (J. Ryūkyū) is spelled without macrons. It is an ambiguous term. Customary meanings of Ryukyu have changed over time and continue to change, and much of this book consists of describing its different configurations.

In terms of physical geography or geology, Ryukyu refers to an arc of islands to the west of the Ryukyu Trench (Ryūkyū kaikō), spanning the space between the southern tip of Kyushu to Yonaguni near Taiwan. In this geospatial definition, Ryukyu is often known as the Ryukyu Arc. Figure 2 details the northern part of this arc.

Moving through the Ryukyu Arc from north to south, first are the Satsunan islands, consisting of Tanegashima and Yakushima, followed by the small but important Tokara island group. Next are the northern Ryukyu islands, consisting principally of Amami-Ōshima, Kikai, Tokunohsima, Okinoerabu, and Yoron. Okinawa is just beyond Yoron. In good weather, it was possible to sail from the Satsunan islands to Okinawa using line-of-sight navigation. One island would be visible at all times, either in the rear or in front. After 1609, it became common to refer to the northern islands of the Ryukyu Arc collectively as Michinoshima

Fig. 2. The northern Ryukyu arc (Michinoshima)

("islands constituting a road"). I prefer this term when speaking broadly of the northern Ryukyu and Tokara islands.

Slightly to the northwest of Okinawa are the islands of Iheya and Izena, and to the southwest is Kumejima. Despite their small size, these three islands become significant points of analysis in parts of this book. Collectively, the southwest part of the Ryukyu Arc, those in the Miyako and Yaeyama groups, are called Sakishima. Figure 3 details this region.

Except for Kikai at times, none of the Ryukyu islands from Amami-Ōshima southward were within the state boundaries of Japan, however defined, until 1609. Culturally, however, the Ryukyu islands functioned as a maritime frontier of Japan, and to some extent of Korea, prior to 1609. As Thomas Nelson has observed, Japan was immensely important in the cultural life of early Ryukyu.[9] One obvious indication is that all Ryukyuan languages are Japonic.[10] It is important to bear in mind throughout this book that, especially during premodern times, cultural and political boundaries often were not congruent.

Defining Ryukyu as a political or cultural entity is more complex than specifying geospatial boundaries. For centuries, the Ryukyu islands were home to inhabitants whose affiliations were to local communities or to nodes along maritime networks. There were many different "Ryukyus"

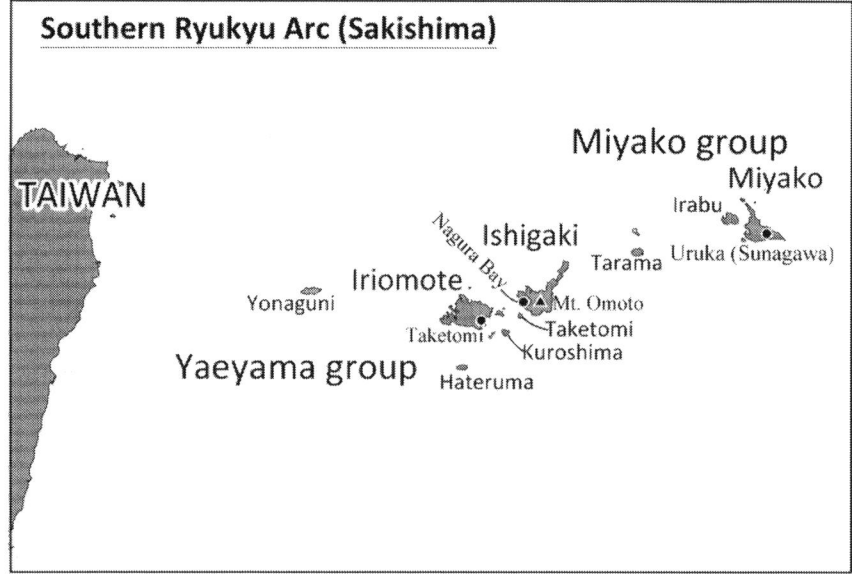

Fig. 3. The southern Ryukyu arc (Sakishima)

throughout history. Unless the immediate context indicates otherwise, I use "Ryukyu" as a general term of convenience, referring to the islands from Amami-Ōshima and Kikai in the north to Yonaguni in the southwest. In certain contexts, "Ryukyu" might also refer to one or more political communities located within these islands.

However, in nearly all premodern documents "Ryūkyū" meant the island of Okinawa, the largest of the Ryukyu islands. Sometimes prefixes like "large" (Dai-Ryūkyū) or "main" (Hon-Ryūkyū) modified Ryūkyū, but it always meant Okinawa. This point should not cause confusion because here I will use "Okinawa" when referring specifically to that island.

After 1609, the northern Ryukyu islands became part of the territory of the Shimazu lords, which is commonly called Satsuma. Today those northern Ryukyu islands are part of Kagoshima Prefecture. In this important sense, therefore, the islands in the Ryukyu Arc from Yoron northward were outside the boundaries of "Ryukyu" as a political entity after 1609, even though the northern Ryukyu islands retained many cultural affinities and maintained contact with Okinawa. They even posed as being part of the Ryukyu kingdom when Chinese officials visited Okinawa.

Between approximately 1500 and 1609, the political entity "Ryukyu" consisted of the islands of Amami-Ōshima and Kikai in the north through Yonaguni in the southwest, with Shuri in Okinawa as the clear center. This territory constituted what I call the Ryukyu empire. The term "empire" may seem peculiar at this point, but its meaning will become apparent in later chapters, especially chapter 11. After 1609, this empire shrunk in size and its geopolitical status changed in important ways, described in chapter 15.

During approximately the fifteenth century, Ryukyu as a state existed mainly in the eyes of the members of the Chinese and Korean royal courts, who usually referred to it as Chūzan. Defining Ryukyu as a political unit from approximately 1500 onward is relatively straightforward. By contrast, the political geography of the fifteenth century and earlier was much more diverse.

The term "Chūzan" can be confusing. According to the official story, from roughly the 1330s to the 1420s three territorial states existed on the island of Okinawa. This book will question that claim. However, conventionally, Chūzan was the area of Okinawa that includes Urasoe, Shuri, Naha, and some adjacent territory. Sanhoku (or Hokuzan) refers to northern Okinawa, roughly synonymous with the term Kunigami. Likewise, Sannan (or Nanzan) refers to the south of Okinawa below Naha, roughly corresponding to Shimajiri. Collectively, these three purported territorial states are called Sanzan, literally "three mountains." However, in many contexts, especially after the 1420s, Chūzan stands for the whole of Okinawa, or even the entire Ryukyu islands.

For our purposes, early modern Ryukyu refers to the period 1609–1879 and corresponds in periodization to the Japanese term *kinsei*. The boundaries of early modern Ryukyu were Iheya island, to the northwest of Okinawa, through Yonaguni, to the southwest. Early modern Ryukyu also included the tiny island of Iōtorishima, to the west of Tokunoshima. The term "old Ryukyu" corresponds to the Japanese Ko-Ryūkyū, and by convention refers to the Ryukyu kingdom prior to 1609.

In this book "early Ryukyu" is not the same as "old Ryukyu." I use "early Ryukyu" to indicate the Ryukyu islands prior to their becoming an organized political entity centered at Shuri. Therefore, "early Ryukyu" means the Ryukyu islands before approximately 1500. After that date, I prefer the term "Ryukyu empire" when referring to Ryukyu as a political unit. I generally avoid the common term "Ryukyu kingdom," because it can be confusing for reasons that will become apparent.

In 1872, Japan's Meiji state began laying the groundwork to annex Ryukyu. Resistance by the king and other elites, combined with circumstances inside Japan, delayed the annexation until 1879. That year, the territory of the post-1609 Ryukyu empire became Okinawa Prefecture, Japan. Between 1945 and 1972, Okinawa Prefecture became "The Ryukyus" under U.S. military occupation and governance. Okinawa Prefecture came back into existence in 1972, following "reversion" to Japan.

China played a crucial role in the formation of Ryukyu as a political entity, as we will see in detail. China influenced early Ryukyuan politics and the economy, much as it influenced most other states surrounding it. That said, however, at no point in the past were any of the Ryukyu islands Chinese territory, politically or culturally. Moreover, although they occasionally functioned as navigational aids for vessels at sea, the uninhabited rocks near the Ryukyu islands, known today by such names as Senkaku shotō or Diàoyútái, are entirely outside the boundaries of this study.

ORGANIZATION AND MAJOR ARGUMENTS

This book consists of four parts and sixteen chapters. For the most part, each chapter can stand on its own, although I include frequent allusions to other chapters.

Part I, chapter 1, situates the Ryukyu islands within a larger network of sea-lanes, migration, and culture. Early Ryukyu was not a self-contained entity, and it cannot be well understood apart from this network. Chapter 2 examines the close links between the development of early Ryukyu and *wakō*. The term *wakō* is conventionally translated as "Japanese pirates," but we will see that *wakō* were much more than pirates and that many of them came from areas other than Japan. Among other points, I argue that *wakō* were inextricably connected with the formation of political communities in the Ryukyu islands. Chapter 3 describes the role of early Ming anti-*wakō* measures in creating Ryukyu as a formal state. This creation corresponded to the appearance of three principalities on Okinawa, and chapter 4 questions the assumption that they were territorial states. Chapter 5 examines power centers in Okinawa and Kumejima, and their relationship with the first and second Shō dynasties of kings.

Part II examines struggles to control the Shuri-Naha area and conflict connected with royal succession. Chapter 6 examines the origin of the first Shō dynasty and its close connection to warfare between Japan's northern and southern courts. I also take up the question of whether the first Shō dynasty kings were all related to each other. Chapter 7 is a close look at warfare and political instability during the reigns of Shō Taikyū, Shō Toku, and Shō En. Chapter 8 examines the origins of Shō Shin's reign, the challenges he inherited and created, and the longer-term legacy of his problems with legitimacy. Chapter 9 pauses the narrative to consider the ways in which the writers of Ryukyu's official histories approached the challenge of connecting unrelated lines of kings.

Part III describes transformations of the Ryukyuan monarchy that took place during the reigns of Shō Shin and Shō Sei. When Shō Shin's partisans seized the throne in 1477, kings of Chūzan ruled in the manner of local *wakō* chieftains. By the end of Shō Shin's reign in 1526, the situation was fundamentally different. Chapter 10 explores the process of making Shuri into a strong center of an extended polity and the military campaigns that brought all of Okinawa and the other Ryukyu islands under Shuri's control. Chapter 11 examines the structure of Shō Shin's Shuri-centered empire from several angles. I also consider definitions of "empire" and argue that the term appropriately describes Ryukyu between 1500 and 1879. Chapter 12 examines the new religious hierarchy that Shō Shin and Shō Sei created in the service of the empire. I argue that Kikoe-ōgimi, the high priestess, subsumed within one person a previous pattern of three sister priestesses, and that Benzaiten became her divine counterpart.

The fourth part examines changes in East Asia and in the world, which put pressure on Ryukyu and ultimately contributed to its subordination to Satsuma. Chapter 13 examines the relationship between Ryukyu's kings and the Muromachi *bakufu*, new world conditions, and increasing tensions with the Shimazu lords. It also discusses the decline in Ryukyu's tribute trade, the importance of silver in the region, and the state of Ryukyu's military forces. I demonstrate that Ryukyu's war with the Shimazu domains was complex in its causes and should not be reduced to a simple story of victimization. Chapter 14 examines the 1609 war itself, a topic surprisingly absent from most survey histories. Chapter 15 explores a select set of postwar developments that set the stage for Ryukyu's early modern era and helped set up conditions that led to the difficult transition from Ryukyu to Okinawa Prefecture starting in the 1870s. Chapter 16 concludes with a reflection on the different Ryukyuan entities that existed as a function of time and perspective. I argue against the modern tendency to posit an essential Ryukyuan political or cultural community that persisted through time.

PART I

RYUKYU'S NETWORK, 1050–1470

CHAPTER ONE

Ryukyu in the East China Sea Network

The official histories begin the story of Ryukyu in Okinawa. According to *Reflections on Chūzan*, the deity Amamiku descends from heaven, creating land and people in Okinawa and then creating sacred groves from north to south. Eventually local lords emerge as leaders, followed by kings, and the other Ryukyu islands submit to these Okinawan kings. Similarly, most modern histories of Ryukyu start with Okinawa as the place of genesis. However, Okinawa did not become the political or economic center of gravity in the Ryukyu islands until the fourteenth century. Similarly, Ryukyuan culture did not spring from the soil of Okinawa. People, culture, and technologies entered from outside, and this chapter argues that north-to-south migrations along maritime routes were at the core of this process.

This chapter situates early Ryukyu within what I call the East China Sea network, which extends in an arc from the Korean peninsula, through western coastal areas of Japan, and down through the islands south of Kyushu to the coast of China (see fig. 4). The concept of such a region is not new, and scholars such a Murai Shōsuke and Tanaka Takeo have written about it extensively. As an arc of islands, early Ryukyu was an integral part of this network. Therefore, when considering people, wealth, and culture in early Ryukyu it is essential to broaden our usual conceptual boundaries. In a very real sense, Ryukyu was part of territory that included islands like Tsushima and Iki, and ports in western Kyushu.

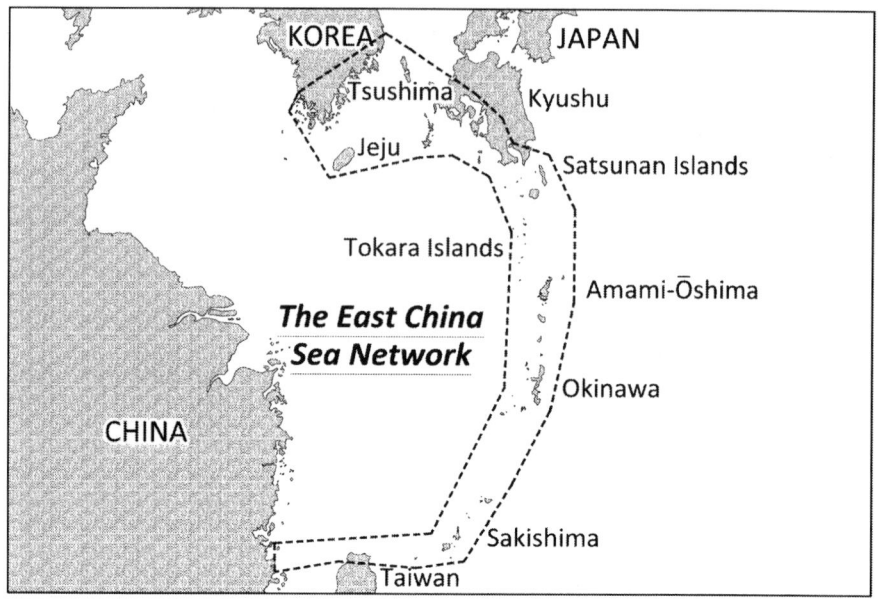

Fig. 4. The East China Sea network

This chapter examines several segments of the network. After a brief discussion of relevant geography, I begin in the northernmost Ryukyu islands, then move on to the economic forces that contributed to a gradual shift in population and power southward to Okinawa during the thirteenth and fourteenth centuries. Subsequently, I discuss Okinawa and its connections to two groups of islands to its north: the northern Ryukyu islands and the Tokara islands. I then link Okinawa, the northern Ryukyu islands, and the Tokara islands with coastal Kyushu, the Japanese islands of Iki and Tsushima, and the Korean coast. Finally, I examine routes to China. In the next chapter, I situate the southern Ryukyu islands within the network.

CURRENTS, WINDS, AND LANDFORMS

Stressing the interconnectedness of exchange networks within the East Asian region during approximately the fourteenth century, historian Angela Schottenhammer points out: "The centers of this exchange doubtlessly lay in China, Japan, and Korea. But also smaller countries and regions in the north and south of the China Sea, such as the Ryūkyūs or even traders from an island as small as Tsushima, participated and were integrated into this supra-regional system. Its initiators were often private organizations and merchants who sought to maintain and cherish their contacts even under politically unfavorable conditions."[1] Maritime routes connected the nodes within the network. Several factors influenced movement around the East China Sea, including currents, winds, and landforms.

The Kuroshio is a strong current flowing northward between Taiwan and Yonaguni and continuing northward to the west of the Ryukyu islands. Northwest of Amami-Ōshima, the Kuroshio turns eastward and flows through the sea between the Tokara islands and Amami-Ōshima, an area known as the Shichitō-nada. In other words, the Kuroshio forms a natural barrier between the Tokara and the northern Ryukyu islands. Its flow created dangerous conditions for shipping, and it defines a biological barrier with substantially different flora and fauna on either side of it. The Shichitō-nada also marks a cultural boundary, albeit a permeable one that people could and did cross. This boundary divides Ryukyuan languages and the Kyushu dialects of Japanese.[2] In 1893, when Sasamori Gisuke sailed from Kagoshima to visit the Ryukyu islands, he was struck by the terrifying power of the current in the Shichitō-nada. A sailor explained to Sasamori that if a typical Japanese-style sailing vessel encountered the current, it might be swept far off course into the Pacific.[3] The Kuroshio surging through the seas around the southern Tokara islands is one reason mariners from that area became especially prized as pilots throughout the network. Likewise, the Kuroshio serves as a marine barrier between Yonaguni and both Taiwan and the southeast coast of China.

Between Okinawa and Miyako, the expanse of sea known as the Kerama gap functioned as a barrier to travel because crossing it required navigation without reference to visible landforms. Despite the significance of these natural obstacles, properly equipped and piloted vessels regularly overcame them. Sailing from Kikai to the port of Naha in Okinawa could be done entirely within sight of land on clear days. Therefore, relatively small ships could travel this route without advanced navigational skills. To sail from Amami-Ōshima to Tokara, or from Okinawa to Sakishima, or to the China coast, on the other hand, required superior ships, knowledge, and skill.

The wind was the main driving force for vessels plying routes around the East China Sea. Storms, of course, could be disruptive, but generally wind patterns were predictable. The winds in the region changed during approximately the third and ninth lunar months.[4] Knowledge of wind patterns even appears in the *Omoro*. For example:

> The ship Suzunari sailing under the south wind
> When we hear the true southern wind
> Load goods from China and Southeast Asia
> And deliver them to the king

and

> When the season changes during the third month
> At my shrine, the shrine of the deity
> I pray to my guardian deity
> Asking that the great priestess
> Cause a true southern wind to speed [our ship]
> Now that the new summer has begun.[5]

The twice-yearly changes in wind direction from north-northwest to south-southeast meant that mariners often resided for several months in or near ports to which they had traveled as they waited for the wind to change.

KIKAI AND THE NORTHERN TIER ISLANDS

The appropriate starting place for early Ryukyuan history is the northernmost Ryukyu islands of Kikai, Amami-Ōshima, and Tokunoshima. These islands formed an economic unit and possibly, at times, a political unit. In this book, my collective term for these islands is Northern Tier (fig. 5). Lacking extant written sources from the Northern Tier during most of its early history, we are unable to identify specific people, social organizations, or institutions. For convenience I sometimes speak of islands acting as willful entities. In all such cases, of course, I am referring to the unnamed human actors residing in those places.

Northern Tier islanders first appear in Japanese sources as "southern barbarians" (*nanban*). They attacked Kyushu in 996 and captured four hundred people in Ōsumi, according to official reports. The next year, they attacked Dazaifu, the center of the Japanese state in Kyushu, carrying off people and goods. The marauding southern islanders attacked the provinces of Satsuma, Higo, Hizen, Chikuzen, and the islands of Iki and Tsushima, capturing hundreds of people in the process. In the confusion of initial reports, Dazaifu officials originally mistook the attackers for Koreans.[6] There were at least two reasons for this confusion of identity. First, throughout much of the tenth century, coastal areas of Kyushu had been subject to attacks by Korean pirates. An especially large-scale attack on Hakata, Iki, and Tsushima took place in 1019.[7] The

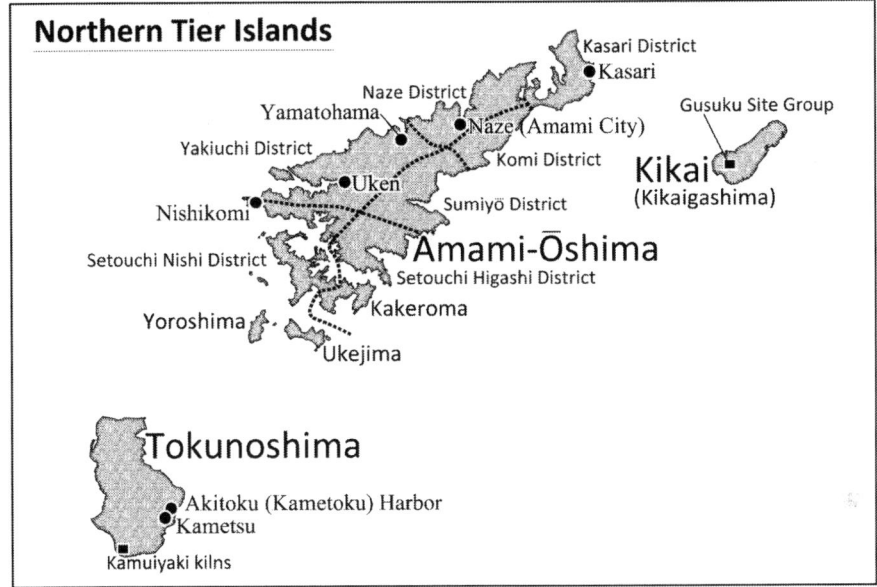

Fig. 5. The Northern Tier islands

other reason is that close ties existed between the Korean peninsula and the Northern Tier.[8]

The southern marauders in 996 and 997 most likely came from, or were based at, Amami-Ōshima. Responding to the attacks, in 998 Dazaifu officials sent orders to officials on "Kikaigashima" to suppress the brigands. Kikai is the small island just to the east of Amami-Ōshima. In 999 Dazaifu reported that indeed Kikai had suppressed the raiders.[9] Although we cannot verify these details, one point to note is the considerable power located in the Northern Tier.[10] Archaeological evidence suggests that Kikai was both under Dazaifu jurisdiction during the tenth century and that the culture of its inhabitants differed from that of nearby Amami-Ōshima.[11] The political geography may have been even more complex, with Kikai and a small portion of Kasari peninsula on Amami-Ōshima forming a single political unit.[12]

In 998, Kikai was part of Japan in the technical sense that it was subject to the jurisdiction of Dazaifu and thus ultimately the Heian court. Kikai's geopolitical affiliation was not stable over time. Roughly a century after the attacks of 996–999, Kikai had drifted out of Japan's boundaries. In 1111, a ship from Kikai that drifted into Kii was dealt with in the same manner as a ship from China or Korea. By then, Kikai had become a place to which Japanese in political or legal trouble might abscond. Japanese texts tended to write the "ki" of Kikai using pleasant characters meaning joy or nobility when the island was, at least nominally, within Japanese jurisdiction. When Kikai ceased to "obey" Japan, however, written materials tended to use the character for "ki" meaning demon (*oni*).[13]

In some medieval Japanese literary texts, the name "Kikai" transformed into boundary zones or lands far across the sea. It sometimes occurred attached to that of other countries, such as "Kikaikōrai" (Kikai + Korea), or as the first term in a list of distant places, as in "Kikai, Kōrai (Korea), Tenjiku (India), Shintan (China)."[14] Both in literary texts and with respect to trade and flows of culture, "at the same time that the waters around Kikaigashima constituted an interstitial space (*hazama*) between the Ryukyu and Japanese islands, they probably functioned even more so as an interstitial space connecting Ryukyu and the Korean peninsula."[15] From the end of the tenth century to the early fourteenth, the Northern Tier was a prominent crossroads.

Notice the places in and around Kyushu that the Amami-Ōshima marauders attacked in the 990s. They map out a regional network linking coastal areas of southern Korea with the islands of Tsushima and Iki, western Kyushu, and the Northern Tier. By the latter half of the eleventh century, this network extended as far southward as Okinawa. In subsequent centuries, it grew to include Sakishima and southern coastal China. Until approximately the thirteenth century, however, there was a disproportionate concentration of wealth and advanced technology in the Northern Tier, with Kikai as its administrative center.

THE GUSUKU SITE GROUP

Discovered in 2006, excavation of the Gusuku Site Group in Kikai has revealed about one hundred and fifty raised buildings, many burial pits, fifty hearths, and thirty ironworking hearths. Goods originating outside of Kikai account for about 70 percent of the total. The Kasari peninsula in Amami-Ōshima contributed raw materials such as timber, water, and stone to the Gusuku Site Group. Iron sand has been discovered at the Maehata and Ōufu sites within the group. The sand provided iron for metalworking. Iron products from Kikai eventually found their way to Okinawa.[16]

Funeral practices are a fundamental marker of culture, and the different sites at Gusuku indicate at least three types: interment, cremation, and the reburial of cremated bones.[17] Significantly, reburial of cremated bones was not practiced in Japan during the eleventh and twelfth centuries, the time corresponding to such burials in Kikai.[18] Moreover, ordinary cremation was not common in the islands south of Kyushu.[19] The coexistence of diverse burial procedures indicates a multiethnic, multicultural society in Kikai.[20]

Archaeologists have divided the history of the Gusuku Site Group into three broad periods. The first was comprised of the ninth and tenth centuries, during which time Kikai was under Dazaifu's jurisdiction. The main economic activity was trade in turbo (turban) shells, used for making mother-of-pearl inlay. The eleventh and twelfth centuries constitute the second period and the peak of prosperity. Kikai was outside of Japanese political control, and economic activity there diversified. Turbo-shell trade and trade in exotic products such as large conch shells and sea-turtle shells remained important, but Kikai also became the distribution center for local and regional manufactured items. Especially significant was *kamuiyaki* stoneware, produced mainly in Tokunoshima and shipped throughout the Ryukyu islands and as far north as Kyushu. During the thirteenth and fourteenth centuries, the Gusuku Site Group gradually declined.[21]

The prosperity of Dazaifu and Kikai varied inversely. As Kikai's economic activity increased during the eleventh century, the island separated from the declining Dazaifu. During approximately the twelfth century, the northern Ryukyu islands benefited economically from an influx of talc stoneware (*ishinabe*) from western Kyushu, the production of *kamuiyaki*, innovations in the technology of making mother-of-pearl from turbo shells, and increasing demand for sulfur. At approximately the same time, Dazaifu suffered because the center of trade in Kyushu shifted to Hakata, and Dazaifu lost infrastructure and functions.[22] As the economic vigor of Kikai and its neighbors gradually declined during the thirteenth century, Okinawa gained in relative power and prominence.

KAMUIYAKI

The origins of *kamuiyaki* had long been a mystery. It was found throughout the Ryukyu islands and in coastal Kyushu such as the Mottaimatsu site in Kagoshima Prefecture. *Kamuiyaki* represented a major technological advance over earthenware, and it was not until 1983 that researchers discovered the main manufacturing site on Tokunoshima near Kumuiyaki pond (Isen Town). "Kamui" corresponds to *kame* (urn) in standard Japanese. Tokunoshima was an ideal site for stoneware manufacturing because of abundant forests to fuel the kilns and sufficient tillable land to provide food for workers and technicians. *Kamuiyaki* production probably deforested the island.[23] Kilns have been found elsewhere in the region, but Tokunoshima was the main manufacturing site, and Kikai served as the chief distribution center for *kamuiyaki*.[24] More generally, Kikai served as a major "exchange terminal" within the East China Sea network for a variety of products and people.[25]

Connections with Korea facilitated the transfer of the technological know-how required to produce *kamuiyaki*. Korean kiln technology existed in Higo (Kumamoto Prefecture) and Tokunoshima during the eleventh and twelfth centuries, and Korean-made celadon and unglazed porcelain appeared in Kikai. The production of *kamuiyaki* corresponded with the peak demand for turbo shells, the main product of the Northern Tier and a likely source of capital for establishing *kamuiyaki* production.[26] The movement of people, including Korean technicians, would have been required to initiate and probably to sustain *kamuiyaki* production. In this context, maritime merchants facilitated the required exchanges. They operated along routes between Korea and the Northern Tier via the islands of Iki and Tsushima.[27]

SHELLS FOR IRON

Prior to the production of *kamuiyaki*, Kikai and Amami-Ōshima maintained their power in part by trading turbo shells for iron. Matsunoto in the Kasari peninsula of Amami-Ōshima was a major turbo shell processing site.[28] Excavation of Matsunoto has revealed eighty-seven items of ironware or items used in ironmaking such as ventilation ports. Likewise, twenty-two iron items have been excavated at the Fuwaganeku site at Kominato in Amami City. Sites at which iron goods have been excavated overlap with large caches of turbo shells. People in the northern Ryukyu islands acquired iron and iron goods mainly via the shell trade.[29]

After demand outstripped local turbo-shell production capabilities during the eleventh century, the Northern Tier began to export *kamuiyaki* to Okinawa and the southern Ryukyu islands in return for turbo shells.[30] This process encouraged the development of powerful centers to the south, such as Katsuren in Okinawa and the island of Kumejima near Okinawa, which also traded extensively with China (fig. 6). At Ikei gusuku on Ikei island in Okinawa's Kin bay near Katsuren, turbo and other shells became objects of veneration. This small island probably profited from the close connection between Katsuren gusuku and the vigorous shell trade at Kasari.[31] One indication of the importance of the turbo-shell trade generally is that, in the *Omoro,* only two physical objects (as opposed to people or deities) are modified by the term *kikoe* (resounding). They are a royal sword, Tsukushi-chara, and turbo shells (*kurokariya*) produced at Kumejima.[32]

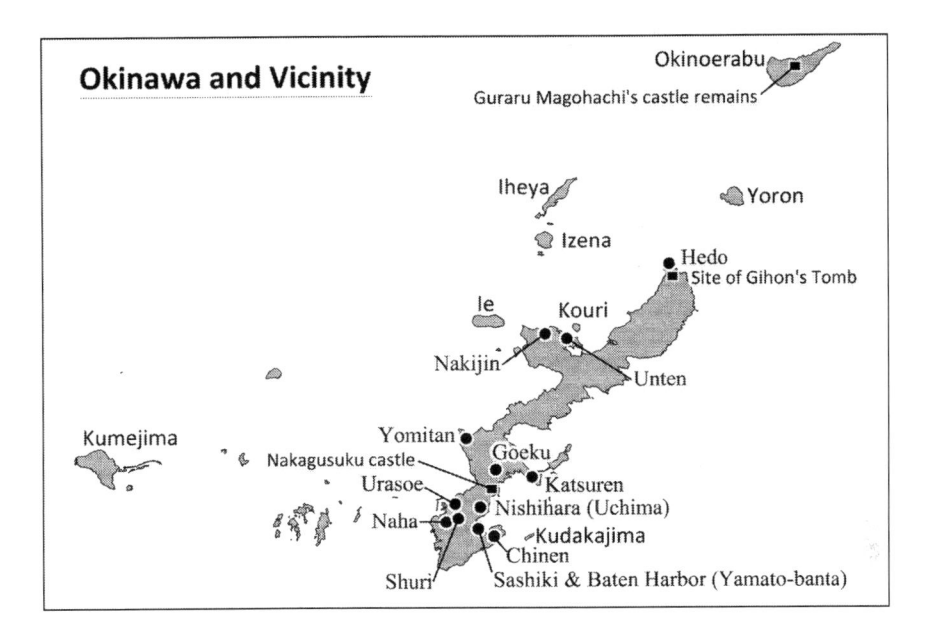

Fig. 6. Okinawa and vicinity

The *Omoro* likened Katsuren to "Kamakura in Yamato" and placed Katsuren's most famous ruler, Amawari, on a par with the king. Amawari's use of a jeweled ladle is the main device for communicating his elevated status.[33] It is almost certain that this ladle would have been made from mother-of-pearl, based on similar extant objects.[34] The ladle was a symbol of the power to control the forces of nature and to confer credibility.[35]

The Northern Tier, in effect, nurtured the turbo trade at points south through the production of *kamuiyaki*. This circuit of exchange set the stage for development of power centers in Okinawa and nearby islands, especially Kumejima (fig. 6). During the fourteenth century, some of these centers began to surpass their predecessors or counterparts in the north, most likely because of profits from private trade with China. The establishment of formal tribute trade between Ming China and Okinawa in 1372 accelerated this process.

NAHA, THE NEW UKISHIMA

During the fourteenth century, three freshwater rivers emptied into Naha harbor. This inflow suppressed the growth of coral reefs and helped Naha became a prosperous international port. Naha was sometimes known as

Ukishima (Floating Island), and by other names. The main part of Naha was an island, Ukishima (fig. 17). To the southwest of Ukishima was Naha harbor, and to its northeast were tidal mudflats, beyond which lay the port of Tomari.[36] The original Ukishima, however, both in the senses of its function as an international port and its name, was Kikai. The topography of Kikai includes a plateau visible from a distance out at sea.

According to the official histories, Shō Toku devoted considerable blood and treasure to pacifying Kikai, which resisted stubbornly. Other Ryukyuan rulers waged war in the Northern Tier. Consider the following *omoro* from the original 1530s compilation:

> The high priestess (Kikoe-ōgimi)
> Conveys prayers made to heaven
> And the pride of Terukawa [a solar deity]
> To King Shō Shin
> Who subdued Kasari
> Acclaimed High Priestess.[37]

Kasari is a relatively flat and agriculturally valuable peninsula located directly across from Kikai. Sho Sei launched an invasion of Amami-Ōshima in 1537, and Shō Gen (r. 1556–1572) might have done so in 1571.

Although we cannot be certain of exactly when Amami-Ōshima first came under Okinawan control, the earliest record of an official taking up residence there as Shuri's agent dates from 1506, the same year Shō Shin subdued Kumejima.[38] The overall picture reflects the economic and military power of Okinawa gradually exceeding that of the Northern Tier. Vigorous resistance in the north and the need for repeated conquests well into the sixteenth century attests to the power once concentrated there. Consider the following *omoro* describing a journey from Kikai to Shuri. Most lines repeat in the original, expressing "to" and "from," but are listed here only once:

> Okishima [Ukishima] of Kikai
> Moishima of Kikai
> From Okishima
> To Biru [Beru village] in Kasari [northern Amami-Ōshima]
> To the Nakasetouchi straits [southern Amami-Ōshima]
> To Kanenoshima [metal island, i.e., Tokunoshima]
> To Seriyosa [old name of Okinoerabu island]
> To Kaifuta [Yoron island]
> To Asumori [sacred site at the northern edge of Okinawa]
> To Akamaru [Tōbaru in northern Okinawa]
> To Sakigyamori [sacred site on Kouri island off northern
>   Okinawa near Nakijin]

To Kanahiyabu [sacred site at Nakijin, northern Okinawa]
To Sakiyoda [Cape Zanpa near Yomitan, central Okinawa]
To Oyadomari [Naha harbor]
To Shurimori [sacred grove inside Shuri castle].[39]

The name "Oyadomari" (literally, "parent anchorage") indicates the superior status of Naha. More important, this list of places nicely maps out a key subset of the East China Sea network.

THE NORTHERN TIER CULTURAL ZONE AND *NORO*

Sakita Mitsunobu has called the area from northern Okinawa to Amami-Ōshima and Kikai the "Hokuzan Cultural Zone."[40] Hokuzan was the northern principality according to the official histories. Sakita and others regard northern Okinawa and all of the northern Ryukyu islands as having been united as a single polity under the lord of Nakijin during the fourteenth century. Although Sakita has identified an important zone of culture, the idea that it was a unified political community is problematic. Therefore, I use the term Northern Tier Cultural Zone to refer to the geocultural space from northern Okinawa to Kikai, via the northern Ryukyu islands (fig. 7).

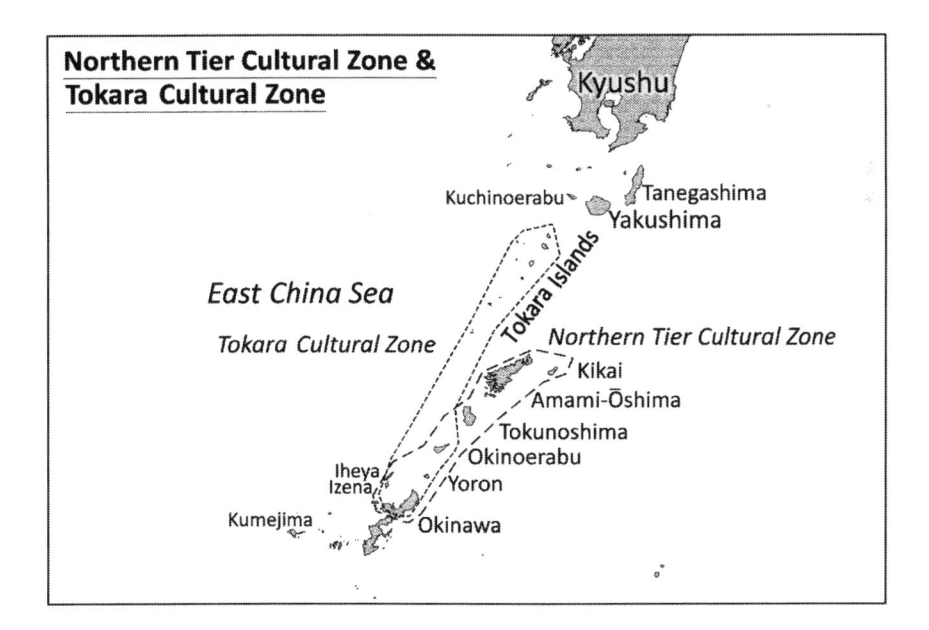

Fig. 7. The Northern Tier Cultural Zone and the Tokara Cultural Zone

Other than one song celebrating Shuri's 1500 invasion of Yaeyama, there are relatively few *omoro* specifically about Sakishima. By contrast, the *Omoro* abounds with songs about locations in Michinoshima. The northern Ryukyu islands, with their ties to Japan and Korea, were the cultural homeland of Okinawa's royal houses and many local rulers. These ties were one reason for the frequent warfare between Okinawa and islands to the north and for trauma at the royal court after the loss of the northern islands in 1609. This loss probably contributed to the final compilation of the *Omoro*.[41]

The oldest extant map depicting Japan encircled by a dragon is in the Kanazawa Bunko Museum. It was drawn around 1305 and probably reflects late thirteenth-century conceptions of Japan's geography. Only the half depicting western Japan is extant. Text at the edge of the map, outside of Japan, states that in "Ryūkyū-Ōshima," there are creatures with the body of a person and the head of a bird. In a different map from the same era, the label "Ryūkyū-koku" includes the description, "Human body, bird head."[42] The bird-head reference likely indicates the religious costume of priestesses who would later become known as *noro*. One *omoro* describes a priestess in Nakijin as wearing eagle feathers.[43]

Noro exemplify the deep northern cultural roots of the Ryukyuan monarchy. After 1609, Satsuma enacted cultural policies aimed at severing the ties between Shuri and Michinoshima. One 1624 edict prohibited *noro* from accepting formal appointment as state officials of Okinawa. This policy engendered so much resistance, however, that Satsuma officials relented. Into the eighteenth century, priestesses from Michinoshima traveled to Okinawa for formal appointment as *noro* by the king.[44] This continued cultural prestige of Shuri is all the more significant in light of the history of military conflict between Shuri and Amami-Ōshima and Satsuma's direct control of the northern Ryukyu islands after 1609.

The *Omoro* speaks of a vast population of *noro* in the northern Ryukyu islands, whose function was to protect sea-lanes. One song mentions thirty on Okinoerabu; another mentions thirty and then forty on Tokunoshima; and another mentions eighty on Amami-Ōshima.[45] Actually, the kings in Shuri appointed far fewer *noro*. Even taking into account the *Omoro*'s tendency to exaggerate, however, this vast population of priestesses in songs suggests a time when the sea-lanes in Michinoshima were very busy.[46]

THE TOKARA CULTURAL ZONE

A second zone partially overlaps the Northern Tier Cultural Zone but is mostly distinct from and parallel to it. This zone includes northern Okinawa and usually the small nearby islands of Iheya and Izena plus the Michinoshima islands of Yoron and Okinoerabu. From Okinoerabu, the zone veers to the west of the Northern Tier islands and encompasses the Tokara islands. It may also include the islands of Yakushima and Tanegashima.[47] I call this subset of the East China Sea network the Tokara Cultural Zone (fig. 7).

One of the Tokara islands is Gajajima, but during the fourteenth and fifteenth centuries, "Gaja" often referred to the Tokara islands collectively. During the 1450s, the Tokara islands appear to have been a boundary region between Ryukyu and Satsuma. According to accounts of Korean castaways and the Hakata merchant Dōan, military forces from Okinawa controlled the southern half of the Tokara islands and Satsuma controlled the northern half.[48]

The Tokara Cultural Zone functioned as a cultural conduit separate from the Northern Tier islands. One example is the term *tonchi* (from *tono*) in the Tokara islands. There, *tonchi* and the related term *tonjū* indicate the abode of locally important households of mainland Japanese origins. The Higo family on Kuchinoshima, for example, can be traced to the thirteenth century.[49] The *Omoro* includes twenty-five examples of people called *"tono/dono"* or *"-ton/-don"* and thirty-five buildings so termed, twenty-one of which are structures associated with Shuri castle. As in Tokara, the corresponding Okinawan term *tonchi* (*tunchi*) indicates powerful people who came south from Japan, or their residences.[50] The next section includes additional examples of the Tokara islands as conduits for culture across a wide area.

ALL THE WAY TO KOREA

This section situates both the Northern Tier Cultural Zone and the Tokara Cultural Zone within a larger geocultural network extending north to the Korean peninsula, and sometimes even farther inland. Here I examine three broad realms, all of which illuminate fundamental aspects of Okinawan and Ryukyuan culture. The first is the idea of *obotsu* and burial practices connected with it. Next is a discussion of sacred sites, known as *yabusa* and by similar names, and their connection with the legend of Minamoto Tametomo sailing to Okinawa and initiating the first royal line. Finally, I discuss the northern Okinawan Aoriyae and its connection with solar worship in diverse locations.

Presenting Bodies to the Heavens

The practice of placing corpses in baskets or cages and leaving them at the top of trees or poles to decompose was characteristic of the Northern Tier Cultural Zone and regions farther north. Within the Ryukyu islands, the practice has been documented in Amami-Ōshima and in parts of central and northern Okinawa.[51] Nagoya Sagenta was a Satsuma retainer. After residing in Amami-Ōshima between 1850 and 1855, he wrote a detailed description of the local culture, *Nantō zatsuwa* (Tales from the southern islands). It explains that, after the death of a priestess, "her corpse is placed in a large box, which is suspended from atop a tree for three years. Then the bones are washed and placed in a jar."[52]

Similar practices have been documented in places along the coastline of the Japan Sea in Akita, Yamagata, and Ishikawa Prefectures. In those places the remains are hoisted aloft after cremation.[53] In Korea, hoisting (non-cremated) bodies into trees was done in the case of deaths from smallpox and other diseases. The practice was both a de facto sanitary measure and was thought to mollify the angry deity who had caused the disease by offering up the body.[54] A broad range of northern Asian peoples, from the Koryaks in Kamchatka west to Mongolia, traditionally disposed of corpses or bones by placing them on platforms or in trees. Bones of humans or hunted animals thus offered up toward the heavens were believed to be reborn.[55]

There is only one known example from Fukuoka, but folklore from the region such as the legend of the "bone-hanging tree" attests to the former existence of the practice. Kashiigū, a shrine in Fukuoka City with ties to Korea, derives its name from the legend that Emperor Chūai's coffin was hung in a *shii* tree (*Castanopsis cuspidata*, Japanese chinquapin).[56]

Anthropologist Ōbayashi Taryō points out that most communities that practiced tree or sky burials possessed a well-developed concept of a heavenly realm mirroring an earthly realm.[57] In northern Okinawa and the northern Ryukyu islands, this concept of verticality in the form of a heavenly realm running parallel to an earthly realm is *obotsu*, a term often paired with *kagura* to form *obotsu-kagura*.

The word *obotsu* is not native to Sakishima.[58] Yoshinari Naoki and Fuku Hiromi have noted a precise overlap between the geographic distribution of *obotsu* as a concept and as a component in names and religious rites, on the one hand, and the practice of tree burials in the northern Ryukyu islands on the other. They regard these tree funerals as presenting bodies to the heavens—that is, up to the realm of *obotsu*. They also hypothesize that such funeral rites are connected with the common Ryukyuan practice of burying bones in sacred groves (*utaki*), a matter I investigate further in chapter 7. Eventually, the royal court at Shuri formalized *obotsu* religious rites; and in this format, they spread wherever royal religious officials such as *noro* operated. However, the roots of *obotsu* lie in the Northern Tier Cultural Zone.[59] The distribution of the practice of placing bodies or bones in trees or other high places is an indication of migration, most likely from Korea, up and down the coast of Japan and into the Ryukyu islands.[60]

Yafusa-san of Higo Travels to Okinawa

I am sometimes asked whether the story of Minamoto Tametomo traveling to Okinawa and his son becoming the first king (Shunten, r. 1187–1237) is a legend. Often the question includes a phrase like "just a legend" or "only a legend." Yes, the story is a legend. As legends often do, however, it mirrors actual events. For example, if we substitute Samekawa for Tametomo, and if we move the time forward about two centuries, to the end of the fourteenth century, the legend reflects migration from Kyushu to northern Okinawa to southern Okinawa. The following discussion is the first of several examinations of this important matter. Its main purpose is to reveal cultural connections between Okinawa, Kyushu, and nearby islands.

The island of Iki, northwest of Fukuoka (fig. 8), is a key junction in the East China Sea network and home to sacred sites called *yabusa* or *yabosa*. At Ishida in Iki City, for example, there are ten *yabosa* sites, most located on top of a hill. They feature rocks piled up near one or two trees, and rites take place atop a stone altar. There is a source of water nearby, and the area receives ample sunlight. Legends connected with the Iki sites indicate that they originated as shrines to the founding ancestors of villages. These Iki sites bear a close resemblance in name, appearance, and function to the Yabusatsu (or Yabusasu) grove in southeastern Okinawa,[61] located in Tamagusugu, just to the east of Sashiki. According to *Reflections on Chūzan*, this Yabusatsu grove was one of the sacred sites that the deity Amamiku founded at the dawn of Ryukyuan history.[62] Iha Fyū has pointed out connections between *yabosa* sites in Iki, funeral practices in Okinawa, and the Yabusatsu grove.[63]

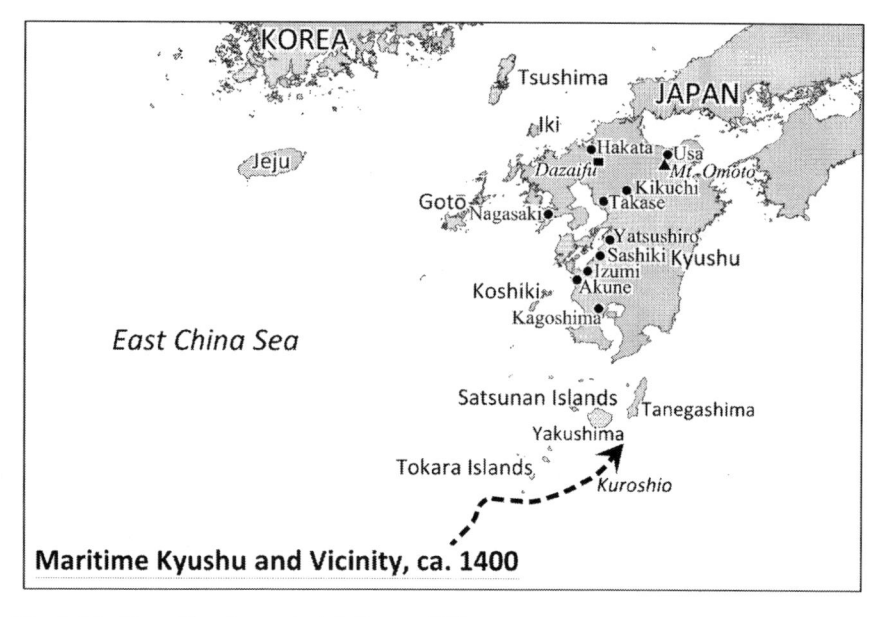

Fig. 8. Maritime Kyushu and vicinity, ca. 1400

Yabusa/Yabosa sites are also found in Tsushima and throughout western Kyushu from Saga Prefecture to Kagoshima Prefecture.[64] In the Matsuura area of Nagasaki, *yabosa* sites enshrined deities that protected settlers and pioneers. These sites date from the 1350s or possibly earlier. Especially important for early Ryukyuan history are two *yabosa* shrines in Higo (Kumamoto Prefecture) facing the Yatsushiro (Shiranui) Sea. They are the Tametomo Shrine at Tsunagi (formerly Sashiki) and the Tametomo Shrine just to the south at Minamata. Both are dedicated to Minamoto Tametomo, known locally as Yafusa-san (from *yabusa*).[65] Herein is almost certainly the geographic origin of Okinawa's Tametomo legend (fig. 8). As we will see in detail later, Samekawa-ōnushi (O. Samikawa-ufushu, Lord Samekawa), father of the first Shō dynasty's first king Shō Shishō (r. 1407–1421), migrated from Sashiki in the Yatsushiro area of Higo to northern Okinawa. He then moved farther south to Sashiki in southeastern Okinawa, near what became the site of Okinawa's Yabusatsu grove.

There is a Yabusatsu grove in Shomi, in Izena, the purported birthplace of Kanemaru, founder of Okinawa's second Shō dynasty. A common route from Iheya or Izena into Okinawa was to land at Unten harbor near Nakijin. That is precisely the path Tametomo purportedly took according to the legend of his journey to Okinawa from Kyushu. In the legend, Tametomo later married the sister of the lord of Ōzato, near Sashiki. According to *Origins of Lord Samekawa* (*Samekawa-ōnushi yuraiki*), an early modern text of unknown provenance, Samekawa, following the same route, married the daughter of a local lord.[66] In other words, the tales of Samekawa's migration from Kyushu to Okinawa and of Tametomo's migration are largely congruent.

Tametomo appears in the *Omoro* as "Teda Hachiro," which comes from the title Chinzei Hachirō Tametomo.[67] The Tametomo legend probably dates from the arrival of the Samekawa family from Higo in the late fourteenth century. As Yoshinari Naoki points out, "Higo was a region with deep connections to the Ryukyu Arc from ancient times. Moreover, it was the knot that connected the Ryukyu Arc and the Korean peninsula."[68]

The ties between Ryukyu and Higo were extensive. Takase (present-day Tamana) on the coast of Higo was the northern terminus of a sea route to Fujian in southern China. The route ran through the Ryukyu islands, and it became especially popular during the fourteenth century as the Hakata-Níngbō route became increasingly dangerous.[69] Hashimoto Yū points out that the shift to the Takase-Fujian route accelerated the development of the Ryukyu islands.[70] Recall that the fourteenth century was when Okinawa surpassed the Northern Tier as the main center of gravity in the Ryukyu islands. The Takase-Fujian route may have been either a cause or an effect of that change.

It is also significant that the *Omoro* frequently mentions Yatsushiro. It is spelled "Yashiro" and almost always paired with "Yamato." *Omoro* scholars have traditionally regarded Yashiro as Yamashiro and Yamato as Japan as a whole. However, Yatsushiro is an equally plausible rendering of Yashiro on linguistic grounds.[71] Moreover, there is historical and anthropological evidence in favor of the Yamato-Yashiro pair specifically indicating locations in Kyushu. Tanigawa Ken'ichi and others have argued that "Yamato" in this context does not mean Japan as a whole, but the Yamato-in territory, located in present day Takano-chō and Noda-chō of the Izumi district in the northernmost part of Kagoshima Prefecture. The old Yamato-in territory had close ties with Higo and with the Southern Court, points I revisit in later chapters.[72] Inamura Kenpu has also argued that Yamato-Yashiro in the *Omoro* indicates Kyushu. He points out that in the 1950s, Okinawans of aristocratic background often referred to mainland Japan as a whole as Ō-Yamato (great Yamato) and used Yamato to indicate Kyushu.[73] An important piece of evidence in support of this interpretation is the 1611 text of an oracle from a sacred grove on Iheya that describes the invaders of 1609, who we know came from southern

Kyushu, as "shaved-forehead men of Yamato [Satsuma], of Yashiro [Yatsushiro]."[74] I examine connections between the Higo coast and Okinawa in detail in later chapters.

Deities of Wind and Rain

This discussion begins with the Aoriyae deity of northern Okinawa and traces its roots northward, through the Tokara Cultural Zone to Tsushima. Based in Nakijin, the Aoriyae priestess was the most powerful woman in Okinawa prior to her displacement by Shō Shin's Kikoe-ōgimi (high priestess) around 1500. The name Aoriyae refers to the deity as well as its priestess. From its likely origins as a water-well deity in Kumejima, Aoriyae became associated with wind, rain, and protection from storms.[75] Control over water in various forms is a theme we will encounter repeatedly in connection with powerful Ryukyuan men and women. This power is also a basic quality possessed by the deity Hachiman and Empress Jingū, as discussed in the next chapter.

Like Hachiman, Aoriyae was also a military deity. For example, in the *Omoro,* she appears as an "island-smashing priestess" (*shima-uchi-gimi*), with "island" meaning any defined community:

> Acclaimed Aoriyae
> Resounding Aoriyae
> Island-smashing Aoriyae forever
> . . . .[76]

and

> Acclaimed Aoriyae
> Because you are an island-smashing priestess
> Aoriyae
> Provide for us a propitious day for our attack
> Acclaimed Aoriyae.[77]

Aoriyae was a combination of deity, priestess, military leader, shaman, and diviner. She was one of several Ryukyuan manifestations of Hachiman.

Aoriyae was closely connected with a sacred space called *shike,* in which she performed her rites. In Tsushima, *shike* is called *shigechi*. It is associated with solar worship, in which the shining sun functions as a mother deity, O-Hideri or Teruhi, whose light gives birth to a child deity. At Tsushima *shigechi* sites, rites called *are* venerate the solar deity O-Teruhi-sama. The term *shige* indicates a divine forest, thick with growth, and a hedge or fence that forms a double enclosure or a detached shrine at a distance from the main one. These sites often feature an altar made from a tall pile of rocks. Moreover, Tsushima solar worship is closely associated with Hachiman.[78]

The term *shike* (often in combination with other elements) occurs in *Omoro* songs, as in the following example:

> Acclaimed priestess Aoriyae
> Performs beautiful prayers in the *shike* space
> The emerging sun
> Is as lovely as a blooming flower
> Acclaimed priestess Aoriyae.[79]

Aoriyae also performs dances within the heavenly *shike* space (*kagura no shike uchi*), bathing her body in the sunlight. This description of a priestess transporting herself to a heavenly space refers to a shamanic trance.[80]

Although not identical, the *shigechi* of Tsushima is similar to the *yabosa/ yabusa* of Iki and western Kyushu. Another similarity with *yabusa* is that the Tokara Cultural Zone was the conduit through which the idea of *shike* entered Okinawa. In the Tokara islands there is a Teruhi shrine with priests (*hōi*) and priestesses (*neeshi* or *nūshi*). The expression for the priestess entering a shamanic trance is "the arrival of *shike*" (*shike ga kuru*). Moreover, a fearsome deity taking hold of the priestess is described as "*shike* is violent" (*shike ga arai*).[81] The term *neeshi* is probably related to *negami* (root deity), a type of female shaman in the Ryukyu islands. Throughout the Tokara islands there are sacred hills and mountains called Negamiyama.[82] In short, the cultural roots of the shamanic women so characteristic of Okinawan religion lie in points north of the Ryukyu islands within the East China Sea network.

North-to-South Migration

The flow of people, culture, and technology into Okinawa, Kumejima, and Sakishima was mainly from north to south. Some of this flow came from Michinoshima, some from Korea, and most of it from Japan, especially western Kyushu and nearby islands. Tanigawa Ken'ichi has metaphorically called it an "attack of northern culture."[83] Subsequent sections and chapters explore this topic further. Here I mention several physical manifestations of the north-to-south flow.

The climate in Okinawa is not suited to preserving skeletal remains, but there has been sufficient excavation and testing to warrant several conclusions. One is a significant break between the physical structure of prehistoric residents of Okinawa and those of later eras. Okinawan skeletal remains from about the eleventh or twelfth centuries onward begin closely to resemble their counterparts in Japan during the Kamakura and Muromachi periods.[84] As Thomas Pellard points out, "The bearers of Gusuku culture expanded within the whole Ryukyu Archipelago, and preexisting foragers, who were few, simply died out or were assimilated without leaving a significant trace."[85] *Omoro* descriptions of the clothing and other aspects of the appearance of local rulers suggest that at least some were direct arrivals from Kamakura-era Japan. Furthermore, excavations of Okinawan weapons and armor reveal that they were the same as those used in Japan during the era of the Northern and Southern Courts (ca. 1335–1392) and the Muromachi period. In general, most military items excavated in Okinawa were made in Japan.[86]

DNA evidence from recent studies is consonant with this situation. Studies of both modern and ancient DNA "tend to show that Ryukyuans form a group closely related to Mainland Japanese." Moreover, despite geographical proximity, "Southern Ryukyuans do not show any particular affinity with the Austronesian populations of Taiwan, and they form a clear subgroup with Northern Ryukyuans." Genetic diversity in the Ryukyu islands is relatively low, which indicates a lack of long-term isolation.[87] In other words, the Ryukyu islands were part of a larger network, and the migration from regions to the north that populated the Ryukyu islands and brought Gusuku culture, "agriculture, ceramics, and the Proto-Ryukyuan language," took place between approximately the tenth and twelfth centuries. Most likely the shell trade was the major economic driving force behind much of this migration.[88]

In devoting so much attention to the East China Sea network, I do not mean to suggest that there was little or no contact between eastern Japan or the Inland Sea region and the Ryukyu islands. The presence of the Kumano gongen cult in Okinawa and other Ryukyu islands since approximately the fourteenth century or earlier is one indication of that contact.[89] During the fifteenth and sixteenth centuries, Ryukyuan ships frequently sailed to Sakai and other ports in eastern Japan. Similarly, the kings of Chūzan enjoyed cordial relations with the Muromachi *bakufu*, whose shoguns referred to them as "Ryūkyū yononushi" (rulers of Ryukyu). When Ryukyu's royal government formally recognized aristocratic households during the eighteenth century, those claiming Japanese founding ancestors hailed from many regions of Japan.[90] Nevertheless, the East China Sea region was of paramount importance in the development of early Ryukyu, and therefore it is the focus of the early chapters of this book.

ALL THE WAY TO CHINA

Early Okinawa's ties with China are well known and frequently discussed, whereas ties with northern areas typically receive less attention in survey histories. China played a vital role in early Ryukyuan history as a conduit of material wealth. Nevertheless, prior to the seventeenth century, Chinese high culture had little impact on Ryukyu. Early Ryukyu's technology (metallurgy, agriculture, weapons), literary and aesthetic culture (including oral traditions), religious culture (including Buddhism), the various Ryukyuan languages, and the vast majority of Ryukyu's people came from the north. Much of the region's economic activity also took place north of Okinawa. One additional indication of the interconnectedness of the northern routes was the fact that distinctive Ryukyuan place-names found in the *Omoro* were known to Hakata merchants and to Koreans and appeared on their maps.[91]

The Takase-Fujian route mentioned above became popular around the 1340s, diverting maritime traffic from the previous route, a line from Hakata to Níngbō.[92] The new route greatly increased traffic through the southern Ryukyu islands, but smaller-scale private trade, piracy, and smuggling based at locations in Okinawa and points to the southwest had been occurring since the twelfth century and probably earlier.

During the thirteenth century, Chinese ceramics began to appear at major *gusuku* sites in Okinawa and the southern Ryukyu islands. Fragrant wine and other products from as far away as Thailand and Vietnam also began to make their way into the Ryukyu islands at this time. For example, a four-eared jar from the Khwae Noi River in Thailand was excavated at Nakijin.[93] After the start of formal tribute relations with Ming China in 1372, the material wealth of several major *gusuku* sites such as Kumejima, Katsuren, Shuri, and Nakijin increased dramatically. Celadon (green ware) ceramic dolls, Buddhist statues, candleholders, and other specialized products have been excavated at these sites, as well as a wide variety of metal goods.[94] China was a source of great wealth, both directly and indirectly. To understand Ming China's role in the development of Ryukyu, it is necessary to undertake a close study of *wakō*, the topic of the next chapter.

CHAPTER TWO

Wakō and the Ryukyu Islands

What would have been the main economic incentive to residing in the Ryukyu islands during the thirteenth or fourteenth centuries? As rugged islands with thin soil and limited sources of fresh water, Ryukyu did not inspire people to come there and stay for the agriculture. Fishing and related harvesting of sea products could have supported small villages, and the shell trade was lucrative into the thirteenth century. Other than seashells, however, local natural resources were not sufficient to support large concentrations of population and power, especially in Okinawa and Sakishima.

More concretely, local resources alone would not have been sufficient to support the many fortresses and castles (*gusuku*). Assuming that there were approximately one hundred fortresses on Okinawa by the fifteenth century, and using some reasonable assumptions to extrapolate the population backward in time from seventeenth-century records, there would have been an average of three hundred to five hundred people per fortress. Moreover, fortresses were overwhelmingly concentrated in the southern part of Okinawa. A model of extracting taxes from an agricultural surplus produced by a local population could not account for such a concentration of power centers.[1] Approaching this matter from the standpoint of archaeological evidence in Okinawa one arrives at the same conclusion. Agricultural surplus cannot explain Okinawa's numerous *gusuku*.[2]

The Ryukyu islands were an ideal abode for international mariners who operated outside of state boundaries and formal law.[3] As indicated in the previous chapter, the Ryukyu islands received people and culture from northern locations within the East China Sea network. It should hardly be surprising, therefore, that the major agents of early Ryukyuan political history were *wakō*. Indeed, it would require explanation had it *not* been the case, as Tanigawa Ken'ichi has explained: "In an age when *wakō* are cited as the reason for Goryeo's collapse and during which the Ming dynasty was threatened by *wakō* attacks, there is no evidence whatsoever that only the southwestern islands [Nansei shotō, i.e., Ryukyu] were outside of the range of *wakō* activity. On the contrary, this path consisting of one island after another would have been a natural route for southward moving *wakō* powers."[4] In addition to constituting political power centers, *wakō* shaped early Ryukyu's cultural and technological development.

Although the importance of *wakō* in early Ryukyu should be obvious, this point is rarely explored in survey histories, or even in most specialized studies. The tendency to focus on Okinawa as the center of Ryukyu at all times, combined with the tendency to regard "Ryukyu" as a natural political community that developed largely on its own, may be one reason. Another, of course, is that *wakō* often functioned as brigands. Furthermore, *wakō* did not record their activities in writing, and the official histories were written well beyond the time when *wakō* dominated the harbors of the Ryukyu islands. Pirates appear in their pages, but only as outside marauders who threaten Ryukyuan shipping.

The word *wakō* was apparently coined in Korea, appearing in a 1223 entry in *History of Goryeo* (K. *Goryeosa*). Actual pirate activity, however, had been taking place in the East China Sea region well before this time.[5] Recall the "southern barbarian" attacks on Dazaifu territory at the end of the tenth century. Maritime historian Tanaka Takeo explains that, for most people, the term *wakō* narrowly denotes "pirate bands consisting of Japanese who fly the flag of Hachiman and who set off to faraway locations across the East China Sea to pillage, burn, and assault."[6] Focusing on the fourteenth century, I refine and expand this overly narrow image of *wakō*. To set the stage, it is necessary to survey the sociopolitical conditions of the region.

THE TURBULENT FOURTEENTH CENTURY

The Mongol Yuan dynasty (1271–1368) in China created conditions of regional military and political unrest. Starting in 1231, the Goreyo state in Korea alternately resisted and appeased Mongol forces, finally becoming a vassal in 1271. Because it became standard practice for Korean kings to marry Yuan princesses at this time, "Koryŏ [Goreyo] became Yuan's 'son-in-law nation,' and the royal house of Koryŏ became nothing more than a branch of the Mongol ruling family."[7]

Consolidation of Mongol power in Korea soon led to two armed incursions into Japan—one in 1274, another in 1281—with a third threatened but that never materialized. These invasions by Mongol soldiers using Korean naval vessels wreaked havoc on Tsushima and Iki, the traditional links between Japan and Korea. Their apparent goal was to force the Kamakura *bakufu,* and thus the imperial court, into at least pro forma tributary relations with the Yuan dynasty. If so, both incursions failed, the second with help from a fortuitous typhoon. For our purposes, the Mongol incursions are less important for what actually happened at the time than for their strong impact on popular imagination in Japan for centuries thereafter. Moreover, the storm element is significant. Although the "myriad deities" of Japan all assisted in the defense effort, Hachiman, lord of storms and water, played the major role, at least in later imagination. Finally, these attacks on Japan were a setback for Korean–Japanese relations. From this time onward, Korea became a legitimate target in the minds of many Japanese.

I should emphasize that the typical medieval Japanese warrior did not fight for "Japan" or some other abstraction. Warriors typically fought for the glory of their households and for a chance to acquire the spoils of war.[8] A problem in the wake of the Mongol incursions was that the Kamakura *bakufu* had few spoils to distribute. The enthronement of the ambitious emperor Go-Daigo in 1318 set in motion events that led to the destruction of both the *bakufu* and the city of Kamakura in 1333. Civil war soon broke out, and after a few tumultuous years of military campaigns, two competing imperial courts emerged by 1337. The Northern Court was located at Kyoto under the de facto rule of Ashikaga Takauji, founder of the Muromachi *bakufu*. The Southern Court, under Go-Gaigo and his successors, was located to the south in the mountains of Yoshino.

Warfare between the two courts lasted until a reunification deal went into effect in 1392. Dissatisfaction over implementation of this arrangement resulted in new outbreaks of fighting during the fifteenth century and a reemergence of the Southern Court, a point missing in many textbook accounts of Japanese history but very important for understanding the history of the southern Ryukyu islands.

Back in Korea, the failed Mongol incursions into Japan helped weaken Goreyo society, if from no other cause than the heavy resource burdens the campaigns imposed. Yuan policies also sowed dissention within Goreyo's royal family, for example, by appointing separate kings of Shěnyáng (Mukden) with jurisdiction over Koreans residing in Manchuria. The 1350s were especially volatile in both Korea and China. Mongol power was on the decline, and in 1352 Zhū Yuánzhāng (1328–1398) joined the anti-Mongol insurgency that was already under way. He founded the Ming dynasty in 1368 as the Hóngwǔ emperor. It is important to bear in mind that Hóngwǔ worked to consolidate power throughout his long reign and that warfare between Ming and Mongol forces continued well after 1368. Among other things, this continuing warfare meant that the Ming court needed outside supplies of sulfur and horses.

Pro-Yuan versus anti-Yuan factions in Korea during the 1350s and 1360s fueled great unrest, with the anti-Yuan King Gongmin (r. 1351–1374) as the central figure. Especially during the 1350s, Gongmin sought to enhance his power by undermining powerful families. The details need not concern us, but one result was to cause locally prominent Koreans to flee to China or elsewhere, almost certainly including Ryukyu. There is considerable evidence of direct Korean presence in Okinawa from the 1350s and for several decades thereafter, a topic I examine later. It is possible that King Satto (or Sado, r. 1355–1397) was one such refugee.

The other important development during the 1350s was a significant rise in the frequency and severity of *wakō* attacks on Korea. The main goal of these attacks was grain, but the pirates made off with anything of value, including people and even boats. Korea's three southern provinces produced the most rice, and transporting it to northern areas is most efficiently done by ship. As we have seen, the fall and winter winds are northerly, blowing across the peninsula from the continent. The winds reverse direction during the spring. Therefore, the state established local storehouses for tax rice and cloth collected during the autumn, which were shipped north toward the capital Gaeseong starting in the late spring.[9] *Wakō* knew of this system and typically attacked the transport vessels at various stages of the shipment process. Before describing their attacks on Korea in connection with Japan's northern and southern courts, I will examine the *wakō* themselves and some aspects of their religion.

SEA PEOPLE OF THE MARGINS

There is no simple definition of *wakō* that covers all cases. In general, *wakō* were seafarers who operated in and around the margins of cultural and state borders and often migrated in search of economic opportunities. They pursued whatever activities might turn a profit, including trade in goods and people, diplomatic activities (often combined with trade), mercenary military service, the provision of security and protection services, and full-scale marauding.[10] Depending on seasons and circumstances, *wakō* might also engage in agriculture and fishing.

Wakō were not necessarily Japanese.[11] Many fourteenth-century *wakō* were Korean,[12] and many sixteenth-century *wakō* were Chinese. Peoples of other backgrounds also filled their ranks. Moreover, some *wakō* were not obviously one nationality or another. Whether from growing up in mixed ethnic communities, having mixed parentage, or resulting from extensive travel across cultural zones, many *wakō* possessed native or near-native multicultural knowledge, a vital tool of their trade. However, Japanese tended to serve as a common language among *wakō*, and most of their bases were in Japan because of the absence of strong central authority there until the end of the sixteenth century.

The term *wakō* overlaps but is not congruent with "pirate" (J. *kaizoku*). It can be difficult to put *wakō* into perspective. One point to bear in mind is that any merchant activity in premodern East Asia over sea-lanes was a dangerous undertaking. Natural hazards were a potential threat, but people typically posed a greater danger. Almost any seafaring merchant in, for example, 1400 had to sail with an armed crew or escort and be willing to deploy violence. Depending on circumstances, merchants might also employ *wakō* to protect their cargo from other *wakō*.

In pirate mode, *wakō* bands attacked other ships, grain boats, and entire communities, sometimes destroying them. They seized people and held them for ransom or sold them into servitude. *Wakō* even maintained cavalry units and were able to attack points far inland. Their depredations in the Korean peninsula extended as far north as Uiju on the Yalu River.[13] Much of this activity was "rational" in the sense that it was designed to turn a profit for the pirate group. However, *wakō* sometimes engaged in gratuitous violence. In any case, they often constituted a menace to coastal populations and even to states.

Wakō were not a menace in every circumstance, however. It was possible to make deals with *wakō* bands. Moreover, eliminating them by sheer military force was nearly impossible. *Wakō* were often well connected over a large geographic zone. They could deliver goods or people, including diplomats, to places located across dangerous waters. If a local ruler in Ryukyu needed a skilled metal worker, or an entire crew of skilled metal workers, tile makers, potters, or shipwrights, *wakō* could usually arrange to transport such people from Japan or Korea to where they were needed. If an early Ming emperor needed several hundred head of military horses and was willing to pay a high price for them, *wakō* groups in places like Jeju island in Korea, Tsushima (four pastures, roughly two thousand horses during the fifteenth century)[14] or Okinoerabu island in Ryukyu had the livestock and know-how to convey them to China. *Wakō* could either produce or deliver superior agricultural tools and weapons to relatively underdeveloped places such as the Ryukyu islands. Local populations or rulers, therefore, might welcome *wakō* because of their knowledge, goods, and capabilities.

Wakō often lived aboard houseboats (*ebune*) in Japan's Inland Sea and in western Kyushu. According to a 1510 Korean description of such vessels in and around the islands near Hakata, entire families lived on board the ships. Moreover, the sailors had a weathered appearance, their language and clothing differed somewhat from that of most Japanese, and though armed with bows and swords, they were particularly skilled at boring holes in the hulls of enemy vessels.[15] Merchants and fisher people dwelled on such vessels, as did adventurers, outlaws, remnants of defeated warrior bands, and others down on their luck.[16] Some of them set sail for the Ryukyu islands at various times.

Although piracy in the East China Sea never stopped, there were two periods of particularly intense activity. The first was circa 1350–1420, and the second circa 1470–1600. It is common, therefore, to distinguish between early (*zenki*) *wakō* and later (*kōki*) or second-wave *wakō*. Tanaka Takeo has created tables of all known *wakō* attacks, which are available in several of his books.[17] With respect to early political communities in the Ryukyu islands, our main concern is early *wakō*. Later *wakō* also influenced Ryukyuan history, as we will see.

Several figures who were either *wakō* or had close ties with them played prominent roles as intermediaries between Korea and Ryukyu during the fifteenth century. I mention them here as examples of mariners who traveled across dangerous sea-lanes in pursuit of profit. Kin Genchin (K. Kim Wonjin) was apparently a resident of Hizen. Korean records describe him as Japanese in some passages and Korean in others, and he operated easily in either place. He served the Matsuura family of Hizen and the Shimazu family of Satsuma as an envoy to Korea, first appearing in Korean records in 1423. He carried a letter from the Korean court to Shimazu Hisatoyo asking for the repatriation of Koreans who had been sold into servitude. Hisatoyo, who was seeking to solidify foreign trade connections, responded by entrusting nine people to Genchin, who repatriated them to Korea. In 1429, a group of shipwrecked Ryukyuans drifted into Korea, and Genchin orchestrated their return. In 1435, while in Korea as an agent of the Matsuura, he allowed the use of his ship for Ryukyuans in Korea to return home. In 1437, he traveled to Ryukyu to repatriate a group of Koreans.[18] Kin Genchin's activities highlight the geographical network linking Ryukyu with Kyushu and Korea, and the importance of Japanese-based intermediates in Ryukyu–Korean connections.

A letter in the name of King Shō Hashi explained that a party of Ryukyuans who arrived in Korea in 1431 had traveled aboard the ship of Sōda Rokurōjirō, an agent of the lord of Tsushima. The Korean court granted the Ryukyuans and Rokurōjirō treatment as foreign envoys. These envoys explained that pirate activity had interfered with the transmission of Ryukyuan embassies to Korea, but they were eager to restore such exchanges. Furthermore, there were over one hundred Koreans in Ryukyu who had been rescued from pirates. It was the desire of Shō Hashi's court to send them back to Korea, but it lacked sufficiently large ships. In 1433, Rokurōjirō repatriated a group of Ryukyuans from Korea to Okinawa. In correspondence, Rokurōjirō sometimes appears as a "pirate chieftain" (C. *zéizhŭ*, J. *zokushu*), suggesting that the drafters of Shō Hashi's correspondence saw the mariner as a *wakō* leader.[19] Rokurōjirō's father, Sōda Saemontarō, was a powerful *wakō* head in Tsushima, and his influence there led to a Korean attack on the island in 1419.[20]

In addition to Genchin and Rokurōjirō, the Hakata merchant Dōan traveled between Korea and Ryukyu during the 1450s. Tanaka describes such men as "trans-national royal envoys" of uncertain citizenship, who served different rulers in the East China Sea region. Moreover, "there were many cases of changing over from *wakō* into merchants or envoys."[21]

HACHIMAN AND *WAKŌ*

By the 1550s, Hachiman flags had become emblematic of *wakō* vessels along the China coast commonly known there as Hachiman ships (*bāfān chuán*). The flags functioned both as religious talismans and as a means to communicate with other vessels.[22] One variety of Hachiman flag originated among Seiseifu retainers, who served the Southern Court government in Kyushu.[23] Long before Hachiman flags came into common use on ships, Hachiman served as the main *wakō* deity.

Today, Hachiman (sometimes, Yahata or Yawata) is a vastly popular Japanese deity housed in over forty thousand shrines. Like many Japanese deities, Hachiman is a complex mixture of Buddhist, local, and international elements. Therefore, Hachiman has a range of qualities and appears in different guises that typically highlight one aspect or another. We need not undertake a full survey of this much studied deity, but a basic understanding of Hachiman's origins and major manifestations is one key to comprehending the *wakō* roots of Ryukyu's early rulers.

During the eighth century, Hachiman resided in northern Kyushu in at least two sites. One was the Usa Hachiman Shrine (Usa City, Ōita Prefecture). This shrine was clearly of great political importance, and it played a decisive role in the so-called Dōkyō Incident of the 760s.[24] The other site was the Daibu Hachiman Shrine in Fukuoka. This region of northern Kyushu had close ties with the Korean peninsula.

Legends connected with the Usa Hachiman Shrine link Hachiman with shamanic transformations involving a golden hawk and Emperor Ōjin and, through him, to his mother Jingū, legendary conqueror of Korea. Other links with ancient Hachiman worship in Japan include maritime activity; the Ama family, which merged with the Usa and worshipped a dragon king; and the Karajima family, immigrants from Korea who brought with them shamanistic religious practices.[25] As the Hachiman cult spread in Japan, Hachiman took on the dual qualities of a deity of war and of agriculture. Moreover, from his earliest manifestations in Japan, Hachiman was also a blacksmith deity. These aspects are all closely related: blacksmiths forge both the weapons of war and the tools that enhance agricultural prosperity. Ryukyuan folk songs and legends frequently speak of blacksmith deities, blacksmiths arriving from Japan, and the military power and productivity associated with them. All of the agricultural deities in Miyako are also blacksmith deities.[26] As we will see, blacksmiths and metal play key roles in the official biographies of many early kings.

Suzuki Mitsuo argues that the likely place of Hachiman's origin was Jeju island and the southern coastal areas of Korea across from it. One feature of the religion of Jeju island is worship of a dragon deity named Halmang. A closely related deity was Yeongdeung, who controlled wind and rain on the sea and appeared either as an older woman with a child or as a dragon. Moreover, Yeongdeung or Yeongdeung-Halmang developed the dual character of a fierce wind deity of the seas and an agricultural deity, like the dual character of Hachiman in Japan. According to Suzuki, the Yeongdeung of Jeju was the oldest version of what eventually became Māzŭ (J. Maso) on the Chinese coast. Māzŭ is a female deity who guides ships, and Tiānfēi (J. Tenpi) is a variant form. Moreover, the idea of a woman exerting a divine protective influence over male relatives—in the Ryukyu islands—may ultimately have come from this Yeongdeung source.[27]

Ōei no Gaikō is the Japanese name for the summer 1419 Korean military attack on Tsushima to suppress piracy. Owing to incomplete information about the event on the Japanese mainland, and a lack of awareness that the Yuan dynasty and the Goryeo kingdom in Korea had fallen decades earlier, rumors quickly spread to the effect that the military campaign had been another Mongol attack on Japan. In this context, Hachiman as a divine reincarnation of Jingū turned back the invasion at Tsushima. She did so by creating a fierce, cold wind that froze the attackers to death and destroyed their ships.[28] Again we see Hachiman as a military deity of wind, water, and storms.

As a deity of wind and water, one of Hachiman's symbols was the *tomoe* emblem.[29] It was also the emblem of Ryukyu's kings. Its standard form (*mitsu-domoe*) consists of three comma-like jewels (*magatama*) in a circle that implies swirling movement (see chapter-opening pages in this book). Excavations of *ryūhai* jewels in Tanegashima suggest a connection between the dragon form of Yeongdeung and the *tomoe* emblem. The likely origin of the *tomoe* was the Korean kingdom of Silla, with a transmission from the Korean peninsula to the Usa Hachiman Shrine.[30]

Hachiman took on secondary qualities derived from his fundamental character as a deity of wind and water. One was that of a protective deity of sea-lanes and rough seas. Similarly, as a deity who could control the weather, Hachiman played a vital role in agriculture. He was also a blacksmith, who might appear in a number of guises, especially as a white-haired old man (*kaji no okina*). The old man we will encounter in Ryukyu's official histories, who gave a rousing speech leading to the enthronement of Kanemaru as Shō En, resembled this manifestation of Hachiman. Biographical legends of several early kings, some of which appear in the official histories, feature metal workers and blacksmiths as facilitating their rise to power. Kanemaru's biography, for example, features blacksmiths appearing at crucial turning points in his life.[31]

From this brief discussion of Hachiman's qualities, his close links with *wakō* should be clear.[32] In the context of the East China Sea network and early Ryukyu, the presence of Hachiman almost always indicated *wakō* connections. Hachiman shrines were present in Tsushima, Iki, parts of coastal Kyushu, and in almost all of the Tokara islands.[33] In other words, the regional distribution of Hachiman shrines closely overlaps *yabosa* and *shike* sites discussed in the previous chapter.

RYUKYUAN MANIFESTATIONS OF HACHIMAN

Origins of Ryukyu explains that Hachiman originally came from heaven to stabilize and defend Japan. "He is the protective deity of that state." It then relates a story of King Shō Toku establishing a Hachiman shrine near Naha to celebrate his successful conquest of Kikai, and it explains that this Hachiman shrine houses a deity that protects the Ryukyuan state.³⁴ Although only one of the seven major shrines in premodern Okinawa is formally a Hachiman shrine, a closer look reveals broader Hachiman influence.

For example, the founding legend of the shrine at Naminoue in Naha recounts that a spirit rock ended up there (details omitted). One night in an oracle, the spirit in the rock announced: "I am Japan's Kumano Gongen.... Build a shrine here, and I will protect the state." Moreover, after the shrine was built, worshippers discovered a bell floating in the sea. They retrieved it and set it up in the main shrine building.³⁵ Floating bells were associated with Hachiman and *wakō*. The actual bell at Naminoue came from a temple in Gyeongsang Province on the southeast coast of Korea. It was cast in 956 and likely arrived in Okinawa in 1467, during the reign of Shō Toku.³⁶ The bell was probably plundered from a Korean temple and eventually made its way to Naha on a *wakō* ship before its installation at Naminoue.³⁷

Tsukishiro is a form of Hachiman. Its origins derive from moon iconography associated with Sōgyō Hachiman (Hachiman appearing as a Buddhist priest) and Hachiman's Buddhist counterpart, Amida. The basic religious idea is that Hachiman is present in moonlight, hence the full-moon images on Hachiman flags. Moreover, it was common practice to conduct rites associated with Hachiman during the night of the full moon because the deity was fully visible at this time.³⁸ Shō Hashi, de facto founder of the First Shō dynasty, maintained a Tsukishiro (lit. "in place of the moon") shrine at in Sashiki in southeast Okinawa. The shrine housed a magic stone, which was the native-place deity of Shō Hashi's family. Recall from the discussion of the Tametomo legend in the previous chapter that Shō Hashi's grandfather, Samekawa, came to Okinawa from Kyushu. As I explain further in chapters 4 and 6, Samekawa migrated from Sashiki in Higo to Sashiki in Okinawa. The Tsukishiro form of Hachiman was the deity he brought to Okinawa.³⁹

Omoro songs mention Tsukishiro in connection with four places: Sashiki and Chinen in southeast Okinawa, places with close legendary connections to the origins of wet-rice agriculture, Shuri, and Okinoerabu island.⁴⁰ Okinoerabu served as a pasture for *wakō* horses, and it was the domain of the *wakō* leader Guraru Magohachi (active early fifteenth century). In one *omoro*, the light of the moon over the Kikuyanaki grove in Okinoerabu links that island with Shuri:

> The acclaimed Sejiarakimi priestess
> Resounding in the east
> From above the Kikuyanaki grove

> The rising moon
> Bathes Shuri grove with its light
> And to my venerable lord [the king]
> Truly, the light reaches.[41]

This *omoro* suggests strong ties between the rulers in Shuri and Okinoerabu.

At Shuri, Tsukishiro appears in connection with a religious rite, most likely a preparation for war:

> The high priestess Kikoe-ōgimi
> Resounding One of Great Spiritual Power
> Wearing red armor
> It is her sword striking, certainly
> That will resound throughout the country
> She has Tsukishiro in the lead
> She has the Knower of Things in the lead.[42]

One interpretation of this song is that the high priestess is dressed as a male warrior participating in a procession. A sorcerer bearing the Tsukishiro stone precedes her.[43]

The Aoriyae priestess of Nakijin often channeled divine power for military purposes. In this mode, she was a northern Okinawan version of Jingū as a manifestation of Hachiman.[44] Aoriyae was also closely connected with the *tomoe* symbol:

> Acclaimed Aoriyae priestess
> Who, wearing the triple-*tomoe*
> Enters into the capital of the divine throne
> Acclaimed Aoriyae priestess.[45]

In other words, *tomoe* jewels worn around the neck facilitate a shamanic connection with the seat of divine power. In one form or another, Hachiman was a prominent deity in early Ryukyu.

KANEYOSHI AND THE SOUTHERN COURT *WAKŌ*

A crucial context for the development of Ryukyu was the warfare between Japan's Northern and Southern Courts, especially in Kyushu. *Wakō* attacks on the Korean coast intensified in 1350 and continued for decades. Attacks occurred on a large scale, sometimes involving hundreds of ships and thousands of combatants. The most intense period of *wakō* marauding was from 1375 to 1388. Some scholars point to lack of agricultural productivity in the classic *wakō* havens as a major reason for these depredations. Paddy land, for example, comprised only 3 percent of Tsushima. Similarly, poverty was also a severe problem in Kyushu at this time.[46] Given the massive scale of *wakō* attacks, however, another impetus was the need for grain to supply Southern Court armies. Prince Keneyoshi, the court's leader in Kyushu, actively collaborated with *wakō* toward this end. In other words, *wakō* based near the coast of Higo and at Tsushima, Iki, and Matsuura supported Prince Kaneyoshi and his Southern Court by providing needed supplies, plundered from Korea. In return, Kaneyoshi provided protection for the *wakō*. In contrast, *Kyūshū tandai* Imagawa Ryōshun, head of the Northern Court in Kyushu, sought to suppress *wakō* piracy.[47]

Envoys from Korea traveled to Japan in an effort to stem the tide of piracy, the first of whom arrived at Kyoto in 1366. The Muromachi *bakufu* sought good relations with Korea, but its control over Kyushu was limited at the time. The piracy problem prompted the *bakufu* to pursue military pacification of Kyushu.[48] It eventually succeeded, but the Southern Court *wakō* became even more active during the 1370s, prompting the following 1375 message from the *bakufu* to the Korean court via the Tenryūji priest Tokusō Shūsa: "Kyushu is broken apart by rebelling subjects and does not pay tribute; the stubborn subjects of the Western seacoast have become pirates. But these are not the doing of the *bakufu*. We are planning to dispatch a general to Kyushu to pacify the area and can promise to suppress the pirates."[49] Success in carrying out this promise required more than fifteen years. Southern Court *wakō* also attacked China, albeit less frequently. While the Korean court had obvious reasons to be gravely concerned with putting a stop to the *wakō* attacks, the reasons for the similarly intense concern by the Hóngwǔ emperor require further explanation.

Notice that Korean envoys courted the *bakufu* even though it lacked the power to suppress piracy. "In contrast to the close association between the Seiseifu lords and *wakō*," explains Miyara Angen, "the *Kyūshū tandai* viewed the combined power of *wakō* and Seiseifu as the enemy." Moreover, *wakō* groups "made their bases in the Matsuura peninsula, Iki, Tsushima, and Amakusa in Higo, from which they seized authority over the sea-lanes from the East China Sea to the Straits of Korea. Seiseifu and the *wakō* had exactly the same plan and vested interests. By plundering Korea and coastal China, the *wakō* and Seiseifu participated in a relationship of mutual profit."[50] It is possible that the Korean court misunderstood the contours of political power in Japan at the time, especially the Seiseifu–

wakō connection. By contrast, the Ming court dealt directly with Prince Kaneyoshi, attempting to make him into king of Japan. Some scholars have taken this move as a sign that Ming officials did not understand Japan's internal conditions. However, it is more likely that the Ming court knew exactly who controlled the *wakō* and thus initially focused on Kaneyoshi.[51]

The basic timeline of the rise and fall of the Southern Court in Kyushu begins in 1348 with a castle on the Higo coast near Yatsushiro that had two names, Hanaoka castle or Sashiki castle. It was in the territory of the Nawa family, who provided naval forces for the Southern Court. Seiseifu headquarters moved around Kyushu with the changing tides of war. Seiseifu occupied the same space as the old Dazaifu between 1360 and 1372, the peak of Southern Court power. It relocated to Kikuchi in the mountains of Higo until 1381. Then Seiseifu migrated, via Take and Uto in Higo, to Nawa-controlled Yatsushiro, where it remained until 1390. Kaneyoshi died in 1383. His son Yoshinari succeeded him and had already been active as the de facto Southern Court leader since about 1375. The Southern Court reunited with the Northern Court in 1392, and in 1405, the Nawa family relocated to Uto.[52]

The defeat of the Southern Court in Kyushu caused migrations of *wakō* into the Ryukyu islands. Miyara explains that, with the defeat of Southern Court forces in Kyushu:

> the power of the Kikuchi, Matsuura, and other families declined, and the *wakō* in whom these military leaders had invested and [had] relied upon sought sanctuary overseas. However, the naval power that they had developed did not decline in the slightest. They gradually migrated southward into the Ryukyu islands, beyond the reach of the power of the Muromachi *bakufu*. There, they established bases of power from which they engaged in piracy and private trade with China and southeast Asia.[53]

The collapse of Seiseifu power during the 1380s and 1390s put pressure on the Southern Court *wakō* in Kyushu to migrate. Moreover, developments in Korea also pressured *wakō* bands to change their tactics.

Analysis of the number and size of *wakō* attacks compared with what they obtained and the losses they incurred reveals that even during the period 1364–1374, they had begun to experience diminishing returns to scale. The trend continued. The number and size of attacks increased during the 1370s and 1380s, but Korean resistance and evasion resulted in fewer per capita gains. For the most part, the effectiveness of *wakō* marauding in Korea tracked the rise and decline of Seiseifu. One result of decreasing *wakō* gains in Korea was an increase in raids on the Chinese coast.[54] An element in this complex mix was increasingly effective Korean defenses, including costal fortifications, coordinated signal beacons using fire, more and better ships, better commanders, and more soldiers along the coast. The founding of the Joseon (Yi) dynasty in 1392 accelerated this process.[55]

By the 1390s Southern Court *wakō* lost their state sponsors and many of their bases. They could still operate from islands such as Tsushima, but a hostile Muromachi *bakufu*, improved Korean defenses, and lower demand for the possible spoils of their attacks on Korea had the effect of pushing *wakō* bands southward. By this time, the busiest harbor in the Ryukyu islands was Naha.

NAHA AND THE TRADE IN CAPTIVES

The port of Naha served as a major intersection within the East China Sea network through which "pirates, captives, fishermen, divers, envoys, monks, traders, and other people traveled" during the fourteenth through sixteenth centuries.[56] Merchants or *wakō* in Japan would have found sailing to Naha for trade more practical or more profitable than journeying directly to the coast of China or farther afield. The result was the creation of "a strange relationship of dependency" between Ryukyuan and Japanese merchants.[57]

The first appearance of Ryukyu as a state in Korean records begins with a 1389 statement that an embassy from Ryukyu returned Koreans who had been captured by pirates.[58] The repatriation of captured Koreans recurred frequently thereafter as a reason for Ryukyu-sponsored voyages to Korea. Although the Korean court granted favorable treatment to these embassies, it did not actively encourage trade with Ryukyu.[59] In this context, Korean people were valuable commodities, whose repatriation permitted potentially lucrative trade embassies. Repatriation was not necessarily an act of benevolence. It constituted "one variety of the slave trade."[60]

In 1453, four shipwrecked Koreans washed ashore in "Gaja" (K. Wasa), a term indicating the Tokara islands in general, not the specific island of Gajajima. Two of them returned home in 1453, but their case was not simply one of rescue and repatriation. First, the four were split, with Shimazu (Satsuma) personnel taking custody of two and Ryukyuan personnel taking custody of the other two. Those in Ryukyuan hands did not travel directly from Tokara back to Korea. Instead, they went to Kasari in Amami-Ōshima and then on to Shuri, where they were given to the king's older brother. By the time the Hakata-based agent Dōan became aware of them, the Koreans had been in Okinawa for three years, where they kept watch over a royal storehouse. Dōan purchased the Koreans from two Ryukyuans during his three-month stay in Okinawa.[61] Murai Shōsuke points out that "Even though Dōan took charge of and repatriated them, the process certainly had the character of human trafficking. Therein lies the reason for the zeal with which Ryukyuan kings repatriated Koreans."[62]

There was a close relationship between pirates and merchants with respect to the trade in captives throughout East Asia. *Wakō* raids on the Korean coast or elsewhere typically resulted in the seizure of people as well as goods. Some of these people ended up as laborers in Japan, but most were resold to Japanese merchants, daimyo, or agents of Ryukyuan kings.[63] In many cases, these parties would repatriate captives to Korea in return for compensation. Some captives were also purchased and returned to Korea by Korean agents who traveled to Japan. Repatriation was an integral part of the trade in captives, and the king of Ryukyu (whoever controlled Naha) was a major operator in this arena.[64]

In 1456, strong winds blew Ryang Seong and other Koreans into Kumejima. Eventually, they made their way to Okinawa and back to Korea. Ryang wrote an account of his sojourn in Okinawa, which appeared in *Joseon Veritable Royal Records* in an entry dated 1462. He describes boarding a "tribute ship" after a month and going to Okinawa, where he resided for a month at an "official hall" near the shore, five *li* away from the royal capital. This facility was probably located at Tomari, the port next to Naha that typically served as anchorage for the relatively smaller ships sailing to Okinawa from the other Ryukyu islands. Ryang also describes a nearby earth-walled enclosed neighborhood that was home to over one hundred households, some Korean and some Chinese. Most likely, the enclosed district was Kumenri, later known as Kumemura. It was located in Ukishima, the island that separated the harbors of Tomari and Naha. Although commonly regarded as Ryukyu's ethnic Chinese enclave, Kumemura was also home to a significant population of Koreans.[65]

Ryang noted that "there is no theft in this country," and then described the punishments for theft. He apparently meant that Ryukyuans did not steal. Those who might do so were "people who arrived here after having been sold from Japan, who frequently take other people's belongings."[66] This intriguing passage hints at the multiethnic composition of Naha and its role as a hub for captives. Ikuta Shigeru has highlighted the flourishing trade in people at Naha, which provided the king and his family with labor to produce the sulfur, horses, and other commodities for the tribute trade. The use of unfree labor probably functioned to keep tax extractions from local residents low.[67]

On Ukishima in Naha were a Chinese community, a Korean community, and a "Japanese" community that "had intermingled and merged with local society to such a degree that it was difficult to pinpoint any specific Japanese settlement. Furthermore, though they used the 'Japanese language' (*wago*) and wore 'Japanese clothes' (*wafuku*), they were not necessarily 'Japanese' in an ethnic sense. Operating within 'pirate-like conditions' in a maritime world, they were hybrid entities referred to as *wajin*."[68] Until the 1620s, Naha remained an international hub in which peoples from throughout the East China Sea network resided and often intermixed.

POWERFUL MEN FROM YAMATO

As already noted, many Ryukyuan legends feature blacksmiths, blacksmith deities, or blacksmiths posthumously deified, who arrived from Yamato (Japan, typically Kyushu). The origin tale of the Sakibaru grove in Ōhama Village in Ishigaki tells of two brothers who sailed for Japan to supply their village with metal tools. Their journey took them to Bōnotomari in Satsuma. Until well into the twentieth century, Bōnotomari and nearby Akime were the home ports of blacksmith shops that conducted business throughout the Ryukyu islands.[69] Kanidono, the deity of Nagayama grove in Irabu island, near Miyako, originated as a sailor from Japan. He made and distributed metal farm tools, and the islanders deified him.[70]

One legend found in Sakishima tells of a fierce, powerful blacksmith who arrived from Japan and extracted forced labor from the local people (Taketomi); another describes a blacksmith deity made of iron whose violent behavior frightened the local population (Yonaguni). In both tales, the residents asked the blacksmith's wife to kill him. She knew of a tiny area of exposed flesh on his otherwise metal body, and stabbed him there, in the neck, while he slept. The people were grateful.[71] In one Yonaguni variant, the stabbed iron deity was Nebara Kanidono, who had come to Yonaguni from Yakushima. He did not die immediately and let out a scream so terrifying that over a thousand of the island's residents threw themselves into the sea and drowned. Thereby, the iron deity reached the western limit of his travels at Yonaguni, the westernmost point of the Ryukyu islands.[72]

Similarly, a legend from southern Okinawa features a Japanese warrior named Sagara Ichirō (suggesting a Higo origin) or Kagoshima Ichirō (Satsuma origin), who landed near Sashiki and made his way to Itoman. There, a local warrior whose body was covered in sharkskin, and thus was as hard as iron, slayed the newcomer. Later, that same local hero met his demise after being stabbed in the space between his fingers, his only area of soft flesh. This local hero may have been based on legends about Shō Hashi, who was closely associated with sharks, the totem animal of his family, the Samekawa, which means "shark river."[73]

Throughout Sakishima, several sacred groves worship a deity known as Kanedono (Kandunu). In the lore of some groves, he arrived from Kumejima. At the Nagayama grove in Irabu and at the Ungusuku grove in Tarama, he arrived from Japan. A sacred song from the Ungusuku grove includes the following lines:

> Venerable blacksmith deity
> Who truly was born on the island of Yamato
> From three mountains of iron nuggets
> ....
> He built a giant bellows and piled up a giant anvil
> He built a giant hammer and a small hammer
> He built giant tongs and blacksmith tools. . . .

In other words, this blacksmith deity created farming tools and then set sail from Japan to arrive in Tarama.[74] At Uruka in Miyako, Uruka Ōtono is venerated for having brought shipbuilding skills and knowledge from Japan.[75]

These summaries are but a few examples of the origin legends connected with sacred sites and harbors in Okinawa and Sakishima. Similar legends are widespread in Michinoshima.[76] The basic message is consistent. Powerful men from Yamato show up at a port or harbor in the Ryukyu islands. Sometimes their arrival causes conflict; but more often these newcomers were a source of benefit. As Mitsugu Sakihara commented:

> We find all over the Ryūkyū Islands . . . folktales recording the coming of outsiders, very often Japanese warriors, with very little disturbance. . . . That they were almost invariably respected and welcomed seems to indicate they had an advanced culture, but the fact that they formed no homogeneous class or group . . . seems to mean that their integration was comparatively easy and without much conflict, due, perhaps, to their essential affinity to the island people.[77]

Sakihara's point resonates with a major argument of this book, namely, that the early Ryukyu islands functioned as a frontier region of Japan.

The following *omoro* is about soldiers landing at Unten harbor near Nakijin, the same place through which the founders of the first and second Shō dynasties passed, as well as an invading army from Satsuma in 1609 and, in legend, Minamoto Tametomo:

> Serikaku priestess
> Akeshino priestess
> Brings down rain
> To soak the armor
> Of arrivals at Unten
> Arrivals at Kominato
> Pour down on the Katsuo grove
> Falling rain
> To soak the armor
> Of Yamato [Satsuma] soldiers
> Of Yashiro [Yatsushiro] soldiers.[78]

After considering several possibilities, Iha Fuyū concluded that this song "tells of the landing of warrior band remnants, *wakō*, et cetera during the middle of the Muromachi period or later."[79]

Here and elsewhere, *omoro* sing of the arrival of armed Japanese. Such arrivals would have taken place frequently between 1380 and 1450 because of the larger political and military events examined above and in the next section. In 1991, an old suit of armor was found in a cave near Tamagusuku (near Sashiki) in southeastern Okinawa. Although badly decayed and rusted, the Japanese imperial court chrysanthemum crest in metal leaf was still evident on the breastplate. It was of early Muromachi period vintage.[80] Based on its age, location, and chrysanthemum crest, the armor probably came to Okinawa with Southern Court remnants, quite possibly with Shō Hashi's family.

THE SOUTHERN RYUKYU ISLANDS

The early history of the Miyako and Yaeyama island groups is subject to the same source-related limitations pertaining to Okinawa and the northern Ryukyu islands. Our main sources are extant legendary accounts, old songs, divination manuals, archaeological finds, and the distribution of place-names. Although legendary accounts compiled during the early modern era provide detailed narratives, we have no way to authenticate them.[81] It is reasonable to conclude that Sakishima was home to local warlords who came into the islands from Japan. They were of *wakō* background, and many or all of them were Southern Court partisans. The period during which they settled into the southern Ryukyu islands was the 1390s through the middle of the fifteenth century. In terms of common archaeological periodization of Sakishima, this influx of migrants corresponds to the Late Suku period (fourteenth to sixteenth centuries) and the Nakamori period (thirteenth through seventeenth centuries).[82]

Miyako

The details of Miyako's early political history come from legends about incessant rounds of warfare between local lords. Because these legends were written during the eighteenth or nineteenth centuries, they take on the qualities of a Chinese-style morality play. Entering the narrative in the middle of the fourteenth century, the Yonabaru family, led by Sata Ufuhito, was at war with the forces of Meguromori, the first leader of Miyako known by the honorific title Toyomiya (Tuyumiya). Initially, Meguromori's forces fared badly, and the situation seemed hopeless. Meguromori was about to kill himself when a dog he had kept, but which had been gone for seven years, suddenly reappeared and attacked the Yonabaru forces. Devouring people's legs and generally wreaking havoc, this dog was obviously no ordinary canine but a divine force. The tide of battle turned, and the remnants of the Yonabaru forces resorted to trickery, but to no avail. As for Meguromori, his virtue was such that "when he prayed for rain, rain fell immediately."[83] Throughout the Ryukyu islands, one mark of a potent ruler was the ability to control rain. In addition to Meguromori and the *omoro* quoted in the previous section, we will encounter many other examples. After their defeat, the surviving Yonabaru fled to various locations.

In the next generation, Masaku, childhood name of Yonaha-sedo Toyomiya, devised a way to revive Yonabaru fortunes by paying tribute to Chūzan, which took place around 1390. The people of Miyako were ignorant of virtues like benevolence, righteousness, loyalty, and filial piety and were constantly at war. Masaku sought to leverage the culture and influence of the great island "Okina" (Okinawa) to end this local misery. He set sail for the northeast, arrived in Naha, could not understand the language, but studied there for three years along with others from Miyako. Impressed with the determination of the Miyako group to learn the advanced civilization of Chūzan, King Satto initiated trade and bestowed other benefits.

This account reflects obvious Confucian values and the political geography of the early modern era. Similar to that of Masaku, Satto's legendary biography was also a rags-to-riches success story thanks to hard work and wise choices. Just as China began civilizing Okinawa via Satto, at least according to the official story, Masaku began civilizing Miyako with Satto's assistance. Yonaha-sedo became the first nominal lord of Miyako and Yaeyama, ushering in the "Toyomiya era," which lasted into the sixteenth century.[84]

All we can say with reasonable certainty at this point is that fourteenth-century Miyako was home to competing local lords. Moreover, the start of tribute trade between Okinawa and China probably brought news of Okinawan prosperity to Miyako and stimulated attempts to trade with Okinawa. Korean records suggest that Miyako was the only part of Sakishima trading with Okinawa during the fifteenth century. Moreover, it is likely that denizens of Sakishima traded directly with the coast of China.[85] It is possible that Shō Shin's military campaign in 1500 to conquer Yaeyama was in part a move to rein in such trade, which Chinese authorities would have regarded as illegal, a matter I consider in chapter 10.

The first leader in Miyako about whom we can be moderately certain was Nakasone Toyomiya. According to legend, he was born between 1457 and 1465, and we know that he was active around 1500, and possibly as late as the early 1520s. As an ally of Shō Shin, Nakasone helped suppress Oyake Akahachi's 1500 "revolt" in Yaeyama. It appears that Nakasone's immediate descendants fell out of favor with Shuri, thus ending the Toyomiya era. Another accomplishment attributed to Nakasone was winning over the loyalty of local people by digging a well to provide drinking water. Once again, notice the importance of water control in legitimizing a ruler.[86]

With this mainly legendary survey as background, we now turn to evidence of the arrival of *wakō* groups in the Tomori and Uruka (modern Sunagawa) districts of present-day Gusukube-chō in southern Miyako. The legend of every historically significant site in Miyako tells a tale of the arrival of people from the outside.[87]

According to one version of the founding legend of Miyako, a man from Japan and a local woman created a society there. Deified, one name for the man is Amarifua Kankanushi, "Heavenly Blacksmith Lord." Waste iron (*kanakuso*), which indicates active smelting or blacksmith work, has been excavated near Uruka. As we have noted, all agricultural deities in Miyako are also blacksmith deities, and all deities in its ancient folk songs have Japanese names. One local deity is Mayamato toki no shu, meaning literally "genuine Yamato divination lord." Mayamato ("true Yamato") was a common childhood name in Sakishima and Okinawa.[88]

There is overwhelming cultural evidence pointing to the arrival in Miyako of groups from Japan during the fourteenth century, and possibly earlier and later. Moreover, both archaeological and cultural evidence indicates that these groups pursued private trade with China.[89] Owing in part to limited resources in Miyako, and to competition for trade, these groups frequently fought each other.

Is it possible to be more specific about any of these groups? A historian of Miyako, Inamura Kenpu, has argued that divination manuals (*sōshi*) from the Tomori and Uruka areas reveal a link with Southern Court *wakō*. These manuals were part of the tradition of yin-yang divination (*onmyōdō*) associated with Abe no Seimei (921–1005). Although fairly complex, the manuals do not require literacy to perform divination, relying on a system of symbols. They also reveal a knowledge of basic astronomy commensurate with the navigational needs of seafarers.

Of particular interest are the prayers written in ordinary Japanese script on the "throne of the deities" section of the manuals. Here is a typical example, translated according to Inamura's analysis:

> Water deity (Mizu no kami ganashi)
> Northern mother country deity (Ne no hō nma terasu ganashi)
> Southern wealth and fortune deity (Uma no hō yononushi ganashi)
> Lord Ryōkai [Kaneyoshi] (Agarinarikane hyakuchōnushi)
> Ruler of the island (Shima no nushi)
> Ruler of the country (Kuni no nushi)[90]

If indeed Southern Court *wakō* ended up in Miyako pursuing unauthorized trade with China, it would have made sense to pray to the water deity first; subsequently to invoke a deity from one's northern place of origin; next to invoke a deity associated with good fortune in the south; and finally to praise the rulers of the island and country, whoever they might have been. The crucial term here is "Agarinarikane." *Agari* means east. Leaving out the details of his analysis, Inamura glosses *-narikane* in this case as the equivalent of Ryōkai, that is, Prince Kaneyoshi, the onetime Seiseifu head and brief "king" of Japan at the Ming court.[91]

Consideration of a wider range of names throughout the Ryukyu islands reveals that Agarinarikane, the *-narikane* element, or the equivalent is fairly common. In Okinawa, the *-kane* (or *-kani*) element indicates metal, and the name is associated with blacksmith sites.[92] The context of the divination manuals does suggest that Agarinarikane might refer to Prince Kaneyoshi, but we cannot be certain about this case. Given the close connection between *wakō* and metal in Ryukyu, it is entirely possible that the two meanings of -*kane*/-*kani* (metal and Kaneyoshi) coexisted. In Miyako, therefore, we find circumstantial evidence for the arrival of Japanese warrior or *wakō* groups in the wake of the Southern Court's initial defeat. In parts of Yaeyama, evidence for a link with Japanese warriors or *wakō* is stronger.

Yaeyama

Although local rulers or chieftains must have existed in the various Yaeyama islands, that region lacks even a legendary narrative for the fourteenth century or most of the fifteenth. According to some accounts, Yonaha-sedo Tomomiya became the nominal head of the Yaeyama islands, but Yonaha-sedo himself is best regarded as a legendary figure. The historical narrative of the Yaeyama islands opens with genuine people, but details about their activities are obscure. These figures, all local warriors or rulers, burst onto the scene toward the end of the fifteenth century.

The great local hero of Yaeyama was Oyake Akahachi (d. 1500), a rough contemporary of Nakasone Toyomiya. Most details of Akahachi's life are legendary, starting with his birth in Hateruma. Naata Ufushu (ca. 1456–1517; pronounced and written in various ways) was Akahachi's childhood friend. As adults, the two moved to Ishigaki. Another power holder from this era was Nakama Mitsukeima Eikyoku (pronounced and written in various ways). According to legend, he was a descendant of Taira remnants who landed at Kabira bay in Ishigaki. Miusuku Shishikadun (pronounced and written in various ways) was born in Hateruma and remained there, becoming its ruler. In the standard narrative, these four men were allies, or at least coexisted peacefully.

According to legend, Keraikedagusuku Yōcho was a descendant of *wakō*, who settled on the island of Iriomote. As his power expanded, Yōcho defeated Hirakubo Kana, ruler of the Hirakubo peninsula area of Ishigaki. Kana had a reputation as a fierce and cruel ruler, and Yōcho's defeating him did not initially upset the local balance of power.

Even the legendary accounts present no clear picture of what transpired to cause the war with Shuri in 1500. A typical explanation is that Miyako's Nakasone attempted to convince the stubborn and fiercely independent Akahachi to submit to Shuri's authority and send tribute. Akahachi began to mobilize a military force from his territory at Ōhama on Ishigaki and sought a military alliance with Hateruma's Miusuku Shishikadun, who refused. Akahachi next sent two agents to convince Shishikadun, but they ended up killing him and throwing his body into the sea. Akahachi subsequently sought an alliance with Kabira's Nakama Mitsukeima. He also refused, and Akahachi ended up killing him too.

Having thus conquered most of Ishigaki, Akahachi next attacked Naata Ufushu, his childhood friend. Two of Ufushu's brothers died in the fighting, but Ufushu himself escaped to Iriomote. From there, he sent a warning to Nakasone, who urged Shuri to send a military force. Thus began the war of 1500.[93] Miusuku Shishikadun was almost certainly a *wakō* leader, and Akahachi headed the Kawara *wakō* in Ishigaki, as we will see in later chapters. The point here is that the Miusuku-Akahachi rivalry was a conflict between *wakō* groups, and the Naata-Akahachi conflict probably was as well.[94]

The cultural evidence for Japanese migration into Yaeyama and *wakō* activity is similar to that of Miyako. We have already seen, for example, legends of powerful blacksmiths or iron deities taking up residence. The names of the sacred groves of Taketomi island, which served as a port, indicate trade between Yaeyama and Yakushima, Tokunoshima, Okinawa, and Kumejima.[95] The earliest evidence of *wakō* activity in Yaeyama goes back to about the 1430s.[96] In other words, the arrival of Southern Court *wakō* groups in Yaeyama was approximately one or two generations later than in Okinawa and Miyako. Moreover, there is an important difference in Yaeyama. Some legends and old songs speak of a return to Japan. This topic probably reflects the brief resurgence of the Southern Court during the first half of the fifteenth century as well as the relative dearth of resources in Yaeyama.

According to legend, Nakama Mitsukeima's father came to Ishigaki from Japan. The basic plot of the story connected with Mitsukeima's father is the same as the Minamoto Tametomo legend. Mitsukeima was the son of a Japanese warrior, pushed south by the tides of war, who married a local woman. While Mitsukeima was a young child, his father and older brother decided to return to Japan. His mother composed *Song of Eagle Island* (*Washi no shima uta* or *Bashi nu shima yunta*) as an expression of her hopes for their safe return and flourishing. The key image is an eagle laying eggs in a banyan tree, the eggs hatching, and the parents flying with their offspring to Japan. Moreover, Inamura has hypothesized that that their specific destination was Yatsushiro in Higo.[97]

The standard narrative of Yaeyama history that developed later puts Mitsukeima's death in the year 1500, because the stories of all of Yaeyama's local rulers became intertwined with Akahachi's "revolt." However, based on the distribution of rewards by Shuri soon thereafter, it appears that Mitsukeima had been dead well before 1500, probably for at least a decade.[98] If so, and if the song indeed reflects his father and older brother's return to Japan, the return would have taken place in the early or middle fifteenth century.

The Southern Court did not vanish after 1392. It remained a force for more than a century later and even played a role in the Ōnin War.[99] Go-Kameyama secretly fled Kyoto in 1414 to create the Latter Southern Court (Gonanchō) at Yoshino. Southern Court military resurgences took place throughout the 1420s and early 1430s. In 1443, Southern Court supporters raided Kyoto and seized the jewel, one of the three imperial regalia. In 1446, Southern Court armies sustained a major defeat, and the Yoshino area calmed down after 1470. In this context, Southern Court *wakō* groups who had migrated into the Ryukyu islands and who remained attached to their cause, or who had been unable to thrive in Ryukyu, would have been especially inclined to return during the 1430s or early 1440s.

I will return to the Southern Court in connection with Shō Hashi and later examine the warfare during Shō Shin's reign in detail. At this point we have seen extensive evidence of *wakō* in the Ryukyu islands during the fourteenth and early fifteenth centuries. Perhaps counterintuitively, *wakō* activity in the region is the main reason Ryukyu came into existence as a state within the Chinese tributary system, the topic of the next chapter.

CHAPTER THREE

A State for Trade Purposes

During the late fourteenth century, political organization within the Ryukyu islands consisted of local rulers based at fortresses near harbors. There were variations in the number and power of these rulers, and a range of possibilities regarding cooperation, competition, and conflict. Ryukyu was not a unified political entity at this time, nor was the island of Okinawa. In this chapter, I argue that the Hóngwǔ emperor provided strong incentives to bring Ryukyuan rulers into the Ming tribute trade to facilitate security policies after failing to make progress with Prince Kaneyoshi. The main issues were piracy and smuggling. Compared to its other tributary states, the Ming court extended favorable treatment to Ryukyu. This treatment did not mean that the Chinese court admired Ryukyu, nor was it a form of generosity. In effect, the port of Naha became the Ming dynasty's shipping terminal at a time when security policies prohibited Chinese merchants from conducting foreign trade under their own auspices.

The Ryukyuans who traveled abroad during the fifteenth century were not known for their refined manners. For example, after a meeting with the shogun in 1466, Ryukyuan envoys in Japan went outside the main gate of Kyoto and began shooting off firearms, terrifying local residents.[1] Those firearms came from China, where disorderly Ryukyuans often strained the patience of Ming officials. The Ming court was well aware that the Ryukyu islands were full of *wakō*. Indeed, its goal was to channel *wakō* through the Ryukyu islands and then into a nominally lawful framework over which Chinese authorities could exercise some control. Though expensive, the Ming court provided inducements designed to tame *wakō* residing in the Ryukyu islands. By roughly 1500, this taming process had largely succeeded. Korea pursued a similar approach vis-à-vis Tsushima beginning in the 1420s.

The Ming dynasty tended to be wary of unrestricted, uncontrolled foreign contact. One manifestation of this caution was a ban on private trade with foreign countries, the Maritime Prohibitions (*hǎijìn*), under which private trade remained illegal from 1374 to 1567.[2] The details, severity, and vigor with which these prohibitions were enforced varied during this period and need not concern us often. To some extent Chinese merchants were able to circumvent the prohibitions, but they nevertheless increased the demand for the goods that ships sailing under the aegis of a Ryukyuan king could obtain from Southeast Asia and elsewhere.

TRIBUTE TRADE

What is often called the "tribute system" became formalized during the early years of the Ming dynasty. Simply stated, foreign courts sent envoys and exotic products from their countries as "tribute" to the Chinese emperor. He responded by showering the "faithful" envoys with gifts and permitting private trade between Chinese merchants and the entourages that inevitably accompanied these envoys. The theoretical logic was that ritual formality (*lǐ*) should express hierarchical gradations of culture and civilization between countries. In practice, the system was a way to buy the passive or active cooperation of potentially problematic states or territories.

Given their location within the East China Sea region, their many small harbors, and the large harbor at Naha, the Ryukyu islands possessed a high potential for causing problems through piracy and smuggling and, conversely, a high potential for benefiting China as a legitimate conduit for trade goods. This situation is the main reason the Ming court invested so heavily in Ryukyu. Setting aside the question of whether this investment eventually paid off for China, it certainly changed the political and economic dynamics of the Ryukyu islands.

Because the terms of the tribute trade were generally advantageous to those who participated, many states were eager to do so. Presenting tribute involved theatrical subordination, but it did not usually entail political subservience. The potential for profit by the participants and the corresponding resource drain on China were such that the Ming court, and the Qing court after it, imposed restrictions on how often foreign countries could send tribute. The usual frequency was once in three years.

To participate in the system a local ruler had to possess the title "king" (*wáng*). There were several gradations of king, but the particulars need not concern us. How did a ruler qualify as king? The details varied with circumstances, but the minimum requirement was for someone in actual or apparent control of a territory to take the title and for Chinese officials to acknowledge it. This acknowledgment took concrete forms such as a crown, an official seal, and formal robes from the Chinese court. In functional terms, a king had to possess sufficient political power to execute his side of the agreement as well as, or ideally better than, any rival. In Ryukyu, whoever controlled the port of Naha was the obvious choice for king, but there was no rigid rule limiting the number or geographic density of kings.

One way to enhance profits was for countries to have multiple kings, all eager to pay tribute. Consider the small sultanate of Sulu, whose former territory is now part of Indonesia, the Philippines, and Malaysia. In Chinese eyes, Sulu came to consist of three little kingdoms, known simply as East, Central, and West. The king of the East was the first to send a tribute mission to China in 1417, presenting the Ming emperor with a giant pearl and a pot of Sulu soil. The array of impressive gifts he received in return either prompted the other kings to do the same or caused the other kings to come into existence and then do the same. This Chinese connection "laid down one of the most enduring foundations of Sulu's strength and allowed Sulu to rise in Southeast Asian affairs."[3] Much the same could be said for Okinawa at approximately this time, with the minor difference that its three kings were arrayed from north to south. I address the question of Okinawa's three small kingdoms in the next chapter.

In 1368, the newly enthroned Hóngwǔ emperor sent messengers to several countries surrounding China asking their rulers to send tribute to the Ming court and in turn to receive formal investiture (recognition) from the court of their status as kings of their countries. As in the case of Sulu, usually the Ming court had no trouble finding kings who were eager to do this. However, it encountered difficulty locating a suitable king in Japan. The main obstacle was the Ming demand that this king be someone willing and able to suppress the *wakō* who were ravaging Korea and finding their way to China as pirates or smugglers.

RYŌKAI, KING OF JAPAN

As part of this initiative, Hóngwǔ sent an envoy to Japan in 1368, but he was killed by pirates in the region of the Gotō islands. The next year, Hóngwǔ sent another diplomatic mission, headed by Yáng Zài, which arrived at Seisiefu headquarters. Yáng presented a strongly worded letter, addressed to "King of Japan Liánghuái" (J. Ryōkai; Kaneyoshi with the characters reversed). It described the ravages of pirate attacks and ordered the king to suppress piracy or face a Ming military attack that would destroy the pirates and capture Kaneyoshi: "On behalf of Heaven, how could I fail to smite such unrighteous people? King, think about this well!"[4] Kaneyoshi's reaction was to behead five of the envoys and imprison Yáng for three months. Instead of sending the threatened army, however, Hóngwǔ instead sent another envoy, Zhào Zhì. His message was largely the same, but it also included a long list of countries that had become Ming tributaries. More important, fifteen Japanese Buddhist priests who had been arrested in China accompanied Zhào. After some wavering, Kaneyoshi agreed to play the role of king. He sent an embassy offering horses and local products and repatriating some seventy Chinese captured by pirates. The Ming court responded favorably.[5] Despite appearing to cooperate with Ming demands, however, Kaneyoshi did nothing to rein in the *wakō*.[6] He simply profited from the tribute trade.

Briefly, Kaneyoshi, as Ryōkai, reigned as Japan's king for tribute trade purposes. He was credible in that role until 1380. In 1374 and 1380, Ashikaga Yoshimitsu sent embassies to China, which the Ming court refused to recognize owing to lack of proper documentation. Shimazu Ujihisa sent a mission in 1374, which Chinese officials rejected because his status was not high enough. Six missions sailed to China under Kaneyoshi's name. The first three, in 1371, 1378, and 1379, proceeded normally. The Japanese ships brought horses, sulfur, weapons, and other items and engaged in the usual diplomacy and trade. A mission in 1380, however, was refused for "insincerity," and missions in 1381 and 1386 were also rejected.[7] It is quite likely that the missions from 1378 onward were only nominally sent by Kaneyoshi, because he stepped down as Seiseifu head in 1374 and died in 1383. For our purposes, however, the key development was the 1380 rejection for insincerity.

At the start of his reign, Hóngwǔ was determined to bring Kaneyoshi into the Ming international order. His reasons for focusing on Kaneyoshi, not the Ashikaga shogun, made sense at the time. Ōta Kōki points out that Ming records indicate an awareness that Japan was embroiled in civil war over issues of imperial succession. Moreover, Hóngwǔ's letter to Kaneyoshi shows that the Ming court knew who controlled the Southern Court *wakō*.[8] Outright *wakō* attacks on China were only part of the story. Prince Kaneyoshi, or people using his name, were also involved in smuggling.

By the late fourteenth century gunpowder weapons had become crucial in warfare. The Hóngwǔ emperor, "the gunpowder emperor" according to Tonio Andrade, embraced this powerful technology. "The extraordinary success of the Ming dynasty," argues Andrade, "was based on the effective use of guns."[9] Sulfur was a key ingredient in gunpowder. Japan produced it in abundance, especially in and around Kyushu. China possessed abundant potassium nitrate (saltpeter) but lacked sulfur in a form that was readily usable. Therefore, sulfur had great profit potential as a trade item.[10]

Hú Wéiyōng was the Ming chancellor between 1373 and 1380, and Hóngwǔ grew suspicious of his vast power. When Hóngwǔ received a report in 1380 that Hú had met with a foreign envoy, Hóngwǔ executed Hú and purged other officials at the same time. Kaneyoshi's reign as Japan's nominal king also ended at this point. Earlier, Hú had falsely accused local Níngbō official Lín Xián of a crime and banished him to Japan. This move was a ruse to get Lín into Japan and open a line of communication with Seiseifu. The "king of Japan," probably Seiseifu officials using Kaneyoshi's name, sent the priest Nyoyō to China with four hundred soldiers and a shipment of giant candles. Concealed inside the candles were gunpowder and swords. The expedition was a failure, and by the time it arrived in the first month of 1380, Hú had already been executed. Lín's involvement was not revealed until 1421. This 1380 incident destroyed the credibility of Japan's Southern Court in Hóngwǔ's eyes.[11]

Ōta argues that this incident was part of a broader problem with illegal trade, and Hóngwǔ's attempts to win the cooperation of Kaneyoshi were part of a campaign to control potentially destabilizing smuggling. Pointing out that Nyoyō probably had *wakō* connections, Kawazoe Shōji notes, "Here we see a pattern by which *wakō* or *wakō*-like forces helped define Ming internal politics."[12] Japan might supply useful items, especially horses, swords, and sulfur, but Ming officials lacked an effective way to obtain these items securely. *Wakō* attacks on China were increasing, and *wakō* had been moving south, into the Ryukyu islands. In 1374, for example, a Ming official received orders to sail to "the sea around Ryukyu" to apprehend pirates.[13] After Hóngwǔ gave up on the Southern Court, the Ryukyu islands presented a possible way to resolve these problems. Ryukyu was Plan B.

RYUKYU AS A RECEPTACLE FOR *WAKŌ*

Yáng Zài heard about Ryukyu during his extended stay in Kyushu. At some point prior to 1372, he journeyed to Okinawa directly from Kyushu, returning to Nanjing via Fúzhōu. At that time, Yáng probably communicated the nature of tribute relations to Satto, ruler of the Urasoe region, including Naha. Soon thereafter, when Yáng returned with the official decree from the Ming court inviting Satto to send tribute, he quickly accepted. Satto became a "king of Ryukyu" for the purposes of trade and diplomacy with China. Mamoru Akamine points out, "It would not be too much to say that it was Yáng Zài who created the conditions for an oceangoing, sea-trading, outward-looking Kingdom of Ryukyu."[14] Akamine is certainly correct that Yáng's activities established the foundation of what, more than a century later, became a state encompassing all of the Ryukyu islands. However, there is no indication that the polity Yáng and Satto created in 1372 extended much farther than the Urasoe-Naha area. Two other Okinawan polities quickly appeared in Chinese records, but they all conducted tribute trade through Naha, assisted by the same group of resident Chinese.[15]

The Ming dynasty extended favorable treatment to early Ryukyuan rulers presenting themselves as kings. In 1372, Hóngwǔ limited tribute activity from Korea and more than six other countries to one embassy every three years. An embassy from Ryukyu arrived soon after this decree, but it had received no such notice. After 1382, the same year the Ming court formally recognized Ryukyuan kings of Chūzan, Sanhoku, and Sannnan, it explicitly permitted unlimited tribute embassies from Ryukyu.[16] Between 1372 and 1398, fifty-seven tribute embassies, an average of about two per year, left Naha for China. Despite its relatively small size and dearth of resources, Ryukyu sent more tribute embassies to China than did any other country. The Ming court provided the personnel necessary to handle tribute-related logistics, large ships, and officers to direct those ships. According to a 1439 *Rekidai hōan* entry, to that point the Ming court had given Ryukyu thirty ships, although only seven remained seaworthy.[17] Unlike for other countries, embassies from Ryukyu were not restricted to certain ports and Okinawan kings authenticated their own tribute missions. Ming preferential treatment toward Ryukyu was especially pronounced starting in 1383, when Satto received a silver seal and a formal message from the Ming emperor encouraging frequent tribute trade.[18]

Ming authorities sought to use Ryukyu as a conduit for *wakō* activity and to convert it into legitimate trade.[19] As Okamoto Hiromichi explains: "After having given up hope of controlling Japanese pirates through Japan, the Ming tried to eliminate Japanese pirates and illegal merchants by controlling more tightly its boundaries with the sea.... Ryukyu was expected to become a Ming foothold in maritime East Asia instead of

Japan and to fulfill the role of 'receptacle' for the maritime merchants who had to be eliminated."[20] These "maritime merchants" were *wakō,* and the Ming policy was a variety of appeasement. For the policy to work in the short term, the Ming court had to make tribute trade more attractive than smuggling or piracy. That logic is the main reason for the generous policy, one that could be and was tightened later.[21] There were other benefits for China. Ryukyuan *wakō* had broad connections throughout the region, so Ryukyu could serve as a conduit for Japanese products and as a channel for diplomatic communication with Japan.[22] Vessels sailing under the auspices of Ryukyuan kings could bring goods to China from faraway places in Southeast Asia, thus reducing the economic pain of the Ming Maritime Prohibitions.[23]

One practical problem was a lack of ships large enough to make long-distance voyages profitably and safely or of the pilots to guide them. The Ming court solved this problem by supplying Ryukyu with Chinese-made ships, initially at no cost.[24] It is likely that most or all of these ships went to Ryukyu after service in the Ming navy. For example, Chóngwǔsuǒ in Quánzhōu (Fujian Province) was a coastal defense installation. Chinese records indicate that a ship named *Courage-59* (*Yǒng-zì wǔjiǔ-hào*), attached to one of the Chóngwǔsuǒ units, was sent to Ryukyu to convey the royal envoy Kaku Sobi (Guō Zǔwěi). Locating the envoy's name and the ship's name in other records, it appears that this vessel became a Ryukyuan ship sometime between 1431 and 1534.[25] At least for tribute voyages and voyages to Southeast Asia, Chinese served as captains, officers, and interpreters aboard what were officially Ryukyuan vessels.[26]

Until well into the fifteenth century, the newly created state of Ryukyu functioned much like a Ming trading company, with the Chūzan king functioning as Ryukyu's greatest merchant.[27] It was as if the Ming court outsourced many aspects of foreign trade to Ryukyu. We should note that "Ryukyu," in this sense, included Chinese personnel residing in Naha. Resident Chinese functioned as de facto officials, and some held official titles based on the early Ming system of royal outposts.[28] Resident Chinese in Naha maintained connections with similar communities throughout Southeast Asia, forming a network.[29] Most histories of Ryukyu portray these Chinese personnel as a gift of the Ming court to Ryukyu. Insofar as they enabled profitable tribute trade to take place, this portrayal makes sense. However, for this very reason, resident Chinese possessed potential political power, which they sometimes used.

PROBLEMATIC BEHAVIOR

Bringing Ryukyuan mariners, many of whom had *wakō* backgrounds, to China as members of tribute missions, even on ships under Chinese command, was bound to cause disturbances. In 1415, Ryukyuan envoy Choku Karo (Zhí Jiālŭ) was arrested while in China. The official decree stated that although Choku had enjoyed fine treatment while in the capital, upon his return to Fujian he and his party ran wild. They stole a ship, killed a police official, assaulted a eunuch and stole his clothes. The decree states that Choku was the ringleader and that, although he deserved the death penalty, Chinese officials were returning him to Ryukyu for punishment. The decree warned the king to take greater care in the future that his envoys not act like criminals.[30]

In 1439, the Investigating Censor of the Fujian Regional Inspector (Xúnàn Fújiàn jiāncháshǐ) wrote to the Board of Rites complaining about Ryukyuans in Fúzhōu. He pointed out that Ryukyuan envoys Rinkei (Lín Huì) and Teichō (Zhèng Zhǎng) were abusing the system by inviting a group of over two hundred people to stay at their official lodging. The local government paid the living expenses of Ryukyuans on official business, and this crowd had cost 796,900 copper cash over less than half a year. Not only were the Ryukyuans and their comrades expensive, their behavior was disorderly, consisting of "freely cursing and brawling." The official recommended that the group be cut off from official support. Moreover, because the two Ryukyuan officials in charge refused to cease their disruptive behavior, they should be punished. The Board of Rites agreed, but the emperor ruled in favor of a warning this time, reserving the possibility of punishment for later should the situation not improve.[31]

The problem of Ryukyuans abusing official policy continued. In 1472 officials in Fujian formally complained that Ryukyuans who had previously arrived with tribute missions had set up households and would not return to their country. The emperor approved a Board of Rites order permitting those who had become de facto long-term residents to have their households registered as Chinese and demanding that the others return to Ryukyu.[32] The behavior of Ryukyuan sailors also generated a complaint from the king of Malacca (southern Malay peninsula) in 1470. A formal letter to the king of Ryukyu stated that rank-and-file sailors did not heed orders and were prone to violence to such a degree that they disrupted the civil authorities.[33] In 1478, the Chinese emperor received a report that Ryukyuan sailors in 1475 cooperated with a local chief in

Champa (coastal southern Vietnam) to launch a military attack on the Vietnamese kingdom of Annam to the north.[34]

It is important to note that not all seafarers in the Ryukyu islands participated in the tribute system. Not until the early sixteenth century did Shuri subdue all or most of the power centers throughout the Ryukyu islands. As a good example of the limits of the tribute trade to tame piracy and illegal trade, consider the Fujian official Yáng Quán. According to a 1430 entry in *Ming Veritable Records,* when pirates attacked Zhāngzhōu, a coastal city near Xiàmén, Yáng did not marshal soldiers in its defense. Instead, he took bribes from local residents and then allowed them to sail to Ryukyu to engage in trade.[35] Yáng's case puts into perspective a 1452 order from the Ministry of Justice (Xíngbù) to residents of the Fujian coast, issued in the context of a local uprising. It prohibited their handling cargo and weapons. Significantly, it also prohibited "dealings with Ryukyu by ship and serving as guides for pirates."[36] In other words, Ming officials were well aware of the nexus between Ryukyu, coastal Fujian, and pirates. Despite decades of favored treatment and many shiploads of tribute, as of the middle of the fifteenth century Ming authorities remained suspicious of Ryukyu.

THE OVERALL PATTERN OF TRIBUTE TRADE

The frequency of tribute trade increased dramatically after 1383. Total Ryukyuan tribute trade, including the number of embassies per year, number of ships, and quantity of goods, reached a peak during the 1420s and 1430s. Subsequently, it began a gradual decline, followed by a sharp decline during the 1520s.[37]

No single metric captures the entire picture of official trade. The number of tribute missions per year is one possible measure, but each mission might consist of variable numbers and sizes of ships with different mixes of cargo. It is more useful to measure the quantity of sulfur, an item shipped with each tribute voyage. Ryukyu had access to a steady supply of sulfur from the island of Iōtorishima.[38] Here, I follow Ikuta Shigeru's analysis, with quantities derived from *Rekidai hōan* documents. Ikuta divides Ryukyuan tribute trade into seven periods, each based on significant changes in circumstances affecting the trade.[39]

Period two was the approximate peak of Ryukyu's tribute trade. The average annual shipment of sulfur to China on Ryukyuan tribute vessels during this time was 38,013 *jīn*.[40] Using this quantity as 100 percent, table 1 shows the decline in Ryukyuan sulfur shipments to China relative to each immediate previous period and to period two, the peak of trade.[41]

Period three marks the start of Ming-imposed restrictions on Ryukyu's tribute trade, the most important of which was limiting tribute missions to one per year. By 1440, once per year was already the typical frequency, so the practical impact on trade volume was small.

Table 1. Ryukyuan sulfur shipments to China

Period	Years	Sulfur (jīn/year)	% of the Previous Period	% of Period 2
2	1425–1439	38,013	–	100%
3	1440–1477	35,300	93%	93
4	1478–1506	28,345	80	75
5	1507–1517	27,272	96	72
6	1518–1544	8,818	32	26
7	1549–1609	6,192	70	16

The fourth period was the result of another instance of Ryukyuans in China acting like pirates. According to Chinese allegations, members of a Ryukyuan embassy in 1474 attacked the Fuzhou household of Chén Èrguān, plundered it, burnt it down, and killed Chén and his wife. After learning of the matter the following year, the Ming emperor responded by ordering Shō En to punish the miscreants and by restricting tribute missions to once every two years, with a maximum size of one hundred people and additional restrictions regarding cargo.[42] The first embassy sent under these restrictive conditions arrived in 1478, and tribute trade declined moderately as a result. Shō Shin worked hard to restore the previous annual rate of tribute, and he succeeded in 1506. That success notwithstanding, the volume of trade declined slightly compared with the previous period. Ryukyuan tribute trade declined precipitously during period six.

Period seven begins with a decline in ship quality. After 1450, Ryukyu continued using Chinese-made ships, but the burden of payment for them began shifting to Ryukyu. The kingdom received its last Chinese ship in 1548, according to Ikuta. After that point, Ryukyu built its own ships, but they were smaller and of lower quality. (As we will see in chapter 10, some of these smaller ships might also have been made in China.) Such ships could not venture to Southeast Asia, but by that time Portuguese traders had taken over most of those routes.

In short, almost as soon as Ryukyu attained its peak prosperity and territorial expanse in the early sixteenth century, its tribute trade began a significant decline. I examine this decline in the context of larger world trends in chapter 13.

SULFUR AND HORSES

Sulfur and horses help illuminate the maritime network in which Ryukyu was embedded and the role of *wakō*. Ryukyu's tribute cargo of sulfur was not simply a token. Elemental sulfur was scarce in China, requiring that it be manufactured from pyrite, an iron sulfide. During the Ming dynasty "the number of areas producing pyrite-derived sulfur greatly increased. Ming dynasty documents (1564) mention that the emperor allowed the central and four local governments to buy about 10,000 *jin* of sulfur per year to replenish their supplies for gunpowder manufacture."[43] With this 10,000 *jīn* figure as a point of reference for the quantities listed in table 1, we can see that early Ryukyu was a significant supplier of sulfur to China. Moreover, Ryukyuan sulfur and *wakō* were closely connected, as Ōta Kōki points out:

> Of the sulfur produced in Japan, it appears that Ryukyu-made sulfur, in particular, was exported. In this connection, Ryukyu served as a route by which *wakō* attacked China. [Ryukyu] was not only a location that supplied sulfur, but it was also significant as a base for *wakō* activity. Therefore, Ryukyuan sulfur was well known to the Ming state, which was on guard against its smuggling.[44]

One again we see the logic of generous Ming tribute trade incentives to Ryukyu. If sulfur from Japan or Ryukyu was going to make its way into China anyway, it would be better that this essential and potentially dangerous commodity arrive through official channels.

In addition to Iōtorishima, Ryukyuans could obtain sulfur from Mount Aso in Higo and Iōjima in the Satsunan islands near Yakushima and Tanegashima. Takase in Higo was the main shipping port for Aso-produced sulfur. The southern route from Takase to Fujian, discussed in chapter 1, also served as a sulfur road.[45] Increased demand for sulfur in China corresponded closely with increased traffic along this southern route.

Wakō cavalry units were especially active during the 1370s and 1380s. They launched at least ten major attacks during these decades. A major source of horses was Jeju island, and the Hóngwǔ emperor was aware of this location as a confluence of pirates and horses. The Gotō islands, Iki, and Tsushima also served as *wakō* pasture.[46]

One reason the Hóngwǔ emperor was interested in horses is that he needed them to wage war against the Mongols and their allies, who remained powerful even after the fall of the Yuan dynasty. In 1383, Liáng Mín went to Ryukyu and arranged to buy almost a thousand horses for the Ming court. Securing so many horses and successfully shipping them to China would have been an immense undertaking. Specialists would have been required to round up the horses, maintain them in a pasture, deal with herds, and transport them in fleets of ships (twenty to twenty-five head per ship). The only entities capable of such logistics, concludes Nagahama Yukio, would have been *wakō* bands.[47] Ryukyu did not regularly supply Ming with such large numbers of horses. Tribute voyages averaged thirty to thirty-eight head of horses between 1374–1464, after which the number dropped off, averaging only ten head during the middle of the sixteenth century.[48] In other words, horses sent as part of the tribute trade were mainly token gifts. Ryukyu's main benefit for the Ming state with respect to horses was to serve as a source and staging area for ad hoc purchases.[49]

The main horse pasture in the Ryukyu islands was Okinoerabu, whose topography is mostly flatland atop a raised coral reef. Kikai and Miyako were also home to horse pastures. According to one *omoro*:

> The lord of Okinoerabu
> Selects a herd of horses
> The herd
> Is at his disposal
> This remote lord
> Attaches a golden saddle
> And rides down to Yowa harbor.[50]

Recall that Okinoerabu had close ties with Shuri. It was one of the four places at which the Tsukishiro form of Hachiman was worshipped, and it was the residence of *wakō* chieftain Guraru (Goran) Magohachi, who flourished during the first half of the fifteenth century. Magohachi had close ties with Okinawa and appears in *Omoro* songs as Magohatsu:

> Magohatsu [Magohachi] of Erabu
> Worships Tamanokyaku [deity of a grove in northern Okinawa]
> *Hitoidjo* [name of a ship]
> Travels in the early morning
> Magohatsu of the outer island [Okinoerabu]
> Bejeweled.[51]

Sulfur, horses, *wakō*, and the trade with China, both official and illegal, all came together within the Ryukyu islands during the fourteenth and fifteenth centuries.

KOREA

Ryukyuan kings relied heavily on Chinese assistance for trade with both the Ming court and Southeast Asia. Chinese merchants residing in Naha managed Ryukyu's trade, which shipped on board Chinese-made vessels under Chinese command.[52] They were Ryukyuan insofar as they sailed under the aegis of a Ryukyuan king, carried diverse goods from throughout the East China Sea region, and included Ryukyuan crew members.

As soon as kings recognized by the Ming court appeared in Ryukyu, rulers with that title, or anyone convincingly posing as an envoy of such kings, also became eligible to conduct official trade with Korea. Ryukyu relied on outsourcing for its missions to Korea. Some Ryukyuans did travel to Korea, but the majority of personnel were Japanese, who traveled as actual or spurious agents of Ryukyuan kings. A 1456 entry in *Joseon Veritable Records* states: "Because the distance between Ryukyu and Tsushima is vast, Ryukyu cannot engage in direct contact with our country. Most of what they send to us relies on Japanese for transmission."[53] The routes to Korea would have been almost entirely controlled by *wakō* groups. Any independent Ryukyuan voyage not made in concert with at least some powerful partners would have been precarious.[54] The Hakata priest Dōan traveled back and forth between Korea and Ryukyu as an envoy in 1453, 1455, and 1457.[55] Japanese priests or merchants headed subsequent Ryukyuan embassies for the next forty years, and the Korean government paid their return stipends, not to Ryukyu, but to their homes in Kyushu.[56]

Spurious Ryukyuan embassies became a serious problem for Korean officials. The first one appeared in 1423. Officials scrutinized the envoy's papers and seal and rejected him. Approximately two years earlier, pirates from Tsushima captured a vessel sailing to Korea on behalf of Ryukyu. This incident may have inspired a subsequent attempt by Tsushima pirates to pose as Ryukyuans.[57] Indeed, the limited descriptions in Korean accounts all indicate that spurious "Ryukyuan" envoys came from either Tsushima, Hakata, or other parts of Kyushu. In part because *wakō* played a prominent role even in legitimate embassies, it was difficult for Korean officials at the time, and for historians today, to discern which embassies were genuine. A majority of the twenty-one embassies to the Korean court from Ryukyu between 1461 and 1524 appear to have been suspicious.[58]

In at least one case, someone even created a fictitious country and posed as an envoy of its king. In 1478, someone posing as an envoy from "Jiŭbiān" arrived in Korea.[59] In the context of trying to determine his legitimacy, minister Yi Seungso pointed out: "In the past, there were people who called themselves envoys of Ryukyu. They were from Hakata. They went to Ryukyu and requested of (the king of) Ryukyu a letter of introduction and came here. The envoy who has now come is perhaps of the same variety."[60]

The techniques of deception used in connection with fraudulent embassies were often sophisticated.[61] In 1479 and again in 1480, vessels carrying documents allegedly from King Shō Toku, who had been dead since 1469, arrived in Korea. Authorities were suspicious in the second case because of inconsistencies regarding the name of the king in envoys' statements.[62] Similarly, spurious embassies from the "king of Japan" (the Ashikaga shoguns), also became a problem for the Korean court, especially during the sixteenth century.[63]

YAMATO

Compared with China or Korea, the political geography of Japan was much less organized around a center. Moreover, security for vessels sailing in Japanese coastal waters often demanded obtaining protection from powerful *wakō* groups.[64] Ryukyuan rulers required no title to conduct trade with powers in Japan. Trade and travel between Japan and the Ryukyu islands was unregulated, at least until the Shimazu lords of southern Kyushu began a decades-long process of wresting control over traffic between Japan and Ryukyu during the sixteenth century.

The most common term for Japan in the Ryukyu islands was Yamato, which appeared often in place-names, childhood names, and the names of local deities.[65] As I argued in chapter 1, the *Omoro* pair "Yashiro" (Yatsushiro)-Yamato (Satsuma) indicate Kyushu. Those with sufficient resources could travel there to conduct trade and obtain valuable goods:

> On a trip up to Yamato [Satsuma]
> What was bought?
> On a trip up to Yashiro [Yatsushiro]
> What was bought?
> Fine turquoise jewels.[66]

Although it often indicated Kyushu, when not paired with Yashiro, Yamato might refer to Japan as a whole or to somewhere in Japan other than Kyushu; recall the example of Katsuren likened to "Kamakura in Yamato."

The beginning of Ryukyu's tribute trade occurred when the Muromachi *bakufu* was nearing the peak of its power and influence. Starting with Shō Hashi, Ryukyuan kings maintained cordial relations with the Ashikaga shoguns. In correspondence, the shoguns addressed the kings in Shuri as "lords of Ryukyu" (*Ryūkyūkoku yononushi*),[67] and Ryukyuan kings usually dispatched a trade ship to the *bakufu* each year. This trade was sufficiently important that, when the Ōnin War (1467–1477) disrupted it, Sakai merchants sailed to Ryukyu to obtain goods from China and Southeast Asia. In addition to the merchants of Sakai, the powerful Ōuchi of Suō (Yamaguchi Prefecture), actively traded with Ryukyu. Technicians associated with the Ōuchi supervised the casting of temple bells in Ryukyu, which was especially frequent during the reign of Shō Taikyū.[68] I examine relations between Ryukyu, Satsuma, and other parts of Japan in detail in later chapters.

WAS RYUKYU AN ILLUSION?

Ryukyu became a formal state in the East Asian international order because of Ming policy to tame the region's *wakō* and the related Maritime Prohibitions. When Yáng Zài traveled to Naha in 1372, Okinawa was an island governed by dozens of local lords. Although many or all of them engaged in private trade, none of them would have been capable of conducting formal tribute trade on their own. The lord of Urasoe became "king" for tribute purposes. Satto, the kings who followed him, and the kings associated with the northern and southern principalities, profited from the situation. Ryukyuan ships began sailing to Southeast Asia, typically via Fuzhou, but they did so in Chinese-made ships with Chinese captains guided by Chinese pilots and supported by Chinese interpreters.[69] Similarly, as we have seen, Ryukyuan ships sailing to Korea were typically Japanese vessels commanded and piloted by Japanese or by mariners of mixed Korean and Japanese origins.

Ships sailed to destinations in China, Southeast Asia, and Korea under the auspices of a Ryukyuan king, and Naha served as an international port. Ryukyuans were actively involved in this maritime activity, but the common image of Ryukyuan mariners independently sailing to a variety of far-flung kingdoms requires some modification. In many respects, during the late fourteenth century and well into the fifteenth, "Ryukyu" functioned much like a shipping company. Its two largest clients were the

Ming court supported by Chinese living in Naha and the Ashikaga shoguns aided by Sakai merchants.

With these points in mind, let us consider Shō Taikyū's famous 1458 Sea Bridge to the Many Countries Bell (Bankoku shinryō no kane). Its inscription states in part that Ryukyu exists in a favorable location within the southern seas. Ryukyu has received the superior qualities (goods and/or people) of Korea, it is a close associate of the Ming dynasty, and it is closely bound to Japan. Likening Okinawa to Pénglái, the legendary Chinese island of the immortals, its ships form a bridge to the many countries. The bell claims that Ryukyu satisfies the needs of China for precious treasures from afar. Ryukyu's land is enchanted, its people prosper, and it is fanned by salubrious winds. Thus, at this place, our king, Great Ruler of the Realm (Shō Taikyū), born in 1410, received the royal rank from high Heaven and nurtures the people on earth.[70] Yano Misako points out that the bell inscription reflects aspirations to foreign trade, not necessarily the prevailing state of affairs.[71] From what we have seen, perhaps the bell functioned as an idealized interpretation of that state of affairs.

Consider the claim of Ryukyuan ships acting as bridges and Ryukyu satisfying China's needs. In a sense, it is quite correct, because Ryukyu's ships did substitute for Chinese ships during the era of Ming's Maritime Prohibitions. Ships under Ryukyuan auspices that traded in Southeast Asia, for example, gave Chinese merchants access to goods from that region. The bell does not mention, of course, that the ships and the know-how needed to sail them to Southeast Asia were of Chinese origin. Moreover, we have seen that at the time Shō Taikyū's bell was cast Chinese authorities in Fujian clearly looked on Ryukyu with suspicion as a source of piracy and smuggling. The claim inscribed on the bell takes Ryukyu's situation as a regional trade conduit and gives it a highly favorable spin—which is, of course, the function of many official monuments. The idealized image of early Ryukyu, exemplified in the bell's inscription as "a thriving and prosperous kingdom with wealth filling its coffers from a vibrant foreign trade,"[72] has flourished in the modern era.

Citing research by Akamine Seiki demonstrating that Ryukyu did not conduct independent trade with Southeast Asia,[73] a hypothesis by Ōta Ryōhaku that Chinese merchants in Naha constituted a shadow government that held the real power in early Ryukyu,[74] and the relatively inferior quality of native Ryukyuan ships, Irei Takashi lamented that the image of Ryukyu's "golden age" as a prosperous, independent maritime kingdom appears to be an illusion. In light of Ryukyu's early modern and modern history of having been controlled by outside powers, Irei concludes, "That the 'golden age' was a falsehood is indeed a gloomy matter, but thinking about the storms of outside pressure that have scoured this cluster of islands, it is something we must accept."[75] Irei's essay addresses the emotive impact for many contemporary people of the idealized image of early Ryukyu.

Early Ryukyu was not an illusion, but its history was more complex than Sea Bridge to the Many Countries Bell, the official histories, or many modern accounts acknowledge. One point to underscore is that although early Ryukyu was never formally part of any other country, it was not a de facto country itself until well into the reign of Shō Shin. Early Ryukyu was a frontier region within the East China Sea network generally and Japan in particular. Until the sixteenth century, there was no Okinawa-wide or Ryukyu-wide government, little or no literary culture outside of a few Buddhist temples, and there was a high level of internecine violence. Ryukyu did eventually become a centralized state and a far-flung empire. Moreover, from roughly 1510 to 1550, this Ryukyu empire enjoyed significant power and wealth. We could reasonably call this period a "golden" age, although it was fairly short and was more golden for some Ryukyuans than for others.

CHAPTER FOUR

The Enigma of the Three Principalities

There is perhaps no more fundamental "fact" of early Ryukyuan history than that from roughly 1314 until the 1420s the territory of Okinawa was divided among three small kingdoms or principalities. Collectively, they are, literally, the "three mountains" (Sanzan). Individually, they are Sannan in the south, Chūzan roughly in the center (including Naha, Shuri, and Urasoe), and Sanhoku in the north. Moreover, many conceptions assume that Sanhoku also controlled the northern Ryukyu islands. These places were peculiar states. Other than records of trade with China and Korea, we have no written documents from any of the principalities. We do not know where their boundaries were, nor do we have any coins, monuments (with one possible exception), or other such concrete items from these places that bear their names. The *Omoro* is full of references to places throughout the region, but not once does "Sanzan" or the name of any specific principality appear in its songs.

These three principalities definitely existed. We have abundant official Chinese and Korean records discussing envoys and tribute from their kings. What we do not have, however, is strong evidence that these places were territorial states. To state my conclusion in advance, it is more likely that the sudden proliferation of kings in late fourteenth-century Okinawa was the result of local rulers rushing to get on board the Ming gravy train. These local rulers obviously occupied territory, so there probably was some correspondence between geopolitical space and the three principalities. Nevertheless, the principalities seem to have existed mainly as something akin to dummy corporations. Given that Ming policy was to channel as many Ryukyu-based *wakō*-led powers into the tribute trade as possible, creating three states on paper may have furthered this goal, especially during the early decades of the trade.

According to the official histories, military conquest ended the three principalities, although they do not all agree on the details. In general, Shō Hashi, local lord of Sashiki in Sannan, conquered Shuri around 1405 and set up his father Shō Shishō as king of Chūzan. In some accounts, he then conquered Sannan and finally Sanhoku. In others, he conquered Sanhoku and then Sannan. There is some variability in the dates, but by roughly 1429 in any account, Shō Hashi had unified Okinawa under his rule.

Most contemporary and modern historians of Ryukyu have assumed that the three principalities existed as territorial states. However, looking even slightly below the surface of the official records reveals anomalies. For example, all three principalities shipped sulfur as tribute. Iōtorishima, supposedly a possession of Sanhoku, must have either allowed other principalities to mine sulfur or provided them with it. This point, plus anomalies such as the location of all relevant local trade documents (part of *Rekidai hōan*) in Kumemura in Naha, prompted one historian to posit the existence of an extraterritorial network that transcended the three principalities.[1] Other historians have taken different approaches to explaining anomalies connected with the three principalities as they appear in Chinese, Korean, or Ryukyuan official records or histories.

The concentration of powerful local rulers was greatest in southern Okinawa, the area later imagined to have been Sannan. There, not only kings, but royal uncles, brothers, and sons also sent tribute embassies to China. This situation was contrary to normal Ming procedure, and was rarely found elsewhere. For example, in 1388, the Ming court accepted tribute from a Shōeishishi, ostensibly the uncle of the Sannan king Shōsatto, and Shōeishishi's younger brother.[2] According to Chinese records, Shōeishishi presented tribute six times between 1388 and 1397.[3] Moreover, Chinese records indicate four different royal lines in Ryukyu between 1380 and 1429, and Korean records indicate five.[4] Every tribute embassy sent by the king of Sanhoku arrived in China in tandem with an embassy from Chūzan, and many Sannan embassies also arrived at the same time as embassies from Chūzan. In light of the Chinese policy of bringing Ryukyu into the tribute trade system to curtail illegal trade, the three principalities appear to have channeled multiple Ryukyuan warlords into the system.

Consider some other points. The successor to Satto of Chūzan was Bunei (r. 1398–ca. 1406).[5] In 1406, *Ming Veritable Records* indicate that tribute arrived on the same day from King Bunei of Chūzan and King Ōōso of Sannan.[6] The next year, Chūzan's "Prince Shishō" (Shō Hashi's father; Samekawa's son) sent envoys announcing the death of his "father," King Bunei, and requesting recognition as Chūzan's king.[7] Later in the century, in entries ranging from 1471 to 1472 in *Ming Veritable Records,* Shō En managed the remarkable feat of becoming the "prince" of a younger king, Shō Toku.[8] Obviously, these Okinawans, with the assistance of Chinese residing in Naha, were presenting themselves to the Ming court in a way that maintained the fiction of orderly, nonviolent royal succession. That is the point. Many of the Ryukyu-related entries in *Ming Veritable Records* reflect self-reporting by Ryukyuans or their handlers. To state the obvious, what appears in official records did not necessarily happen as recorded.

Conversely, consider the purported unification of the three principalities by Shō Hashi's military campaigns. *Reflections on Chūzan* contains a lengthy passage claiming that in 1423, Shō Hashi sent an envoy to the Ming court. The envoy's letter explained that for a century Ryukyu had been divided into three regions at war with each other, much to the detriment of the common people. Grieving for their sake, Shō Hashi launched military campaigns to pacify Sannan and Sanhoku, whose kings indulged in luxurious living and militarism. *Reflections* then reports that the emperor replied, praising Shō Hashi for raising a "righteous army" and relieving the people of their misery.[9] Setting aside the formulaic Chinese tropes, the key point is that there are no extant Chinese records from the 1420s indicating that anyone informed the Ming court of the unification of Ryukyu's three principalities.[10] It appears that this purported act of reporting to the Chinese court took place only within the seventeenth-century pages of *Reflections.*

In 1534, for example, investiture envoy Chén Kǎn was unaware of what had happened to the principalities in any detail. He pointed out that *Account of the Great Ming Unification (Dàmíng yītǒng zhì)* was completed in 1461. It states that during the reign of the Hóngwǔ (1368–1389), Ryukyu was divided into three kingdoms, all of which sent tribute embassies. Afterward, only Chūzan sent embassies. Therefore, "probably the other two kingdoms were annexed."[11] Chen commented cryptically on this passage saying, "Perhaps it was because Wò was strong and Jìn was weak,"[12] referring to complicated events connected with the eventual conquest of the state of Jìn by Duke Wǔ of Qūwò in approximately 677 BCE. Chén's conjecture that complex events had resulted in unification by Chūzan was a sensible guess, and it may have reflected what he heard while in Okinawa. However, if a Ryukyuan envoy had indeed informed the Ming court in the 1420s of Shō Hashi's unification, that notification would have appeared in Chinese texts and Chén would have been aware of it.

WERE THEY TERRITORIAL STATES?

Writing in 1940, Higashionna Kanjun stated: "The name Sanzan first appeared in Ming historical records and was not a native Ryukyuan entity." When "Satto, Lord of Urasoe" first sent tribute to the Ming court, he did so as "King of Ryukyu." When the lord of Ōzato sent tribute the following year, he called himself "King of Sannan" to distinguish himself from Satto. The names Chūzan and Sanhoku subsequently arose in contrast to Sannan. These royal names were for tribute trade purposes and were not native to Ryukyu, in contrast with terms like *yononushi* (ruler) or *anji* (*aji*, lord).[13] Despite such initial skepticism, Higashionna followed the basic narrative of the official histories. Noting that the same person went to China as an envoy from Sannan in 1424 but was back in China as an envoy from Chūzan in 1427, Higashionna suggested that Chūzan conquered Sannan sometime between 1424 and 1427.[14] However, we can find a reverse case. An envoy for Chūzan in 1424 turned up as an envoy for Sannan in 1427.[15] Moreover, taking different transliterations of what appear to be the same names into account, as many as five envoys represented both Chūzan and Sannan during these years.[16] Is it possible that the three principalities were, in effect, different brands of the same shipping corporation?

The official narrative explains Chūzan's unification of the three principalities starting with the rise in 1392 of (Shō) Hashi, a relatively obscure lord of the small territory of Sashiki in Sannan. He conquered Shimasoe-Ōzato gusuku in 1402. Then the narrative diverges. The more common story today follows the chronology that Sai On proposed in his 1725 revision of *Genealogy of Chūzan*. In it, Hashi next deposed the Chūzan monarch Bunei (r. 1396–1406) and placed Hashi's father, Shishō, on the throne. To complete the unification, Hashi's forces conquered Sanhoku in 1416 and Sannan in 1429.

Based on a comparative reading of Chinese, Korean, and Ryukyuan official histories, Wada Hisanori proposed a somewhat different narrative. He argued that Hashi conquered Sannan first, then Chūzan, and finally Sanhoku. In Wada's view, Hashi's conquest of Shimasoe-Ōzato was in fact the conquest of Sannan. The putative Sannan king, Ōōso (r. 1402 or 1403–1413), was none other than Hashi himself. In 1405, Hashi conquered Chūzan, deposed its ruler Bunei, and placed his father Shishō on the throne. At this point Chūzan and Sannan were in fact the same polity, but Sannan continued to exist as a subordinate entity to Chūzan under a new king, Tarumi (Taromai), who was Hashi's oldest son. This situation accounts for the substantial overlap of their tribute missions and envoys to China. In 1422, Hashi succeeded his father as king of Chūzan and destroyed the king of Sanhoku. After Tarumi's death in approximately 1429, Sannan simply ceased to exist in any sense.[17] Thus Chūzan, with its capital at Shuri (Urasoe castle burnt down in 1406), was the only royal polity remaining.

Wada's revised narrative came out in the 1980s and generated debate. The precise details are less important than some broader features Wada brought into relief. One is Chinese authorities' unfamiliarity with the particulars of Okinawan politics. The information supplied by the tribute embassies needed only to appear to be consistent for the tribute trade to proceed. In this context, Shō Hashi may have posed as King Ōōso of Sannan, while also having conquered Chūzan. If Wada was correct, then Sannan existed at this time only to facilitate trade.

Soon after Wada, Ikuta Shigeru proposed a major revision in the conception of the three principalities. He explicitly argued that they were Chinese creations for the purpose of making tribute trade easier.[18] The most important element in locating the principalities was the presence of resident Chinese who could process tribute trade. Such a community resided on Ukishima when that island separated the ports of Tomari and Naha. In Ikuta's view, the heart of Chūzan was a nexus between Tomari and Shuri, and the heart of Sannan was a nexus between Tomigusuku and Naha. Functionally, these "principalities" were the northern and southern extensions of the resident Chinese community in Naha. Ikuta also proposed that the center of Sanhoku was not Nakijin but the nearby port of Unten, where a community of Chinese merchants must have resided.[19]

Ikuta proposes that the Chūzan and Nanzan kings were father and son respectively who eventually came into conflict. Moreover, similarly to Wada's assertion of a father and son relationship, Ikuta states that Shō Hashi and the Sannan king, Tarumi, were close associates.[20] In Ikuta's view, the apparent flourishing and fall of the three principalities mainly reflected fluctuations in the population of resident Chinese capable of handling tribute trade.[21] He concludes, "I cannot accept as historical fact the 'division' into and 'unification' of the so-called three principalities."[22] Shō Hashi eventually consolidated all of the tribute trade into his hands, probably with the assistance of powerful resident Chinese. It is likely, then, that the consolidation or unification of the three principalities was more a reorganization of the tribute trade than a result of military campaigns between the armies of three different states.

A CLOSER LOOK AT TEXTUAL EVIDENCE

Many *omoro* sing of the lords of places like Nakijin or Ōzato, commonly hypothesized as the capitals of Sanhoku and Sannan respectively. *Omoro* language typically portrays the power or fame of important people or places as sonically resounding over a large area. There is no indication in the *Omoro*, however, that Nakijin, Ōzato, or some other prominent castle was the capital of a broader state during the late fourteenth century. That it does not mention the three principalities suggests that Okinawans themselves did not recognize these places as territorial states. Moreover, insofar as *Omoro* songs do suggest military hostility between different locations, the lines of conflict do not always fit the three principalities narrative. Consider Nakagusuku. Based on its location, Nakagusuku would have been a major component of the Chūzan military forces, according to the usually hypothesized borders of the three principalities. With this point in mind, consider the following *omoro*:

> Acclaimed Nakagusuku
> Should the many lords think to come north from Shuri
> And attack
> We will use our stone and iron weapons
> To fight them and push them back
> Acclaimed Nakagusuku.[23]

In this song, Nakagusuku functions as a bulwark to prevent the northward movement of military forces. It appears antagonistic toward Shuri, contrary to the hypothesized boundaries of the principalities. Of course, it is impossible to date this song, so it might refer to a time outside of the era of the principalities.

There are anomalies in the official Chinese and Korean records. Consider Sannan. An entry for 1394.9 in *Joseon Veritable Royal Records* indicates that a tribute embassy arrived in Korea sent by Satto, king of Chūzan. The mission presented tribute items and repatriated rescued Koreans. In addition, it "requested the return of Sannan prince Shōsatto, currently in exile [in Korea]."[24] However, during the first month of the same year, *Ming Veritable Records* lists a tribute mission arriving from "Sannan King Shōsatto," along with tribute from Chūzan's Satto.[25] Strangely, Shōsatto is a king at the start of 1394, dispatching tribute to China; but he is a prince in exile in Korea several months later. From Iha Fuyū onward, scholars of Okinawa have worked to resolve this apparent contraction. A simple strategy is to claim that the Korean text really intended to say "King Shōsatto's son."

Even if we accept that the text does not mean exactly what it says, however, explaining why this son of Shōsatto was in exile in Korea remains difficult.[26] Ikuta hypothesizes that Shōsatto was actually the prince of the Chūzan king, who handled trade at Naha and posed as "king" of Sannan. Eventually the two men grew antagonistic toward each other, and the prince sought to make himself the genuine ruler of the area south of Naha. The Chūzan king threatened to attack or actually did so, and the "Sannan Prince" fled to Korea.[27] Based on a close reading of Chinese records, Ikuta points out that Satto, Bunei, and Shōsatto appear to have been siblings.[28]

One possible explanation addresses another peculiarity of the three principalities: the curious names of many kings. Satto (C. Chádù) was king of Chūzan at the same time that Shōsatto (C. Chéng-chádù) was king of Nanzan. Bear in mind that the Chinese officials recording Ryukyuan names probably did not know how to pronounce them, nor did they know much about Ryukyuan society. As Sun Wei and others have pointed out, "Satto" and its variants was a *generic* name for Ryukyuan nobles. Indeed, a better spelling would be Sato, especially because an old version of *Ming Veritable Records* uses characters that would be pronounced that way in modern Japanese (C. Zhādōu). In short, there might have been several different kings appearing in Chinese records under the generic name "lord" (*sato/satto*) or "lord of———." "Prince Shōsatto" in the Korean records, therefore, might have been someone other than the Nanzan king.[29]

Sato/satto might refer to the generic Ryukyuan term for ruler, *satonushi*. In a Korean context, *sado* indicated a local magistrate or locally powerful family.[30] Moreover, according to *Ming Veritable Records,* in 1392 King Satto sent an envoy to China named either Satto or Sato (C. Chádōu).[31] Regardless of its precise provenance, the element *satto/sato* in the names of monarchs, nobles, and envoys during the era of the three principalities makes most sense as a generic term.

Space does not permit a lengthy discussion of the other royal names during this era, but it is worth mentioning the three purported kings of Sanhoku: Haniji (r. 1322–1395); Bin (r. 1393–1395 or 1400); and Han'anchi (r. 1401–1416). Haniji, with a remarkably long reign of seventy-three years, first appears in Ming records in 1383.[32] His name probably refers to or derives from Haneji, a northern Okinawa place-name. Han'anchi's name likely does as well, although it is possible that the *-anchi* element is *anji* (local lord). Bin may have been a childhood name or derived from a place-name.[33] These generic names for monarchs, derived from localities (Sanhoku) or social position (Chūzan and Sannan), underscore the localized nature of power in Okinawa at this time.

Are there any documents from Ryukyu during or soon after the era of the three principalities stating that Okinawa was divided between three kingdoms? There are two, but both were written by Chinese. In 1383, Ming envoys Liáng Mín and Lù Qiān traveled to Ryukyu and reported: "At this time, three kings in Ryukyu are vying for supremacy and attacking each other."[34] The second item is a monument inscription from 1427. Its author was Shō Hashi's top official, Kaiki (C. Huái Jī), who was Chinese. Kaiki's Monument to the Garden that Benefits the Country (Ankoku zanju kaboku no kihi) mentions that Ryukyu had been divided into three parts and that Chūzan was the central capital.[35]

These two documents do not constitute strong evidence that the powers within Okinawa at the time understood the island's geopolitical landscape as consisting of three territorial states. Because we know virtually nothing about these purported states other than what the official Ming and Joseon records say, there is considerable room for speculation. Perhaps the most creative scholar in this respect has been the archaeologist Asato Susumu. His hypothetical model of the power structures of Chūzan and Nanzan during the period of roughly 1370–1430 is quite plausible if one accepts as axiomatic that Okinawa consisted of three territorial states. Asato's model also sets the stage for the linear development of royal authority from Satto to Shō Hashi and then from the first Shō dynasty to the pivotal reforms of Shō Shin.[36] Although most historians of Ryukyu continue to maintain that the three principalities existed as territorial states, not everyone agrees.[37]

In my view, existing evidence is insufficient to warrant a strong claim that Okinawa consisted of three warring or potentially warring states from circa 1314 until the late 1420s. The idea of the three principalities may have derived in part from the fact that powerful lords resided in the north, central, and southern regions of Okinawa. Given the profitability of the tribute trade, it is certain that multiple Okinawan powers were eager to participate. Operating as three royal states may have created a framework for maximizing that participation. The inclusion of Sannan crown princes and even other royal relatives as dispatchers of tribute in the official records reflects the higher concentration of local powers in southern Okinawa. Moreover, we should also bear in mind that although individual ships left Naha under the auspices of a particular king, prince, or royal relative, any number of local power holders might have contributed to the cargo and have expected eventually to share in the profits.

What about Shō Hashi's rise to power after 1405 and the "unification" of Okinawa during the late 1420s? There was no reduction in tribute quantity or quality during these decades, so the "fall" of Sannan and Sanhoku had no material impact on trade volume. In other words, it is likely that the same Okinawans who had been contributing to tribute cargoes before approximately 1420 continued to do so after the three principalities ended. We will see that Shō Hashi likely seized Naha and surrounding areas in a Chinese-sponsored coup that represented a change of management. Using a corporate metaphor, which I think is appropriate for the early Naha tribute trade, it is quite possible that the end of the three principalities was actually the advent of a new organizational structure.

THE THREE PRINCIPALITIES AS SYMBOLS

We have seen that the three principalities were closely connected with official trade between Okinawa and the Chinese and Korean courts. Most likely, by the time the royal court began to compile official histories during the seventeenth century, scholars assumed that these places had been territorial states corresponding roughly to the regions of Kunigami, Nakagami, and Shimajiri, as Kaiki's 1427 monument stated. In addition to their role in facilitating the tribute trade, and less probably as actual polities, the three principalities also functioned symbolically.

In 1958 Georges Dumézil argued that the mythology of Indo-European peoples displays a tripartite ideological division. For example, the three twice-born (*dvija*) castes of the Indian subcontinent, although arranged in a hierarchy, also embody three essential functions: spiritual power to rule, military power, and economic productivity. Variations of this tripartite division of functions can be found across wide areas of the Eurasian continent.[38] In 1984, Ōbayashi Taryō applied Dumézil's scheme to Okinawa's three principalities. Based mainly on the legendary accounts of Shō Hashi's eventual conquest of all three, Ōbayashi argued that Chūzan represented the locus of spiritual power and thus political legitimacy. Sanhoku, whose last king, Han'anchi, was known for his military prowess, represented military power. Sannan, with its abundant fresh water, represented economic productivity in the form of agricultural bounty.[39]

Chūzan embodied the first function, symbolized in the *Omoro* by the drum. The world of the *Omoro* is a realm of powerful sounds. Priestesses tap into divine power by merging their voices with those of the deities. Rulers manifest their power through the shamanic drum. For Shō Hashi, for example:

> At the Yoriage grove at Sashiki
> The lord posessing the drum that governs *shima*
>   [islands, communities, domains]
> At the Yoriage grove of the base country.[40]

Torigoe Kenzaburō points out that the "lord" (*aji*) in this song is Hashi when he was still lord of Sashiki gusuku. "According to the ideas at the time of the *Omoro*, it was thought possible to amplify spiritual power by beating the drum vigorously. Therefore, he is portrayed as a castle lord with spiritual power that subdues other domains."[41] Precisely because he possessed the drum, Hashi went on to conquer widely. The official histories' portrayal of Shō Hashi as Okinawa's first full king, embodying all three functions, mirrors the qualities of the Chinese emperor.[42]

Through conquest, Shō Hashi acquired the military power associated with Sanhoku and the agricultural wealth of the south. According to *Kyūyō,* "I hear that there is a spring in Ōzato called the Kadeshi Spring," Shō Hashi said to Tarumi, the last king of Sannan (or Hashi's son, according to Wada). Knowing that Tarumi coveted wealth and beauty to a fault, Hashi offered to trade his gold-plated screen for the spring. Tarumi happily agreed, thus sealing his fate. For Hashi now controlled the water that made agricultural wealth possible. He prohibited access to it, the people of Sannan rebelled against Tarumi, and Hashi completed his conquest of the south.[43] In this way, the screen (*byōbu*) symbolized the third function: economic wealth. It was the instrument by which Shō Hashi was able to control water, a recurring theme in Ryukyuan legend and history, and thereby the agricultural wealth of the south.[44]

Chapter 6 examines the migration route that Shō Hashi's family took from Sashiki in Kyushu to Sashiki in southeastern Okinawa. Looking at the route only within Okinawa, it started with Samekawa entering Nakijin (Sanhoku) from the north and eventually settling in Sashiki (Sannan). Samekawa's son Shō Shishō, and his grandson Sho Hashi, ended up in Shuri (Chūzan). In other words, the Samekawa family dwelled at the central region of each principality, with Chūzan as the final destination. In this sense, Shō Hashi quite literally came to embody all three principalities. As we have seen, this migratory path was also the same as the legendary route of Minamoto Tametomo, who came ashore near Nakijin and migrated to Ōzato in the southeast, near Sashiki.

Ikuta points out that the purported unification of the three principalities under Shō Hashi also served another symbolic function. When Shō Shin actually unified Okinawa in the early sixteenth century, he built roads and the Madan bridge (Madanbashi) to link Shuri with the Shimajiri region, in part to facilitate military defense of Naha harbor. It turns out that the place-names listed on Shō Shin's 1522 monument commemorating the bridge (monument G in chapter 8)—Haebaru, Shimasoe-Ōzato, Chinen, Sashiki, and points south (see fig. 16)—became the territory of Sannan in *Reflections on Chūzan*. In other words, the lack of centralized control in Okinawa that prevailed during the three principalities era continued until Shō Shin's regime. Much later, in 1650, Shō Shōken transposed what was in fact Shō Shin's unification of Okinawa backward in time to the reign of Shō Hashi.[45] My own conclusions about the chronology of Okinawa's unification accord with those of Ikuta.

THE BIG PICTURE

In the official histories, Okinawa's first ruler was Tenson, descendant of a deity. According to *Genealogy of Chūzan*, Tenson has the qualities of mythical Chinese sage kings. He taught the people how to cook, to dwell in dens, and to use the moon to keep time. His reign coincided with agriculture, including the fermenting of wine. Among other activities, he built a castle at Shuri and divided "the realm" into three parts, whose names happen to have been Chūzan, Sanhoku, and Sannan.[46]

The first human king of Okinawa was Shunten, son of Tametomo, whose reign purportedly began in 1187. As the story goes, by then society had degenerated from the state of unity and harmony that had prevailed during Tenson's era. "The people of the country became fond of warfare," and swords, bows, and spears became abundant, brought in from other countries because Ryukyu lacked metal. Shunten restored a substantial degree of order; but disorder returned during the reigns of his two successors. Shunten's short line ended when Gihon (r. 1249–1259) abandoned his throne and wandered north to Hedo, at the northern tip of Okinawa. We will revisit Gihon's alleged northward trek, which was of crucial importance for the authors of the official histories as they attempted to weave together disparate royal lines. Gihon abdicated his throne to Eiso (r. 1260–1300), who restored order to the point where criminal law was no longer necessary. Moreover, Eiso's moral authority was so potent that northern islands such as Amami-Ōshima submitted to his rule.[47]

Notice that Eiso ruled over a well-governed kingdom that purportedly included Okinawa and the northern Ryukyu islands. Recall from chapter 1 the economic and military power shift from the Northern Tier islands to Okinawa. Eiso's ostensible reign occurred right in the middle of this transition, when power centers such as Katsuren were developing in Okinawa in connection with the expanded turbo-shell trade. Even if there had been a powerful lord at Urasoe who became the model for Eiso, there could not have been a unified, centralized state during the thirteenth century. Indeed, the majority of historians of Ryukyu regard Eiso as a local lord, not a king of a unified Okinawa. Asato Susumu is a conspicuous exception. He holds to the same metanarrative as the official histories—namely, that Okinawa was a unified kingdom, then broke into three principalities, and became reunified under Shō Hashi.[48]

Most historians regard Eiso as a semilegendary harbinger of the rise of powerful local rulers and large-scale *gusuku*. They see the formation of the three principalities during the fourteenth century as a step toward political consolidation and the eventual development of a centralized monarchy. In other words, assuming that the three principalities were indeed territorial states, most historians regard them as confederacies of local rulers, with the lords of Nakijin, Urasoe, and Ōzato as the leaders of each confederacy. In this view, Shō Hashi of Sashiki unified Okinawa, and Okinawa subsequently began to expand its power northward and southward, eventually encompassing all of the Ryukyu islands by the early sixteenth century.

My analysis leads to a different and more complex big picture. First, the story begins not in Okinawa but in the Northern Tier islands. The next major development is the rise of large-scale *gusuku* at various locations in Okinawa, Kumejima, and elsewhere. There is insufficient evidence to conclude that the three principalities were organized territorial states and therefore that they represented a significant move in the direction of the centralization of power. They may have corresponded in some way to coalitions of local lords, but we cannot be certain of any details. What we can say is that the three principalities functioned as a framework to facilitate wide participation in the tribute trade with China, precisely the outcome that Hóngwǔ sought. The existence of such a framework may have been necessary or desirable in part because of patterns of local rivalries and alliances. Our ultimate evidence for such matters, however, is legendary in nature. Archaeological evidence has shed much light on technologies, possible trade networks, and the locations of local power centers. Such evidence has not, however, been able to tell us what the three principalities were.

I examine the end of the three principalities further in chapter 6, but, briefly, Shō Hashi's seizure of the sole authority to conduct tribute trade was a significant change. For one thing, it set the stage for future warfare aimed at controlling Naha and valuable trade routes. More important, the wealth available to rulers who controlled Naha became a foundation for the eventual development of a centralized, bureaucratic state during the long reign of Shō Shin. In this sense, Shō Shin, not Shō Hashi, and certainly not Eiso, was the first king of a unified Okinawa.

Based on an analysis of the *Omoro*, Fuku Hiromi points out that: "Prior to the Ryukyu kingdom taking the appearance (*teisei*) of a kingdom, there was no Okinawa-wide political hierarchy. Those who called themselves kings, those who called themselves rulers (*yononushi*), and those who called themselves lords (*tono*) must sometimes have forged friendly connections and sometimes come into conflict as they pursued wealth and power for their bases."[49] When did Ryukyu take "the appearance of a kingdom," to use Fuku's terminology? For the purpose of conducting official foreign trade and diplomacy, different Ryukyuan rulers simultaneously used the title "king," or derivatives of it, during the time of the three principalities. Domestically, effective rule over all of Okinawa from a clear center became reality around 1500 or slightly later. In other words, I locate the emergence of a genuinely unified Okinawan state approximately one century later than do most modern survey histories.

CHAPTER FIVE

Geographies of Power

The previous chapters have examined different aspects of the larger international network in which the Ryukyu islands were enmeshed. We have seen that within the Ryukyu islands the preponderance of power gradually shifted from the Northern Tier to Okinawa during approximately the thirteenth and fourteenth centuries. To complete our understanding of the geopolitical environment in which Ryukyu developed, this chapter focuses on power centers within Okinawa and Kumejima (see fig. 6).

WAKŌ, WARFARE, AND OKINAWAN RULERS

Warfare was endemic to the Ryukyu islands, as archaeological excavations of fortifications and weapons attest. Physical evidence includes arrow- and spearheads, firearms, swords, cannonballs, stone projectiles, armor, and helmets, as well as descriptions of these items from Korean accounts.[1] A precise reconstruction of Ryukyuan military history is difficult. We know of the time and general location of some major conflicts, but we do not know the precise outcomes or the exact reasons for many of those conflicts. In this realm, the official histories are deceptive. They record only some of the actual warfare, and they transpose it into a Chinese-style morality play or into the style of medieval Japanese military dramas.

We have seen that early Ryukyuan "kings" were powerful local rulers with a license to trade with China within the structure of the tribute system. Moreover, we have observed that the generous terms the Ming court extended to Ryukyuan kings, including recognizing so many of them during the three principalities era, was done primarily for the purpose of *wakō* control. We have seen additional evidence that Ming officials regarded the Ryukyu islands as home to pirates and smugglers during the 1450s or even later. Do we have any evidence from within Okinawa of rulers sailing forth to engage in raiding or pillaging? We do, and it comes from the *Omoro*. Consider the following song:

> Masarikyo [the captain] pilots the ship
> The king of Okinawa resplendently present
> Ukiagari [the captain] pilots the ship
> Do not think the oarsmen lack vigor in their rowing
> Do not think the oarsmen row dangerously
> The lord of the south is present
> The lord of the lords is present
> The impressive lady lord
> Spiritually powerful lady lord
> We offer splendid goods to our ancestors
> Offer splendid goods to our ancestors
> We did not obtain them by asking
> Did not acquire them by asking
> But by stealth
> By pilfering [*nosude*] we attained them
> And stashed them in wine jars
> Stashed them in sacred wine jars.[2]

The two lines about the oarsmen are not entirely clear, but the translation here captures the general sense. The part about seizing the goods and offering them to the ancestors is quite clear. The verb written as *nosude*, and pronounced more like "*nusude*," would be *nusunde* (robbing, stealing, taking improperly) in modern Japanese. In other words, either the king himself, or close associates, have returned from a voyage during which they obtained valuable goods illicitly, which they hid in wine jars.

The lord of the south was apparently a powerful ruler in Okinawa and a close associate of one of the kings.[3] The song implies that the king prospers because of this powerful lord. Wine and wine jars are a common symbol of wealth in the *Omoro*. This frank song suggests that the parties to a successful raid are celebrating and thus free to proclaim their exploits. Recall Iha Fuyū's speculation that during the early modern era Ryukyuan officials began to regard the *Omoro* as dangerous thought. This song is a good example of the *Omoro* contradicting the official histories, at least in spirit.

In another *omoro*, a bard sings of the exploits of the lord of the south, who occasionally takes "the goods of other harbors," with harbors in this context indicating communities:

> Aka-no-etsukiya [an *omoro* bard, who sings of]
> Other people's harbors [villages, islands], where there are
> Valuable goods that are taken and taken
> Neha-no-etsukiya [the same bard, who sings of]
> The lord of the south
> The lord of lords.[4]

The syntax in translation is awkward, but the meaning is that the *omoro* bard Aka-no-etsukiya sings of the lord of the south, who adds to his wealth by taking the valuable goods of other people's communities (*hito no ura*). It is not clear precisely how this outside wealth might come into the lord's hands, but some variety of forcible appropriation is likely. Extraction of tribute is one possibility, and raiding is another.

LARGE-SCALE *GUSUKU*

The "lord of the south" and the other lords mentioned in these songs would have been based in large-scale *gusuku*. We have seen that *gusuku* is a generic term for Ryukyuan castles, fortresses, or enclosed encampments. Not all *gusuku* housed local lords, but all did include one or more sacred spaces. The nature and developmental trajectory of *gusuku*, especially large-scale *gusuku*, is a major topic for debate in Ryukyuan archaeology and early history.

Gusuku ranged in size from just over 100 square meters to 20,000 square meters (or 40,000 counting the entire complex). Multiple rings of impressive stone walls enclosed the largest *gusuku*, whereas others featured a single stone wall or simple earthworks. Large *gusuku* were castles in every sense, with a main keep, courtyards, moats, gates, and powerful armaments. Others were little more than encampments on high ground. Okinawan *gusuku* emerged mainly during the thirteenth century, reached their highest numbers during the fourteenth century, and declined in number but tended to increase in size and complexity during the fifteenth century.[5]

From north to south, the most powerful *gusuku* sites in Okinawa include Nakijin, Nago, Katsuren, Goeku, Chatan, Nakagusuku, Urasoe, Shuri, O-mono gusuku, Ōzato, and Tamagusuku, which is closest to Sashiki. O-mono gusuku, in Naha harbor, literally means "fortress of things." Based on descriptions by Korean castaways from the middle of the fifteenth century, it contained wine cellars, where large pots were arrayed in rooms that smelled of fermentation broth. Wine was stored in three different areas based on vintage. Moreover, O-mono gusuku contained military storehouses in which armor, spears, swords, and bows and arrows were arrayed. O-mono gusuku functioned as a warehouse for trade goods, as an armory, and as a fortress to defend Naha harbor.[6]

SHURI CASTLE

Shō Hashi established Shuri castle as a base for himself and his father in approximately 1406, following Bunei's downfall and the burning of Urasoe castle. We do not know who built Shuri castle, but Shō Hashi's prime minister, Kaiki, supervised landscaping of the surrounding grounds according to the official histories and the Monument to the Garden that Benefits the Country. According to the official record, Kaiki traveled to China in 1417 to study medicine and to observe famous mountain garden sites. Soon thereafter, he oversaw the digging out of what became Ryūtan pond, just north of Shuri castle. He also had flowering trees planted there. Most likely using the soil from this project, Kaiki created an artificial hill to the west of the castle. The placement of the pond and the hill indicate landscaping following geomantic principles.[7]

Moving ahead several decades to the time of Shō Taikyū, Korean castaway Ryang Seong, although initially lodged at Naha or Tomari, soon relocated to the vicinity of Shuri castle. It is important to bear in mind that the elaborate Chinese-style main hall of Shuri castle that stands today is a reconstruction of a structure built in 1768. The Shuri castle of the fifteenth century was located at the same place, but it would have been a very different set of structures.

According to Ryang's account, Shuri castle consisted of three walls. The outermost wall enclosed storehouses and a stable. Inside the second wall lived approximately two hundred soldiers. The innermost wall enclosed a three-story tower, which was the center of government. The bottom story held wine and food, and the top story contained precious items. Its roof consisted of boards soldered together. The king dwelled within the second story on select lucky days, and approximately one hundred women served as his attendants. Further, one hundred favored male attendants served the king in five-day shifts.[8] Ryukyuan envoys visiting Korea in 1462 provide an interesting detail about the women in attendance. Armed with swords, they served as the king's bodyguard when he moved around within the castle. Ordinary soldiers did not live inside the palace.[9]

Ryang also pointed out that Shuri castle resembled castles in Korea, with tall, winding walls and many buildings within them. The king also dwelled in a two-story building, which was probably connected with the central three-story tower via a corridor. The structures created a courtyard. Soldiers resided nearby, and during morning assemblies or criminal trials they wore full suits of armor. Based on Ryang's description, this armor came from Japan.[10] Ryukyuan envoys to Korea in 1462 also described their country's military equipment as being similar to that of Japan.[11]

During the middle of the fifteenth century, Shuri castle was the site of metalworking, carried out within the outer wall on the western side and possibly at other sites. Richard Pearson points out that excavation of this area, called Iri no Azana, has revealed "the remains of a furnace for extracting metal that was connected to a shallow trench, crucibles, tuyeres (bellows valves), large amounts of iron and bronze filings, molds for the production of temple bells, and other metal objects."[12] From the remains of molds, we can also conclude that large temple bells were cast at this site.[13] Experts from Japan supervised bell casting, and it is important to note that both technological know-how for such projects and a distribution network for iron had developed in Japan during the Kamakura period.[14]

More broadly, we know of roughly one hundred and fifty ironworking sites in villages unconnected with large *gusuku*. These sites produced "Weapons, armor, agricultural tools, fishing tools, building tools, knives, and iron cauldrons."[15] In 1376, Chinese Ministry of Justice Vice Minister Jì Hào returned from Ryukyu after purchasing forty horses and 5,000 *jīn* of sulfur. He reported a low demand there for luxury items such as silk, figured cloth, or gossamer fabric. Instead, Ryukyuans valued porcelain and metal axes.[16] It makes sense, of course, that most Ryukyuans of the time would have prized items of practical utility.

NAKIJIN AND ITS CONNECTIONS

In the official histories, Nakijin was the capital of Sanhoku. Its last king was violent, ill-tempered, and dull-witted. In this portrayal, Nakijin was associated with raw military power. Nakijin is also prominent in the *Omoro*, although not specifically for its military power. In the *Omoro*, Nakijin is Miyakizen. It was a key crossroads in both the Northern Tier Cultural Zone and the Tokara Cultural Zone. According to *Omoro* songs, the most prominent features of Nakijin were its location, function, and associations. It was the gateway into Okinawa from points north. It was also the location of powerful priestesses who served as models for Shō Shin's high priestess, the Kikoe-ōgimi. Finally, the Nakijin of the *Omoro* was the likely homeland of the second Shō dynasty.

Han'anchi's Sword Points North

Han'anchi's sword, formally known as Chiyoganemaru, became one of three sacred objects of Ryukyu's royal court. These objects, all swords, functioned roughly like the regalia of Japan's imperial court.[17] The official histories provide a dramatic account of Han'anchi's final battle. In it, Shō Hashi's coalition of military forces destroyed Han'anchi at Nakijin, aided by the use of shrewd stratagems. The account reads like a popular Japanese military drama. As part of the story, Han'anchi's sword ended up in the Shikema River. An anonymous person who hailed from the island of Iheya later recovered the sword and presented it to the king.[18]

The sword Chiyoganemaru was made in Japan during the early Muromachi era and had a short handle for use as a cavalry weapon. Its popular name is Chibugani. Kaneseki Takeo has argued that this name derives from Korean and that the sword itself probably made its way to Ryukyu via Korean merchants. Both the meaning of the sword's name and the symbolism connected with its legends indicates that it possessed the supernatural power to control water, a theme we have seen repeatedly in early Ryukyuan contexts.[19] The legend of Han'anchi's sword associated it with Nakijin's sacred grove Kanahiyabu. Putting this information together, once again we find traces of a network from Nakijin across to Iheya and Izena, north through Michinoshima, and northwest to Korea.

Gateway to Okinawa

When *wakō* bands, refugees, merchants, fortune seekers, or others arrived in Okinawa from Japan or other northern locations, they typically entered via the Nakijin area. Consider the following consecutive *omoro* about a talented arrival from Japan:

> Acclaimed Nariomoi of Ginka
> In an acclaimed jewel of a castle
> Dwelled a Yamato-wizard (*Yamato no oni*)
> Nariomoi of Ijieki[20]

> Acclaimed Nariomoi of Ginka
> Went up to Miyakizen [Nakijin]
> And built the acclaimed Tokumitsu [storehouse]
> Nariomoi of Ijieki.[21]

When referring to people or places, the suffix or prefix *oni-*, conventionally translated "demon," indicates someone of superior, even magical, talent or power. Ginka is in Nago, south of Nakijin on the Motobu peninsula. Nariomoi apparently arrived in Okinawa from Japan with superior knowledge and skills. Putting his abilities to work, he engaged in trade at Nakijin and became wealthy. We cannot correlate Nariomoi with a specific historical figure. The broader point is that Nakijin and nearby areas functioned as a gateway into Okinawa from the north.

Closely Linked with Shuri

As far as we know, the second Shō dynasty's founder, Shō En, devoted no energy to symbolic or ideological matters other than by casting coins. He governed in the manner of a powerful *wakō* leader. Shō En's Shuri castle, and the polity based there, probably bore a close resemblance to what Ryang Seong and other Korean observers described slightly earlier. Shuri was a center of power, and Shuri castle housed several hundred retainers, but it did not tower above the other large-scale *gusuku* in Okinawa. This situation changed during the long reign of Shō En's son, Shō Shin, when Shuri became the administrative center of an expansive empire and the new symbolic and religious center of a network of spiritual power. The most important connection within this network was the Shuri-Nakijin link.

Shō Shin built the Kanahiyabu (Kanahyan) grove in Nakijin for this purpose, and its counterpart in Shuri was the similarly named Sonohiyabu (Sonohiyan) grove near the Shureimon gate of Shuri castle. So closely linked were these two sites that their names overlapped. Consider this example from the *Omoro:*

> Acclaimed Aoriyae priestess
> Prays to the central deity
> Even his highness the king
> Prays and flourishes
> Acclaimed Aoriyae priestess
> Prays to Kanahiyabu.[22]

Here, Shuri (the king) and Nakijin are so closely interrelated that it is difficult to be certain of the geographic orientation because the term "Kanahiyabu" can indicate either the Kanahiyabu shrine in Nikijin or the Sonohiyabu shrine in Shuri.[23] In other words, Kanahiyabu in this song can indicate the Sonohiyabu site at which the king would be worshipping, the linked site in Nakijin where the Aoriyae priestess performed her rites, or both simultaneously.[24]

In another *omoro,* the king, though in Shuri, taps the power of Nakijin's deity so that he may rule his realm:

> The Sun-king [Lord of the east direction]
> Prays to Nakijin's Kanahiyabu
> So that the king
> Rules and prospers
> The Sun-king [Lord of the hole-of-the-sun].[25]

Notice that in this song Nakijin is a source of the power that enables the kings in Shuri to rule.

According to the official histories, Kanemaru (Shō En) was born on the island of Izena, although he later fled to northern Okinawa. I examine parts of his biography in detail elsewhere, and it is a far-fetched tale. Although the details of Kanemaru's origins are more obscure than those of Shō Hashi, it is likely that Nakijin, not Izena, was the homeland of the second Shō dynasty.[26] In addition to the Kanahiyabu-Sonohiyabu link, Shō Shin appointed his third son as overseer of Hokuzan (Hokuzan kanshu). Although usually regarded as a military overseer to guard against rebellions, the main function of the office was to facilitate the Nakijin Aoriyae in the performance of religious rites that were a replica of those conduced at Shuri.[27] In chapter 7, I present additional evidence that Nakijin was the likely ancestral homeland of the second Shō dynasty.

SOUTHERN OKINAWA

Okinawan legends, including those written into the official histories, often feature powerful outsiders arriving from the north, entering Okinawa near Nakijin, and then traveling to the south. Like Nakijin in the northwest, southeast Okinawa was an area associated with wealth, technology, and religious power. More specifically, the deity Amamiku (Amamikyo) moved from northwest Okinawa directly to southeast Okinawa before moving westward again, around and up to Shuri. This legendary divine migration corresponds to migrations of deities from the Tokara Cultural Zone to Nakijin and finally to southern Okinawa. It also corresponds to legendary and human migrations, Shō Hashi's family being the outstanding example.

As an example of deity migration, consider Okinawa's Sasukasa (Sashikasa in the Tokara islands). Aoriyae is closely related to Sasukasa, and in both cases their names indicate both the priestess and her deity. On the Tokara island of Akuseki, the deity of Mount Negami (Mount Root Deity) is Sashikasa-no-mikoto, and a Takarashima deity is named Negami yaemori sashikasa-no-goze. These Tokara Sashikasa deities are served by male (*hōi*) and female (*neeshi*) shamans, discussed in chapter 1 (fig. 2).[28] It is not entirely clear whether the Tokara Sashikasa migrated first to Kumejima and from there to northern Okinawa (Hedo and Nakijin), or first to northern Okinawa, or to both regions separately (fig. 6). In any case, in both Kumejima and Okinawa, Sasukasa and Aoriyae are migratory deities from across the sea.[29] In Kumejima, the Ryukyuan Sasukasa and Aoriyae are a single deity, Sasukasa-aoriyae, although in the *Omoro* they are separate entities.[30] Iha Fuyū pointed out that the Sasukasa and Aoriyae of northern Okinawa both possess the quality of being able to control or moderate the wind.[31] In her *Omoro* iteration, Sasukasa thrusts the "peg of the world" (*yo no kugi*) to defend Shuri-mori.[32] The phrase "thrust the peg" is found in the texts of sixteenth-century monuments to structures integral to the military defense of Naha harbor.[33]

We have seen that Aoriyae functioned as a template for Shuri's high priestess, Kikoe-ōgimi. Aoriyae remained at Nakijin, but Sasukasa migrated south. The two deities Aoriyae and Sasukasa, originally the single Sashikasa deity of the Tokara islands, became northern and southern counterparts of each other in Okinawa.[34] Specifically, Sasukasa became associated with Ōzato in the south and with decorative screens (*byōbu*), a symbol of wealth.[35] Sashikasa/Sasukasa's southward migration also traces a path similar to that of the legendary Minamoto Tametomo, the deity Amamiku, and the Samekawa family. The founders of the second Shō dynasty also had close ties to both Nakijin and Kumejima, which I examine in detail in later chapters.

The rugged mountains of northern Okinawa are not suited to agriculture. *Wakō* groups entering Okinawa from the north probably migrated to the southern end of the island in search of land for rice cultivation. Shō Hashi's home base of Sashiki was among the best places in Okinawa for rice, and *Omoro* songs praise Sashiki's fine white rice and water.[36] By the early fifteenth century, double-cropping had developed in southeast Okinawa, subsequently spreading to other rice-growing areas in the Ryukyu islands.[37] Based mainly on Ryang Seong's 1456 account, the typical pattern was to sow seeds during the tenth through twelfth lunar months, transplant the seedlings during the first month of the next year, and harvest the grain during the fifth month. The cut stalks left in the field would sprout new shoots, and a second round of harvesting took place during months seven through nine.[38]

According to legend that became an integral part of royal religious rites, seeds of rice and the other "five grains" originated at Kudakajima, a small island just off the coast from the Chinen peninsula in southeastern Okinawa (today's Nanjo City, which includes Sashiki). The seeds spread from there to the closest coastal areas. Therefore, Tamagusuku and Chinen were the sites of the first wet-rice agriculture. Well into the seventeenth century, the king visited the island each year during the second lunar month, along with the kingdom's leading priestesses, to venerate the origins of Ryukyuan agriculture.[39] The arrival of grain seeds from Kudakajima is a variation of the broader theme of outsiders bringing valuable technology.

Southeast Okinawa stands out not only in agriculture but also with respect to metalworking. Okinawa's legendary first king, Shunten, became lord of Shimajiri because he was able to have a blacksmith make a sword from iron pieces for which he had traded. Moreover, Shunten traded a metal screen (*byōbu*) that he had obtained for territory along a river.[40] We have seen that Shō Hashi's legendary biography includes similar elements, set in the same approximate location of southeastern Okinawa.[41] Indeed, Shunten legends connect southeastern Okinawa with Nakijin in much the same way as does Shō Hashi's biography or the Tametomo legend.

One royal treasure is the sword Tsukushi-chara. Tsukushi (often pronounced Chikushi) was also an old name for Kyushu. "Chara" indicates a locally powerful family. Therefore, the sword is named after a locally powerful household in Kyushu. Particularly when called Tsukushi-chara, not its alternate name Teganemaru,[42] this sword is associated with the lord of Ōzato. In the *Omoro*, for example:

> At esteemed Ōzato
> [The lord] takes the
> Esteemed Tsukushi-chara
> And prospers
> Esteemed Ōzato
> Esteemed Tsukushi-chara.[43]

Ōzato was the location of blacksmith sites where swords were manufactured from imported iron or were remanufactured and modified. In the latter case, swords or sword blades from Japan would be refitted with hilts and handles wrapped with the skin of sharks or rays.[44]

Swords from Okinawa became popular export items during the fifteenth and sixteenth centuries. There is a famous passage in which Tomé Pires, a Portuguese merchant writing in Malacca in about 1512, states: "The Lequeos are called Gores—they are known by either of these names. Lequeos is the chief one." Pires later describes the large cargo of swords Ryukyuans typically brought for sale.[45] Scholars of Ryukyu have been interested in this term "Gores" since the 1920s and have proposed a variety of hypotheses. According to Uezato Takashi, the terms "Lequeos," and "Gores" in Pires' famous passage derived from these Ryukyuan swords. Omitting many details, his essential point is that swords from the island of "Gōru" (probably Borneo in the Celebes Sea) were known in Javanese as "Rikiiuu" (Ryukyu). In other words, Japanese swords carried by Ryukyuan traders, some possibly modified in southern Okinawa, became associated with Ryukyuans arriving in Java via Borneo.[46]

FORTRESS KUMEJIMA AND ITS CONQUEST

In *Omoro* songs about seizing other people's harbors, one plunderer is the powerful lord of Kumejima:

> The chief Fukudi-gima
> Grabs
> The valuable goods of other people's harbors
> And offers them up to the ruler
> The young lord Kasasu
> Offering up the valuable goods from other people's harbors
> To the genuine young lord.[47]

Kumejima is a small island to the west of Okinawa that was the abode of powerful *wakō* groups. This song and others indicate that Fukudi-gima, of Nakazato Village in Kumejima, is a subordinate to the Kasasu lord of that island. In another *omoro*, the influence of the Kasasu lord, expressed in sonic terms as a roaring echo, extends all the way to Yamato.[48]

At the northern edge of Kumejima is the crescent-shaped Mount Ōtake ridge whose high points exceed a thousand feet (305 meters).[49] Although some peaks in northern Okinawa and Mount Omoto in Ishigaki are slightly higher, the position of Mount Ōtake at the northwestern edge of Kumejima, and the position of the island itself, provide a commanding view of local sea-lanes. As the song suggests, Kumejima was perfectly situated to profit from, impose tolls on, or raid, commerce between Japan, various Ryukyu islands, and China. Mount Ōtake and other peaks in Kumejima also provided ideal terrain for fortifications. Owing to accidents of geography, the island was a perfect base for *wakō*. A natural fortress, Kumejima was a strong power center, and it remained independent of Shuri's control until Shō Shin's reign.

Like most of Ryukyuan history of the fifteenth century and earlier, the biographical details of local lords have come down to us from legends. According to such accounts, the key figure in uniting Kumejima under a single ruler was Ishiki'nawa (conventional modern pronunciation), who lived into the fifteenth century. His four sons all became lords of castles. During their generation, forces from Shuri attacked Kumejima. Some accounts give the reason as betrayal of the brothers by underlings.[50] For now it is sufficient to note that Shō Shin conquered the island at some point, bringing it into Shuri's orbit. Moreover, this intervention led to the fall of Gushikawa gusuku and contributed to important institutional developments connected with the *hiki* system, explained in chapter 10.

In legends and religious geography, Kumejima had close ties with Miyako and Yaeyama. For example, Kōntofushi-kawara, a deity worshipped in Taketomi, came from Kumejima. Moreover, a brother and sister deity from Kumejima came to be worshipped as the deity of Mount Omoto in Yaeyama.[51] On Kumejima's northwestern shore, just below Mount Ōtake, was Yamato anchorage (Yamato-domari). This anchorage and Gushikawa gusuku functioned as a *wakō* base.[52] The lord of Gushikawa was part of the Kawara lineage of *wakō*. Shō Shin destroyed another branch of the Kawara lineage in the war against Akahachi (Honkawara) of Yaeyama in 1500. He conducted military campaigns in Kumejima in 1506, at least according to the most common date.[53]

Kumejima is rich in place-names and deity names connected with metalworking. Even its chief priestess, Kimihae, sometimes called Oni-Kimihae in the *Omoro*, was closely connected with metalworking.[54] During the era of Shō Shin's reign, the island's thirteen furnaces specialized in different types of iron products, and they lit up the night sky with a red glow.[55] Noting that Kumejima was known as "metal island" because of its abundant iron sand and ironworks, Iha Fuyū suggested that one reason Shō Shin invaded in 1506 was to gain control of its iron industry.[56] We revisit Kumejima in later chapters.

WAKŌ CHIEFTAINS: GAARA AND KAWARA

This section revisits the matter of *wakō* migration via the distribution of distinctive names, which I call Gaara group names. The distribution of Gaara group names overlaps substantially with the Northern Tier Cultural Zone. Moreover, these names are found in Goeku and Nishihara in Okinawa, as well as in Kumejima and Sakishima, where they often take the form of Kawara or Gawara and overlap with place-names containing the word *omoto*.[57]

Along the Higo coast, the word *gora* means the head atop one's shoulders. By extension, it came to mean leader.[58] *Gaara* and its numerous variants are related to *gora* and imply a *wakō* chieftain.[59] With the passing of generations, the Gaara names lost their specific association with *wakō* chieftains, but they retained a strong flavor of "Yamato" or "Japan." Gaara group names include Gōra, Gorira, Goriya, Guriya, Guri, Goraru, Guraru, Goran, and other variants. One example we have encountered thus far is Guraru Magohachi of Okinoerabu.[60]

Gaara group place-names are common throughout Michinoshima. Examples include the Goriya River, Goriyahara, Goriyagusuku, and Goriya in Amami-Ōshima, Agariguran in Tokunoshima, and Guraru and Gurarubaru in Okinoerabu.[61] The title "Yamato no ikusa taishō" (Great Yamato general), appears in Amami-Ōshima place-names and legends. Places associated with this Yamato general usually overlap with wet-rice agriculture, good harbors, and the element *goriya* and variants in nearby personal and place-names. Nagara-Hachiman is another variety of this Yamato general. In Okinoerabu, the home village of Gararu Magohachi is located in that island's wet-rice zone. As Ōyama Ringorō points out, wet-rice agriculture and other technologies came south from one island to another along with "the *wakō* lineage name 'Goriya.'"[62]

There are other cultural remnants of what were probably Gaara group *wakō* in Amami-Ōshima. Certain festival floats in Setouchi, for example, are called Goriya boats. A sacred grove in the same town is called Mount Guri. It was home to a temple where a local lineage worshipped, but that building was converted into the community shrine during the Taishō era. About forty years earlier, old military gear was excavated from around the foot of the mountain. "We can regard the existence of *wakō* as background to the word Goriya," concludes Takahashi Ichirō.[63]

Moving south to Okinawa, Gaara group names have a limited distribution and are found mostly in Nishihara (Nishihara-chō, central Okinawa, south of Nakagusuku) and Goeku (Okinawa City, central Okinawa, north of Nakagusuku). These locations are significant, and we return to them when examining connections between Shō Taikyū and Kanemaru in the next chapter. Here, I point out a close overlap between Gaara group place-names in Nishihara and the presence of northern-style funeral rites. The main archaeological evidence is a distinctive type of small bone jar found in both Nishihara and the Kominato district of Amami City on the northeast shore of Amami-Ōshima. In other words, these bone jars were connected with funeral customs that arrived from the north with Gaara group *wakō* lineages.[64]

In Miyako and Yaeyama, Gaara group names are especially common in old childhood names.[65] *Origins of Ryukyu* regarded Oyake Akahachi and Honkawara as two different people, both of whom rebelled against Shuri in 1500. In the context of stating that this point is incorrect, Iha Fuyū explained that the name Kawara, a variant of Gaara, means "head" and the Yaeyama nickname Ponkawara means "big head." Honkawara was Akahachi's deity name meaning "big leader."[66] Kawara names are prominent in several locations in Sakishima. One group associated with the Kubamoto (or Kōnto) sacred grove in Taketomi island was the Kubamotoshishi Kawara, whose deity was Yamato-dono (lord Yamato). Moreover, this group came to Taketomi from Kumejima.[67] The likely origin of Kawara names is northern Kyushu, in the vicinity of Fukuoka.[68]

Mount Omoto in Ishigaki is the highest peak in Yaeyama. In northern Amami-Ōshima, Mount Yuwan is commonly known as Mount Obotsu. Leaving out several other examples, high places with *obotsu* in their names are common in the Northern Tier Cultural Zone, and mountains with *omoto* in their names are found in Sakishima. Both names are related, ultimately to the Mount Omoto that figures prominently in Usa Hachiman legends (a young child received Hachiman's oracle at the foot of this mountain).[69] The *obotsu* versus *omoto* difference in pronunciation corresponds with Gaara and its variants versus Kawara, and to geography (northern versus southern Ryukyu islands). Putting everything together, it is likely that these groups of names indicate two lineages of *wakō*. The Gaara/*obotsu* lineage settled mainly in the Northern Tier Cultural Zone. The Kawara/*omoto* lineage settled in Kumejima and Sakishima. The war that eliminated Akahachi's Kawara group in 1500 and the 1506 invasion of Kumejima were probably connected.[70] I will examine this topic further in chapter 10.

PART II

DYNASTIC TURBULENCE, 1400–1600

CHAPTER SIX

The First Shō Dynasty

The chapters of the previous part examined the cultural, political, and economic geography of early Ryukyu. The chapters of this part examine the first Shō dynasty, the transition to the second Shō dynasty, and the kings of the second Shō dynasty up to and including Shō Nei (r. 1587–1620).

ROOTS OF THE FIRST SHŌ DYNASTY

We have already encountered the argument that Shō Hashi's grandfather, Samekawa, was a Southern Court *wakō* from the coast of Higo who migrated to Okinawa. This evidence is circumstantial, of course, but there is much of it. If we insisted on certainty with respect to early Ryukyuan history, we would be able to say very little about anything. My argument, and that of many others, rests on the preponderance of evidence. On the one hand, there is abundant evidence that Samekawa migrated to Okinawa from Kyushu. Conversely, the evidence that Samekawa was born in tiny Iheya island is that the official histories say so. This assertion is especially suspicious in light of the strategy the official histories employed for linking different royal lines, which I examine in chapter 9. While it is likely that Samekawa passed through Iheya as he migrated south, all indications point to Sashiki in Higo as the starting point for that migration.

The first writer to state that Shō Hashi's roots were in Higo was Kyokutei (Takizawa) Bakin, in *Chinsetsu yumiharizuki* (1807). Bakin's main reason for asserting a Higo–Ryukyu link was the presence of the same place-names, especially Sashiki (present-day Ashikita in Kumamoto

Prefecture) and Hamamura (in Higo and Katsuren).[1] Today Sashiki in Kumamoto survives mainly as the name of Ashikita's Sashiki station. In Shō Hashi's day and for many years later it was an active seaport. *Yatsushiro nikki,* a local chronicle covering the period 1484–1566, mentions Sashiki at least thirty-seven times.[2]

In the 1930s, Orikuchi Shinobu (1887–1953) expanded this analysis of names, further linking Sashiki in southern Okinawa with Nakijin, Iheya, and coastal Kumamoto.[3] Orikuchi linked the village of Nawashiro in Okinawa's Sashiki, where Shō Shishō and Shō Hashi resided, to the Nawa warrior family of Yatsushiro. Moreover, Orikuchi first proposed that "Yashiro" in the *Omoro* refers to Yatsushiro. He linked the migration of Samekawa to Okinawa with the arrival of the Tametomo legend and speculated on the origins of the names of Shō Hashi and Shō Shishō. Orikuchi also explored the close connections of the Samekawa with Hachiman worship and *wakō*.[4]

Some details of Orikuchi's analysis have not held up to subsequent scrutiny, but the main point has fared well. As we have seen, it is highly probable that the Yamato-Yashiro pair in the *Omoro* and other old songs and oracles means Kyushu in that it indicates Yamato-in in Satsuma and Yatsushiro in Higo, not Japan and Yamashiro as many *Omoro* translators maintain.[5] Yamato-in territory had close ties with Higo at precisely the time of the early Chūzan kings. During the war between the northern and southern courts, Kaneyoshi's army invaded and held this territory. Between 1400 and 1448 the Sagara of Hitoyoshi in Higo received income from the Yamato-in territory. The Sagara traded with China and Ryukyu, most likely using the port of Ichiki in the north of Satsuma.[6] An extensive corpus of legends also links places and symbols connected with Shō Hashi and his family in Okinawa with Kyushu.[7] Other connections are more general, but still significant. A distinctive type of flower-petal-shaped celadon porcelain has been excavated from fourteenth- and early fifteenth-century sites in Okinawa and Kyushu, especially Kumamoto.[8] Moreover, the Yatsushiro (Shiranui) Sea was the locus of an especially vigorous foreign trade and regional information network during the fifteenth and sixteenth centuries.[9]

These general and specific links between Kyushu and Okinawa with respect to the founders of the first Shō dynasty are especially compelling because of the broader history of the Southern Court *wakō* and their southward migrations, which I have discussed at length in chapter 2. Samekawa arrived in Okinawa when the position of the Southern Court *wakō* along the Higo coast had seriously eroded or soon thereafter (see fig. 9).

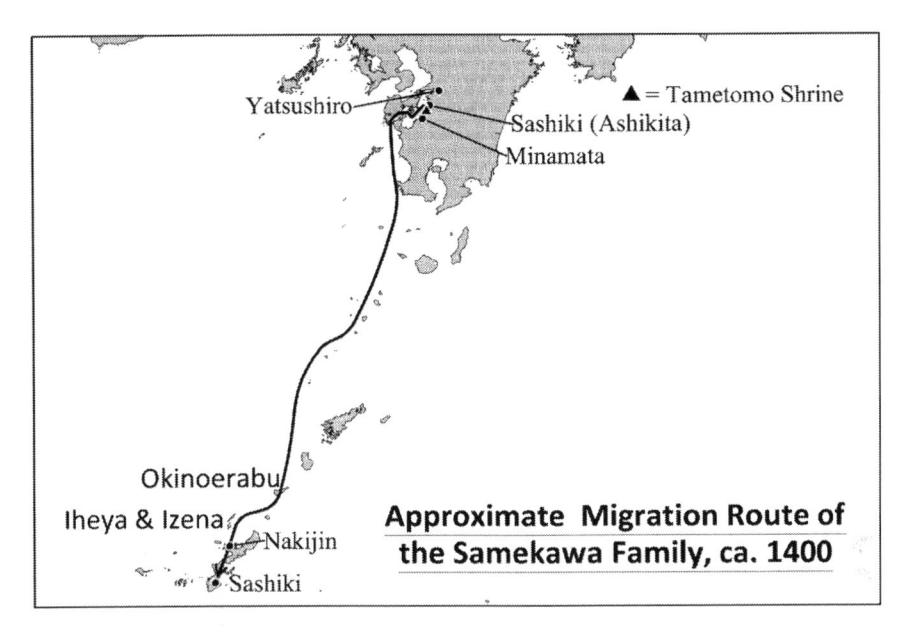

Fig. 9. The approximate migration route of the Samekawa family, ca. 1400

That Samekawa came to Okinawa from Higo is nearly certain. The precise route he took is less clear. It is possible that he passed through Okinoerabu, Yoron island, and locations in northern Okinawa. The main evidence for Okinoerabu is the close association of Samekawa and his family with the Tsukishiro form of Hachiman. As we have seen, Tsukishiro appeared in the *Omoro* in four places: Okinoerabu, Sashiki, Chinen, and Shuri castle.[10] Okinoerabu also has close legendary links with northern Okinawa. A divine song from Hedo, *Shima-watari no umui* (Recollection of island crossings), claims that Okinoerabu was the original Ryukyu island. It formed from a floating mass in the sea, and from Okinoerabu islands spread north to Tokunoshima and all the way to Japan. Islands also developed in the other direction, including Iheya and Okinawa. Legends connected with the song explain that the ancestral founders of Hedo migrated from Okinoerabu to Yoron, to Iheya, and finally to Hedo, whence the history of Okinawa began.[11] Recall that Hedo was where the deity Amamiku entered Okinawa, moving from there to Nakijin. Putting everything together, "the footsteps of Amamiku were probably the footsteps of *wakō*."[12] Whether they were the specific footsteps of Samekawa is open to speculation, of course, but his route almost certainly included one or more of the locations Iheya, Hedo, and Nakijin.

According to his legendary biography, Samekawa had two children. His son became Shō Shishō, and his daughter became the priestess of Baten. Several related legends link the Baten priestess with Kyushu via Yamato-banta, the inlet near Sashiki ui gusuku and Baten. Leaving out many details, the Baten priestess traveled to Kyushu and brought back to local waters a favorite fish, called *kibinago* in Kyushu and *gajoku* (and other names) in Okinawa. Local festivals commemorated this and related events, including the hill where Samekawa hung his fishing nets to dry. A landslide in 1959 destroyed that hill and other sites associated with Samekawa.[13]

KATSUREN AND SHŌ HASHI

Excavations reveal that during the middle of the fourteenth century, Katsuren suddenly became a center for trade in high-quality Chinese porcelain. It was also one of the few large *gusuku* in Okinawa that made use of Korean roof tiles.[14] A major power in Okinawa between the fourteenth and fifteenth centuries, Katsuren also maintained close ties with locations in the northern Ryukyu islands.[15] *Record of East Sea Countries* records a message sent to the Korean court in 1418 by a "Katsuren-gusuku," second son of the king of Chūzan. It explained that, because his older brother had recently died, Katsuren-gusuku was making contact for the first time.[16] This message was approximately three years before Shō Hashi formally became king. The same year, *Joseon Veritable Records* states that Katsuren, second son of the king of Ryukyu, sent an envoy bearing a letter and a variety of gifts.[17] This son of the king may have been Shō Hashi, operating under the name Katsuren. If not Hashi, it was nevertheless a member of his household.[18] According to Ōyama Ringorō, two songs in the *Omoro* state that Shō Kinpuku and Shō Furi, both sons of Shō Hashi according to the official histories, were lords of Katsuren.[19]

Katsuren gusuku (the place) was probably under the control of Shō Hashi and his descendants during the early fifteenth century through the 1440s. If so, then it is likely that Amawari in the 1450s was either a relative of Shō Hashi or a close ally. That said, however, from textual sources we know almost nothing about Amawari other than that he probably died in battle in 1458, that the official histories regard him as evil, and that the *Omoro* sings his praises and places him on a par with the king.

CHINESE AGENTS AND THE DEMISE OF BUNEI

In the official histories, righteousness always prevails, albeit sometimes after the delay of a generation or more. According to *Kyūyō*, Shō Hashi and his father enjoyed reputations in Sashiki as upright rulers. When King Bunei of Chūzan indulged himself in excesses of luxury, paying no heed to the suffering he inflicted on the common people, Hashi raised a "righteous army" and went to "inquire about this crime." The local lords ended up acclaiming Hashi and his father as their ruler.[20] Hashi destroyed Bunei and set up Hashi's father, Shishō, as king of Chūzan. Indulgence in luxury to the point of causing the common people to suffer is a cliché in East Asian official histories. Nevertheless, Bunei may indeed have been wicked. His demise almost certainly was the result of an incident involving eunuchs.

During the first month of 1406, Chūzan sent several castrated men to China to serve as eunuchs. The Yŏnglè emperor reacted with anger. He ordered the men returned and said that it was "intolerable" that people who had committed no crime should be punished in this manner. He further demanded that Bunei ensure that such an occurrence never happen again. In a case of the pot calling the kettle black, Yŏnglè ended his communiqué by stating that emperors and kings must not interfere with the creative force of heaven and earth.[21] As usual in such cases, we have no record of what happened on the Ryukyuan side. It is reasonable to surmise that somebody connected with tribute trade had miscalculated badly. Later that year, Bunei was gone. During the fourth month of 1407, Shō Shishō suddenly appeared in Ming records as crown prince, ostensibly as the son of Bunei, having sent an envoy to report his fictive father's death.[22]

Direct Chinese influence in Ryukyuan domestic politics was strongest from around 1406 or 1407 through the 1440s, and the sudden demise of Bunei looks very much like a Chinese-sponsored coup, with Shō Hashi as the beneficiary. The rise of Shō Hashi and the Chinese who served as his highest ministers also corresponded with the end of the three principalities. Whatever its actual political geography or administrative structure may have been, Ryukyu as a trading entity came under new management at this time.

At this point we should pause and consider the triumvirate of Chinese officials who headed the governments of Shō Shishō and Shō Hashi. Their posts were prime minister (*ōsō* or *kokusō*) and left and right head envoys (*chōshi*). According to *Origins of Ryukyu*, the right head envoy managed the tribute trade documentation and functioned as the head of Kumemura (Kumemura-okite).[23] According to *Genealogy of Chūzan*, the first prime minister was A Ranpō (Yà Lánpáo), appointed during Bunei's reign.[24] Also according to *Genealogy*, Ōmo (Wáng Mào) served Shō Shishō concurrently as prime minster and right chief envoy, a point confirmed in *Ming Veritable Records*.[25] Ōmo carried over into Shō Hashi's administration, but having served so long, he petitioned the Ming court to be allowed to return to his hometown. To assist Ōmo, Teifuku (Chéng Fù) served concurrently as prime minster and left head envoy in charge of matters of state. Later in Shō Hashi's reign, Kaiki became prime minister. According to the official histories, he remained in office during the reigns of Shō Chū, Shō Shitatsu, and Shō Kinpuku.[26]

The main point is that concurrent with Shō Hashi's rise to power we find powerful men appointed by the Ming court "serving" the Chūzan kings. These Chinese "were extraordinary appointments as political and diplomatic directors," according to Higashionna Kanjun.[27] Kaiki was especially influential. Even before Hashi's purported unification, Kaiki "transcended the boundaries of the three principalities as a superintendent of all of Ryukyu."[28] Not only did he oversee the landscaping around Shuri castle, he served as a Daoist longevity adviser to Shō Hashi and as a diplomat to Chinese outposts in Southeast Asia.[29] Indeed, during his time in power, Kaiki overshadowed the Chūzan kings by functioning as the main orchestrator of exchanges of goods between Ryukyu the Ming court.[30]

Consider the convergence of several changes. Shō Hashi's overthrow of Bunei corresponded to a relocation Chūzan's capital from Urasoe to Shuri, closer to Naha. Urasoe castle burnt down at this time, possibly in connection with Bunei's demise. The timing and close ties between Kaiki and Shō Hashi suggest that Hashi allied with powerful Chinese to overthrow Bunei. Moreover, after Shō Hashi took the throne, Ryukyu's king received a rhetorical upgrade in Chinese documents that included a higher rank and more elevated language.[31] What strengthens the circumstantial case for a Chinese-sponsored coup and de facto change of management was the ill-fated eunuch incident of 1406. In light of these points, it may have been a change of administration, not clashes of armies, that led to the disappearance of the three principalities.

The emergence of a triumvirate of Chinese officials at the top of the governments of the early first Shō dynasty kings was a significant development. However, these Chinese officials fade from the official records rather quickly. *Genealogy* lists Kaiki as carrying over into Shō Kinpuku's reign but gives no details, nor do we know whether head envoys continued as royal officials instead of residing in Kumemura. Starting with Shō Kinpuku's reign, we see royal younger brothers, fictive or real, playing roles in politics similar to that of Kaiki during Shō Hashi's reign.[32] The most prominent such younger brothers, Shō Furi and Shō Sen'i, did not fare well, as we will see. During Shō Shin's reign, the royal government came to be headed by a triumvirate of top officials, the Council of Three, none of whom were Chinese.

THE AWKWARD FIRST SHŌ DYNASTY

The first Shō dynasty was a time of frequent warfare. This warfare took place at the level of kings, aspiring kings, powerful lords, and probably among local forces too obscure to merit register in either the official histories or later lore. In 1453, Shuri castle burned down in what the official histories describe as a succession struggle between the forces of Shiro, son of the deceased King Shō Kinpuku, and Kinpuku's younger brother Furi. In the aftermath, which left both claimants dead, "Prince Goeku" ascended the throne as Shō Taikyū. *Genealogy of Chūzan* portrays Furi as aggressively seeking to usurp Shiro, the designated royal heir. At one point in a dialogue between the two, Shiro chastises Furi for seeking to misappropriate his older brother's legacy. *Genealogy* also suggests that Shō Taikyū ascended the throne with the approval of local power holders (C. *guórén*; J. *kokujin*).[33]

Most details of the 1453 battle are obscure, but we know from archaeological evidence that there was a major fire in Shuri castle that year.[34] A *Ming Veritable Records* entry from the second month of 1454 states that an envoy from Ryukyu reported the death of Shō Taikyū's "older brother" Kinpuku. It also mentions the battle between Furi and Shiro, which caused both of their deaths and the destruction by fire of the royal storehouse. The royal seal received from Hóngwǔ had melted and Taikyū had stepped in to deal with state affairs.[35] It is certainly possible that the conflagration later attributed to a struggle between Furi and Shiro was actually connected with Shō Taikyū seizing power.

Mitsugu Sakihara points out that "after Shō Hashi died in 1539 at the ripe age of 67, all of his successors (as many as four in about fifteen years) were short-lived and quarrelsome."[36] Two of these quarrelsome kings were Shō Taikyū and Shō Toku. The official histories list them as kings of the first Shō dynasty, but they do not seem to fit into the family. Indeed, much of the dynasty is suspicious as a lineage of biological relatives. According to the official histories, Shō Shishō reigned from 1406 to 1421 and Shō Hashi from 1421 to 1439. The remaining kings all had short

114   Dynastic Turbulence, 1400–1600

reigns, averaging six years (fig. 10). During this era, men became kings of Chūzan by virtue of military might, not biological heredity. "With enough political power," explains Takahashi Kimiaki, "anyone could become a king."[37] Whoever became king duly reported to the Ming court that he was the son of the previous king. Not until the 1530s did Chinese officials begin to require confirmation in return for investiture.

SHŌ TAIKYŪ AND HIS ERA

According to the official lineage, Shō Chū (r. 1439–1444) was Shō Hashi's son, and Shō Shitatsu (r. 1444–1449) was Shō Chū's son. The branch pauses at that generation, and the next king, Shō Kinpuku (r. 1450–1453) was another of Shō Hashi's sons. When Kinpuku died, his son Shiro and his brother Furi killed each other in a succession dispute. Shō Taikyū was the next king, but official sources disagree on his pedigree. *Reflections on Chūzan* says Taikyū was Kinpuku's first son.[38] However, the Bridge to the Many Countries Bell inscription gives Taikyū's birth as 1410.[39] If so, and if

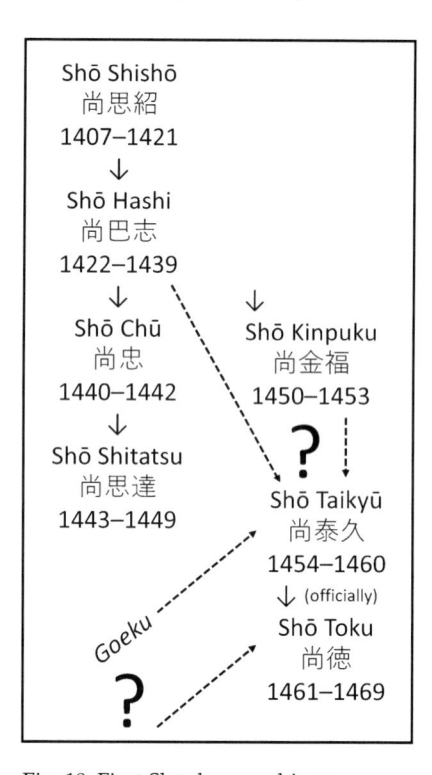

Shō Shishō
尚思紹
1407–1421
↓
Shō Hashi
尚巴志
1422–1439
↓   ↓
Shō Chū   Shō Kinpuku
尚忠   尚金福
1440–1442   1450–1453
↓   ?
Shō Shitatsu
尚思達   Shō Taikyū
1443–1449   尚泰久
             1454–1460
             ↓ (officially)
             Shō Toku
             尚徳
             1461–1469

Goeku
?

Fig. 10. First Shō dynasty kings

the official date of 1398 for Kinpuku's birth is correct, then Kinpuku fathered his first child at age eleven or twelve. *Ming Veritable Records*, however, lists Taikyū as a "royal brother."[40] Sai On had access to this source, which is probably why his 1725 *Genealogy of Chūzan* lists Taikyū as yet another son of Shō Hashi and thus Kinpuku's brother.[41] Taikyū appears to have been an awkward case for the authors of the official histories.

Shō Taikyū enjoys a good image in both the official histories and the *Omoro*, probably because of his connection with Kanemaru, founder of the second Shō dynasty. As the official story goes, Kanemaru was a peasant and a refugee. He fled his birthplace of Shomi in Izena island owing to a dispute over water with other farmers, arriving in northern Okinawa in 1438. In 1441, however, he fled from there to Shuri, where he found work as an official in charge of Naha harbor, serving Shō Taikyū. Such a position would probably have entailed record keeping and dealing with overseas commerce. On the one hand, such duties would seem beyond the ability of a peasant refugee. On the other hand, Shō Taikyū was probably "king" only of the Shuri-Naha area, even if he controlled other territory such as Goeku and Uchima in Nishihara (fig 6; there are several other places named Uchima in Okinawa). In other words, Shō Taikyū more closely resembled a powerful *wakō* chieftain than the head of a centralized, bureaucratic state. In that setting, formal education and training might not have been necessary for officials like Kanemaru. Although Kanemaru's legendary biography is not reliable in any particular detail, we will see that other evidence links him with Shō Taikyū.

The same year Shō Taikyū purportedly put Kanemaru in charge of Naha harbor he also appointed him lord of Uchima in Nishihara. It is quite possible, of course, that Kanemaru had already established a base at Uchima and from there allied with Shō Taikyū. Continuing with the official story, during Shō Toku's reign, Kanemaru went into seclusion or hiding at Uchima. From there, by popular demand, he came out of retirement and took the throne as Shō En. Kanemaru's rapid rise from refugee peasant to high official to king is one of many amazing tales in the official histories.

These histories refer to Shō Taikyū as "Prince Goeku" prior to his taking the throne, although such a title would not have existed in the mid-fifteenth century. In the *Omoro*, Shō Taikyū does not appear as a blood relative of Shō Hashi. Instead, Taikyū was actually born in Goeku as the son of its ruler.[42] Moreover, an inscription dated 1456 on a bronze bell stored at Ankokuji states that Taikyū had the bell cast and then sent it to Goeku gusuku.[43] Taikyū's roots were in Goeku, not Shuri.

116   Dynastic Turbulence, 1400–1600

Taikyu's successor as ruler of Goeku was Oni-Ōgusuku. As the official story goes, the scheming Amawari, lord of Katsuren, convinced Shō Taikyū that Gosamaru, lord of Nakagusuku, although he was actually loyal to the king, had been plotting against him. Surrounded by his enemies, Gosamaru dramatically proclaimed his loyalty to the throne in 1458 before taking his own life. Thereby Amawari was able to eliminate his main rival. The final step in Amawari's plan was a surprise attack on Shō Taikyū. Fortunately for the cause of righteousness, Amawari was married to Shō Taikyū's daughter, the filial Momoto-fumiagari, a powerful shamanic dancer in the *Omoro*. Oni-Ōgusuku was one of Amawari's generals. When he heard of the plan to betray the king, he alerted Momoto-fumiagari, and they fled to her father's court at Shuri. Their warning came just in time for Oni-Ōgusuku to amass military forces on the king's behalf. In the meantime, Oni-Ōgusuku had been singing divine songs, which miraculously conjured up a fierce storm that interfered with Amawari's advance. These moves saved Shō Taikyū's life and throne.[44] Recall many previous examples of powerful rulers able to control water or storms.

What actually took place in 1458? We cannot know in detail. There was a struggle between powerful lords and their allies. Shuri, Nakagusuku, and Katsuren were involved, and possibly Goeku and other locations (fig. 11). Moreover, as we will see, this warfare was at least in part a

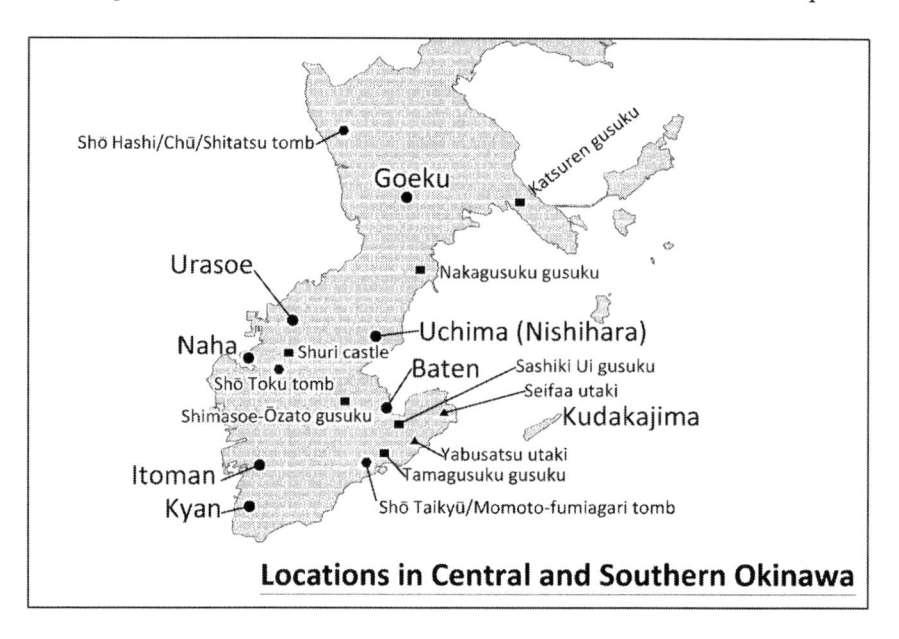

Fig. 11. Locations in central and southern Okinawa

contest to see who would control northern sea-lanes. The 1440s and 1450s were a time of conflict between certain Okinawan powers and northern locations such as Kikai.

Shō Taikyū had his famous Sea Bridge to the Many Countries Bell cast in 1458, most likely as a reaction to the violence of that year. He had many temple bells cast, and one reason for these projects may simply have been Buddhist piety or interest in leveraging Buddhist power. Sea Bridge to the Many Countries Bell, however, hung in Shuri castle, and its main purpose was to enhance the image and legitimacy of Shō Taikyū, a king who most likely was the first and last of his line.

Similarly, Shō Taikyū was the first Ryukyuan ruler to have coins cast bearing his reign name (Taisei, also pronounced Ōyo). These Taisei copper coins (*Taisei tsūhō*) were of poor quality compared with Chinese copper cash at the time, and they may have been made from recycled Yǒnglè-era coins with the characters replaced.[45] The two other kings who had coins minted were Shō Toku and Shō En. Otherwise, there was no minting of coins in Ryukyu until the production of *tōmasen* circa 1715. As outsiders taking over the throne, all three of these kings would likely have sought to bolster their legitimacy. The coins minted during Shō En's reign were of high quality, suggesting that he had access to superior technology.[46] Coins minted during the reigns of Shō Taikyū and Shō Toku have been excavated in Echizen in western Japan (Fukui Prefecture). As we will see, Echizen forged important connections with Ryukyu during the sixteenth century. The coins suggest that trade connections may have existed earlier.[47]

SCATTERED REMAINS

Oni-Ōgusuku did not survive Kanemaru's seizure of the throne in 1470. This outcome makes sense, because both of these men occupied the same sociopolitical niche as claimants to Shō Taikyū's legacy. Shō Taikyū's remains never found their way either to the Shō family tomb in Sashiki (Sashiki yōdore), which houses Shō Shishō, or to the tomb in Yomitan in central Okinawa commonly called "Sashiki grove" (see fig 11). Sashiki grove claims to be the resting place of the bones of Shō Hashi, Shō Chū (r. 1440–1442), and Shō Shitatsu (r. 1443–1449). Both Shō Taikyū and Shō Toku's tombs are in separate locations from each other and the other Shō kings. In other words, most of the first Shō dynasty kings are geographically dispersed in death. This situation probably reflects in part the tumultuous transition to the second Shō dynasty and in part the lack of biological relatedness of at least some members of the dynasty.

After his death, Shō Taikyū's bones were moved to Goeku and hidden there in a type of tomb ordinarily used for those who died of leprosy.[48] His remains did not come to rest in their current location at Tamagusuku in the Chinen Peninsula until 1908. Although we do not know the details, the start of Shō Toku's reign does not appear to have been a peaceful father-to-son succession. Indeed, both the ostensible father, as bones or a corpse, and his former harbor manager went into hiding in central Okinawa after Shō Toku came to power.

SHŌ TOKU AND HACHIMAN WORSHIP

Officially, Shō Toku (r. 1461–1469) was the last monarch of the first Shō dynasty. As such, one would predict a portrayal of him as deeply flawed. He is depicted as an active *wakō*, although the official histories do not use that word. One indication is Shō Toku's divine title, a name bestowed on Okinawan rulers and their kin by divine oracle. Shō Toku had two titles, one of which was Hachiman-no-Aji, "Lord Hachiman."[49] Moreover, Shō Toku's half-brothers had Hachiman in their divine titles.[50] More significant than his title was Shō Toku's behavior. The official histories portray him as angry and reckless. After an invasion force he dispatched to conquer Kikai failed, Shō Toku personally led an army of two thousand to complete the task. While moving through the village of Asato before setting sail, the king spied a bird flying overhead. He took out his bow, looked up to the heavens, and took aim. Shō Toku declared that if his arrow were to shoot down the bird, his army would surely be successful. He then shot the bird out of the sky.

While at sea, Shō Toku's force encountered the miracle of a large temple bell floating in the waves. The crew hauled it aboard his ship. Back in Okinawa after subduing Kikai, Shō Toku erected a shrine on the spot where he had shot the bird, had the bell installed there, and dedicated the structure to Hachiman.[51] He also placed his weapons and armor in the shrine. The floating bell, the connections with Hachiman, and the shooting of the bird all come from *wakō* lore.[52] If the official accounts are accurate, then "Shō Toku himself was a *wakō*."[53] Writing in 1940, Higashionna Kanjun pointed out that in the 1460s it was *wakō* who worshipped Hachiman. Therefore, the establishment of the Hachiman Shrine may have been connected with "a group of Japanese residing in Ryukyu."[54] It was probably inconceivable to Higashionna that the king himself was a *wakō*.

There is a twist to this matter. Ryukyu's first official history was the 1650 *Reflections on Chūzan*. Like later official accounts, it portrays Shō Toku as violent and morally depraved. However, the *Reflections* account leaves out the *wakō*-specific details about shooting the bird, the floating bell, and the military shrine dedicated to Hachiman. Those details are, however, found in a slightly earlier account, Taichū's 1605 *Ryūkyū shintōki*.

Shintōki relates the difficulty an Okinawan army encountered in subduing the "small but well-defended island" of Kikai, and it includes an account similar to what we have seen about shooting the bird, encountering a floating bell, and establishing a shrine to Hachiman. Taichū, however, describes all these events as having occurred "around the time of the fifth king, Shō Taikyū," not during Shō Toku's reign.[55] This discrepancy may be the reason these details do not appear in *Reflections*. In any case, later compilers of official histories during the eighteenth century designated Shō Toku as the king who shot the bird and so forth. Certainly, Taichū may have been confused about Ryukyuan political chronology, but Shō Taikyū's reign was a time of considerable military activity. Let us take a closer look.

INVASIONS OF KIKAI

Are there any other sources that attest to Okinawan invasions of Kikai? In 1456, the Korean castaway Ryang Seong wrote that there are two islands to the east of Okinawa that did not submit to it. One is called Ushima (Ōshima); the other, Jiso (Korean pronunciation).[56] Shuri had subdued Ushima, but Jiso had not submitted, despite being attacked yearly. Higashionna argued that it is difficult to regard this Jiso as Kikai. His main reason is that three of the official histories state that it was Shō Toku who invaded Kikai.[57] If we suspend faith in the veracity of the official histories, then Ryang's account suggests that Shō Taikyū was waging an ongoing campaign to subdue Kikai. Two household records from Kikai describe warfare and contact with Shuri prior to 1466, roughly sometime in the 1450s. For example, the lineage of Amami official Kantarugane begins with a statement that a distant ancestor by the same name organized the people of Kikai to resist "repeated attacks" by Chūzan military ships. Eventually their defenses failed, they surrendered, and Kantarugane was taken to Okinawa.[58] The typical interpretation of this material is that the 1466 fighting between the Chūzan king and Kikai was the final, decisive battle in a longer series of wars.[59] This interpretation may well be correct. Nevertheless, there is some reason to question it.

First, *Ryūkyū Shintōki* was the earliest source to explain the *wakō* lore described above. Taichū clearly attributed these actions to Shō Taikyū, not Shō Toku. Moreover, what little corroborating evidence we do have for invasions of Kikai, Ryang's account, indicates the 1450s as the approximate time period, roughly corresponding to Shō Taikyū's reign of 1454–1460. Therefore, if Kikai was conquered by a king who acted like a *wakō*, and Chinese-style historiography requires the last king of a dynasty to be evil, then moving the *wakō* details Taichū recorded from Shō Taikyū's reign into Shō Toku's reign would solve several problems. It would reinforce the evil nature of the last king while simultaneously burnishing the reputation of the previous monarch, a ruler closely linked with the Second Shō dynasty. In other words, the conquest of Kikai may have been the work, in whole or in part, of Shō Taikyū.

THE AMAWARI-GOSAMARU CONFLICT AND MICHINOSHIMA

As Iha Fuyū pointed out in 1937 and others have reiterated, whatever the details of the Gosamaru-Amawari-Taikyū conflict may have been, a major issue was control of or access to trade with Michinoshima.[60] One *omoro* describes Nakagusuku as a nexus or base (*nekuni*, central location), whose ships connected it with Tokunoshima and Amami-Ōshima. The song implies political control by Nakagusuku over a network connecting it with several northern islands.[61] Two other songs say much the same about Katsuren. The first is about the voyages of Katsuren's sailors. In it, the tiny Amami islands of Ukejima and Yoroshima (just south of Amami-Ōshima; fig. 5) function as bridges linking Katsuren with Tokunoshima and Okinoerabu. The next song states that the voyages of Katsuren's sailors bring forth tribute and link Katsuren with Kikai and Amami-Ōshima.[62] In other words both Nakagusuku and Katsuren had close ties with, and possibly military control over, certain routes and locations in Michinoshima.

The 1458 conflict, therefore, may have been a three-way battle for military and economic supremacy over Michinoshima, with Shō Taikyū as the apparent winner in Okinawa. However, it is likely that further military action by Taikyū, and possibly by Shō Toku as well, was required to assert Shuri's control over Kikai and Amami-Ōshima. We will see additional invasions of the north by kings of the second Shō dynasty.

WAKŌ AND THE FIRST SHŌ DYNASTY

During the time of the first Shō dynasty, armed mariners were common throughout the Japanese islands and beyond. Depending on circumstances, they behaved like pirates, military personnel, diplomats, or merchants. A common term for such mariners was and is *wakō*. During the modern era, the word has become strongly marked with the negative connotations of its stock English translation, "Japanese pirates." Stated differently, the close association of the term *wakō* with brigands or outlaws, typical of Korean and Chinese perceptions, has persisted to the present. These perceptions obscure the multiple roles *wakō* played. Peter Shapinsky has rechristened *wakō* leaders "sea lords," and certainly in a general way this term could be applied to kings of the first Shō dynasty and other powerful local rulers such as Gosamaru, Amawari, and Oni-Ōgusuku.[63]

While almost any territorial state or polity ultimately rests on a base of military power, early Ryukyuan kings and local rulers were themselves active warriors. Otherwise they would not have been able to take or hold the throne or their territories. Because their power was based at harbors, these warrior-rulers functioned as *wakō*. It was precisely people like the first Shō dynasty kings that the Ming court was trying to bring into what it regarded as a lawful political order by means of generous tribute-trade terms. The lure of tribute-trade profit, however, was also a powerful incentive for violence within Ryukyu. Because of the tribute trade, Naha became an especially valuable prize for the ambitious to try to seize.

Despite their royal titles, kings of the first Shō dynasty were local rulers, albeit especially powerful ones. They conducted official trade with China to the exclusion of any other local ruler, although it is likely that in the process they cooperated with allies behind the scenes. Rulers of the Shuri-Naha area used the Shō name in dealing with China, and the official histories later wove them into a dynasty of biologically related men.

Recall that Gaara group names are prevalent in Michinoshima and also found in Goeku in Okinawa, Shō Taikyū's likely birthplace. Shō Taikyū was probably not Shō Hashi's relative but an outsider associated with Gaara group *wakō*. If so, then it makes sense that he and Amawari would have come into conflict. With its Michinoshima connections and great wealth, Katsuren occupied a niche that Taikyū sought to wrest from Amawari's control. That Shō Hashi was closely linked with Katsuren makes this antagonism more plausible, if indeed Shō Taikyū put an end to Shō Hashi's line. This hypothesis is speculative, of course. Moreover, Amawari's praise in the *Omoro* is still difficult to explain. We will need to factor in the turbulent early history of the second Shō dynasty and its problems with legitimacy to obtain a fuller picture.

CHAPTER SEVEN

Seizures, Erasures, and Resurgences

Reflections on Chūzan explains Shō Toku's alleged wickedness in detail. Fond of war, irreverent, and greedy, his arrogance also made him prone to killing innocent people. Wise ministers hid themselves in the forests and kept a low profile.[1] After Shō Toku died, a white-haired old man addressed a crowd of officials who had gathered to consider the royal succession. He declared that Shō Toku had been a disgrace to his ancestors, immersing himself in debauchery in the manner of King Jié of the (legendary) Xia dynasty. Jié allegedly had created a forest of meat and a pond of wine, a metaphor for depravity from the Chinese classics. Next, the old man compared Shō Toku to another bête noire of ancient China, King Zhòu of the Shang dynasty. The old man declared that Heaven despises evil and elevates goodness. Therefore, "Quickly kill the crown prince, elevate the virtuous [Kanemaru], and bring peace to the country!"[2]

After this rousing speech, a delegation headed to Uchima in Nishihara to ask the "greatly surprised" Kanemaru to become king. According to all the official accounts, Kanemaru was astonished that anyone was considering such a thing. At the same time, soldiers set off to hunt down the "seven- or eight-year-old" crown prince who, along with his queen mother and wet nurse, was hiding in Madama[-mori] gusuku, a sacred site. Finding them there, the soldiers slaughtered them and left their corpses in place.[3] In discussing these same matters, *Genealogy of Chūzan* adds a Chinese rhetorical flourish: "Ah, is not a ruler without heaven's mandate (*tiānmìng*) just like a bird?"[4]

Such a stark contrast between idealized virtue and brutal violence might seem to be a case of awkward editing. However, all the official histories give substantially the same account. Here we see a bloody displacement of one king and his family inserted into the framework of a morally sensitive cosmos in which virtue is rewarded and vice punished. The white-haired old man was almost certainly a manifestation of Hachiman, and the narrative easily appropriates him as the voice of moral reason. It is the slaughter at Madama-mori, however, that stands out uncomfortably. Why mention such details? The answer is connected with an older conception of rulers as shamans who can control the forces of wind and rain, much like Oni-Ōgusuku did when he used his voice to create the storm that stalled Amawari's advance. Royal bones, implied in the name Madama (True Jewel), attract rain. Human bones have been found at all or most Okinawan sacred sites at which rainmaking ceremonies took place.

ROYAL BONES ATTRACT RAIN

Origins of Ryukyu includes a tale from the village of Makabe (in present-day Itoman City) about two brothers who were lords of a castle. They acquired a particularly fine white horse, and another lord attacked their fortress to acquire it. They both fought valiantly but went down to defeat. One brother died, along with the horse, at a mountain called Kobamori. When a later descendant visited the area, he found a rock in the shape of a human skeleton and three round rocks endowed with the ability to leap into the air. Of course, that descendant established a shrine at the location.[5] In this case, lordly bones in a mountain grove became powerful rocks worthy of enshrinement.

Miyazato grove in the village of Maehira (also in Itoman) derived its power in part from the presence of two skeletons, those of a wet nurse and the child in her care (reminiscent of Shō Toku's infant). More potent, however, was a skull secretly stolen from "Kundagusuku" in Shuri, described more fully below.[6] The Kubadō grove in Ōzato district (present-day Yonabaru-chō) enshrines the bones of a radiant heavenly maiden. The story is a version of Japan's Hagoromo tale, except that the woman died on earth.[7] Human bones, apparently, can influence cosmic forces.

A 1728 *Kyūyō* entry declares: "Since long ago, in back of Shurikinjō [an area adjacent to Shuri castle] and the [nearby] dam, beneath groves used for rain prayers (*amagoi utaki*), tombs have accumulated. The tombs are near people's houses. For this reason, interring corpses at such sites is prohibited. Moreover, owners of the tombs shall construct tombs at new sites and transfer the remains to them."[8]

There is more to this passage than its surface indicates. This directive occurred amid a flurry of Confucian-inspired reforms in connection with

Sai On's rise to power. For example, earlier that year the royal government prohibited sorcery.[9] The prohibition against bones at sacred sites connected with rain and water was part of the same campaign against what Sai On and his supporters regarded as superstitious practices. The government framed the matter as one of aesthetics or hygiene, but why were sites connected with water and rain also locations for tombs? The basic reason is a widespread belief that bones attract rain.

Noble bones are particularly effective in attracting rain. This idea probably has its roots in the Korean peninsula and was manifest in Silla's "bone rank system" (*golpumjedo*). Its two highest ranks were "sacred bone" and "true bone." The name Madama literally means "true jewel," and in Ryukyuan contexts, it was common to refer to human bones as jewels. Moreover, in parts of Korea, China, and in Ryukyu, we find the belief that good bones attract rain.[10]

The royal bones of Shō Toku's family were among those true jewels. *Kyūyō* passages are revealing. One explains that Shō Toku's son and heir was killed and then buried outside of the inner palace residence (C. Jìn-chéng, "forbidden city"). That area became known locally as Kundagusuku. The next passage explains Kundagusuku, saying that Shō Toku's queen, wet nurse, and son were buried under the royal castle. Because their remains possessed tremendous spiritual power, people were attracted to the burial site. Ordinary people would come to Shuri and seek employment as servants in elite households as a way of gaining access to this potent location. That is how one villain from Makabe managed to pilfer a skull and take it to Miyazato grove, where it is celebrated each year. The passage suggests that such an intense interest in these bones is an ignoble custom and then goes on to explain more details about the Miyazato grove, including the other skeletons mentioned above.[11] This passage sheds light on the 1728 attempt to rid the Shuri castle area of bones. It also explains why the official histories link the corpses of Shō Toku's family with Madama grove, which almost certainly was the same place as Kundagusuku.

AMAMIKYO AND THE SECOND SHŌ DYNASTY

Amamikyo and Shinerikyo are primordial deities in the *Omoro*. There are several variations in their names, omitted here, and Amamikyo is the same deity as Amamiku in *Reflections on Chūzan*. We have already seen that legends about the arrival of powerful blacksmiths from the north are found throughout the Ryukyu islands. Moreover, blacksmiths and metal play crucial roles in the legendary biography of every early king from Satto onward. Tanigawa Ken'ichi has pointed out that, from Kanahiyabu in Nakijin southward, the sacred groves Amamiku created in *Reflections* were all enclosed by stone walls that would have required iron tools to create.[12] The paths trod by the footsteps of Amamiku/Amamikyo in legend corresponded with the southward spread of advanced technologies.

In the *Omoro*, Amamikyo was a divine carpenter who created countries, islands, *gusuku*, and sacred groves.[13] The tools for accomplishing this task included iron axes and *kanahetsu*, an iron tool for piling up stones.[14] Amamikyo created Goeku gusuku, a place of great importance for Shō Taikyū and Kanemaru, and the Amamikyo-Shinerikyo pair also established rice cultivation.[15] Stated concisely, they created the world; then islands or countries; and then rice, groves, and *gusuku*. This creation took place from north to south, whether in *Omoro* songs or in other songs or legends.[16]

Tracing place-names connected with Amamikyo throughout the Ryukyu islands reveals that such names are especially concentrated in northern Okinawa, and from there disseminated to the south. They coincide with points of political power, royal authority, and protection of sea-lanes. Amamikyo-related terms also overlap with other *wakō* markers we have seen, such as Gaara group names or the *tomoe* symbol.[17] Although its deeper roots are obscure, the local roots of the second Shō dynasty are in the Nakijin area, with later migration to Nishihara in connection with Shō Taikyū.

KANEMARU'S CONNECTIONS

Recall that according to the official biography Kanemaru was born in Izena to a farming household. He got into trouble over water use and fled with his wife and younger brother to northern Okinawa. This section further explores connections between Nakijin and the second Shō dynasty. One sequence of *Omoro* songs makes this connection especially clear. The first praises Nakijin as the pinnacle of the country, and the next praises "acclaimed Kanemaru." The subsequent song is one we have already encountered, in which the Nakijin Serikaku priestess causes rain to soak the armor of newly arrived warriors. The next song in the sequence praises the acclaimed priestess of Okinawa who dwells at Uchima (in Nishihara). Even though the 1709 royal palace fire disrupted some of the original *Omoro* sequences, for the most part the songs are not randomly ordered. Their position vis-à-vis other songs is often significant. These four songs create the following linkage: Nakijin ◊ Kanemaru ◊ Serikaku Priestess ◊

Uchima.[18] Here and elsewhere, we see Nakijin, not Izena, as the homeland of the second Shō dynasty.[19]

Recall that Goeku and nearby Nishihara are the two locations in Okinawa with extant Gaara group names.[20] In the *Omoro*, Goeku is one of only four *gusuku* associated with the primordial creator deity Amamiku/Amamikyo. Moreover, Goeku is associated with control of and wealth from *momoura* (hundred harbors/communities). *Momoura,* in other words, indicates a widespread maritime network. Goeku's rulers achieved this control over a maritime network by the beating of a drum, a shamanic power object in the *Omoro* that symbolizes political control. *Omoro* songs reveal that a deity named Enochi (J. Inochi) was also found in Goeku.[21] Worship of this deity involved bow twanging, indicating religious practices from Japan or farther north.[22]

Moving from Goeku and looking for references to Uchima in the *Omoro,* there is one odd result. The *Omoro* songs usually occur in groups organized according to place. Many of the Uchima songs, however, are embedded in the Nakijin *omoro* group, even though the two places are spatially far apart. For example, found in a cluster of Nakijin songs is the following:

> The administrator of Uchima
> Onisanko [Kanemaru]
> Let him boast
> In far mountains
> Inside hedges
> He plants mulberry trees
> He plants waving trees [mulberry trees]
> And makes drums
> And makes sounding-and-calling-things [drums].[23]

There are others, but this song nicely illustrates the key points. First, in the *Omoro,* there is a close link between Nakijin and Uchima. The link is one of qualities, not geographical proximity. The songs surrounding this example include references to powerful priestesses from Nakijin. In the next song, for example, the Akeshino priestess pounds on the drum, which has precisely the same function as the drum that supported Goeku's power.[24] While the proximate geopolitical origin of the second Shō dynasty was Uchima in Nishihara, its spiritual home and roots were in Nakijin.[25] Its deepest roots probably extended northward along the path of Gaara group names and other links with the northern Ryukyu islands, Japan, and possibly other areas.

SHŌ SHIN

Survey histories tend to treat Shō Shin's long reign as an idyllic age. Ryukyu prospered as an international trade hub, peacefully engaging in commerce throughout a large part of the world. Trade wealth contributed to cultural vitality. Shō Shin ushered in Ryukyu's golden age, the "Great Days of Chuzan," in the oft-repeated words of George H. Kerr.[26] The empire Shō Shin created was indeed larger, wealthier, and more powerful than any previous iteration of Ryukyu. The institutional framework that Shō Shin initiated and Shō Sei completed lasted until 1879 and even later. Shō Shin was Ryukyu's most important king by almost any definition. Why, then, is the man who brought about the Great Days of Chūzan missing in *Reflections on Chūzan*?

Reflections is organized in de facto chapters, most corresponding to a royal reign. There are chapters for many of the actual and legendary kings before Shō Hashi, for the first Shō dynasty kings (except Shishō), one for Shō En, and even one for the brief reign of Shō Sen'i. The chapter after his jumps to Shō Sei, skipping Shō Shin. The 1701 *Genealogy of Chūzan* includes a brief chapter on Shō Shin, even though ostensibly the 1701 *Genealogy* was simply a Chinese translation of *Reflections*.[27] Likewise, the 1725 *Genealogy* includes a chapter on Shō Shin, and there are extensive *Kyūyō* entries covering the events of his reign. Is it possible that his chapter was irretrievably lost in our extant editions of *Reflections*? Yes, but it is unlikely that a chapter of such importance would disappear without any comment or attempt to reconstitute it later from *Genealogy*.

Throughout his reign Shō Shin worked to consolidate power. Military conquest was essential, of course, but so too was what we might call "soft power." The king and his officials erected temples, shrines, monuments, stands of trees, and other structures not only to proclaim the glory of royal rule but also to create a new political geography, with Shuri as the undisputed and comprehensive center of a Ryukyuan empire. Shō Shin also worked to erase, minimize, or transform the legacies of potentially problematic predecessors, of which there were several. His reign was prosperous, and it was a time of momentous change. One price for this prosperity and change was bloodshed on a scale greater than that under any predecessor. Moreover, internal family problems and questions of legitimacy dogged Shō Shin, and to some extent the entire line down to Shō Nei. These points probably explain why Shō Shin is missing, for the most part, from *Reflections:* his reign included too many skeletons in too many closets.

128   Dynastic Turbulence, 1400–1600

SEIZING THE THRONE

Shō Sen'i was the younger brother of Shō En. During his brother's reign Sen'i became lord of Goeku, the likely origin place of Kanemaru's apparent benefactor Shō Taikyū. That Sen'i became lord of Goeku was an indication of his older brother's favor and probably of Shō En's intention that Sen'i would become the next king. Such favor alone, however, counted for little amid the maelstrom of Ryukyuan royal politics.

Working through the brief and rather awkward entry on Shō Sen'i in *Reflections* is revealing. The text explains that Shō Sen'i left his parents at age five and was raised by his brother, the future Shō En. Sen'i became lord of Goeku at forty-one. From there the text jumps to the second month of 1477, the year Sen'i ascended the throne. As if to contrast with an earlier sentence explaining that "heavenly deity Kimitezuri" manifested itself to congratulate Shō En, the text describing Shō Sen'i states that if "solar deity Kimitezuri" were to appear, it would certainly indicate that Sen'i was the choice of the deities.[28] Incidentally, Kimitezuri properly indicates a religious ritual. *Ryūkyū shintōki* misunderstood it as the name of a deity, which is probably why it appears that way in *Reflections*.

Continuing the passage, with Sen'i seated on the throne and Prince Kume Nakagusuku (Shō Shin) standing beside it, the enthronement ceremony began:

> In all previous cases, the high priestess and lesser priestesses left Uchihara and stood facing east in front of the Kimihokori [building]. This time, however, contrary to the norm, they stood facing west. Then, starting with the ruler above and spreading downward, all present wondered what was happening. Spirits chilled, they clasped their hands, and their mouths turned dry. [Speaking through the priestesses, the deities] declared in an *omoro:* "Beloved child of the king in Shuri dances with the deities splendidly."[29] Hearing this song, Shō Sen'i regarded himself as lacking in virtue. He said that his bringing disrepute to the throne had pulled down heaven's wrath upon him. Having reigned for six months, he abdicated.[30]

The enthronement ceremony enacted Uncle Sen'i's doom. He might not have incurred heaven's wrath in the classic Chinese sense of a morally attuned universe, but Sen'i lost the struggle for power in the wake of his brother's death. Shō Shin was only thirteen when his mother, Ogyaka, successfully engineered a coup.[31]

The eastern direction is called *agari* in Okinawan, a term closely linked with the rising sun and the renewal of life. Looking to the east in the early morning from Urasoe castle, Shuri castle, the Seifaa grove near Sashiki, or other significant sites of political power, an observer can watch the sun emerge above the sacred island of Kudakajima. That is why the priestesses normally faced east when conducting state rites. By contrast, west is the direction of the setting sun and death. Everyone watching his enthronement ceremony knew that the sun had set on Sen'i. *Reflections* explains that he "retired" to Goeku but lived less than a month.

Perhaps in the spirit of protesting too much, *Reflections* ends the chapter on Sen'i by ruminating about the legendary Chinese sage king Yáo passing on his throne to the unrelated but virtuous Shùn, who passed it on to the unrelated Yǔ. It concludes: "If the virtue of Shō Sen'i of our court indeed had exceeded that of Shō Shin, then why on earth would the deities have acted contrary to people's desires and cast Shō Sen'i out? Certainly, Shō Shin was one of the sages."[32] Here, Shō Shōken appears to be struggling to work these matters out, so much so that volume (*kan*) four ends there and volume five begins some fifty years later, with Shō Sei.

Although *Reflections* uses the term "designated heir" (*seishi*) in connection with Shō Shin, the word occurs only after Sen'i abdicated. Younger brothers of kings had played prominent roles in the recent past.[33] It would have been perfectly reasonable that that Sen'i was Shō En's designated heir, or in any case that he plausibly saw himself as such. In *Reflections*, however, there is no clear statement about whether Shō En had formally designated a successor. *Genealogy*, in contrast, declares Shō Shin to have been Shō En's designated heir, but that, because he was so young, "the various officials" selected Sen'i instead. Moreover, it eliminates the drama of enthronement rites gone awry, including the peculiar *omoro* with no obvious meaning in the quoted passage from *Reflections*. Instead, *Genealogy* briefly mentions that Sen'i received an oracle to the effect that "Shō Shin, though young, has truly received the mandate to rule," which Sen'i shared with the court officials.[34] Notice the greater skill with which later generations of Ryukyuan historians handled the internecine struggle.

BANISHING THE FIRST SHŌ DYNASTY

Albeit via different approaches, the official histories attempt to portray more or less smooth transitions between the first and second Shō dynasties and between Shō En, Shō Sen'i, and Shō Shin. Local histories, however, complicate the picture. In chapter 6, we encountered a place in Yomitan called Sashiki grove. Though far removed geographically from Sashiki in southeast Okinawa, Yomitan is where many associated with the first Shō dynasty went into hiding in the wake of Kanemaru's seizure of the Naha-Shuri area.

As part of his consolidation of power, Shō Shin eliminated Goeku as a power center. This move makes sense given Goeku's close association with Shō Taikyū, Oni-Ōgusuku, Kanemaru, and Shō Sen'i. Although posing as legitimate heirs of the first Shō dynasty vis-à-vis China, the kings of the second Shō dynasty neither recognized the deities of the first Shō dynasty nor maintained its physical infrastructure or memorial sites. Over the centuries, for example, Shō Hashi's Tsukishiro shrine crumbled away, along with his castle, Sashiki ui gusuku. Not until 1938 was the Tsukishiro shrine rebuilt amid the ruins of the castle site.[35]

We also encountered the Baten priestess in the previous chapter. Closely associated with Samekawa and the early kings of the first Shō dynasty, she is mentioned in only one *omoro*.[36] In this and most other respects, the Baten priestess faded into obscurity as the second Shō dynasty established itself. The top priestess in the new political order was Kikoe-ōgimi. The legend of the Baten priestess in *Origins of Ryukyu* tells an anachronistic story of Kikoe-ōgimi being blown off course when sailing to Kudakajima. Her ship landed in Kyushu, and the Baten priestess sailed there to bring Kikoe-ōgimi back to assist in alleviating a drought. Upon her return, Kikoe-ōgimi dwelled at a hut on the coast of Yonabaru slightly north of Baten. Moreover, whenever a new Kikoe-ōgimi took office, she made a pilgrimage to this site and formally adopted the deity name Tedashiro, which originally belonged to the Baten priestess.[37] Just as Kanemaru and his successors took over the Shō name from the previous line, or pseudo-line, so the newly created Kikoe-ōgimi took over the name Tedashiro from the defunct Baten priestess.

In the realm of Buddhism, Shō Toku built Shintokuji and cast several bells. His major contribution to Ryukyuan Buddhism was his obtaining of sutras, possibly the entire canon (Tripitika), from Korea.[38] Sutras were potent power objects, as Shō Shin, another promoter of Buddhism, well understood. It is hardly surprising that Shō Shin would have wanted to possess the Buddhist canon, but he apparently found Shō Toku's set problematic. The potent rainmaking bones of Shō Toku's family suggest lingering spiritual power. In any case, for Shō Shin, sutras from the previous dynasty posed a problem of disposal. To understand Shō Shin's peculiar solution to this problem, we must examine the official histories, supplemented by *Origins of Ryukyu,* Korean records, and the physical remains of Enkakuji.

Shō Shin entombed the problematic sutras in a vault in the shallow pond in front of Enkakuji. A 1502 *Kyūyō* entry explains that Shō Toku had acquired a complete Buddhist canon from Korea. "After the king [Shō Toku] died, the sutras still remained. Therefore, King Shō Shin had a shallow pond constructed near the main [Shurei] gate to Shuri castle." Inside the water of the pond he constructed a vault-like shrine to Benzaiten into which he placed the sutras. As the years went by, the enclosure rotted away into the earth.[39] *Origins of Ryukyu* gives a similar account, but describes the shrine enclosure as having been destroyed in 1609, the year of the war with Satsuma.[40] The shrine may indeed have sustained damage during the war, but by that time the sutras almost certainly would have decayed. Shō Hō (r. 1621–1640) ordered the shrine rebuilt.[41]

The key point here is that Shō Shin's move was an attempt to neutralize or quarantine powerful but potentially toxic material associated with a recent previous king whose line had been violently terminated. It was one act in a larger process of delegitimizing recent past kings. Significantly, the artificial pond was flanked on one side by the powerful Sonohiyabu grove, another of Shō Shin's creations. On the other side of the water was Enkakuji, the new center of Buddhism in the kingdom that also served safely to neutralize Shō En. As Shō Shin's father, Shō En was a crucial figure despite his problematic connections to both Shō Toku and Shō Sen'i. The deity Benzaiten, associated with water and storms, appears to have been a new arrival to Ryukyu during Shō Shin's era. We will see that Benzaiten became the supreme protective deity of Ryukyu in the new religious hierarchy, a function for which she was well suited. Flanked by Enkakuji and Sonohiyabu, Benzaiten guarded Shō Toku's sutras or whatever remained of them.

Putting sutras in a pond was almost certainly not a peculiar act of piety on Shō Shin's part, because he acquired a new set and housed them properly in his temples. Chén Kǎn noted that on both sides of the Buddha images at Enkakuji and nearby Tenkaiji "thousands of volumes of sutras are stored."[42] Clearly, Shō Shin had obtained new sutras, although we do not know exactly when and how. Most likely they also came from Korea. *Joseon Veritable Royal Records* indicates that envoys ostensibly representing Shō En asked for sutras in 1483 and 1491. These envoys were almost certainly fraudulent, using forgeries of old documents and the name of a deceased king. A legitimate embassy from Shō Shin arrived in 1500 and requested the entire Buddhist canon, although there is no independent verification that the volumes arrived in Ryukyu at this time.[43] The important point, however, is that, whether in 1500 or at some other time, Shō Shin replaced the entombed sutras of a problematic predecessor with new ones of his own. Compared with the sutras, however, his oldest son presented an even greater challenge.

AWKWARD MARRIAGE, AWKWARD SON

The death of Shō Sen'i in 1477 did not end conflict within the royal family. Sen'i had a daughter, Kyojin, and Shō Shin eventually made her his queen (fig. 12). Perhaps his mother told Shō Shin to take Cousin Kyojin as his queen for the sake of appearances, but we do not know what went on behind the scenes. The pair produced a son, Shō Ikō (1494–1540). He unwittingly played a prominent destabilizing role that came back to haunt the kingdom in connection with the war of 1609, as we will see in more detail. As of 1501, Shō Ikō had become excluded from the family inner circle. Apparently regaining favor, Ikō became crown prince in 1507. However, Shō Shin's consort Kagō, mother of Shō Sei, worked to destroy Shō Ikō's reputation. Her efforts bore fruit in 1509, and an angry king ordered the sixteen-year-old Ikō to be executed. In the end, though, Ikō survived after seeking refuge in Urasoe, thereby creating the Urasoe branch of the royal

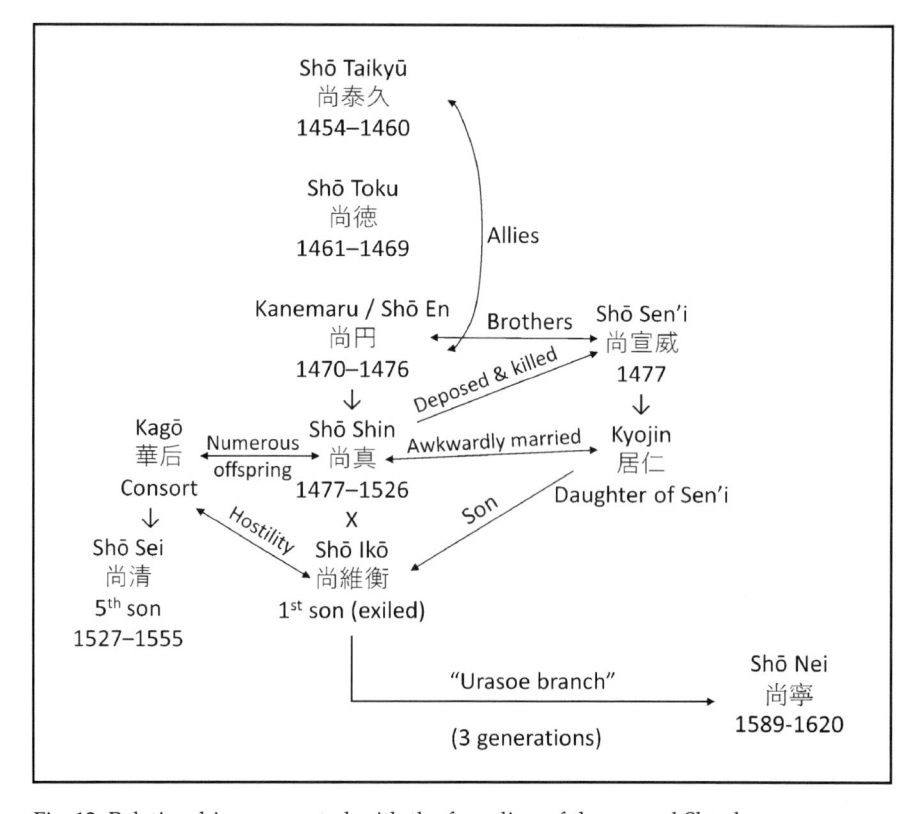

Fig. 12. Relationships connected with the founding of the second Shō dynasty

family. Shō Ikō remained in exile and out of favor until his death. Shō Shin's fifth son, Shō Sei, became crown prince around 1508 or 1509. Aware of Shō Shin's legitimacy problems, the Chinese Board of Rites required that Ryukyuan officials certify that Shō Sei was indeed Shō Shin's legitimate heir.[44] Subsequently, all Ryukyuan kings had to submit written proof of their legitimacy before receiving investiture.

Reflections includes a dialogue in which Shō Sei declares that his older brother, Prince Urasoe (Shō Ikō) is blameless. In accord with heavenly principles, therefore, Prince Urasoe should become king. Shō Ikō responded by declaring himself morally corrupt and stating that following his father's orders is the way of the ancient sages. Therefore the virtuous Shō Sei must become king.[45] *Genealogy* sensibly contains no such dialogue drawing attention to the royal rift. Family problems and legitimacy were only part of the many challenges Shō Shin faced.

CHAPTER EIGHT

The Second Shō Dynasty's Challenges

Despite the tendency to characterize Shō Shin's reign as a golden age, in reality it was a time of severe challenges. In addition to warfare on several fronts, tribute trade with China declined gradually throughout the reign and sharply at the end. Because of the Ōnin War, Ryukyu's main Japanese trading ports shifted from Sakai to Hakata and Bōnotsu, thus giving the Shimazu of Satsuma and adjacent territories greater influence over Ryukyuan shipping. Portugal occupied Goa in 1510 and Malacca in 1511. Trade with Southeast Asia continued, but only minimally, mostly being conducted at places like Patani in the south of Thailand and the eastern Malay peninsula. The frequency with which Hakata and Tsushima merchants posed as envoys from Ryukyu became a major impediment to direct contact between Ryukyu and Korea. Finally, the rise of second-wave *wakō* hindered Ryukyu's international trading activities.[1]

Throughout the sixteenth century, Ryukyuan kings faced challenges from within the capital area, from other parts of Ryukyu's empire, and from changing regional and world conditions. This chapter outlines many of those challenges. The focus is on Shō Shin. I also introduce some of the turbulence connected with later reigns, which I discuss in greater detail in subsequent chapters.

TROUBLE WITH CHINA

"King," began an edict from the Ming emperor to Shō En in 1475, "your envoys have already presented tribute at the capital and returned with the usual imperial largesse. Recently, officials in Fujian . . . have reported that the [Ryukyuan] delegation member Cài Zhāng [Sai Shō, 1445–1504, third-generation Kumemura resident] and others engaged in extreme unlawful acts such as murder and the theft of property upon their return to Fuzhou." The edict goes on to demand that these rogue Ryukyuans be held accountable for their crimes. It states that henceforth Ryukyu may only send one tribute mission every two years and specifies other restrictions on tribute trade.[2]

The edict refers to the 1474 incident, mentioned in chapter 3, in which Ryukyuan envoys murdered Chén Èrguān and burned down his household compound. Taking place during the final years of Shō En's reign, this event caused the first major structural limitation of Ryukyu's tribute trade. It threatened the economic well-being of the court at Shuri at a time when trade with Japan had also become more difficult.

Ryukyu responded vigorously to the 1475 edict. In a lengthy 1476 communiqué, for example, the Ryukyuan court explained in detail why it would not have been possible for Ryukyuans to have committed this crime. Switching its tone from excuse making to obsequiousness, the text then praises the Chinese court as the source of civilization. Just as neglect of filial duties for even one day would cause a person's heart to become unsettled, so too, the new one-in-two-year tribute schedule is insufficient for Ryukyu properly to express its reverence for the "heavenly court."[3]

The pleas were spectacularly unsuccessful. In 1478, for example, an envoy from Shō Shin arrived in China to report Shō En's death and to ask for permission to resume annual tribute missions. The reply from the Board of Rites asked rhetorically how it could possibly allow "outside barbarians" to profit from trade with China after Ryukyuan envoys had committed such serious crimes of murder and arson and then fled? It denied the request.[4] That document was explicit about tribute-trade functioning as a source of wealth for the Ryukyuan court.

In 1480, an imperial edict to Shō Shin pointed out that changing the tribute frequency to once every two years was a punishment, not a move to save Ryukyu trouble and expenses. The edict went on to complain about past behavior, including murder and arson of course, but also of Ryukyuan envoys incurring excessive expenses and "sullying China" by inappropriate behavior such as secretly making prohibited silk clothing decorated with a golden dragon emblem worn by Ming officials. Clear proof of illegal activities such as these is stated as the reason for the change to a once-per-two-year tribute frequency.[5] The illegal clothing refers to a 1471 incident in which Ryukyuan envoy Sai Ei (C. Cài Jǐng) prompted an official investigation. Chinese officials caught him with the prohibited clothing, and Sai falsely claimed that Ryukyu's previous king

(Shō Toku) had been allowed to use such cloth.[6] "Ryukyu's efforts to restore the old system," concludes Tomiyama Kazuyuki, "had the opposite result of prompting an enumeration of Ryukyu's shortcomings one after another."[7]

The Ming court originally brought Ryukyu into the tribute system on favorable terms in an attempt to tame piracy and smuggling. Approximately a century later, it had clearly become less tolerant of Ryukyuan illegal behavior and abuses of the system. One of Shō Shin's challenges, therefore, was to up Ryukyu's game vis-à-vis China. Ryukyu's misbehaving envoys typically came from Kumemura, much of whose population, by the time of Shō Shin's reign, was two or more generations removed from the Chinese who originally settled there. Exerting stronger royal control over Kumemura and the tribute-trade process was probably high on Shō Shin's agenda. Likewise, the processes of expanding Shuri's control over the Ryukyu islands as a whole and creating a centralized state undoubtedly enabled stronger royal control of the tribute trade in addition to the obvious domestic benefits of strengthening what had hitherto been an unstable kingship.

TRANSFORMING THE MONARCHY

The unstable condition of Ryukyuan kingship probably constituted Shō Shin's most pressing early challenge. His own rise to power, of course, had been a violent intervention. During the fifteenth century, reign changes based on personal military power had been the norm. Local rulers maintained their own armies, ships, and trade networks. In Okinawa, perhaps a dozen lords possessed significant military power. Remnants of deposed rulers from the first Shō dynasty and rulers based in other islands constituted additional potential sources of instability. The monopoly on tribute trade was an advantage to whoever controlled Shuri, but it also made that person a target.

Shō Shin struggled for supremacy and legitimacy throughout his long reign. Military campaigns included local warfare not appearing in the official histories, as well as invasions of Yaeyama in 1500, Kumejima (1506 and possibly earlier), and continuing military tensions in Sakishima that included an invasion of Yonaguni around 1522 (or earlier) by forces at least nominally allied with Shuri.

Perhaps the greatest act of power consolidation was Shō Shin's causing Okinawa's major warlords (*aji*) to give up their castles and relocate to Shuri in 1525 or 1526 in return for high noble status—at least according to the common story. Survey histories routinely present this relocation as a simple fact, but we have no indication that it happened as a discrete, orderly event. It is not mentioned in any monument, in the 1701 *Genealogy of Chūzan*, or in any other text until Sai On's 1725 *Genealogy*. Even there, the claim occurs with no explanation, only in the introductory material, and not under a specific year. The 1725 *Genealogy* text states that the presence of warlords had long been a source of uprisings and disorder. Shō Shin relocated all of them to Shuri, disbanded their military forces, and sent his own officials out to govern their territories. *Kyūyō* goes into more detail, but its only basis is Sai On's assertion in *Genealogy*.[8] Perhaps Sai On had in mind Japan's early modern *sankin-kōtai* system.

The relocation of the warlords to Shuri makes logical sense within the overall trajectory of Shō Shin's reign. We know that he stored weapons in a central armory under his control and reorganized military forces and other key state functions into the *hiki* system. There was plenty of turbulence and factionalism in the royal court after Shō Shin's time, but there is no indication of an independent regional power elsewhere in Okinawa that could rival Shuri. Shō Shin brought potential regional rivals such as Nakijin, the Sashiki area, and Kumejima into orbits around Shuri. Regardless of whether and how he relocated or displaced regional rulers, Shō Shin succeeded in concentrating power at the capital to such an extent that no other entity in Okinawa or within the rest of the Ryukyu islands could seriously challenge it by the end of his reign.

Shō Shin's reign marks the first known use of written documents for government administration. He also created an eclectic ideology in support of royal power. These measures had the effect of transforming Ryukyu's monarchs and their governments. Before Shō Shin, kings of Ryukyu resembled powerful *wakō* chieftains. After Shō Shin, they resembled Chinese-style heads of a centralized bureaucracy. The official histories, and most modern ones, project this later, sixteenth-century model of the monarchy back to previous generations. Historians often perform this type of maneuver.[9]

Shō Shin's centralizing project did not stop with his death. His successor, Shō Sei, further enhanced Shuri's military capabilities and continued to systematize the bureaucracy and official state rituals. He created a new type of military *gusuku* and developed the religious ideology of royal authority known later as *tedako shisō* (son-of-the-sun thought). Shō Sei also brought out the first volume of the *Omoro sōshi*. Later chapters will discuss these matters.

SHŌ SHIN'S MONUMENTS

Recall Shō Taikyū's Sea Bridge to the Many Countries Bell and Kaiki's 1427 Monument to the Garden that Benefits the Country. The idea of creating memorials and monuments to record accomplishments and portray them as glorious was not new with Shō Shin. More so than any previous ruler, however, Shō Shin systematically and in detail proclaimed his accomplishments and their significance. Taken together, his monuments outline the main features of the new order he put into place. They also constitute our main body of written sources from the era. It is useful, therefore, to survey these monuments, because they will come up in later discussion. I present summaries of them here in chronological order.

A. Enkaku Zenji ki (1497)

Shō Shin erected Enkakuji as a Rinzai Zen temple to memorialize his father, Shō En. Built between 1492 and 1495, the temple's name literally means "En's enlightenment." The priest Shūyō wrote the monument inscription in Chinese. It states that Shō Shin has "pacified the core region of the country" (*bāngjī āndìng*), laying the foundation for myriad peaceful generations. The creation of Enkakuji brings prosperity to the people, all of whom gladly supported its construction, even though they were not forced to do so. The king has planted a young pine for each segment of society as a symbol of his desire to nurture the growth of the kingdom.[10]

B. (1) Kanshōrei ki and (2) Mansairei ki (1497)

These two monuments, written in Chinese, commemorate aspects of two adjacent scenic hills in Shuri. Kanshōrei means "Official Pines Peak," and Mansairei means "Longevity Peak." The former name comes from Shō Shin's ordering officials in Shuri to plant thousands of pine seedlings at the site, which also served as a recreation area for officials. Pines were a classic symbol of longevity, and their sturdiness made them useful for landscaping. Particularly significant is the Mansairei ki monument text statement that Shō Shin initiated a system of official ranks (*jué*) that was a revival of ranks used during the Qín dynasty (221–206 BCE).[11]

C. Kokuō shōtoku hi [1] (1498)

This monument, which bears an inscription in Chinese, stood inside Enkakuji. It describes Shō Shin's Buddhist piety as the reason for his establishing the temple.[12]

D. Sashikaeshi matsuo no himon (1501).

This monument is also known as Sashikaeshi matsuo no hi no mon and Ufudōmō no himon. Enkakuji abbot Shūkei inscribed the text placed at the top of a hill called Sashikaeshi-matsuo, located in what is now the Daidō section of Naha. In the sixteenth century, this area was located between Naha and Shuri. The monument states that Shō Shin established Enkakuji to extoll the merit of his ancestors for the benefit of posterity and proper cultivation. To ensure sufficient lumber for upkeep and repairs of the temple, the king had ten thousand (probably meaning "many") pine seedlings planted in the area. Should any future descendant dare to disrupt this lumber supply, there could be no less filial grandchild or less loyal minister.[13]

E. Tamaodon no hi no mon (1501).

Tamaudun (J. Tamaodon) was Shō Shin's royal mausoleum. This monument stood in the outer courtyard, and its text is written in *kana* script. The mausoleum and the monument functioned to clarify Shō Shin's family inner circle in light of continuing disruptions. The monument text specifies that descendants of eight people shall be interred in Tamaudun: Shō En's queen, Shō En's oldest daughter, Shō Shin's oldest daughter, and Shō Shin's third through seventh sons. Conspicuously absent are Shō Ikō and Shō Shin's second son. Most likely, therefore, the second son came from the union of Shō Shin and his first queen, the daughter of Shō Sen'i (see fig. 12). In other words, the monument text excludes the descendants of Sen'i.[14]

F. Momourasoe rankan no mei (1509)

This lengthy Chinese inscription appeared on the front balustrade of Momourasoe hall in Shuri castle. It lauds Shō Shin and explains at length eleven great achievements of his age. Briefly, Shō Shin has (1) been a great patron of Buddhism; (2) managed the country well to the benefit of all; (3) conquered Yaeyama, thus strengthening "our country"; (4) ensured Ryukyu's fiscal and military strength; (5) created formal status ranks, official posts, and caps and hair pins to go with them; (6) adorned the palace with exotic flowers and goods; (7) created an artificially landscaped garden in the palace; (8) created a palace overflowing with elegant food, drink, scrolls, music, and other indications of wealth; (9) caused relations with China to flourish; (10) created Chinese-style ceremonies at court for the king's longevity; and (11) carved blue stones to form the balustrades of the lower section of the palace.[15] In connection with the ninth item, the text states that, since the Yǒnglè era (1402–1424), Ryukyu had been submitting tribute once every three years. Now, however, the frequency has been revised to once a year.[16] This statement is, of course, inaccurate. Perhaps characterizing the frequency of past tribute as once in three years functioned to enhance the impressiveness of Shō Shin's having arranged, briefly as it turned out, a once-yearly frequency.

G. Madama minato himon (1522)

This monument is also known as Madama minato hi no mon. Written by an unknown scribe, it explains the origins of Madama road and Madan bridge. Madama harbor is the area near the mouth of the Kokuba River as it empties into Naha harbor. Madama road was a ring road, which, along with the bridge, was part of the military infrastructure Shō Shin created within the capital area. It explains that in the event of an attack on Naha, soldiers from Shuri, Haebaru, Shimasoe-Ōzato, Chinen, and Sashiki would cross over the bridge and, along with forces from Shimajiri, defend the southern shore of Naha harbor. The monument itself was located on the west side of the Shurei gateway to Shuri castle.[17]

H. Kokuō shōtoku hi [2] (1522)

This monument is the second of two proclaiming Shō Shin's virtue. It was located on the east side of the Shurei gateway to Shuri castle, thus forming a pair with Madama minato himon (monument G). Written mostly in Chinese, it extols Shō Shin's power by celebrating his having received the sword Teganemaru and other valuable items as gifts from the ruler of Miyako. These gifts may have been tokens of surrender or defeat on the part of Nakasone Toyomiya or his son. *Genealogy of Ryukyu* links the receipt of Teganemaru with the receipt of taxes and tribute from throughout Okinawa and "the thirty-six islands."[18] The monument also outlaws the practice of taking one's life after the death of a ruler, what the official histories call *junshi*. The text states that during the ancient reigns of the Shunten, Eiso, and Satto lines of kings, this practice did not occur, but that during the past century it has become commonplace, and it is henceforth forbidden.[19] A *Kyūyō* entry for 1522 cites the monument and repeats its message.[20]

BUDDHISM

Many of Shō Shin's monuments were connected with the establishment of Buddhist temples. In early Ryukyu, Buddhism functioned, not as an austere religious practice or a complex cosmology, but as a potent force to protect the state and ensure its prosperity. Buddhist temples, temple bells, texts, and rites protected society and enhanced the prestige of rulers. The wealth and know-how required to erect Buddhist structures made them concrete symbols of both a monarch's wealth and his piety. In this context, a wealthy kingdom indicated a ruler with superior karmic status. Several of the monuments make this connection, but it is especially clear in monument F (Momourasoe rankan no mei, 1509).

According to legend, the first Buddhist temple in Ryukyu was Gokurakuji, located near Urasoe castle and built in the time of Eiso. At some point it was moved and soon thereafter burnt down. Shō En rebuilt Gokurakuji south of Urasoe castle, changed its name to Ryūfukuji, and installed Kaiin, a Rinzai priest from Kyoto, as its abbot.[21] Early Buddhist or quasi-Buddhist structures appearing in the official histories are Satto's Gokokuji (1384), Shō Hashi's Taianji (1430) and Senbutsu-reikaku (1433), and Chōjuji (Longevity temple, 1451).[22] Shō Taikyū was a major patron of Buddhism, and he is credited with establishing Kōganji, Fumonji, Tenryūji, Tenkaiji, Tennōji, and with casting twenty-three temple bells.[23]

Although we cannot be certain, Shō Shin was probably the first Ryukyuan king to receive formal education in his youth. The Kyoto-born Rinzai priest Kaiin (d. 1495) was his main tutor. Kaiin also wrote monument inscriptions and supervised much of the physical infrastructure of Shō Shin's Buddhist projects, especially Enkakuji. Kaiin served several earlier kings. As a "black-robed minister" (*kokue no saishō*), he had inside knowledge of, or was an active participant in, the political upheavals of the era.[24] Starting approximately with Shō Taikyū's reign, Buddhist priests became increasingly close confidants and advisers to Ryukyuan rulers.

Throughout his reign, Shō Shin sought to sacralize royal authority. Buddhism provided a powerful layer of religious protection to augment the power of priestesses, and Shō Shin incorporated Buddhist rites into a religious state defense system. When he sent envoys to Korea in 1500 to seek a copy of the Buddhist canon, the letter they carried explained that, should Ryukyu receive such a gift, "chanting [of the sutras] would long ensure the pacification of the state."[25] Several monuments from the sixteenth century describe "three hundred" or "more than three hundred" Buddhist priests participating in state ceremonies.[26] This number seems to be a figure of speech meaning "many," much like the number one hundred does in the *Omoro*. By 1603, there were forty-six temples (*jiin*) in Ryukyu dedicated to a total of twenty different deities. Of the temples, seventeen existed by the start of Shō Shin's reign, twenty-four were established during the reigns of Shō Shin and Shō Sei, and one was established after Shō Sei.[27]

THE LONG SHADOW OF SHŌ SEN'I

There do not appear to have been any smooth transitions among the first seven kings of the second Shō dynasty. We have seen that Shō Sei's reign began in the shadow of his older brother, Shō Ikō. Chinese officials required proof that Shō Sei was the legitimate heir to the throne before agreeing to his investiture. According to *Genealogy*, when Shō Sei's illness reached a crisis point in 1555, he called Council of Three members Aragusuku Anki (Mō Ryūgin), Kunigami Keimei (Wa Ibi), and Gusukuma Shūshin (Katsu Kashō) into his presence. When they were assembled in front of the dragon throne, Shō Sei ordered the three to support his designated heir, Shō Gen, and thereby "preserve the country." Later, however, Kunigami and Gusukuma had a change of heart. Declaring Shō Gen to be weak, they convinced other officials to support Prince Ie (Shō Kanshin) instead. Hearing of this matter, Aragusuku angrily declared that Shō Gen was a son of the "legitimate queen" and long-standing heir. Furthermore, conformity to heavenly ethics was "the eternal Way for all time." Aragusuku went on to chastise those who would disobey royal orders, again invoking heavenly ethics, and declared his commitment to enforcing the king's decree. *Genealogy* states that all of the loyal and righteous ministers sided with Aragusuku and Shō Gen inherited the throne.[28] In 1559, after the Chinese emperor ordered the investiture of Shō Gen as king of Ryukyu, Kunigami and Gusukuma were exiled to Kumejima and Iheya respectively.[29]

The events described here are found only in the 1725 *Genealogy*, and using only the information provided in the passage it seems clear that two factions arose among Ryukyu officialdom, each supporting a different claimant to the throne. Shō Gen's faction ultimately prevailed and exiled rival leaders to remote locations after the consolidation of power.[30] The narrative sequence in *Genealogy* of the Ming court granting investiture, followed by the exile of the two "criminal" members of the Council of Three, serves rhetorically to emphasize Shō Gen's legitimacy.

The circumstances surrounding Shō Gen's death are unclear. One possibility is that he died as a result of wounds or sickness contracted while invading Amami-Ōshima in 1571. In any event, his death seems to have been a protracted affair, with the end point listed as 1572.4.1 in *Genealogy*. His successor Shō Ei (r. 1573–1586) did not become king until sometime in 1573; *Genealogy* provides only the year. Contrary to these official dates, household records list Shō Gen as having appointed officials in 1572.8.30

and sometime in 1573.³¹ In other words, it is not clear exactly when the transition from Shō Gen to Shō Ei took place. Among other things, this relatively long period of transition contributed to diplomatic problems with Satsuma, as we will see.

Shō Nei's struggle to solidify his power was long and divisive, and he never completely succeeded. According to the 1725 *Genealogy*, Shō Nei's father was the previous king, Shō Ei (fig. 13). An appended section explains that Shō Nei was the great-great-grandson of Shō Shin via the Urasoe line of Shō Ikō. It also states that Shō Ei adopted Shō Nei.³² However, the 1701 *Genealogy* lists Shō Nei as a son of "king" Shō I of the Urasoe line, rhetorically elevating his biological father to kingly rank.³³ No text other than the 1725 *Genealogy* mentions the adoption, so it may have been a literary device for smoothing the transition. A sister of Shō Ei was Shō Nei's mother, which probably aided his case. On the other hand, Shō Ei had two brothers, at least one of whom was alive when the king died.

Shō Nei was childless and therefore Shō Hō, fourth son of Shō Kyū (1560–1620), inherited the throne. The 1701 *Genealogy* describes Shō Hō's

Second Shō Dynasty

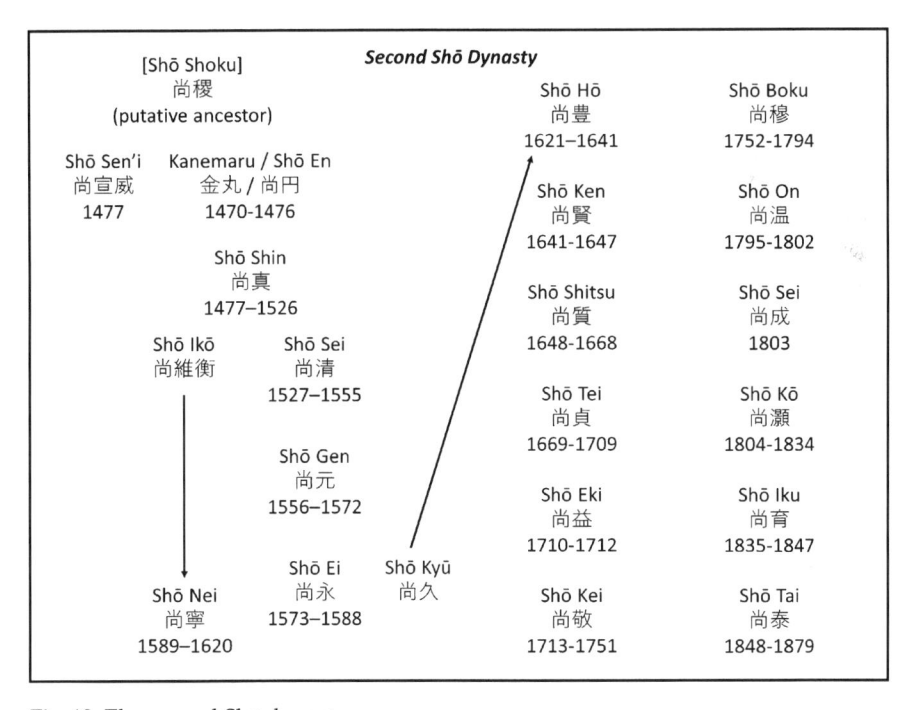

	[Shō Shoku] 尚稷 (putative ancestor)	Shō Hō 尚豊 1621–1641	Shō Boku 尚穆 1752–1794
Shō Sen'i 尚宣威 1477	Kanemaru / Shō En 金丸 / 尚円 1470-1476	Shō Ken 尚賢 1641-1647	Shō On 尚温 1795-1802
	Shō Shin 尚真 1477–1526	Shō Shitsu 尚質 1648-1668	Shō Sei 尚成 1803
Shō Ikō 尚維衡	Shō Sei 尚清 1527–1555	Shō Tei 尚貞 1669-1709	Shō Kō 尚灝 1804-1834
	Shō Gen 尚元 1556–1572	Shō Eki 尚益 1710-1712	Shō Iku 尚育 1835-1847
Shō Nei 尚寧 1589–1620	Shō Ei 尚永 1573–1588	Shō Kyū 尚久	Shō Kei 尚敬 1713-1751	Shō Tai 尚泰 1848-1879

Fig. 13. The second Shō dynasty

father, Shō Kyū, as "true younger brother" of Shō Ei, whereas the 1725 *Genealogy* describes Shō Kyū as the "third child of Shō Gen."[34] I am not suggesting that this difference in terminology is of great significance. However, by relating Shō Kyū to Shō Gen, not Shō Ei, and by positing the adoption of Shō Nei, the 1725 *Genealogy* smooths out any sign of succession conflict. Although we have no record of it, amid the intense factionalism prevailing at the time, a struggle between partisans of Shō Nei and those of Shō Ei's younger brother, Shō Kyū, would have been likely. The status at this time of Shō Kōhaku, Shō Ei's older brother, is unclear.

Shō Nei was a direct descendant of Shō Ikō. Recall that Shō Ikō was Shō Shin's first son by his cousin, queen Kyojin (fig. 12). Kyojin was the daughter of Shō Sen'i, from whom Shō Shin and his partisans seized the throne. The official histories do not discuss whether and to what extent this situation may have impeded Shō Nei or weakened his support, but there was serious internecine conflict. A 1592 *Kyūyō* entry describes an armed revolt. In response, Shō Nei appointed Mō Hōgi (Ikegusuku Peechin Anrai) and Kin Ōshō (Mabuni Peechin Ankō) to attack "the Jana family of Shuri Saishū." The precise location is not clear, although there is an Irijima (same characters as Saishū) in Urasoe. In any case, the account states that the king's men led "righteous soldiers" and that Jana and family resisted vigorously from within their compound. The king's forces used *hiyaa,* a type of three-barreled hand cannon typical of Ryukyuan firearms. They shot into the compound, causing it to catch fire, which forced everyone outside. After a fierce battle, the enemy "general" was killed, and the royal force prevailed.[35]

There are numerous other indications of divisions within Shō Nei's reign. Understanding them, and the 1592 revolt, requires a more extensive context. I revisit the matter in chapters 13 and 14. At this point, it is sufficient to note that factional disputes and trouble with legitimacy greatly weakened Shō Nei at precisely the time when Ryukyu's court needed unity to face unprecedented challenges to its existence.

TROUBLE WITH SATSUMA

Shō Shin ousted Shō Sen'i just as the decade-long Ōnin War was drawing to a close. The postwar Ashikaga shoguns were much diminished with respect to domestic power. As "kings of Japan," however, they remained nominally important, because only the king could authorize trade with the Chinese and Korean courts. The Ashikaga shoguns did not actually control trade at this time. Other powerful lords did the trading, either as legitimate agents of the "king" or posing as such. In the face of military pressure from Oda Nobunaga (1534–1582), the fifteenth shogun Ashikaga Yoshiaki (1537–1597) fled Kyoto in 1573. In the late 1560s, prior to his becoming shogun, Yoshiaki resided in Echizen under the protection of its lord, Asakura Yoshikage (1533–1573). Echizen had close ties with Ryukyu, and I return to this matter in chapter 13.

The main point here is that the decline and demise of the Muromachi *bakufu* changed the geopolitical dynamics in the seas around Ryukyu. Amid the power vacuum, the Shimazu lords of southern Kyushu sought to control shipping between Japan and Ryukyu. From their standpoint, this control furthered several interrelated goals. Obviously, it might benefit Shimazu coffers. Furthermore, denying trade with Ryukyu to merchants in other domains, especially enemies in Kyushu, was part of Shimazu military strategy. The Shimazu lords also sought to forge a direct trade connection with China, and Ryukyu was in a position to facilitate this project.

Shimazu pressure on Ryukyu, therefore, was not a simple case of aggression, and it was certainly not a case of aggression against an unarmed, pacifist kingdom. Shimazu's goal was to work with Ryukyu to promote trade with China in the absence of *bakufu* power. The Shimazu obviously saw themselves as the senior member of any such partnership, and Shimazu goals were not always in Ryukyu's best interests. Timing matters. During Shō Shin's reign, Ryukyu was a significant regional military power and the Shimazu were embroiled in warfare in southern Kyushu. Therefore, when Shimazu Tadaharu (1489–1515) attempted to convince Shō Shin to agree to confiscate the cargoes of vessels entering Ryukyu without a license from Shimazu, Shō Shin remained politely noncommittal.[36]

As we will see in detail, however, changing circumstances impeded Ryukyu's ability to act independently. Although warfare raged in Kyushu throughout much of the sixteenth century, the Shimazu lords gradually consolidated their power. They probably would have conquered all of Kyushu had it not been for the rise of Toyotomi Hideyoshi. Recall that Chinese-made ships sailing under the auspices of Ryukyu's kings conducted international trade within the constraints of Ming Maritime Prohibitions. As these prohibitions relaxed, and as Europeans moved into island Southeast Asia, that aspect of Ryukyu's official trade declined rapidly.

Throughout much of the sixteenth century, Shimazu power strengthened as Ryukyu's power weakened. Moreover, Ryukyu came to depend heavily on merchants from Japan, mostly based in Kyushu, to support investiture rites. The royal court and Ryukyuan elites were unable to purchase all the goods Chinese investiture envoys and their large entourage brought to Ryukyu for sale. Investiture envoys generally would not leave

Naha until they had sold all their goods. The royal government paid all the expenses of their lodging, so the longer the envoys stayed, the greater the financial drain. In this context, visiting Japanese merchants were essential to the process, but the royal government struggled, and often failed, to maintain order when they were in port. Furthermore, the Shimazu lords regarded trade in Ryukyu by other Kyushu domains as a security threat and put pressure on Ryukyu to cooperate in stopping it. The rise of Hideyoshi exacerbated an already difficult situation, as we will see.

FACTIONALISM

This situation aggravated factionalism in the royal government. There were probably several political fault lines, but by the time of Shō Gen's death in 1572 or 1573, the pro-Satsuma versus anti-Satsuma divide had become supremely important. For simplicity, in this section I refer to the Shimazu domains as "Satsuma," even though Shimazu rule usually encompassed all or most of the provinces of Satsuma, Ōsumi, and Hyūga (Miyazaki Prefecture).

I examine details in later chapters, but for now let us consider the demand that Ryukyuan authorities conduct careful inspections of Japanese ships and confiscate the cargoes of any not authorized by Satsuma.[37] Based on this yardstick, Shō Shin, Shō Sei, and Shō Gen were all anti-Satsuma in that they did not cooperate with the demand. After Shō Ei's rule became firmly established in the late 1570s, Shuri pursued policies much more favorable to Satsuma. As he was merely fifteen years old when he became king, it is unlikely that Shō Ei crafted the policy change personally.[38] A comparison of correspondence from the reigns of Shō Gen and Shō Ei reveals small but significant differences. A letter from Shō Gen, for example, is dated "Great Ming [year, month, day]," whereas Shō Ei's letter simply lists the date without referring to Great Ming. In Shō Gen's missive, Ryukyu is "Kyūyō" (beautiful Ryukyu), but it is "Shōkoku" (small country) in Shō Ei's letter.[39] There was also a significant difference in substance between these two reigns.

In contrast, although he cooperated with Satsuma early in his reign, after 1593 Shō Nei became unwaveringly anti-Satsuma. Apart from the required visit he made to Japan in connection with his surrender in 1609, Shō Nei refused to cooperate with Satsuma or the Tokugawa *bakufu* until the end of his life. In 1616, for example, he warned the Ming court of an impending attack on Taiwan by a fleet of thirteen ships of Nagasaki *daikan* Murayama Tōan.[40] It is interesting to note that his successor, Shō Hō, realized that cooperation with Satsuma was the only viable path if Ryukyu was to maintain any autonomy. He even meted out severe punishments to certain anti-Satsuma Ryukyuan officials.[41] In other words, from Shō Gen through Shō Hō, each reign alternated between pro- and anti-Satsuma stances.

CHAPTER NINE

Assembling a Royal Line

I have called into question the official portrayal of the first and second Shō dynasties. The Samekawa family did not originate on the tiny island of Iheya, and it is unlikely that Kanemaru originated on the nearby island of Izena. His roots were probably in Nakijin, although it is likely that his ancestors came from somewhere farther north. It is useful to consider why the official histories locate the origins of these dynasties at what initially appears to be improbable locations. One possible reason is that, except for tiny Iōtorishima, Izena and Iheya were the northernmost extremities of the post-1609 Ryukyu kingdom. However, the more important key to answering the question comes from the geographic end point of Shunten's short royal line. After abdicating the throne, Gihon wandered north. As the story goes, he died in Hedo, at the northern tip of Okinawa, where his remains purportedly rest.

This chapter pauses the narrative to consider how and why Ryukyuan elites were able to splice unrelated royal lines together, as well as some related topics. Recall that the image of an unbroken royal line had typically been the way Ryukyuan kings presented themselves to the Chinese court. The current king, strictly speaking a "crown prince" before investiture, was always the biological son of whomever the previous king had been. The early modern writers of the official histories may also have had Japan's imperial line in mind as a normative model. Regardless, given their function of unifying and organizing a diverse and turbulent past, it makes sense that the official histories would have sought to merge different groups of kings insofar as possible, especially those of Shunten and the two Shō dynasties.

The story of Tametomo founding the Shunten line is false simply because Minamoto Tametomo never journeyed to Okinawa. On the other hand, if we replace Tametomo with Samekawa, then the basic plot describes that family's migration as discussed in chapter 6 and elsewhere. We have seen that the first Shō dynasty functioned as a framework for pulling together kings from Shō Shishō to Shō Toku, at least two of whom were probably not biologically related to each other or to the rest of the line. My interest here is not to point out that the official histories are inaccurate, but to historicize the process whereby those official accounts came into existence. I read the official histories against the grain to shed light on the issues and problems relevant at the time they were written. My argument is that the narrative in the official histories about the origins of the first and second Shō dynasties reflects the sensibilities of early modern Ryukyuan Confucian intellectuals, not, or not always, the realities of fifteenth-century Ryukyuan geopolitics.

THE IDEA OF A ROYAL LINE

The idea of sets of past royal lineages that, in combination, might create a long line of monarchs seems to have emerged vaguely during Shō Shin's reign and more specifically with Shō Sei. Recall that monument H (Kokuō shōtoku hi [2], 1522) mentioned "the past reigns of Shunten, Eiso, and Satto" in the context of discussing loyalty suicides. This phrase may be the oldest textual manifestation of a Ryukyuan consciousness of a heritage of royal lineages.[1] A monument with the same title (also known as Katanohana no hi) from 1543, this one proclaiming Shō Sei's virtue, is more specific. It declares "Shō Sei, Chūzan king of Great Ryukyu" to be the twenty-first descendant of Sonton [Shunten].[2]

The practice of maintaining memorial tablets at Sōgenji for each past Chūzan king began during Shō Shin's reign. The tablets indicate a single unbroken line of rulers.[3] Prior to that time, royal tablets lodged in a variety of temples. By the end of Shō Shin's reign, Enkakuji served as the second Shō dynasty family temple, and the newly built Sōgenji served as the memorial temple for all of the kings of Ryukyu collectively, creating the image of an unbroken royal line.[4] As we have seen, problems concerning legitimacy dogged both Shō Shin and Shō Sei. These problems undoubtedly served as catalysts to their conceiving of and formalizing a royal line in outline form.

Claiming to be the twenty-first descendant of a putative founder of the line or listing the names of each past king were relatively easy tasks compared with writing a narrative history that wove these kings together in a plausible manner and explained awkward transitions. This latter task is what confronted Shō Shōken in the years leading up to 1650, Sai Taku at the end of the century, his son Sai On in the years leading up to 1725, and the scholars of Kumemura who compiled *Kyūyō* soon thereafter. These efforts to weave a continuous fabric from diverse and sometimes incongruous fibers produced much of the framework for the official version of early Ryukyuan history that I examine critically in this book.

SETS OF KINGS

There are five sets of kings who, ideally, might be integrated into a whole. First are Shunten, Shunbajunki, and Gihon. Second are Eiso and his four obscure successors. Third are the two Chūzan kings Satto and Bunei, and finally the two Shō dynasties (fig. 14).

Eiso outshines the others in his group. Because Gihon relinquished the throne to Eiso owing to his virtue, the transition appears valid. Satto and Bunei are somewhat more awkward. The transition from Seii (r. 1337–1354) to Satto is presented much like that of Shō Toku to Kanemaru. Seii's

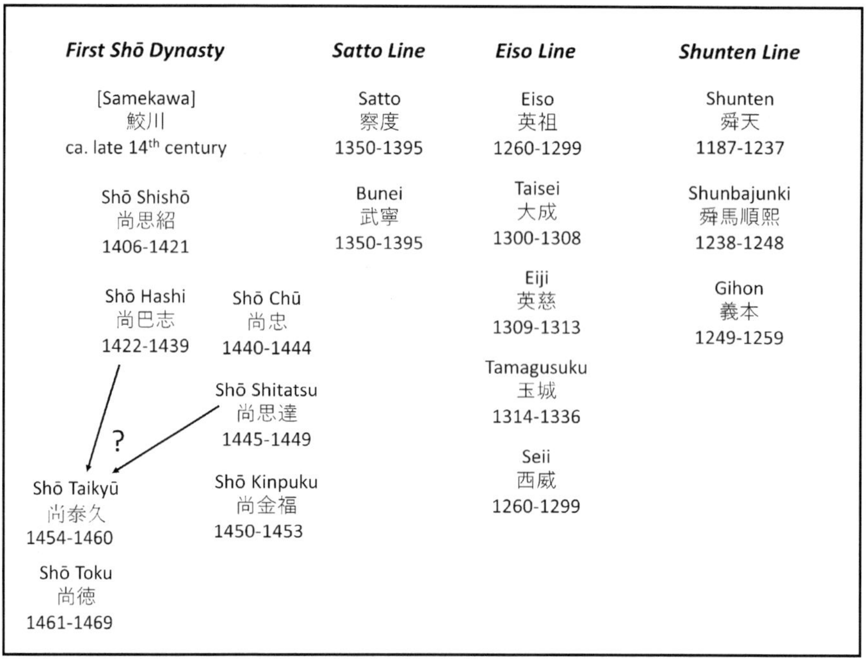

First Shō Dynasty	Satto Line	Eiso Line	Shunten Line
[Samekawa] 鮫川 ca. late 14th century	Satto 察度 1350-1395	Eiso 英祖 1260-1299	Shunten 舜天 1187-1237
Shō Shishō 尚思紹 1406-1421	Bunei 武寧 1350-1395	Taisei 大成 1300-1308	Shunbajunki 舜馬順熙 1238-1248
Shō Hashi 尚巴志 1422-1439	Shō Chū 尚忠 1440-1444	Eiji 英慈 1309-1313	Gihon 義本 1249-1259
	Shō Shitatsu 尚思達 1445-1449	Tamagusuku 玉城 1314-1336	
?		Seii 西威 1260-1299	
Shō Taikyū 尚泰久 1454-1460	Shō Kinpuku 尚金福 1450-1453		
Shō Toku 尚徳 1461-1469			

Fig. 14. Major royal lines according to the official histories

reign was characterized by disorder; and after he died, the local rulers cast out his heir and enthroned the virtuous Satto.

Establishing Satto's excellence required a lengthy hagiographic biography. It extolls his sincerity, humility, virtue, wisdom, and broad learning to make him appear the obvious choice for a legitimate king. The biography invokes the venerable *Classic of Changes* (J. Shūeki; C. Zhōuyì) to liken Satto to the mythical sage kings Shùn and Yǔ, who came to the throne because of their virtue and accomplishments despite being biologically unrelated to their predecessors. His wise and virtuous wife alerted Satto to the value of metal, and the couple prospered by using gold and silver to buy iron from Japanese merchant ships. They used the iron and their wealth to benefit the local community.[5]

Alas, this virtue did not transform their son Bunei, who "turned his back on his father's final instructions, was addicted to sensual pleasures at home, and absorbed in hunting while away."[6] Therefore, his downfall at the hands of Shō Hashi was a natural event within a morally attuned cosmos. As we have seen in chapter 6, it is likely that Bunei fell because of the ill-fated eunuch incident of 1406 and subsequent Chinese intervention. In this sense, Bunei may indeed have met his demise because of wicked behavior. It is worth pausing to note that violent behavior would have been quite likely on the part of any early Ryukyuan ruler, king or otherwise. Conversely, Confucian sagacity would have been highly unlikely. To make this point is simply to be realistic about the rough environment in which all early Ryukyuan rulers operated.

The second and third sets of kings, the lines of Eiso and Satto, fit together well, in part because they were located in or near Urasoe. Linking Bunei and Shō Hashi, however, is nearly impossible in anything other than positive and negative moral terms. In a purely Chinese intellectual environment, this situation might not have been problematic. However, the authors of the official histories strove to connect sets of Ryukyuan kings by birth. Connecting all five was impossible, but a satisfying result could be obtained by linking Shunten's original line with the second Shō dynasty in terms of birth and connecting the others by their levels of virtue and vice. Later, the first Shō dynasty also entered what I will call the plausible procreation zone.

THE PLAUSIBLE PROCREATION ZONE

The ill-fated Gihon was the lynchpin in this linkage. Gihon's tomb is located in Asumori, in Hedo at the northern edge of Okinawa (see fig. 6). Where his bones may be, or whether he even existed in the flesh, of course, is a different matter. Asumori was the first place where the deity Amamiku/Amamikyo established a sacred grove. According to local tradition in northern Okinawa and in Izena, Shō Shoku, Kanemaru's father, was a descendant of Gihon.[7] The official histories all imply this connection, with varying explicitness. The key geographic link is Gihon/Hedo (Asumori) ◊ Shō Shoku and Shō En/Izena. Moreover, after 1725 *Genealogy* and *Kyūyō* stated that Samekawa and Shō Shishō originated in Iheya; then all three lines came within plausible procreation distance of each other, given the frequent boat traffic between Izena, Iheya, and Hedo.

Taking a closer look in chronological order, *Reflections* includes a paragraph at the beginning of the section on Shō En explaining that his parents were peasants in Izena. It states that his family situation in previous generations is unknown, but it is possible that Shō En's parents were descendants of earlier kings and that these descendants crossed over to Izena and became peasants. "Otherwise, how could [Shō En] have suddenly encountered such good fortune?"[8] In Sai Taku's 1701 *Genealogy*, Shō En's father became "King Shō Shoku," with a short section of his own explaining that he was from Shomi in Izena. The passage does not speculate about who Shō Shoku's ancestors might have been, but it states that his tablet is in the royal temple.[9]

Sai On's 1725 *Genealogy* includes a longer section on King Shō Shoku. It states explicitly what *Reflections* hinted at: "Some say Shō Shoku was a descendant of Gihon, and some say he was a descendant of Tenson. We do not know which is correct." This skillful rhetoric leaves room for uncertainty while affirming that Shō Shoku, and thus Shō En, were indeed descendants of ancient kings. To reinforce the point, the passage ends with a paraphrase of *Reflection*'s logic, namely that it is hard to imagine that Sho En could have become a king had he not been of royal ancestry.[10] *Reflections* placed the royal lines within a plausible geographical range, and later official histories helped readers connect the dots.

It is possible that tying the first Shō dynasty to this plausible procreation zone was Sai On's idea. *Reflections* does not even include a chapter for Shō Shishō. The text mentions Shishō at the start of the chapter on Shō Hashi for the purpose of situating the latter. In other words, in *Reflections*, the father-and-son pair come to readers' attention already located in Sashiki. In the 1701 *Genealogy*, Shō Shishō has a short chapter of his own. He appears as lord of Sashiki, and his father, mother, queen, and birth year are listed as "unknown."[11] A parenthetical addition to the 1725 *Genealogy*, however, says that, according to legend, Shō Shishō's father was Lord Samekawa of Iheya, who moved to Baten, in the village of Shinzato, in Sashiki district. Samekawa's daughter became the priestess of Baten.[12]

Kyūyō unambiguously states that Shō Shishō was the son of Lord Samekawa of Iheya and that they moved to Sashiki.

In other words, the idea that the geographic locus of the first Shō dynasty was Iheya seems to have developed relatively late, sometime early in the eighteenth century. It is possible that this development was nothing more than an acquisition of greater knowledge in the form of local legends about Samekawa. *Origins of Ryukyu*, for example, mentions the Samegaa (J. Samekawa) Ōnushi taketsukasa sacred stone in the upper Baten grove.[13] In any case, locating Samekawa at Iheya placed him within the plausible procreation zone. Neither the 1725 *Genealogy* nor *Kyūyō* states or hints at a link between Gihon and the first Shō dynasty. Whether or not this absence of explanation was a conscious editorial decision we cannot say. It is easy to imagine, however, that anything beyond simply locating Samekawa's origins in Iheya might weaken or confuse the tenuous link between Gihon and the second Shō dynasty. The essential task, in other words, was to link the current dynasty with the putative founding dynasty.

THE TAMETOMO LEGEND

Although *Reflections* goes into the greatest detail, all of the official histories state that Ryukyu's first king, Shunten, was the son of Chinzei Hachirō Minamoto Tametomo and the sister of a local lord in southern Okinawa. This Tametomo legend also appears in the discourse of Japanese Gozan Zen priests circa the 1520s or 1530s owing to their connections with Ryukyuan temples. Yano Misako draws the reasonable conclusion that the main reason the legend spread to Gozan priests in Japan at this time was that it was a byproduct of internal Ryukyuan concern about defining the royal line.[14] Although the legend that Tametomo was the father of Ryukyu's first king appeared in Japan during the early sixteenth century, it probably started in Okinawa slightly more than a century earlier.

It is worth noting that this legend, implicitly or explicitly, appears in the household records of locally prominent lineages in Amami-Ōshima.[15] The Shidama lineage traces its descent from Tametomo, through Gihon. Taruyoshi was Gihon's son, born in 1249, the year Gihon took the throne. Taruyoshi was "Prince Urasoe," and his lineage deity (*ujigami*) was Iwashimizu Hachiman in Kyoto.[16] Most lineage records were compiled during the early modern era, and the claim of a specific ancestor born in 1249 is purely legendary. The point is simply that the Tametomo legend permeated many segments of Ryukyuan society.

154　Dynastic Turbulence, 1400–1600

Legends of Tametomo setting sail for Ryukyu exist throughout western and southern Kyushu.[17] The Tametomo legend and the Samekawa migration route also overlap with the movements of the deity Amamikyo/Amamiku. Recall, moreover, that Tametomo was worshipped at two shrines near Sashiki in Kyushu, and that the story of the father of Ishigaki's Nakama Mitsukeima also follows the plot of the Tametomo legend. The legend probably came to Ryukyu around 1400, or slightly earlier, and flourished.

The Tametomo legend also appears in the *Omoro,* linking Shō Shin with Tametomo. For example:

> The sun of Shuri [the king]
> And the sun shining in the heavens
> Become one
> The beloved sun [the king]
> The sun Ichiro-ku [the king]
> And the sun shining in the heavens
> The sun Hachiro-ku [the king]
> And the sun shining in the heavens.[18]

The names Ichiro (J. Ichirō) and Hachiro (J. Hachirō) refer to the king. In this context, "Teda Ichiro-ku" indicates the eldest male child and refers to Shō Shin. Its paired term, "Teda Hachiro-ku," almost certainly refers to Chinzei Hachirō, that is, to Tametomo. In other words, Shō Shin was the first son of his mother, and he was also the descendant of Tametomo.[19] Another *omoro* uses these terms in connection with the creator deities Amamikyo, who created the island (or islands), and Shinerikyo, who created the country.[20] Yet another song likens the rows of pine trees Shō Shin planted to the actions of the same creator deities, Amamikyo and Shinerikyo.[21] Finally, the *Omoro* links Shō Shin with Shunten, the legendary first king and scion of Tametomo.[22] These and other examples root Shō Shin deeply in Ryukyu's primordial royal past. Therefore, the *Omoro* and the official histories are in general agreement about royal roots. Both explicitly link Shunten's lineage with the second Shō dynasty.

At the end of Shō Shin's reign, Ryukyu took an active role in attempting to restore relations between China and Japan. One side effect of this diplomacy, which played out between approximately 1525 and 1530, was to transmit the Tametomo legend from Ryukyu to Japan. One priest who served as an envoy in the diplomatic exchanges was Gesshū Jukei (d. 1533). He wrote the legend down, explaining that he had heard it from the Ryukyuan priest Kakuō of Tenkaiji. From approximately 1530, the legend became known among Japanese Gozan priests and a few others. The

Tametomo legend became an item of lore about Ryukyu, but it was of no practical importance during the early and middle sixteenth centuries. Insofar as Japanese powers interacted with Ryukyu, they did so for entirely for pragmatic reasons. Nor was the Tametomo legend of any practical importance with respect to the 1609 war with Satsuma except that it appeared in the context of rhetoric justifying Satsuma's attack.

Nanpo Bunshi (1556–1620) was a Buddhist priest and Confucian scholar in Satsuma who also handled much of the domain's diplomatic correspondence and served as an adviser to its government. A common literary format for Buddhist priests was to write lines of verse in classical Chinese about a person or topic, with a prose preface explaining the context. Bunshi wrote *Verses and Preface on the Chastisement of Ryukyu* (C. Tǎo Liúqiú shī bìng xù, J. *Tō Ryūkyū shi narabi ni jo*) to justify Satsuma's military action. The preface begins with a fairly detailed account of Tametomo's journey to Ryukyu. It includes the claim that the name "Ryukyu" came from Tametomo's telling the ship's pilot who was taking him from Kyushu to "rely on the current" (*ryūkyū*).

Bunshi's account mentions that Tametomo improved the primitive conditions of the islands, ultimately permitting the Chūzan king to receive investiture from the Ming court. Immediately after making that point, Bunshi explains that "for several tens of generations" Ryukyu has been part of the territory of the Shimazu lords. Moreover, Ryukyu had never failed to send tribute to Shimazu and obey his orders until recently, when the wayward official Jana led Ryukyu down the path of disloyalty and disaster.[23] One of the verses states that Naha was originally part of Kawanabe district, referring to the southern part of Satsuma. Other than mentioning that Seiwa was the fifty-sixth emperor of Japan at the beginning of several lines explaining Tametomo's lineage, terms like "Japan" or "Yamato" are nowhere to be found in Bunshi's text. This absence of Japan is significant. Bunshi's point was that Ryukyu was part of the Shimazu domains, along with Satsuma, Ōsumi, and Hyūga. In this sense, Bunshi may have been the earliest non-Chinese scholar who sought to downplay Ryukyu's connections with Japan.

Was there any historical validity to the claim that Ryukyu had been part of Shimazu territory long before 1609? There was not.[24] In other words, this claim appeared in the context of justifying the 1609 war. Whether that war was actually justifiable based on prevailing norms and circumstances at the time is a more complex matter that I examine in detail in later chapters.

JAPONIC RYUKYU

Except for Kikai at times during the tenth or eleventh century, Ryukyu was outside of any formal Japanese state boundary until 1609. In terms of people and culture, however, it should be abundantly clear by this point that Ryukyu was closely connected with Japan. The departure point for many or most of the people who became Ryukyuans was, at least in proximate terms, Kyushu and nearby islands. The *wakō* groups who migrated south to Ryukyu often departed from ports in Kyushu, but their more distant roots included many parts of Japan, coastal Korea, and in some cases even inland northeast Asia. Of course, many regions of coastal Japan also had historical connections with the Korean peninsula and elsewhere on the continent.

Keeping in mind that, in a cultural sense, "Japan" includes elements from Korea and possibly elsewhere on the Asian continent, let us consider early Ryukyu as it had developed up to approximately 1600. For this purpose, it is helpful to broaden the term "Japonic," which normally refers to a family of languages. Here I apply "Japonic" to the base culture of early Ryukyu, including language, of course, but also realms like religion and material culture.

Owing to trade between China and Ryukyu, some forms of Chinese popular culture, especially folk religion, were present in parts of the Ryukyu islands. Moreover, Chinese cosmological concepts and political rhetoric became increasingly known among elite Ryukyuans during the sixteenth century. Of course, basic Chinese cosmological concepts were also widely known and acknowledged in Japan and throughout East Asia. In general, however, I stress that Chinese culture of any variety was limited and superficial in Ryukyu, even as late as 1600. Many elite Ryukyuans during the subsequent early modern era acquired basic literacy in Chinese high culture and a small number attained a high level of mastery. We will see that this partial sinification of elite Ryukyuans began during the seventeenth century as a direct result of the 1609 war. Similarly, the development of a distinctive Ryukyuan culture accelerated at the same time for the same reason.

With early Ryukyu's Japonic roots in mind, we should consider a final point about the Tametomo legend. Because of its political uses during the seventeenth century and into the modern era, there is a tendency for modern or contemporary people to overlook the inherent appeal of the Tametomo legend, or of similar legends such as that of Yuriwaka, in frontier areas like Ryukyu. The rulers of the various harbors of the Ryukyu islands, their families, and many of the nearby inhabitants were the descendants of people who had arrived fairly recently from Japan. Their forebears arrived as refugees, defeated southern court *wakō*, adventurers, or other categories of (often) marginal people seeking opportunities or simply survival. A heroic but marginal figure who had ventured far from his homeland, someone like Tametomo or Yuriwaka, would have resonated with the circumstances and cultural sensibilities of early Ryukyuans. Tametomo was an outlaw hero, or "anti-hero," a larger-than-life, idealized version of the seafarers within the East China Sea network.[25]

PART III

WAKŌ TO KINGS, 1477–1556

CHAPTER TEN

Centering Shuri and Forging an Empire

Consider the three functions of spiritual power and therefore political legitimacy, military prowess, and wealth discussed previously in connection with Shō Hashi and the three principalities (chapter 4). This chapter examines aspects of those three functions in the context of a transformation of the monarch at Shuri from a regional lord with a license to trade with China to a strong centralized monarch ruling a vast territory. Shō Shin's reign spanned this transition.

In a comparative study of medieval Kyoto and Shuri, Takahashi Yasuo argues that these two cities shared key characteristics that distinguished them from continental capitals of the region such as Nanjing, Beijing, or Seoul. For example, Kyoto and Shuri were not surrounded by defensive walls. Shuri and adjacent areas such as Naha formed an organic unit designed to enhance royal glory and authority (fig. 15). Buddhist priests, most arriving from the Kyoto area, directly contributed to the built environment of Shuri.[1]

SHURI, THE THREEFOLD CENTER

Shō Shin established a Council of Three (Sanshikan, Hōshi, Yoasutabe, and other names) to head his government.[2] Other male officials were organized according to a tripartite scheme in which several *hiki* formed one watch (*ban*). There were three watches, each supervised by a member of the Council of Three. Among female officials, Kikoe-ōgimi functioned analogously to the king, and under her were three Ōamu (or Ōamu-shirare), analogous to the Council of Three. Each of the three highest male and

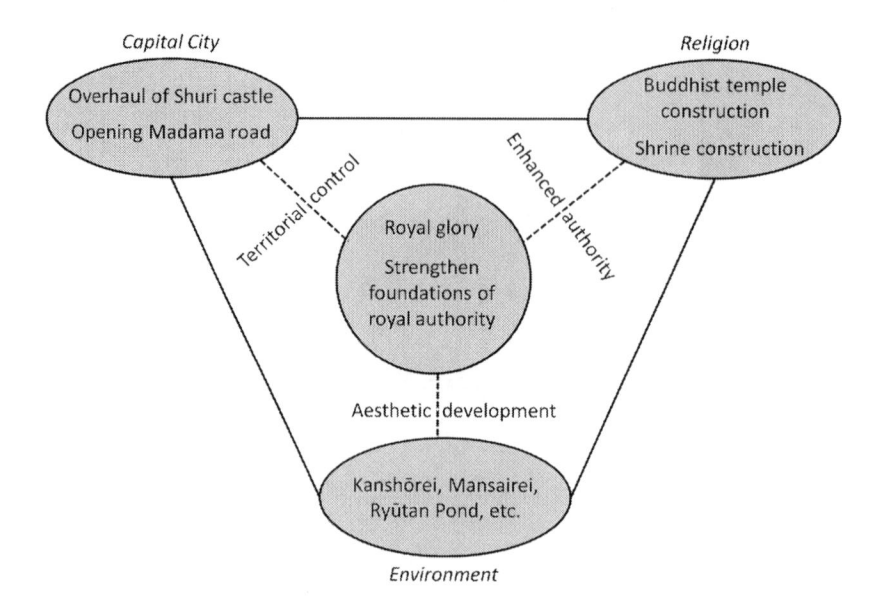

Fig. 15. Components of Shuri as the center of a Ryukyu empire. Based on Takahashi, *Umi no "Kyōto,"* 352, fig. 53.

female officials was linked with the three core districts surrounding Shuri: Mawashi, Haebaru, and Nishihara.

The division of the Ryukyu islands into administrative districts (*magiri*) also dates from this era (fig. 16). Although based on earlier territorial zones, Shō Shin formalized the arrangement. He and his successors organized all of the territory of the Ryukyu islands into units subordinate to and under the control of Shuri as a strong center. By organizing the land in this way, Shō Shin created a *kinai,* a classical term for a geopolitical central region of a large state or empire. This term, or its equivalent, appears in some of Shō Shin's monuments. *Bāngjī* (J. *hōki*) in monument A (Enkaku Zenji ki, 1497) is one example.[3] We have seen that Shō Hashi embodied the geography and symbolic qualities of the three principalities via the migrations of his family and the trajectory of his conquest. Moreover, Kaiki began the process of surrounding Shuri castle with an aesthetically pleasing and geomantically potent landscape. Shō Shin took this process much further by organizing the whole capital city, broadly defined, to embody all three aspects of power represented by the principalities. Shuri-Naha itself became the physical manifestation of royal power and authority, not simply the place where the local ruler's castle and harbor were located.

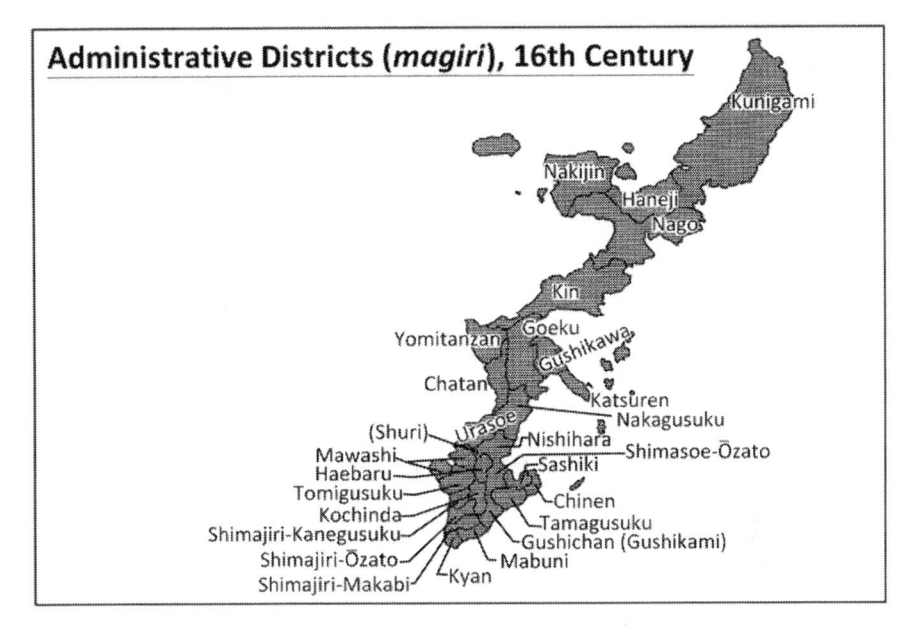

Fig. 16. Administrative districts (*magiri*), sixteenth century

As part of this process, new military infrastructure supported the defense of Naha, Shuri, and surrounding areas. New religious rites for the prosperity of the empire all became centered at Shuri. Other powerful geographic locations became linked with and subordinate to Shuri. For example, some of the Shuri priestesses periodically visited Kudakajima and other outlying locations imbued with religious power, but they did so from their base at the new political and religious center. New temples and shrines supported the new rites and further connected Shuri with key administrative or symbolic locations in the empire. A good example is the Sonohiyabu grove, which linked Shuri and Nakijin, and which eventually linked Shuri with newly conquered territories in other islands.

The new Shuri folded into itself Ryukyu's temporal past and spatial expanse, as many *omoro* proclaim. For example:

> Shuri grove
> Creates splendor and beauty
> All realms north and south
> Come together in the castle
> The Madama grove
> Creates splendor and beauty.[4]

Following the headnote in the Nihon shisō taikei version, I translate *yo* in line three as "realms" in a spatial sense, which add up to all of the Ryukyu islands. However, this word can also indicate temporal realms, such as reigns of rulers.[5] In other words, Shuri castle united both space and time.

The making of Shuri into a comprehensive center was part of Shō Shin's lifetime effort to legitimize himself and erase or minimize traces of problematic predecessors. By centralizing all symbolic and pragmatic functions of royal authority at Shuri, the king was able to neglect some older centers of power, such as Sashiki/Baten. Like Shō Toku's sutras, much of Shō Hashi's old base of power began literally to rot into the earth. Other locations outside of Shuri were too important to neglect, so Shō Shin linked them formally to the capital via shrines and religious rites. As we have seen, he maintained close ties with his likely ancestral homeland of Nakijin. Similarly, the island of Kudakajima and the Seifaa grove across from it on Okinawa received regular royal attention.

NEW OFFICIALS

The precise hierarchy of male officials that developed during Shō Shin's reign is not clear. Indeed, it is difficult to locate the exact date on which any particular royal official first appeared during the sixteenth century. The general picture is that the members of the Council of Three supervised three (or possibly four) officials known as *sedo*, a term that originated from *sentō*, ship's captain. *Sedo* were heads of *hiki*, a term that literally means "pulling together." *Hiki* were bands of government workers with multiple functions as guards, soldiers, religious workers, civil engineers, and construction workers. The other major type of official that appears during Shō Shin's time is the *satonushi*, literally "village lord." Despite the literal meaning of their titles, initially these officials oversaw large territories such as harbors or districts. The *satonushi* of Shō Shin's era became the *jitō* (district-level administrators) of the early modern era. At least in terms of function, early *satonushi* overlapped with powerful local rulers. The appearance of *satonushi* might have been what prompted Sai On to declare that Shō Shin successfully relocated the warlords to Shuri. After Shō Shin's era, *satonushi* declined in relative status as other elite categories came into existence above them.

A hierarchy of female officials matched their male counterparts. Kikoe-ōgimi was a new official in Shō Shin's time. Just as the king stood above a Council of Three, so Kikoe-ōgimi stood above the three Ōamu priestesses of the three core districts of the capital. As we will see in chapter 12, the three-in-one Benzaiten was the Kikoe-ōgimi's deity.

Kikoe-ōgimi became the human spiritual guardian of the Ryukyu empire, and Benzaiten likewise became its guardian deity. Corresponding to the *satonushi* were the "Thirty-three Kimi," a group of high-ranking priestesses such as the Aoriyae, Sasukasa, Serikaku, and Akeshino priestesses of Nakijin and nearby areas.[6] Kimihae in Kumejima was one of these elite territorial priestesses, the only one not a royal household relative. The term *kimi* referred to a high-ranking priestess. Along with Shō Shin's hierarchy of *kimi*, the royal court began appointing local priestesses at the district and village level, the *noro*.

During Shō Sei's reign, the system of male officials and their associated status ranks became more elaborate. Chén Kǎn explained the social hierarchy as "not as severe as that of China." After the king came princes, "who although of exalted status, are not involved in governing." Next was the governing council (Council of Three); and after them judicial officers, the Satokan. Below the Satokan was an official in charge of the port of Naha, followed by a variety of lesser "ear and eye" officials in charge of "visiting," which probably meant governing areas outside of the capital. Finally, there were military officials. Kumemura had its own officials who dealt with the tribute trade. From top to bottom they were Taifu, Chōshi, and Tsūji.[7] This last group consisted of general purpose officials who also functioned as interpreters.

Variation in the terminology and descriptions in monuments, household records, and the accounts of Chinese envoys makes a detailed listing of official ranks and statuses during Shō Sei's era difficult. Moving to the end of the century, however, allows us to see an outline of the mature system before it again changed during the seventeenth century. Based on the text of the monument Urasoe gusuku no mae no hi (1597)[8] and other sources, there were six categories of elite social status. These statuses were not specific government offices, but they corresponded with eligibility for official positions. I have included the approximate corresponding early modern term in parentheses in the following list:

Omoigwabe (Ōji [prince])
Anjibe (Aji)
Kanasome hachimaki (Ueekata)
Sanban no ōyakumoi (Peechin/Peekumi)
Satonushibe (Satonushi)
Gerae akukabe (Chikudun).[9]

Clothing and hairpins helped visually to distinguish these status ranks. Chén Kǎn explained that the color of caps corresponded to official status.

Yellow was the highest (Kanasome hachimaki in the above list means "dyed golden cap"), followed by red, blue/green, and finally white. Like caps, belt color also differentiated official status ranks.[10]

The king's male and female officials managed the center of the empire and the territory it controlled. Beyond the human infrastructure, Shō Shin and Shō Sei created new military infrastructure, discussed in the next chapter, and new politico-religious rites. The regularly conducted rites were known generally as *shikyoma* (also *mishikyoma*). They celebrated the first grains and were held at different times of the year depending on the cycle for each grain. Especially important were the Rice Ear festival (Ine-no-ho matsuri), conducted during the fifth lunar month (fourth in some accounts), and the Barley Ear festival (Mugi ho matsuri), held on the fifteenth day of the second lunar month. In keeping with the mythical movements of deity Amamikyo, three days prior to the start of the Rice Ear festival, water from Hedo was shipped to Shuri. In connection with this festival and a related harvest festival during the sixth month, the three Ōamu led processions of priestesses to perform rites before the hearth deity at each of the three central districts. Separately, the king and *hiki* officers led processions of male officials to perform rites at the Shimo-kūri, a large palace storehouse.[11]

Agricultural rites typically marked the sowing of the first seeds, the initial ripening, and the harvest, as well as the arrival of grain in Okinawa. Although some of these rites included processions to southern districts and, once a year, to Kudakajima, they all functioned to make Shuri the center of the kingdom's material prosperity. Moreover, although there were older precedents for some rites, as formal functions of government they all originated during the reigns of Shō Shin or Shō Sei.

One rite created during Shō Sei's time was Kimitezuri. Recall that this term appears erroneously in *Reflections on Chūzan* as the name of a deity in connection with Shō Sen'i's ill-fated enthronement ceremonies. Kimitezuri was a rite to enhance royal power, and Makishi Yōko argues convincingly that its essential quality was integrative in that it pulled together diverse practices and focused them on Shuri. Like many of the new rites, Kimitezuri took the form of a royal procession. It was connected with the idea that an outside deity, Benzaiten, had arrived and subsumed the local deities into a prosperous and fertile new entity. This entity is centered at the royal palace in Shuri and its representatives are the king and Kikoe-ōgimi, the human counterpart of Benzaiten. There is also a connection with the Aoriyae in Nakijin. Both the new Kikoe-ōgimi and the newly linked-in Aoriyae descended from Kumejima's Sasukasa deity.[12] Recall from chapter 5 that Sasukasa came into the Ryukyu islands from the Tokara islands.

DESTROYING THE KAWARA LINEAGES

Origins of Ryukyu is typical of the official sources in discussing Yaeyama circa 1500. After a brief lead-in about the need to regulate benighted religious customs that waste resources, we are told, "During the reign of Hóngwŭ [1368–1398], this island belonged to our country and sent annual tribute." A detailed description of Akahachi's revolt and its suppression follows. Akahachi's revolt is often called the Honkawara revolt, and *Origins* states, erroneously, that Oyake Akahachi and Honkawara were two different people.[13]

The narrative details of Yaeyama's early history are based on legend that found its way into the official histories and other written accounts of the early modern era. What we can say with certainty is that Shō Shin and Nakasone Toyomiya together fought a war against Ishigaki's Oyake Akahachi and defeated him. Nakasone profited from this action, and Yaeyama came under Shuri's relatively firm control in 1500. Moreover, the local political and military situation in the years just prior to the war was complex. The tales of rival chieftains almost certainly reflect struggles between different *wakō* groups. To gain insight into the 1500 invasion of Yaeyama, we should pause to consider Kumejima.

According to *Kyūyō*, Shuri invaded Kumejima and attacked Gushikawa gusuku, whose lord had defied Shuri's authority and was (of course) abusing the people. The Gushikawa lord refused to leave his powerful castle and do battle with the Okinawan army. However, an insider betrayed Gushikawa by pointing out to the Okinawans that the castle's sole source of water was a ditch from outside. The besiegers filled in the ditch, which forced Gushikawa's forces to come out and fight. The account ends by explaining that Kumejima had been a vassal of Chūzan since the Hóngwŭ era, and Shuri had never invaded the island before now (1506).[14] This final statement is part of several lines justifying the invasion on moral grounds. Whether Shuri had invaded in the past, however, seems irrelevant to such justification. Was there a previous invasion that this passage seeks to deny? Based on developments in the official religious hierarchy, in place by 1501, it is likely that Shuri either invaded or threatened to invade Kumejima during the early part of Shō Shin's reign.[15]

A *Kyūyō* entry for 1500 links the invasion of Yaeyama with Kumejima. It explains that the Kimihae priestess of Kumejima led the force invading Yaeyama. There were three sisters in Kumejima with religious power. The eldest went to Shuri to reside at Benzai grove, a shrine to Benzaiten. The second sister was based at Agari grove in Kumejima, but she later went to live at Mount Omoto in Yaeyama. The third sister became Kimihae, the highest-ranking priestess in Kumejima. As the Shuri forces were preparing to invade, a deity explained that "Originally, the deities of Kumejima and Yaeyama were sisters." Therefore, appointing Kimihae to lead the invasion would facilitate pacification of Yaeyama. Sure enough, seeing a reuniting of the Mount Omoto priestess/deity and her sister Kimihae, the "pirates" resisting the Okinawan forces were shocked into submission, and the people of Yaeyama finally were able to enjoy the benefits of peace. For her role in the process, the position of Kumejima Kimihae became hereditary.[16]

As explained in chapter 5, Gaara group names of the form Kawara or Gawara often overlap with place-names containing the word *omoto*, which is also connected with *obotsu* (the high abode of a deity) and Usa Hachiman. Whatever else it was, Shō Shin's invasion of Yaeyama was an attempt to neutralize a rival *wakō* group, the Honkawara, the "pirates" of the *Kyūyō* accounts. Kumejima was another Kawara location, indicated by sister priestesses and deities. Perhaps the Fukudi-gima we encountered in the *Omoro,* who grabbed the valuable goods of other people's harbors, was one of these *wakō*.[17] Like Yaeyama, Kumejima was a key point along the sea-lanes connecting the coast of China to the Ryukyu islands and points north. Kumejima was also home to a thriving iron industry. For all of these pragmatic reasons, Shō Shin would have wanted control over the island.

WARFARE AND EMPIRE

Although military tales frequently mention defeated generals killing themselves on the battlefield, we have no record other than monument H (Kokuō shōtoku hi [2], 1522) that any officials took their own lives upon the death of their lord. Local lore suggests the opposite. For example, recall Sashiki grove in Yomitan, one of the sites to which those affiliated with the first Shō dynasty fled after Kanemaru took power. The 1522 monument H claims that such suicides had become common during the past century. This period would have covered four royal transitions that were violent, or probably violent: Shō Taikyū, Shō Toku, Kanemaru/Shō En, Shō Sen'i, and Shō Shin. By the end of 1522, the last of the wars to pacify Sakishima, Nakasone Tomomiya's invasion of Yonaguni to oust its ruler Onitora (Unitura) had ended. The juxtaposition in the monument of Nakasone's act of subordination to Shō Shin with the prohibition of loyalty suicides was probably not accidental. When we consider the local wars that Shō Shin undoubtedly waged but have been omitted from the official histories,[18] the past century had been a time of great bloodshed. Characterizing this bloodshed in terms of loyalty suicides, and then prohibiting them on moral grounds, was yet another maneuver by Shō Shin to present himself and his reign as both morally superior and the sole source of political and military authority. Similarly, the monument also functioned to proclaim that the disorder of the recent past was now over.

Shō Shin either initiated or was involved with several military campaigns. The ostensible reason for the invasion of Yaeyama was that Akahachi had rebelled against Shuri, refused to send tribute, and had attacked loyal local lords. The official histories refer to Akakachi's soldiers as "pirates" (C. *zéibīng*, J. *zokuhei*), whose defeat resulted in peace for the peasants.[19] Akahachi himself is a "pirate leader" (C. *zéishǒu*, J. *zokushu*).[20] Another reason for the conflict, mentioned in some later documents, was the prohibition of popular religious festivals in the name of suppressing superstitious practices that squandered resources. In some accounts, these cultural policies caused the revolt, and in others they gave Akahachi leverage in fomenting an uprising.[21]

Kyūyō entries for 1500 are revealing. One focuses on the competence of Shuri's general, Zenihara (or Jinbaru), who commanded the nine "watches" (*ban*) constituting an army of roughly three thousand soldiers. Next is a detailed explanation of Akahachi's belligerence vis-à-vis other local rulers in the region. Eventually Shuri sent a force to chastise this uncontrollable brigand, and local leaders such as Nakasone who assisted the Okinawan forces contributed to a great victory. Interestingly, several tens of wives of the "pirate soldiers," holding leafy branches, looked to the heavens and attempted to repel the Shuri force by sorcery. Recall Miusuku Shishikadun from chapter 2. His story comes next. According to the *Kyūyō* account, Shishikadun repeatedly refused the call to join Akahachi's rebellion, remaining loyal to Shuri. Agents of Akahachi took Shishikadun prisoner, stabbed him to death while at sea, and threw his body overboard. His remains were later found and returned to Hateruma for a formal funeral. The royal government bestowed honors on Shishikadun and appointed his six children as local officials on Hateruma.[22]

Starting with the reasonable surmise that the invasions of Yaeyama and Kumejima were related events, we know that the military action in Yaeyama took place in 1500, and it was Shuri's largest undertaking ever in terms of the mobilization of resources. It seems unlikely that Shō Shin would have invaded Yaeyama without first securing Kumejima. Whatever warfare occurred in 1506, therefore, was part of a broader, ongoing diplomatic and military process. Monument F (Momourasoe rankan no mei, 1509) reflects the apparent end of this conflict. It may also be significant that according to household records, Tameharu, the first agent of Shuri to settle in Amami-Ōshima and govern as Shuri-ōyako, arrived there in 1506.[23]

Overseas warfare, however, did not end in 1506 or 1509. Either in 1513, slightly earlier, or in 1522, Nakasone Toyomiya invaded Yonaguni and destroyed its lord, Onitora. A 1513 *Kyūyō* entry states that Kaneshigawa Toyomiya returned to Miyako from Shuri with a copy of the *Prajñāpāramitā sutra* (*Dai-Hannnya kyō*), suggesting that Kaneshigawa was the ruler of Miyako in 1513. If so, then Nakasone's invasion of Yonaguni would have taken place prior to 1513. Neither the terminal dates for either person nor the date of the war are known with certainty. Whether Onitora was the last gasp of the Honkawara or part of an unrelated conflict is also unclear.

Although dated 1500, another *Kyūyō* entry discusses post-invasion developments. It explains that Miyako's "shark ancestor," Nakasone Toyomiya,[24] and several of his relatives rendered heroic service in connection with the invasion of Yaeyama. Chūzan made Nakasone chief of Miyako as a reward, but he had died of illness by the time the official envoy arrived to convey the appointment. Therefore, Nakasone's eldest son, Kanamori, assumed the post, but "he violated the law and destroyed the basis" for his ruling Miyako. Shuri sent an official to chastise Kanamori, who had died of illness by the time the official arrived. The official confiscated Kanamori's household wealth, seized his two daughters, and returned to Shuri with them. After three years, the crime was forgiven and the two daughters set sail for Miyako. However, violent winds drove their ship onto a reef off the island of Tarama, destroying the vessel and killing all on board. The bodies of the two women floated (the substantial distance) to the vicinity of their home village, where they were recovered from the sea and buried. The same passage explains that Nakasone's second son, Makarigane, became the head of Yayeyama after the invasion. Contradicting other passages about the war having brought the benefits of peace to the people, here we are told that Makarigane cruelly oppressed them. Upon learning of the situation Shuri removed Makarigane and sent him back to Miyako.[25]

Setting aside the red-herring details in the *Kyūyō* passages summarized above, notice the basic plot. Nakasone in Miyako became very powerful, having teamed up with Shuri to wipe out his potential Sakishima rivals. However, soon after Nakasone became the predominant military power in Sakishima, he and his family were all dead, disgraced, or both. The government in Shuri had confiscated the family's wealth at just about

Centering Shuri and Forging an Empire 171

the time Shō Shin acquired a fine new sword and other valuable items from Miyako.

Recall Shō Shin's failure to restore annual tribute missions at the start of his reign. In effect, the Ming court was demanding that the king assert firm control over Ryukyuans in China. Although a point for speculation, it is possible that warfare against Kawara opponents in Sakishima and Kumejima was in part connected with the goal of restoring annual tribute. The timing fits. The Ming court granted a restoration of annual tribute in 1507, which according to the usual date would have been just after the conclusion of the campaign in Kumejima. In 1522, however, the Board of Rites once again ordered Ryukyu to send tribute only once every two years, with a limit of one hundred fifty people per ship. Mirroring the terse statement in *Ming Veritable Records*, *Genealogy of Chūzan* suggests that the reason was the new Jiājìng emperor's desire to act "in accordance with the regulations of previous reigns."[26] This time there is no record of protest by Ryukyu. Despite the restoration of annual tribute between 1507 and 1522, the volume of tribute actually declined slightly during this period.[27] It is likely that by the end of Shō Shin's reign, the tribute trade had become less profitable and more burdensome for Ryukyu owing to the changing world conditions discussed in chapter 13.

SHIPS AND SHIPBUILDING

The drop-off in the volume of tribute trade corresponded to a significant downsizing of the ships in Ryukyu's official fleet circa 1520. At this point, it is useful to summarize the overall trajectory with respect to Ryukyuan ships and shipbuilding. I will begin with a brief description of five periods. My descriptions for periods one through three, about which there is academic consensus, relies mainly on the work of Okamoto Hiromichi.[28]

Period One: 1483–1450

These decades corresponded to the favorable treatment of Ryukyu by the Ming court and the highest volume of trade. Ryukyuan kings received used Ming naval ships free of cost and also relied on Ming shipyards to repair some of these vessels. The ships varied in size, ranging from a capacity of approximately 209 kiloliters (1159 *koku*) and a crew of about a hundred to ships twice that capacity or even larger (crews between 200 and 300). For reference, the *kaisen* (tribute-trade ships) of the early modern era were approximately the same size as the smallest Chinese-made vessels during this period.

Period Two: 1450–1520s

During period two, Ryukyu continued to obtain vessels from China. However, instead of receiving used military vessels for free, Ryukyu bore the costs of vessel construction and subsequent repairs.[29] Ship size did not change, an indirect indication of the continuing vigor of the tribute trade. During this period and the previous one, each ship received a single-character name such as "vigor," "wisdom," "courage," or "longevity" at the shipyard when built. After arriving in Ryukyu, the ship received a Japanese name ending in -*maru*. Probably from around the late fifteenth century onward, ships also received a Ryukyuan name ending in -*tomi*. These names of ships are found in the *Omoro,* and vessels appearing in the songs would usually have had alternative Chinese and Japanese names.

Period Three: 1520s–ca. 1550

The royal court continued to buy ships from China, but the average size shrunk by about half, almost certainly in connection with the drop in the volume of tribute trade that took place during Shō Shin's reign and accelerated during its final decade.

Period Four: ca. 1550–ca.1570

During this period, the Ryukyuan fleet continued to consist of relatively small ships, possibly even smaller than before. The question is whether Ryukyu continued to purchase ships from China or whether it built its own. The first ship of the designation "small ships of [our?] country" (*honkoku shōsen*) appears in documents in 1541, and ships with this description, as well as other terms with "small" in them, were common from 1549 onward. Okamoto and Tomiyama Kazuyuki regard these ships as having been made in China. However, it is likely that they were civilian merchant ships. Tomiyama points out that in 1555 Shō Sei asked to purchase such a ship from the Ming court with the express proviso that "it need not be large."[30] By contrast, Mamoru Akamine states that during Shō Sei's reign (1527–1555), "the shipbuilding industry shifted to Ryukyu itself and Ryukyuan-built hulls came to be used in the tribute trade."[31] Recall from chapter 3 that Ikuta Shigeru also regarded the smaller ships built after 1548 as Ryukyuan-made vessels.

We cannot be absolutely certain where ships were made during this period or precisely when the first Okinawan-made ship (other than vessels of a relatively simple dugout design) was built. Nevertheless, Okamoto and Tomiyama present good evidence that the 1540s or 1550s marked a transition from smaller military ships to somewhat smaller Chinese-made merchant ships as the mainstay of Ryukyu's fleet. It is likely that the first Okinawan-made ships used in trade and diplomacy were built in the 1570s, during the reign of Shō Ei (r. 1573–1586). In documents, these ships are called "local ships" (*tsuchibune*), "small ships," and possibly by other terms.

Period Five: ca. 1570–1609

It is possible that some Okinawan-made ships were produced before the 1570s. From the late 1570s onward, it appears that most or perhaps all of the ships in the royal fleet were locally made. The last Ryukyuan voyage to Southeast Asia took place in 1570, and the Ming Maritime Prohibitions were significantly relaxed in 1567. European control of the Southeast Asian trading ports and the revival of direct international trade by Chinese merchants undoubtedly even further reduced the volume of Ryukyu's tribute trade. Moreover, Tomiyama points out that as early as the 1540s there was competition, possibly including violence, between Ryukyuan ships and Chinese merchant ships in Southeast Asia. Also, the community at Kumemura had drastically declined by the 1570s. These circumstances influenced the royal fleet, causing it to shrink significantly in terms of total capacity.[32]

The "decorated ships" (*ayabune*) that, as we will see, figured prominently in diplomacy with Japan from the middle of the sixteenth century until 1609, were built in the Chinese manner.[33] Therefore, insofar as some or all of them were made in Okinawa, they were probably copies of the Chinese merchant ships mentioned above.

Locally Manufactured Dugout Vessels

As we have seen, *Omoro* songs often mention ships. One describes the ship of an elite lord (*aji*) as having a cloth sail and the ship of a low official as having a sail made from matting.[34] The details of local boat and ship manufacturing in the Ryukyu islands are unclear in most cases. However, extrapolating backward from the early modern era and piecing together other information such as the *omoro* mentioned here, it is almost certain that early Ryukyuans manufactured boats and small ships (known by *sabani* and other terms). These were dug out from large trees to form canoe-like hulls that could be rowed or sailed. Tying four of these hulls together and placing boards across the top created a *henzabune*, which during the early modern era were sometimes used to transport liquor (*awamori*) to Amami-Ōshima and return with as many as eight head of cattle.³⁵ It is almost certain that Ryukyuans manufactured a variety of dugout vessels for use in local and island-to-island transport between Okinawa, Amami-Ōshima, and other northern Ryukyu islands.

Did Ryukyuans manufacture ships more complex than dugout vessels before the 1570s? A shipbuilding tradition in Uruka in Miyako began in approximately the early fifteenth century and continued into the early modern era. These Uruka ships (*Uruka-miuni*) were built mainly in the Japanese manner by attaching two layers of planks to a keel, with the mast located in the middle of the ship and capable of being lowered during severe weather. Uruka ships conducted trade and transported tribute shipments across the Kerama gap to Okinawa, and Inamura Kenpu regards them as part of the *wakō* legacy in Sakishima.³⁶ There is some evidence that mariners from Miyako were able to sail as far as Southeast Asia during the fourteenth century.³⁷

Shipbuilding and Ryukyu's *Wakō* Legacy

Other than Uruka ships, however, we know little about shipbuilding knowledge and capabilities in Ryukyu before the early modern era. *Omoro* songs sometimes mention shipwrights. In one song, the king gathers shipwrights at Shuri.³⁸ In another, the Kimihae priestess at Kumejima raises a pine tree that a shipwright makes into a vessel.³⁹ It is difficult to determine the level of shipbuilding or maintenance know-how from such sources. In any case, other than Uruka ships, there is little evidence of the manufacture of complex vessels in Ryukyu until the middle of the sixteenth century. This point may seem odd given early Ryukyu's extensive *wakō* legacy. It is important to bear in mind, however, that the Ryukyu islands were not an isolated unit. They were part of the East China Sea network in which ships were manufactured at several locations, including the vicinity of Akune in Kyushu (fig. 8). The nearby Tokara islands functioned as a source of maritime knowledge and skill, and a community of Tokara mariners resided in Naha to help manage commerce and navigation across the treacherous Shichitō-nada through which the Kuroshio current flows.⁴⁰ The apprehended crews of vessels suspected of illegal activities along the China coast around the end of the sixteenth century sometimes consisted of sailors from the Tokara islands, the Ryukyu islands, and sometimes also sailors of Chinese origin.⁴¹

In short, knowledge of shipbuilding and navigation was always present in the Ryukyu islands or readily available from nearby areas. If we consider the period from approximately 1380 to 1570, it is not entirely clear whether local Ryukyuan shipbuilding knowledge and capabilities increased, decreased, or followed a more complex trajectory. Setting aside the case of Uruka ships in Miyako, that ships capable of reaching Japan or China began to be built in Okinawa around the 1570s and possibly earlier may suggest increasing capabilities. On the other hand, reliance on China for large ships and repairs for nearly two centuries likely caused whatever shipbuilding knowledge, skills, and facilities that existed in Okinawa as of circa 1380 to atrophy. Indeed, to bring about such a situation was probably one of the goals of the Ming court.[42] Uehara Takashi points out that the large increase in disabled Ryukyuan ships drifting into the Chinese and Japanese coast from the 1570s onward suggests a serious decline in maritime skills.[43] Ryukyu's economic decline may also have contributed to a declining quality of ships.

Timber resources constituted another limiting factor. The timber to build Uruka ships, for example, probably came not from Miyako but from islands in the Yaeyama group. Okinawan-made ships of the 1570s and later were probably limited by a dearth of large timbers, regardless of whatever other factors may have been at play.[44] During the seventeenth century, Ryukyuans began formally to study shipbuilding in China, and during the eighteenth century Sai On initiated a forestry program capable of producing the lumber necessary to build large ships.

Finally, Ryukyu possessed significant naval capabilities as late as the 1550s, as we will see. Between then and 1609, however, Ryukyu's naval power seems to have faded. There is no indication of any naval warfare involving Ryukyuan ships in 1609.

THE HIKI SYSTEM AND KUMEJIMA

Chinese-made and Chinese-named ships, which also acquired Japanese and Ryukyuan names, were closely connected with the *hiki* system. Consider this *omoro*, which illustrates several preceding points:

> Your majesty
> Fame resounding everywhere
> Deigning to reside in the Gold Island
> In the Eastern Direction
> Your majesty
> Fame resounding everywhere
> Deigning to stay at Shuri grove
> At Madama grove
> As the Solar Deity keeps shining
> May you deign to rule and live [as long as the world may exist]!
> O Kikoe-ōgimi
> Famous and rich in spiritual power

> May you deign to sail the exalted ship Ura-toyomi, Nari-toyomi
> O Kikoe-ōgimi
> May you deign to sail the exalted ship Ura-mawari
> In all the realm
> And may you rule and live as long as the world may exist![45]

Here the sacred groves of Shuri and the power of the king and high priestess reverberate throughout the entire realm via ships. "Gold Island" (*kane no shima*) in the fifth line may also simply mean metal or iron island; the term often indicated Kumejima, with its valuable iron industry. However, in this context, Gold Island also refers to Shuri.[46] Why was Kumejima so closely connected with Shuri during Shō Shin's reign, so much so that it served as the model for Kikoe-ōgimi herself?

A full answer requires further research. It would certainly be helpful, for example, to know Shō En's genuine family tree, even just one generation back. Part of the answer lies in the warfare that took place around 1500, which was connected with *kawara*-lineage *wakō*. This warfare was also connected with the origins of the *hiki*. As we have seen, this term indicates hierarchical organizations that served the king as guards, religious functionaries, palanquin bearers, construction laborers, soldiers, and civil engineers. It was the rank-and-file members of *hiki*, for example, who planted those pine seedlings mentioned in several monuments, and their officers directed the process.

Hiki were named after ships; or possibly, ships were named after *hiki*. The names of several *hiki* appear in the *Omoro* and other sources.[47] Sejiaratomi, for example, is the name of both a *hiki* and a ship. At their core, Ryukyuan military forces were naval forces. The *hiki* of the Shuri-Naha area were organized into three watches on active duty on a rotating basis. In a military emergency, one watch defended Naha, one defended Shuri castle, and one combined with forces from the southern districts to defend the southern shoreline of Naha harbor.[48]

Several local histories produced in the early modern era discuss cases of people brought to Okinawa during Shō Shin's time as prisoners to work at Shuri. One document from Miyako refers to the children of criminals sent to work at shrines in Shuri as *"oyakego"* (reminiscent of Okyake Akahachi). A man from Yaeyama named Nishitō was purportedly a general in the forces opposing Shuri in 1500. Several sources report that he was brought to Shuri as a prisoner and worked for the Council of Three, where he displayed impressive abilities. He was put in charge of constructing a stone gateway for the Sonoyiyabu shrine, a typical *hiki* function. In 1524, Nishitō returned to Yaeyama as Shuri's official in charge of Taketomi island, where he built a version of Sonohiyabu near the storehouse for taxes. There, he initiated formal religious rites praising the king in Shuri.[49] Moreover, household records indicate that the grandfather of a member of the Council of Three came to Okinawa as a prisoner in connection with Shō Sei's invasion of Amami-Ōshima. Later, like Nishitō, this man returned to his home area to serve as a royal government official in charge of Yuwan. Local women working for Shuri also served as the chief priestess in Miyako.[50]

Even though the details of these cases are obscure, it made sense that Shuri would have sought to use people like Nishitō. Unlike Nakasone, Nishitō depended mainly or entirely on Shuri as his source of authority, yet he was local to Yaeyama, where much of the population remained hostile to outside control.[51] Locally influential people from other islands whom Shuri had been able to coopt would have been ideal for service as agents overseeing the empire.

Mainly through an analysis of *Omoro* songs about *hiki*, Makishi Yōko argues that military campaigns by Shuri to subjugate Kumejima, most likely prior to 1500, brought Kumejima's top three priestesses to Shuri and emphasized their military qualities. Prisoners from Kumejima were also incorporated into *hiki* as rank-and-file members. Shō Shin created Kikoe-ōgimi as a figure who embodied all three of these Kumejima priestesses and their power.[52] Clearly the military campaign or campaigns in Kumejima had a large impact not only on that island but on the formation of Ryukyu's empire, its officials, and its capital. In addition to economic and political reasons for invading Kumejima, Shō Shin also sought to conquer and appropriate the spiritual and symbolic power of the island.

CHAPTER ELEVEN

The Ryukyu Empire

By the late 1520s, the Ryukyu islands had become an empire with Shuri at its center. From Kikai and Amami-Ōshima in the northeast to Yonaguni in the southwest, Shō Shin and Shō Sei's Ryukyu spanned approximately a thousand kilometers from east to west and approximately five hundred kilometers north to south. This geographic span corresponds to Tokyo in the northeast to Fukuoka in the southwest.[1] The territory was a potential source of strength for the royal government, which extracted taxes ("tribute") from it. Because this expanse of territory did not constitute an organic political unit, however, some parts of the empire required frequent attention. Ryukyu as an empire consisted of territory united by military conquest and governed by officials loyal to Shuri.

Governing an area that large required written documents and centralized records. It should not be surprising, therefore, that our earliest extant written product of a centralized bureaucracy dates from 1529, at the end of Shō Shin's reign. The document is a *jireisho*, a writ of appointment for an official in Kasari (Amami-Ōshima). Tens of thousands of these documents would have been produced over the course of the sixteenth century, but less than 1 percent are extant. *Jireisho* all begin with "Orders of Shuri" (*Shiyori no o-mikoto*). Such language is one manifestation of the truly central role that Shuri began to play during Shō Shin's reign.[2] Indeed, the Ryukyu empire could also be called the Shuri empire.

The purpose of this chapter is to examine key aspects of the Ryukyu empire. First, I examine relationships between the capital and outlying areas, with a focus on Amami-Ōshima. The next topic is military power, warfare, and military campaigns in Amami-Ōshima. Subsequently, I consider definitions of empire as applied to sixteenth-century Ryukyu. Finally, I examine Ryukyu's military infrastructure as it had developed by approximately 1550 and compare it with military capabilities at the start of the seventeenth century.

SHURI'S ISLAND OFFICIALS

The official histories place the Ryukyu empire much further back into the past than Shō Shin's reign. Therefore, when Shō Shin and Nakasone invaded and conquered Yaeyama in 1500, *Kyūyō* and other official sources describe it in terms of putting down a revolt by local brigands. Certainly, informal relationships of travel, commerce, and competition connected the Ryukyu islands well before 1500, and we have seen repeatedly that the Ryukyu islands were part of a larger network. Firm political control over the various Ryukyu islands from the center at Shuri, however, was an early sixteenth-century development.

We have seen that soon after 1500 Shuri eliminated the power of Nakasone and his family and appointed its own agents to govern the major southwestern islands. Moreover, according to *Kyūyō*, Shuri also appointed priestesses in Yaeyama in 1500 and Miyako three years later. Both were local women who went to Shuri to receive their appointments.[3] Even if the many details in the *Kyūyō* accounts about the piety and loyalty of these women are embellishments, the basic point is that Shuri moved quickly to appoint agents and implant institutions of control in the conquered territory.

Possible conquest of northern territories during Shō Shin's reign is less clear. According to the official histories, Shō Sei invaded Amami-Ōshima in 1537, and Shō Gen did so in 1571. Recall that one song in the original first volume of the *Omoro* indicates that Shō Shin conquered Kasari in Amami-Ōshima.[4] We have no major corroborating evidence, but as we have seen, household records place Tameharu in the Kasari area in 1506 as Shuri's agent. He appears in several different records, all of which agree that Tameharu "came from main Ryukyu" (Okinawa), that he died in Chūzan (Okinawa) at age sixty-one, and that his wife was from Okinawa.[5] The Ushuku-ōya household records date its second generation of Shuri's agents in charge of Ushuku (Kasari district) as receiving appointment from the Chūzan court in 1528. The first generation has no specific date, but the household founder was appointed as Shuri's agent in charge of Ushuku, almost certainly placing him within Shō Shin's reign.[6] The records of the Kishitō-Ueekata lineage place its founder in Kasari district around 1522. He frequently visited the Chūzan king, eventually attained high status, and his descendants "also prospered in Ryukyu"—that is, in Okinawa.[7] Around 1526, Hanagusuku Masaburō arrived in Yoron from Shuri to govern that island.[8] In short, during approximately the 1520s, Shō Shin installed Shuri loyalists as male and female officials throughout all or most of the Ryukyu islands.

Renkanshi, an 1825 history of officials in Amami-Ōshima, describes the basic system that prevailed before 1609. It states that during the Wànlì era (1573–1620), the "Shuri emperor" (*Shuri-tei*) ordered that people of Ueekata and Peechin status govern Amami-Ōshima. There were seven illustrious households on the island, and they sent children to Shuri to serve in the castle. After they grew up, they were appointed as officials of *ōya* (or *ōyako*) rank, each placed in charge of one district (*magiri*) (fig. 4). Below them were assistant officials known as *yohito*.[9] The usual titles for district officials in the northern Ryukyu islands in descending rank order were *Shuri-ōyako, ōyako, okite*, and *mezashi*. The relatively late date of the "imperial" order in *Renkanshi* may be a misunderstanding or a segue into the 1609 war, which is the next topic. It may also, however, hint at change during the 1570s, which I discuss later.

Looking more closely at the comparatively well-documented Kasari lineage, it seems to follow this pattern. Tameharu came to Amami-Ōshima in 1506 at age twenty-three, according to the records. Apprenticing sons to a powerful official in Shuri served educational purposes and instilled in them an orientation toward the capital. Tamemitsu (1508–ca.1568) served as an apprentice to Prince Nakagusuku in Shuri and assumed duties in Amami-Ōshima as *ōyako* in Higa (Setouchi Higashi) district in 1533.[10] His wife appears to have been a local woman, daughter of the head of Beru Village in Kasari district.[11]

Tameaki, the third-generation lineage head, also went to Okinawa as a youth. There, he received the yellow cap, a formal marker of high status, and worked as a "servant to the emperor" in Shuri castle. The language of the main record is classical Chinese, and the term for the monarch here is *tiānzǐ* (J. *tenshi*), "son of heaven." There are numerous ways in which Amami-Ōshima household records refer to the king, but it was not unusual for his title to be some variation of "emperor." Tameaki was appointed *ōyako* in Kasari district in 1568, during the reign of Shō Gen.[12] Notice that in addition to the apprenticeship in Shuri, the lineage members served in different districts. The apprenticeships at Shuri castle and the assignment to different districts helped maintain an orientation toward the political center of the empire.

Tameyoshi, the adopted son of Tameaki, was the next lineage head. He set sail for Okinawa to request that he inherit Tameaki's position, and there he "received the yellow cap from the emperor." As he was returning to Amami-Ōshima, without warning a violent wind blew away his ship, never to be seen again. Tameyoshi had a "legitimate son," Tamekoro, in Shuri studying at Enkakuji, who at age thirteen became an apprentice at Shuri castle. "After that," he returned to Amami-Ōshima to take charge of Ushuku in Kasari district. In 1588, Tamekoro became ōyako in Higashi (Setouchi) district and later Kasari district. When did Tameyoshi disappear? Piecing together information from different records, it seems that Tamekoro was born in 1570, and "because he had been orphaned, he went to Shuri at age nine to reside and study at Enkakuji."[13] It is highly likely, therefore, that Tameyoshi met his tragic end in approximately 1579.

The second-generation head of the Ushuku-ōya lineage, Chiyagumori, held several ōyako posts during the Jiājìng era (1521–1566). His son, Inutarugane, also met a tragic end in 1579. He was on his way to Shuri to receive an additional appointment, but his ship encountered a violent storm and was blown away to parts unknown. Moreover, Inutarugane had a son, Omotarugane (or Umitarugane), who had been studying diligently at Enkakuji. After hearing of his father's tragic fate, Omotarugane returned to Amami-Ōshima.[14]

Notice that two ōyako-level officials appointed at the time of Shō Gen vanished at sea around 1579. The language describing their fates is nearly identical. Given that local rulers traveled back and forth to Shuri, they were exposing themselves to the dangers of a sea voyage, albeit within a relatively safe zone. If indeed a sudden wind swept their ships away it would have been a noteworthy event, because in the household records only one other local official met with such an end. In other words, I have found only three cases of ships vanishing during this era or earlier. Is it possible that both Tameyoshi and Inutarugane were on the same ship? Possibly, except the records describe Tameyoshi as returning from Shuri and Inutarugane as traveling to Shuri.[15]

As for the third case, when Umi-Kyōtaru of the Shidama lineage sailed to Shuri to pay his respects to the Ryukyuan king after being appointed ōyako in Higashi district, his ship also encountered sudden violent winds and was never found. This record lacks dates. However, Umi-Kyōtaru came along two generations after someone active during the 1530s, and he was three generations back from someone who was alive in 1673 (no terminal dates). It is entirely possible, therefore, that Umi-Kyōtaru disappeared around 1579.[16]

Shō Ei, on the throne since sometime in 1573, received investiture in 1579. He had consolidated his power and was actively repairing a rift between Satsuma and Ryukyu that had taken place during the confusing period of transition from Shō Gen. Moreover, in 1574, Shuri ordered detailed land reorganization in Nishi (Setouchi) district in Amami-Ōshima. Between 1577 and 1579, it had appointed *ōyako*-level officials in each of five districts of Amami-Ōshima with harbors.[17] Is it possible that Tameyoshi, Inuratugane, and Umi-Kyōtaru were purged in the late 1570s? The evidence is entirely circumstantial, and I as far as I can tell, extant documents do not permit a full reconstruction of official appointments in Michinoshima during the 1570s and later. Too many *jireisho* are missing. Furthermore, as we have seen, the 1570s were the beginning of a period of several decades during which maritime mishaps involving Ryukyuan ships increased. On the other hand, we know that Shō Ei's government began to move in a pro-Satsuma direction during the late 1570s. As a matter for further inquiry, I raise the possibility that a substantial reorganization of Amami-Oshima took place in this context. It may also be significant that during the war, Shuri's military forces in Michinoshima fought vigorously only on Tokunoshima, not Amami-Ōshima, where the successors (or replacements?) of Tameyoshi and Inuratugane surrendered immediately and fared well under Satsuma's rule.

SHURI'S MILITARY POWER

A 1493 entry in *Joseon Veritable Royal Records* describes a Ryukyuan envoy to Korea reporting that Ryukyuan forces "have prevailed in eight or nine out of ten battles," with forces from Satsuma trying to encroach on Amami-Ōshima.[18] At the other end of the empire a few years later, *Kyūyō* describes the invasion of Yaeyama in detail. For example, a general named Ōzato led a contingent of forty-six ships that broke into two squads. One attacked Tōno gusuku and the other attacked Arakawa (possibly the southern shore of Nagura bay). Unable to respond effectively to this two-pronged attack, Akahachi went down in defeat.[19] Whether the account in either text is accurate we cannot say. In a general way, however, these passages indicate Shuri's capacity to project military force to distant locations.

Roughly thirty years later, Chén Kǎn discussed Ryukyuan weapons. "Both their blade weapons and archery weapons are strong and sharp. Bows are slightly longer than those used in China." Two hands were required to remove an arrow that had been shot into the ground. The range of arrows was two hundred steps. Armor was made of leather, and gongs and drums regulated military retreats and advances. "Neighboring countries regard[ed] Ryukyu as a strong opponent."[20]

In 1556, Chinese military forces had repulsed a *wakō* force that attacked Zhejiang Province (number of ships not specified). Driven off from its primary objective, the force sailed for Ryukyu. The new king, Shō Gen, sent his navy to intercept it. According to *Ming Veritable Records*, the Ryukyuan force crushed the pirates, rescued six Chinese who had been captured earlier, and returned them with the next tribute voyage.[21] A message from the Chinese emperor to Shō Gen preserved in *Rekidai hōan* summarizes the battle. When the *wakō* entered Ryukyuan waters, Ba Hitsudo (Mǎ Bìdù) and others "projected fire" into the *wakō* vessel or vessels. In subsequent fighting, the Ryukyuan forces killed most of the pirates and rescued Chinese captives. The emperor praised the "loyal labor" of the "crown prince" (Shō Gen had not yet been invested) and sent silver to reward the Ryukyuan sailors.[22]

In official records, Ryukyuan military forces typically defeat pirates decisively and valiantly, and it is unclear precisely what happened during the 1556 battle. Regardless of the details, the battle nicely illustrates Ryukyu's sixteenth-century transformation. Recall the 1452 order from the Ministry of Justice prohibiting residents of the Fujian coast from "dealings with Ryukyu by ship and serving as guides for pirates."[23] The Ryukyu of the 1450s was a collection of local powers comprised, in many cases, of pirates or potential pirates. A century later, in contrast, Ryukyu was a centralized kingdom that possessed an empire whose broad interests coincided with those of other states in the region, and Ryukyu occasionally took up arms against pirates. These pirates were the latter-period *wakō*, who consisted mainly of Chinese and Japanese with a variety of other ethnic groups in the mix.

Although Ryukyuan defenses could respond effectively to a clear attack, Ryukyuan authorities were not able to prevent large groups of armed Japanese merchants, de facto *wakō*, from pouring into Naha in 1579 and 1606 and intimidating members of the Chinese investiture embassy. As we have seen, these merchants were necessary because the investiture embassies would not leave Naha until they had sold all of their merchandise.[24] The standard protocol since Shō Gen's reign, and probably earlier, was that when ships authorized by Satsuma arrived in Naha, harbor officials stored their weapons until their departure. In connection with Shō Ei's investiture in 1579, vice envoy Xiè Jié noted that hundreds of Japanese waited for the arrival of the Chinese ships. They set up markets, came and went freely armed with swords, and intimidated local people. Satsuma dispatched Yamashita Chikugo to Naha in 1579 to gather intelligence. He observed that Ryukyuan officials appeared powerless to control the situation. One of Satsuma's goals was to sever this connection between Ryukyu and *wakō* and to gain control of shipping between Japan and Ryukyu.[25] Notice that, once again, albeit in a different context than in earlier centuries, *wakō* activities helped to shape Ryukyuan history.

WARFARE IN THE NORTH

Kyūyō has much to say about the warfare in Yaeyama and its aftermath, but its coverage of warfare in Michinoshima is comparatively sparse. Official histories record Shō Sei invading Amami-Ōshima in 1537 and Shō Gen doing so in 1571. However, they are sufficiently inconsistent regarding details that it is difficult to garner a clear picture of the sixteenth-century military situation in the north.[26]

One reason *Kyūyō* discusses Shō Sei's invasion only briefly may be to avoid dwelling on a royal error. Although he was actually loyal to Shuri, "the other chieftains" accused local official Yuwan of plotting rebellion, and as a result Shō Sei invaded. "Because Ōshima is so far across the sea, it is difficult for the king to distinguish between truth and falsehood," *Kyūyō* states. In the typical dramatic fashion of the official histories, Yuwan is said to have looked up to Heaven and declared his innocence before killing himself. His son was taken to Shuri as a prisoner and his descendants later became the Ba noble family. The text is vague, but the son himself "achieved military accomplishments" and returned to Amami-Ōshima to reclaim his father's legacy or territory.[27] The 1725 *Genealogy of Chūzan* contains exactly the same account.[28] If reliable, it appears that Shō Sei intervened in a dispute between local rulers. If the military accomplishments of Yuwan's son were connected with his return, there may have been two rounds of fighting.

Reflections on Chūzan and the 1701 *Genealogy* provide a somewhat different story. *Reflections* states that, in 1535 a report arrived that the "Ōshima northern barbarians" (*hokui Ōshima*) had rebelled, and the king determined to oppose the uprising in the manner of his predecessor, Shō Toku. Shō Sei led three generals northward with an invasion force of fifty ships. After the fleet arrived in Naze harbor, the rebels surrendered without a fight, which reflected the king's sagacious moral power. Or so the text asserts. However, in the midst of pacifying the island, the king fell gravely ill. Council of Three member Kunigami implored Heaven to take his life instead of the king's. The king recovered and sailed back to Naha safely. Kunigami sickened and died, and the king wept.[29] We will see this story again.

There is extensive local lore about the war. Kanehisa Tadashi has collected different versions and condensed the common elements into a core plot. The Guriya family and the Nangumori family were rivals in southern Amami-Ōshima. The Guriya benefited from royal favoritism because the king (or a high minister) had become smitten by a beautiful *noro* from the Guriya serving at the court in Shuri. Resenting the situation, the Nangumori joined forces with Nagara Hachimaru of Uken. They repeatedly interdicted "tribute" (tax) payments bound for Shuri, but when a royal military force arrived, Nangumori and Nagara used their knowledge of the complex local geography to flee in small boats to remote islands and remain in hiding long enough to cause the Okinawan force to become frustrated and withdraw. Victorious, Nangumori and Nagara seized power over a large part of Amami-Ōshima, prompting a second, larger invasion. This time, the Okinawan force pretended to withdraw in order to lure the Nangumori leaders out of hiding, and then quickly returned to destroy them.[30]

We cannot verify the details of these legendary accounts or the versions of events found in the official histories. I would point out that Guriya and Nagara are Gaara lineage names associated with *wakō* groups. All accounts mention shipments of tribute to Shuri. If indeed their interdiction caused the invasion, then by Shō Sei's time Shuri was extracting taxes from Amami-Ōshima in a formal manner. A household record from the Shidama lineage refers to Shuri's opponents as brigands or traitors (C. *zéi*, J. *zoku*) and includes the story about the beautiful *noro* and the seizing of tribute. It ends by stating that the invasion returned governance to its proper path and pleased the people. Another result of the war was that male children of local rulers could "return" to Shuri and take charge of one of the seven districts after becoming adults.[31] Based on the approximate timing that we can glean from household records, it is possible that the practice of sending sons to Shuri as apprentices became formalized during Shō Sei's reign. As with so many aspects of early Ryukyuan history, many details are lost to us, but clearly some kind of struggle between local powers in Amami-Ōshima and Shuri took place during Shō Sei's reign, probably resulting in modifications of Shuri's governance system.

I have found no evidence of Shō Gen's 1571 invasion of Amami-Ōshima in local household records. If that war did happen, perhaps it was a defeat for Shuri, or at least less than a full victory. Moreover, it may have killed Shō Gen. According to *Genealogy* and *Kyūyō*, after the death of Yuwan ōya, Shuri's agent in Amami-Ōshima, his colleagues rose in revolt and refused to pay tribute. Shō Gen personally led an invasion force that totaled fifty ships. After several battles, the rebel leaders were defeated and beheaded, and the king appointed a new local leader, thus "putting the common people at ease." Insofar as Yuwan was loyal to Shuri and the other local officials rebelled, the account of the alleged 1571 invasion reads like a repeat of 1537. That is not the only repetition.

Genealogy and *Kyūyō* also point out that Shō Gen became ill while in Amami-Ōshima. Council of Three member Ba Juntoku (Kunigami Ueekata Seikaku) formally implored Heaven to take his life in exchange for that of the king. The king recovered and returned to Okinawa, but Ba soon died. Out of gratitude for this loyal deed, the king ordered that Ba's descendants hold the title Kunigami Aji.[32] Of course, this sequence is precisely what happened to Shō Sei in 1537 according to *Reflections*. Moreover, the official who sacrificed himself for Shō Gen was a descendant of the Kunigami Ueekata who purportedly saved Shō Sei's life. Perhaps the 1571 invasion never happened. Or perhaps both the 1537 and 1571 invasions were sufficiently problematic or unsavory that at least one official account saw fit to transfer the king's real or symbolic invasion-related illness to a loyal official.[33]

In any case, Shō Gen died soon thereafter. Kuroshima Satoru proposes the most likely scenario is that Shō Gen was wounded on the battlefield and ultimately died of those wounds. He might even have died in Amami-Ōshima. Kuroshima hypothesizes that the story of Ba Juntoku was part of an attempt to delay announcing the king's death. When Ryukyu sent a belated diplomatic embassy to Satsuma in 1575, the envoys presenting King Shō Ei's diplomatic letter to Satsuma stressed that Shō Gen's death had thrown the country into confusion.[34] Kuroshima's speculation makes sense, if the 1571 invasion actually took place. However, no mention of it appears in extant household records, and the official histories present the event as a replay of the Yuwan versus evil local officials story of the previous generation. It is certainly possible that an older conflict flared up again and followed a similar trajectory. Given the many uncertainties, however, I would draw only the broad conclusion that some kind of intervention or interventions by Shuri, possibly only of an administrative nature, occurred in Amami-Ōshima during the 1570s.

TRIBUTE

The "tribute" that Ryukyu regularly sent to China was an investment, not a tax. The shipments of tribute from the other Ryukyu islands to Shuri, although described by the same word in official documents, were tax payments. Did the common people who ultimately paid such taxes derive any benefit from it? Official documents claim or imply that they received good government. That imperial subjects are better off under "our" rule is a standard claim of imperial centers. I am not aware of any way to test this claim in the case of Ryukyu. Moreover, we know little about the details of taxation before 1609. We do, however, have a window into this important realm.

Ryūkyū shintōki author Taichū stayed in Okinawa between 1603 and 1606. He recorded tribute-ship arrivals for one of his years in residence (which one is unclear) and the goods they brought to Shuri. In descending order of the total number of ships, they are:

[Amami-]Ōshima (twenty ships): newly made tools, liquor, vegetables, and tax rice;
Miyako (eighteen ships): superior cloth, lesser cloth, coarse hemp, and rope for ships;
Yaeyama (ten ships): white rice, barley;
Kumejima (nine ships): cotton cloth, millet (*awa*), and millet (*kibi*);
Kikai (five ships): polished rice, millet (*hie*), and buckwheat.[35]

It is possible that the Amami-Ōshima ships included items from other northern Ryukyu islands. There is no mention of the quantities of goods or the size of the ships, but it is likely that these sixty-two ships bringing goods to Shuri made a significant contribution to royal wealth.

For the most part, we do not know the details of how an item like "tax rice" was collected and processed. Several detailed *jireisho* from 1574, however, provide a glimpse. One deals with reorganization of the wet-field holdings of someone called Netachi of Sukomo on Kakeroma Island (part of Setouchi Nishi district in Amami-Ōshima). Leaving out some details, the royal court reallocated nearly a dozen plots of land, apparently to rectify a gap between Netachi's expected tax payments and his (or her) actual productive capabilities. The document also specifies that one-third of the fields were exempt from taxation, and the others were taxed at a fixed rate. In 1574, Shuri also issued similar documents for other parts of the district. These *jireisho* indicate that officials in Shuri possessed detailed land and productivity records and that they paid close attention to tax accounting.[36]

EMPIRE

Based on what we have seen in this and previous chapters, consider the following brief definition from *Empires,* Michael W. Doyle's classic work. An empire is "a relationship, formal or informal, in which one state controls the effective political sovereignty of another political society. It can be achieved by force, by political collaboration, by economic, social, or cultural dependence."[37] How would sixteenth-century Ryukyu appear in light of this definition?

Let us make the reasonable assumption that Okinawa, with Shuri at its political center, constituted a state, which sources of the time typically called "main-Ryukyu" or simply "Ryukyu." The other islands, or possibly subdivisions of them, constituted different political societies. From about 1500 onward, the domains of Oyake Akahachi, Nakasone Toyomiya, Onitora, and the lord of Gushikawa in Kumejima fell to the military forces of Shuri, sometimes with assistance from allies. In the end, Shuri was the only state left standing. As we have seen, it developed a system for leveraging "economic, social, or cultural dependence." By Doyle's definition, the sixteenth-century Ryukyu kingdom looks like an empire.

The process whereby Shuri emerged as the sole political center closely resembles the general empire-building process described by Jane Burbank and Frederick Cooper:

> The only way for a would-be king or tribal leader to become more powerful is to expand—taking animals, money, slaves, land, or other forms of wealth from outside his realm rather than from insiders whose support he needs. Once this externalization of sources of wealth begins, outsiders may see advantages in submitting to a powerful and effective conqueror. Emboldened kings or tribal leaders can then use their new subordinates to collect resources in a regular—not raiding—way and to facilitate the incorporation of new peoples, territories, and trade routes without imposing uniformity in culture or administration.[38]

Recall Ikuta Shigeru's point in chapter 2 that the trade in people at Naha likely functioned to keep tax extractions on local residents low during the fifteenth century. "Externalization of sources of wealth" well describes the creation of a Shuri-centered empire, a centralized monarchy, and the co-opting of local agents to work for Shuri. The transition from *wakō*-like government to a centralized bureaucracy went hand in hand with collecting "resources in a regular—not raiding—way." Finally, although local officials in Amami-Ōshima, and elsewhere, were often socialized and educated in the empire's center, there is no evidence that Shuri made any attempt to impose cultural uniformity or identical governmental structures on the population of the Ryukyu islands.

Was Ryukyu an empire within an empire? In other words, was Shuri's relationship to the Ming court similar to that of the other Ryukyu islands to Shuri? The short answer is no. Of course, vis-à-vis China, the ruler of Ryukyu positioned himself ritually and rhetorically as a vassal of the

Ming empire. In return for ritual subordination, the Ryukyu kings gained wealth and prestige, which helped them create and then maintain their empire. Certainly, China was in a position to exert influence on Ryukyu after its kings had come to depend on investiture and the tribute trade. On the other hand, except for the era of Bunei, Shō Shishō, and Shō Hashi, the Ming court did not insert itself into Ryukyu's domestic politics, nor did it control Ryukyu's foreign policy. Obviously the same could not be said for Shuri's relationship with the other Ryukyu islands.

Is it possible that the Ryukyu islands as a whole did not consist of disparate political communities but instead constituted an organic political community? In other words, is it possible that the entire Ryukyu islands constituted what in modern terms we could call a nation-state? Setting aside the cultural landscape, the extensive warfare needed to create Shuri's empire and to hold it together is a strong indication that the Ryukyu islands did not comprise a natural political community.

There is a tendency to regard empires as large and powerful. Ryukyu was large in the sense of sheer expanse, and during the first half of the sixteenth century it possessed significant wealth and military capabilities. Nevertheless, here size and power are largely beside the point; what matters is the nature of the relationship between Shuri and the other territories under its control. Based on what we have seen thus far, I argue that it is appropriate to regard the sixteenth-century Ryukyu kingdom as an island empire.

MILITARY INFRASTRUCTURE

In this chapter and several others, we have examined the extensive warfare that took place in early Ryukyu. In this section I examine Shuri's overall military organization, weapons, and infrastructure. In the interest of brevity, rather than describing the origins of Shuri's military forces, here I mainly describe those forces as they stood at approximately 1550. I also compare that situation to Ryukyu's military capacities on the eve of the war with Satsuma.

The previously discussed *hiki* system was the core of Shō Shin's new military organization. Recall that *hiki* were organizational structures that pulled together hundreds of people to provide military, labor, and civil engineering functions. Structurally, four *hiki* constituted each of three watches. It is possible that the heads of these three watches evolved into the Council of Three.[39] *Hiki* were multifunctional organizations. They helped build the military infrastructure around Naha (fig. 17) and served as rapidly deployable land or sea military forces.[40]

Figure

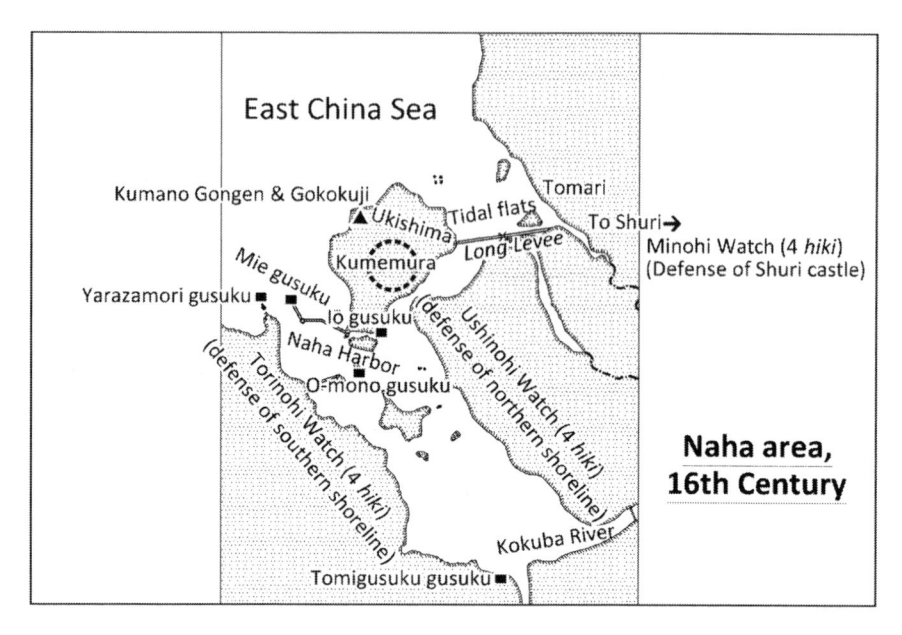

```
                        East China Sea

        Kumano Gongen & Gokokuji
                          Ukishima  Tidal flats  Tomari
                                          To Shuri →
                    Mie gusuku  Kumemura  Long Levee
        Yarazamori gusuku ■                        Minohi Watch (4 hiki)
                            Io gusuku              (Defense of Shuri castle)
                         Naha Harbor
                          O-mono gusuku
                                                    Naha area,
                                                    16th Century
                                        Kokuba River
                    Tomigusuku gusuku ■
```

Fig. 17. Naha area, sixteenth century

In conjunction with these rapid deployment networks, Shō Shin sought to strengthen the underlying military infrastructure, a policy his immediate successors continued. He established a central armory near Naha harbor and constructed a wall across the northern face of Shuri castle. In 1522 Shō Shin built the Madama road to facilitate the deployment and supply of the military forces around Naha. At about the same time, he established an official to oversee artillery deployment and technology. Shō Sei extended the network of defensive walls around Shuri castle, and this work was complete by 1546. He also constructed Yarazamori gusuku and Mie gusuku as artillery platforms to defend the entrance into Naha harbor. Located at either end of the narrow mouth of the harbor, these two fortresses also functioned as anchors for the two ends of a large metal chain that could block ships from entering. Yarazamori gusuku featured sixteen gun ports. In terms of function, these fortresses resembled the *daiba* artillery platforms built much later in Edo bay. In terms of structure, Yarazamori gusuku closely resembled the Chinese Penglai Water Castle (Pénglái shuǐchéng) off of the Shandong coast. Although *gusuku* in early Ryukyu often served as military fortresses, Shō Sei created a new type of *gusuku* that was exclusively military in function.[41]

As part of the centralizing policies we have seen in detail, Shō Shin and Shō Sei hardened the central state infrastructure against military attack. Concentrating military capability at the center fits logically with the larger project of these kings, but it carried potential risks. An invasion force approaching from any other avenue than through Naha harbor would have faced few obstacles. Another problem was that, although the harbor defenses worked well against an obvious attack, they were not effective in regulating the swarms of armed merchants who gathered in Naha whenever Chinese envoys arrived.

The infrastructure that resulted from an overwhelming focus on protecting the Shuri-Naha area from overt military attack was a network of fortresses connected by the Madama road. In addition to Yarazamori gusuku and Mie gusuku, Iō gusuku (Sulfur fortress), nearby but located deeper within the harbor, functioned as the main arsenal, distributing weapons to the *hiki* soldiers as they assembled at their defensive positions. Tomigusuku gusuku, deep inside the harbor, was the command and control center. Madama road connected these fortresses to each other and to Shuri castle (fig. 17).[42]

Ryukyu manufactured some of its own weapons and acquired others from China and especially Japan. There is abundant evidence that Ryukyuans traded in weapons between these places, most commonly bringing Japanese swords to China, where they were in great demand.[43] Ryukyuans often made adaptations to foreign weapons. For example, many sword blades came from Japan, but the handles were of Ryukyuan design to facilitate wielding with one hand.[44]

Moving ahead to the eve of the war with Satsuma, Ryukyu's major port was well fortified and defended by artillery pieces. The *hiki* in Okinawa were able to muster a force totaling as many as three thousand soldiers on relatively short notice.[45] Ryukyuan swords were of effective design. Moreover, albeit in a haphazard manner, during the years just before 1609, Ryukyu had been storing up weapons and making some preparations for warfare. Its arsenal included bows, arrows, swords, pikes, halberds, and small-bore personal firearms. Ryukyuan forces also possessed armor, cavalry horses, and signal banners.[46]

Investiture envoy Xià Zǐyáng regarded Ryukyu as militarily unprepared for a likely war with Japanese forces. Writing in 1606, he noted that Ryukyuan swords and armor were "hard and sharp." However, pikes were weak and mainly for decoration. The length of bows was approximately the width of house eves. Although arrows hitting the ground required the use of both arms to pull out, the arrows did not travel very far.[47] The extent to which Xià studied Ryukyuan weapons or had the requisite knowledge to evaluate them is not clear, but he was impressed only with the swords.

Ryukyu possessed significant military power until the middle of the sixteenth century. On the eve of Satsuma's invasion, Ryukyu was superficially the same in terms of its military capabilities, except that its ships had become fewer and less capable. In fact, however, the situation was far worse. The Ryukyuan armies of 1609 were of Muromachi-era vintage in terms of their equipment. They consisted of five archers to every two soldiers armed with firearms. By contrast, the archers-to-musket bearers ratio of the invading Satsuma force was one-to-seven. Perhaps more important, other than the large artillery pieces, Ryukyuan firearms proved nearly useless in battle against Satsuma forces. Circa 1500, Ryukyuan firearms had been effective weapons. By 1609, however, soldiers were still using *hiyaa*, the same type of firearms they used a century or more earlier. *Hiyaa* might be effective against fixed targets such as the household compound at the center of the 1592 revolt described in chapter 8, but not against mobile invaders. By contrast, soldiers in the Shimazu forces carried the latest firearms and were experienced in their use.[48]

A final consideration regarding Ryukyuan military ability is spiritual power. The hierarchy of priestesses and new rituals that Shō Shin and Shō Sei created were part of both the process of centralization and the defense of the center. It is quite likely, as we will see, that Ryukyuan officials were willing to oppose Satsuma and defy the Tokugawa *bakufu* because of confidence in Ryukyu as a *shinkoku*, a land protected by its deities. The king's forces had prevailed, or appeared to have prevailed, in every battle since 1500. Therefore, correlation between military success and the new religious system was strong, and people routinely mistake correlation for causality. It made some sense, therefore, for officials in Okinawa to have been confident to a fault regarding divine protection.

CHAPTER TWELVE

Politics and Religion

We have seen politics, religion, and society inextricably linked throughout most of this book. The purpose of this chapter is to interrupt the narrative and examine the religious infrastructure that Shō Shin created and his successors refined. I argue that Kikoe-ōgimi subsumed within one person, but did not eliminate, an older pattern of three sister priestesses. Likewise, Benzaiten became the divine counterpart of Kikoe-ōgimi and therefore the supreme protector deity of Ryukyu. Benzaiten subsumed within herself, or manifested herself as, triple sets of deities. One of these deities was the enigmatic Demon Deity associated with the Second Shō dynasty.

BUDDHISM

Ryukyu's temples were either Shingon or Rinzai Zen. Until approximately the sixteenth century, all or most of their abbots and priests came from Japan. During Shō Shin's reign, native Ryukyuan priests became increasingly common, although the leadership posts in large temples typically remained in the hands of priests from Japan. As part of their training, Ryukyuan priests often resided in Japan. Therefore, Buddhist temples constituted an important network linking Ryukyu with Japan. Geographically, the most important of these priest-mediated connections to locations in Japan were Kagoshima, Suō Province in western Honshu (the domain of the Ōuchi), and especially the Kyoto Gozan temples.

Buddhist priests served as Ryukyu's diplomats to powers in Japan, and they typically drafted and transmitted diplomatic correspondence.

Because well-trained Buddhist priests could write classical Chinese, they were also in a position to facilitate trade and diplomacy with China. When in 1525 Ryukyu intervened to reduce tensions between Japan and China, priests served as the envoys. During the sixteenth century, priests performed many of the functions that resident Chinese had performed in the previous century. Recall that the population of Kumemura declined significantly during the sixteenth century.

Priests with diplomatic experience sometimes served as foreign-policy or general political advisers. For example, it is likely that the Ryukyuan Rinzai priest Kakuō (dates unknown) of Tenkaiji served as a political adviser to Shō Sei circa the 1530s.[1] We have seen that the Satsuma Rinzai priest Nanpo Bunshi was an influential political adviser and diplomat during the years leading up to the 1609 war. When that war broke out, the king called on the Ryukyuan priest Kikuin (d. 1620) to serve as lead negotiator, in part because he had lived in Satsuma and was on good terms with Bunshi and several leaders of the invading force. Trusted by both Satsuma and the king, Kikuin served as Ryukyu's prime minster (*kokusō*) until 1616.

Buddhist temples functioned as academic centers that could provide knowledge and know-how to Ryukyuan rulers. Priests were involved in culture, scholarship, and essential functions of state. Their activities included inscribing Shō Taikyū's bells, creating the *Omoro sōshi* by writing down the songs, inscribing many of the monuments of Shō Shin and his successors, and drafting letters from the king to send to powers in Japan. During the sixteenth century, Buddhist priests served as tutors to elite Ryukyuans, Kaiin being the outstanding example (chapter 8). Moreover, we have seen that Enkakuji played a role in the education of the sons of elite families in Amami-Ōshima, and it likely functioned similarly vis-à-vis other islands.

Although Buddhism, Chinese thought, and native religion often occupied separate textual, rhetorical, and ritual realms, Shō Shin and his successors combined all three into a potent synthesis to enhance royal authority and defend the state. Some priests undoubtedly pursued Buddhist enlightenment through their own study and practice. Nevertheless, Buddhism in Ryukyu functioned mainly as a public state institution, not as a private spiritual path.

SONS OF THE SUN

The *Omoro* abounds with terms for the sun and solar deities. We have also seen that the solar religion of the *Omoro* has deep roots in the East China

Sea network, especially in Tsushima and the Tokara Islands.² Late twentieth-century scholarship on native Okinawan religious ideas and their political implications often considered outside influences. For example, in separate essays Higa Minoru and Nakamura Akira pointed out that substituting the word "Heaven" (C. *tiān*, O. *teni*) in the *Omoro* for *teda* (sun) is almost always possible.³ China Teikan and Sakima Toshikatsu have highlighted Buddhist influences on the *Omoro*.⁴ More broadly, these and other scholars have debated the nature of *wakateda shisō*, veneration of the vigorous, rising "young sun," and of *tedako shisō*, the idea that the king is a "son-of-the-sun." The main issue was whether they coexisted or whether the former gave way to the latter during the reigns of Shō Shin and Shō Sei.

Albeit with significant variation, it was once common for scholars to point out that the son-of-the-sun idea, combined with the notion that the king's sister, as Kikoe-ōgimi, functioning as his protector, implied the king's dependence on priestesses for his spiritual power. I have examined these matters at length in earlier work, and I refrain from recapitulating the discussion here because this formulation is out of date.⁵

The work of Yoshinari Naoki and Fuku Hiromi has shed new light on the realm of religion and politics in early Ryukyu. For example, the ability to substitute "Heaven" for "sun" probably reflects the idea of the heavenly realm of Obotsu-Kagura, which we have traced northward to the Korean Peninsula and beyond. The *Omoro* frequently refers to kings and local lords as some kind of *"teda,"* and powerful priestesses and female shamans appear in its songs. Spiritually powerful male rulers also appear in the songs. Moreover, the early modern idea of a sister protecting her brother as an *onarigami* should not be read backward in time either to the *Omoro* or to Shō Shin's religious hierarchy, as has been common practice.⁶

RYUKYU'S DEMON DEITY

The word *oni* generally means "demon," often carrying a negative connotation as something malevolent and fearsome. Such demonic power is dangerous, but it can work to the benefit of a person or group if properly channeled. Certain esoteric Shingon Buddhist rites, for example those involving the deity Dakini, are examples of harnessing demonic power. Rites connected with Bishōmon functioned similarly, perhaps most famously in the case of the warrior Uesugi Kenshin (1530–1578).⁷ Rites invoking Dakini, Bishōmon, or other demonic deities channel potent though dangerous (if mishandled) power for the benefit of a ruler. The Demon Deity (Kijin) of the Second Shō dynasty was another such example.

Probably a form of Hachiman, the Demon Deity was a variation of the divine power by which *wakō* acquired fearsome power in the minds of many Chinese.[8]

Ryukyu's Demon Deity was associated with shamanic divination. It tended to lurk behind the scenes of official rites, appearing occasionally until the end of the kingdom. For example, *Ōshima hikki*, a 1762 Tosa account of conditions in Ryukyu based on interviews of the crew of a disabled ship, mentions that "Since long ago, veneration of the Demon Deity has deep roots in Ryukyu. Its government is based on oracles from this deity."[9] Moreover, when Ryukyu's last king Shō Tai (r. 1848–1879) received the order to vacate Shuri castle in 1879 and saw no way that human power could save his throne, he turned to divine power as a last resort. Kishaba Chōken (1840–1916), a member of Shō Tai's inner circle, reported that he and the king withdrew to a room and examined documents describing the origins of Ryukyu's shrines, presumably in order to find the most potent deity for preserving the state. The king asked Kishaba for his opinion, and he recommended the Demon Deity. When the king asked for assurance of this deity's suitability and power, Kishaba explained that the Demon Deity had a long record of solving thorny political problems.[10]

THREE-IN-ONE DEITIES AND BENZAITEN

Consider the situation at approximately the time of Shō Sei's reign during the 1530s and 1540s. By this point, the hierarchy of male officials and priestesses initiated by Shō Shin had matured. Kikoe-ōgimi resided at the pinnacle of the Thirty-three Kimi, the elite stratum of priestesses. Buddhism was thriving, and solar deities were prominent in native Ryukyuan religion. The newly created Kikoe-ōgimi and the newly imported deity Benzaiten united these various religious strands (fig. 18).[11]

Benzaiten is a Buddhist goddess derived from the Hindu goddess Saraswati. Moving from China to Japan, Benzaiten merged with Japan's Ugajin, whose body was a snake. Benzaiten is closely associated with snakes, and in Japan especially, she functioned as a protector deity. She is also associated with sea-lanes and bodies of water, and her shrines tend to be found on islands and in coastal areas. There are several possible iconographies for Benzaiten. In typical Japanese Buddhist guise, she often is depicted with six or eight arms. A small version of Ugajin's head sits atop her head, and around her halo are three three-mirrored jewels, indicative of a three-in-one quality of Benzaiten discussed below.

For the purposes of the following discussion, it is necessary to bear in mind the fluid boundary between Buddhism and local religions. The

Fig. 18. Benzaiten at Hōgonji, Nagahama (Shiga Prefecture), Japan. Photo by 663highland (Wikimedia Commons)

main doctrine that contributes to this fluidity is *honji-suijaku* (original ground, manifest traces). The basic idea is that Buddhas, Bodhisattvas, or wisdom kings manifest themselves as local deities to benefit people not yet able to grasp the profound truths of Buddhism. The logic of *honji-suijaku* permitted deities to combine in a variety of ways. One of the most common combinations in premodern Japan was a trinity, what I call a "three-in-one deity." In this format, one deity was the *honji*, which could manifest itself as three forms (*suijaku*). Benzaiten was the *honji* of several three-in-one deity combinations. In her case, the three *suijaku* are usually female deities. Several sets of deities in Ryukyu fit this three-in-one pattern, although the discussion below leaves out many examples and details for the sake of clarity.

BENZAITEN, DAKINI, AND THE DEMON DEITY

What about Ryukyu's secretive Demon Deity, to whom Shō Tai turned in desperation as his kingdom came to an end? To state the conclusion in advance, it was probably Benzaiten in a combination called "three heavenly deities" (*santen*) or "three-jewel women" (*sangyokunjo*). This combination was associated with yin-yang magic (*onmyōdō*) and esoteric Buddhism. Just as the sun, moon, and stars comprise the "three lights" and heaven, earth, and humans comprise the "three forces," the three heavenly deities are (1) Benzaiten; (2) Kangiten, an elephant-headed deity related to Ganesh and often called Shōten; and (3) Dakini, a fox-riding deity associated with the power to rule.[12]

Benzaiten subsumed Kangiten and Dakini. Both Kangiten and Dakini were known as demon deities (*kijin*) in medieval Japan in the context of esoteric Shingon rites that conferred military and political power. These rites collectively constituted the "method of cultivating the demon deity" (*kijin no shuhō*), and Emperor Go-Daigo deployed them in his bid to destroy the Kamakura *bakufu*.[13] The demon deity of the Second Shō dynasty, therefore, was most likely some flavor of the Benzaiten-Kangiten-Dakini three-in-one deity.

THREE SISTER DEITY LEGENDS

Recall the *Kyūyō* version of the legend of the three sisters/deities in Kumejima. One settled near Mount Omoto in Ishigaki. Another went to Shuri's Ben[zai] grove. The third sister became the Kumejima Kimihae, but she also led the invasion of Yaeyama to awe the local inhabitants. Recall also that the place-name Omoto is a variation of *obotsu* and is related to Mount

Omoto in Usa, where the blacksmith version of Hachiman resided. In a different version of the legend, all three sisters came from Japan, with one settling in Shuri at the Ben[zai] Grove, and the other two moving on to Kumejima, each residing at a different mountain there. One Kumejima sister later manifested herself as the deity of Yaeyama's soaring Mount Omoto.[14]

In the background of these legends is Shō Shin's conquest of other islands, especially Kumejima and Yaeyama, and his appropriation of their deities. Moreover, these three sisters closely resemble Benzaiten as part of the three-in-one deity configuration Benzaiten-Kangiten-Dakini. Kimihae, sometimes known as Oni-no-Kimihae, and the Hachiman-related Mount Omoto deity are gods of political power and conquest, like Kangiten and Dakini. And at the center, at Shuri's Benzaiten grove, is the sister who, in effect, became Kikoe-ōgimi.

BENZAITEN AS *HONJI*

There are other legends of three sisters/deities in the Ryukyu islands. Their content includes creation stories, the arrival of blacksmiths, the intermingling of humans and divine animals (boars and snakes), giant snakes devouring people, and many other elements that are beyond our scope.[15] The relevant point is that during the sixteenth century, Benzaiten became the *honji* of several deity triads in the Ryukyu islands. For example, it was relatively easy to subsume Miyako's Harimizu deities under Benzaiten because they were already female. In the case of Ishigaki's Mount Omoto sister, however, there is a large gap between the original character of the native deity, a male blacksmith, and the Shuri-imposed overlay in the form of a sister of the Benzaiten priestess.[16]

Konkōkenshū (1711) is Ryukyu's earliest dictionary of classical terms. Its introduction states: "Our country is a *shinkoku*. Its *honji* is Benzaiten."[17] In other words, Ryukyu is a land of various deities, and ultimately they are manifestations of Benzaiten. Chén Kǎn pointed out the shamanic nature of the religion of Ryukyu's royal court, whereby a deity possesses the body of a priestess, but he did not specify the name of that deity.[18] Later Chinese envoys consistently identified the highest deity of the royal court, the one that manifests itself through the body of the high priestess, as some variety of Benzaiten. The *honji* of Shuri's Sonohiyabu was also Benzaiten.[19] In the context of describing the kingdom's top priestesses and the various lesser priestesses in remote areas, *Ryūkyū shintōki* points out that the deities who have arrived from Nirai-Kanai (across the sea) and Obotsu-Kagura (from the heavens) are all manifestations of Benzaiten.[20]

Owing to connections with water, agricultural prosperity, warfare, and judicial matters, Benzaiten was ideal for the role of Ryukyu's supreme deity, and she also fit well with the Chinese-derived Tenpi worship common among Ryukyu's sailors.[21]

Benzaiten had long existed in Japan as a three-in-one deity with Kangiten and Dakini. Kangiten and Dakini had benign forms, but when deployed as part of the method of cultivating the demon deity, they became powerful weapons. It was dangerous for rulers themselves to perform such rites, because only expert priests could correctly channel the power generated by them. Nevertheless, Emperor Go-Daigo did perform at least some demon deity rites himself.

If indeed Benzaiten subsumed Ryukyu's demon deity within her, we have no details about how this practice arrived in Ryukyu. We have seen that southern court *wakō*, supporters of Go-Daigo, settled into the Ryukyu islands during the late fourteenth and early fifteenth centuries. Shingon Buddhist priests from Japan resided in Ryukyu from the time of Shō Hashi, if not earlier. In short, there would have been ample opportunity before the sixteenth century for esoteric Shingon rites to take root in Ryukyu.

MAKING HACHIMAN AND RYUKYU RESPECTABLE

Recall that we have seen several varieties of Hachiman derivatives, often functioning as deities of wind, water, and warfare and often associated with blacksmiths. In the context of discussing religion, Chén Kǎn related a story that "long ago, *wakō* plotted to kill the king of Chūzan." Reminiscent of the imagined appearance of Jingū/Hachiman at Tsushima in 1419, the Ryukyuan deities halted the *wakō* ships at sea, turning their water to salt and their rice to sand, thus permitting their capture. "Therefore, the king reveres the deities and the people fear the deities."[22] Chén's account is yet another example of Hachiman or Hachiman-like deities connected with Ryukyu.

Arranged in approximate chronological order these varieties of Hachiman are:

1. Aoriyae and Sasukasa;
2. Tsukishiro, associated with Samekawa and Shō Hashi;
3. Hachiman of the Hachiman shrine of Shō Toku or Shō Taikyū;
4. The Demon Deity of the Second Shō dynasty.

Tsukishiro makes several appearances in the *Omoro*. Because it was so closely associated with the founders of the First Shō dynasty, however, Tsukishiro had no place in Shō Shin's system. The Hachiman shrine fared better. It became attached physically and spiritually to the Shingon Buddhist temple Shinkokuji, which venerated Hachiman as a bodhisattva. As we have seen, Aoriyae and other Kumejima and Nakijin priestesses became closely linked with Shuri via the Kanahiyabu and Sonohiyabu shrines, and they took their place among the highest priestesses. After Shō Shin's creation of the hierarchy of priestesses, the Demon Deity, who never appears in official records, probably became subsumed by the Benzaiten-Kangiten-Dakini variety of three-in-one deity.

Wrapping the Demon Deity in the mantle of Benzaiten effectively put distance between Ryukyu and its Hachiman/*wakō* roots. Moreover, appropriating other Hachiman-like deities such as Aoriyae, linking them into the official religious network, making them subordinate to Kikoe-ōgimi/Benzaiten, and ultimately to the king, all brought potentially unruly spiritual power under firm central control. The same goes for linking the Hachiman shrine with a Buddhist temple and worshipping Hachiman as a bodhisattva.

Shō Shin was a transitional figure in every sense. His early life was rooted in the turbulent world of *wakō*-derived Ryukyu, in which kings and other rulers came and went based on the tides of military power and political intrigue. Hounded by the dubious legitimacy of his own ascent to power, Shō Shin crafted power, in all of its forms, into stable structures that would perpetuate themselves and support royal rule. Just as he conquered geographic territory, brought it into Shuri's orbit, and organized it for the extraction of resources, so Shō Shin did the same with divine territory.

PART IV

THE NEW ORDER, 1550–1650

CHAPTER THIRTEEN

A Changing World and the Road to War

This chapter examines the challenges Ryukyu faced during a time of rapid changes taking place in Japan, East Asia, and the world. As the sixteenth century progressed, Ryukyu's relations with the Shimazu lords of southern Kyushu often became strained, factional politics within Ryukyu intensified, and Ryukyu's range of viable options narrowed. Here I examine the complex constellation of events and circumstances that eventually led to war between Shō Nei and Shimazu in 1609. I argue that Shō Nei and the anti-Shimazu faction that eventually dominated his administration had no ideal options. Nevertheless, by steadfastly refusing to serve as a mediator between the Ming court and the Tokugawa *bakufu*, and by ignoring the danger inherent in that stance, Shō Nei brought about a disastrous war that was not inevitable.

RYUKYU AS MEDIATOR

In 1523, combat between trade representatives of the Ōuchi and the Hosokawa domains took place in Níngbō, causing serious damage to the port. The Ming court cut off relations with the Ashikaga shoguns as a result. By this time, the shoguns had lost most of their domestic military power, but remained necessary as nominal kings of Japan under whose cover official trade could take place.

In response to this situation, Ryukyu ventured into active diplomacy, serving as an intermediary between the Ming court and Kyoto. In 1525, the Ming court sent a letter to Japan through Ryukyu, which initiated two further rounds of diplomatic correspondence. One result was that the Ōuchi and other daimyo showed an interest in forging closer ties with Ryukyu.[1] Having demonstrated its ability to serve as an intermediary with the Ming court, Ryukyu later faced severe pressure to play a similar role in the wake of Tokugawa Ieyasu's rise to power at the start of the seventeenth century. An immediate result of Ryukyu's diplomatic activity in the 1520s was a series of attempts by Satsuma to control trade between Japan and Ryukyu.

A CHANGING WORLD

Between 1463 and 1511, ships under the auspices of Ryukyu's kings sailed to Siam (Thailand), Malacca, and other parts of Southeast Asia eighteen times. In 1510, Goa fell to Portuguese conquerors, and Malacca fell the following year. Ships under Ryukyuan auspices continued to sail to other port cities in the region, but the frequency of such voyages dropped significantly (fig. 19). Spanish conquest of the Philippines, completed in 1571, coincided with a nearly complete cessation of official Ryukyuan voyages to Southeast Asia, although there was one in 1577 and another in 1606, both to acquire sappanwood (Indian rosewood). By the 1570s, Spain and Portugal had captured most of the trading ports in this region, and networks of overseas Chinese communities conducted trade within those

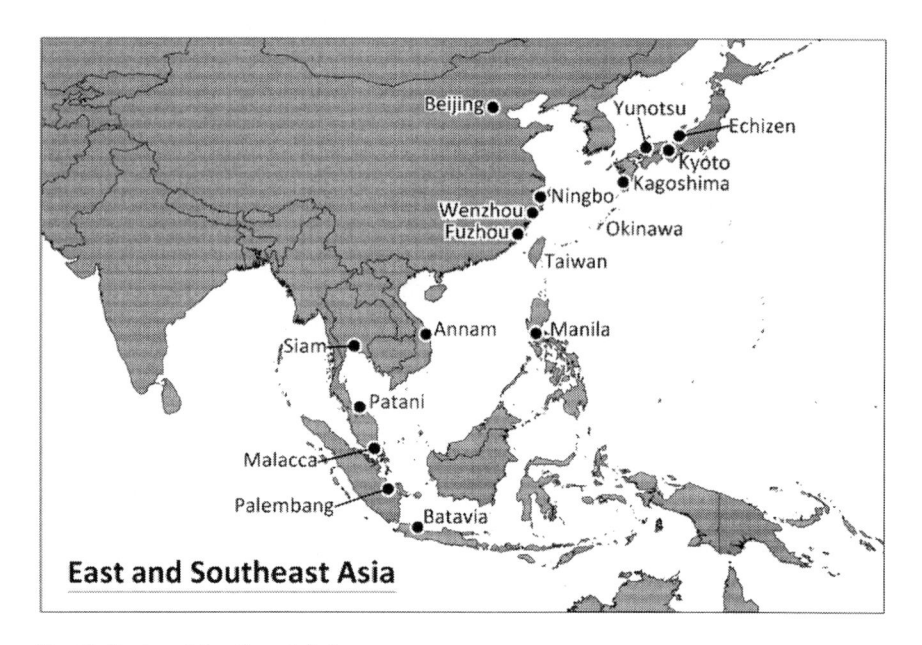

Fig. 19. East and Southeast Asia

ports. Significant relaxation of Ming Maritime Prohibitions from 1567 onward facilitated what amounted to a shift from official trade between governments to private trade between favorably placed merchants.[2] We have also seen that a substantial downward trend in the volume of Ryukyu's official trade began late in the reign of Shō Shin.

Lack of Ryukyuan protest against the 1522 Ming reimposition of the policy of one tribute voyage every two years may have been connected with these circumstances. As private trade crowded out official trade and Ryukyuan ships sailed to Southeast Asia less often, the Ryukyuan court had to obtain sappanwood and pepper through private trade networks at a higher cost. Obtaining these items was necessary because they were on the official list of tribute goods Ryukyu had to present to China.[3] Over the course of the sixteenth century, Ryukyu's tributary trade with China became less a source of profit and more of a burden.

The decline in official trade from approximately 1520 did not mean that Ryukyu's wealth declined at the same rate. Silver from Spanish mines in the Americas was rapidly becoming a world currency. The 1494 Treaty of Tordesillas prohibited Spain from trading with China or other parts of Asia from its base in the Philippines. Communities of Chinese merchants therefore became essential as intermediaries, trading Spanish silver for Chinese silk. Japan was also producing silver at this time, and the ratio of gold to silver was 1:13 in Spain, 1:6 in China, and 1:9 in Japan. Although Chinese and Ryukyuan sources are largely silent about this matter, between 1519 and 1738 the name, location, and other information about Ryukyu appears often in Spanish records. There was even mention of the war with Satsuma. It is likely, therefore, that Ryukyuan merchants conducted private trade using Japanese silver to purchase Chinese silk, and possibly to trade silver for gold, exploiting the differences in exchange rates. In short, private trade within a regional economy based on silver probably compensated to some degree for the decline in official trade.[4]

SILVER EXTENDS THE NETWORK

Circulation of silver not only enabled Ryukyuan traders to profit from private trade between Japan, China, and the Philippines, it also began to modify the East China Sea network discussed throughout this book. Silver mines in western Japan created a trade route that extended from Ryukyu northward along western Kyushu. Instead of turning toward Korea, however, the route continued north to the port of Yunotsu (Shimane Prefecture) and further to Echizen (Fukui Prefecture). Yunotsu was the shipping port for Iwami Ginzan, the largest silver mine in Japan.

Numerous ships from Kyushu began to gather in the vicinity of Yunotsu to transport silver southward.

Shō Nei encouraged men from Japan with useful skills or knowledge to live in Ryukyu. Taichū, author of *Ryūkyū shintōki,* is one example. Kian Nyūdō (1566–1653), who served in Shō Nei's court as a diplomat and expert in several Japanese arts, is another. Kian accompanied Shō Nei to Japan and later became Ryukyu's first Chief of Tea (*sadō kashira*). Late in the sixteenth century, a physician from Echizen named Yamazaki Nikyūshusan (1554–1631) set up residence in Naha. Slightly later, the Echizen priest Sōmi Nyūdō (Sakamoto Fuki) came to Ryukyu and planted mulberry trees on Kumejima to establish silk production there.[5]

There was more to the Echizen connection than these two men. In 1567 its lord, Asakura Yoshikage, wrote to Shimazu Yoshihisa (1533–1611) requesting permission to trade with Ryukyu, and Yoshihisa agreed. The man who would become the last Ashikaga shogun, Ashikaga Yoshiaki (r. 1568–1573), was residing in Yoshikage's domain at the time. Given the close ties between Ryukyu's kings and the Ashikaga shoguns, it is possible that Yoshiaki was exploring a way to revive trade with Ryukyu. In the end, Yoshikage did not trade with Ryukyu and soon died as a result of warfare. A key point here is that Yoshikage asked Yoshihisa for permission to trade with Ryukyu. It is quite possible that he and Shimazu were collaborating to revive Ryukyuan trade with parts of Japan, but to also to keep that trade under their control.[6]

THE SHIMAZU LORDS

The Shimazu family had traditionally been lords of the three provinces of Satsuma, Ōsumi, and Hyūga, present-day Kagoshima and Miyazaki Prefectures. During the much of sixteenth century, they struggled to consolidate power. One aspect of this struggle was the curtailing of the autonomy of subordinate and allied lords in Shimazu territory. For example, in 1582 Shimazu prohibited Tanegashima Sanrōjirō (Hisatoki), lord of Yakushima, Erabushima, and Tanegashima, from selling lumber in Kyushu or from sending unauthorized ships to Ryukyu. The next year, Shimazu restricted the ability of the Ei family of Yamakawa to conduct independent trade.[7]

The Shimazu lords also waged war with non-allied polities holding territory in Kyushu. Initially, the goal was to secure their hold over the three traditional provinces. Later, Shimazu power expanded northward until almost all of Kyushu was in Shimazu hands. However, Shimazu forces suffered defeat in 1586 at the hands of Toyotomi Hideyoshi. Warfare stopped in Kyushu at that point and, under Hideyoshi's watchful eye, Shimazu control shrunk back to the traditional home provinces.

Shimazu Yoshihisa was domain head at that time, but as a gesture of surrender he took the tonsure in 1586 and moved to Kyoto. Hideyoshi granted him permission to return to Kagoshima in 1588. Somewhat remarkably, Yoshihisa governed in close partnership with his brother Yoshihiro (1535–1619) and nephew Tadatsune (1576–1638), who changed his name to Iehisa in 1602. Although Yoshihiro formally succeeded Yoshihisa in 1586 and Iehisa succeeded Yoshihiro in 1602, in practice all three governed jointly. They did not always agree, but they worked together effectively nevertheless.

It is common practice to use the term "Satsuma" as a shorthand for the Shimazu domains. However, because this chapter and the next examine regional geopolitics in some detail, for clarity I refer to the Shimazu family or Shimazu domains in general or, depending on context, to specific Shimazu lords or territories.

DIPLOMATIC TENSIONS

In 1481, Ryukyu began dispatching official ships to the shogun's court. Known as decorated ships (*ayabune*), images of blue sparrows and yellow dragons adorned these vessels. Shuri dispatched decorated ships for special occasions such as a new shogun taking office. A letter from Ryukyu's Council of Three to Shimazu Takahisa (1514–1571), probably from 1557, states that, while Ryukyu does send decorated ships to the *bakufu*, it had never sent one to Kagoshima. Moreover, pirates based in Japan have recently become a serious menace. Therefore, Ryukyu was busy administering defense measures at its ports and did not have the resources to maintain regular diplomatic relations with nearby countries. The Council of Three apologized in advance for being unable to accede to Shimazu's wishes.[8] From the contents of the letter, it is clear that Shuri had come under pressure to maintain regular diplomatic relations with Shimazu. Despite this initial refusal, in 1559 Ryukyu did send a decorated ship to Kagoshima. This embassy established a precedent. Thereafter, the Shimazu lords expected Ryukyu to dispatch diplomatic embassies at appropriate times such as when a new domain lord took office.

In 1568, a disabled ship from Miyako drifted into Kaseda in Satsuma, and Shimazu returned its crew and cargo to Ryukyu. The fact that he returned the cargo was significant. According to the prevailing custom at the time in Japan, when ships drifted into someone else's territory, the lord of that place was entitled to keep the cargo.[9] The next year, Ryukyu dispatched a priest from Tenryūji as an envoy of thanks to Shimazu.

In 1570, a messenger arrived in Ryukyu with the news that Yoshihisa had succeeded to the headship of the Shimazu household. Based on the usual rules of diplomacy, Ryukyu would have sent a decorated ship to congratulate Yoshihisa within a year or so. However, that ship did not arrive in Kagoshima until 1575. In 1570, Shimazu also repeated a long-standing demand that Ryukyu reject any Japanese merchant ships not bearing formal papers of authorization from Shimazu. In 1572, the priest Sesshin brought to Ryukyu letters from the Shimazu elders (*rōjū*) addressed to the Council of Three. They stated that in recent years there had been an increase in unauthorized trade. Assuming that the letters were accurate, Ryukyu had not acted on Shimazu's earlier demands.[10]

Notice that the timing of these events and messages mainly coincided with the period of several years between Shō Gen's likely illness or injury and Shō Ei's becoming established as king. It is also important to note that during much of the 1570s Shimazu was almost constantly at war. From its point of view, Shimazu's attempts to regulate maritime traffic sailing to Ryukyu were part of its ongoing battle to consolidate power.[11]

In 1575 Ryukyu sent a belated diplomatic embassy to Kagoshima to congratulate Yoshihisa on his becoming lord of the three provinces back in 1570. The Ryukyuan envoys were greeted with fireworks and a banquet, but Satsuma officials were not pleased. They quickly presented the Ryukyuans with a list of complaints: (1) allowing unauthorized ships; (2) generally slipshod treatment of the recently dispatched priest Sesshin; (3) bringing very few gifts this time; (4) the Council of Three treating Sesshin poorly; (5) irregularities in the etiquette of document exchange; (6) beheading of the first mate of the Satsuma ship *Kuniyoshi-maru*; (7) not sending a congratulatory embassy when Yoshihisa succeeded to the headship; and (8) inappropriate statements from an unofficial envoy in 1573.[12] The full context of some of these items, the beheading for example, is unclear. Shimazu officials demanded answers, and the Ryukyuan envoys demurred. In response, the officials pressed even more vigorously. Moreover, unsatisfied with the initial answers they pressed the Ryukyuans for clarifications.

Although belligerent, it is clear from these exchanges and other sources that Shimazu was genuinely insulted by the five-year delay in sending the embassy and by the enumerated issues. Japanese warrior society was acutely sensitive to matters of ritual and symbolism, hierarchies, and real or imagined insults.[13] Before 1559, Ryukyu had had little or no experience with rigorous diplomatic standards in a Japanese context.

The relatively casual and friendly nature of the relations between Chūzan kings and the Ashikaga shoguns and Sakai merchants was not applicable to Ryukyu's subsequent dealings with the Shimazu lords and Hideyoshi, who expected a much higher level of formality and ritual precision.[14]

In the course of this diplomatic wrangling, Yoshihisa explicitly mentioned that Ryukyuan trade had been given to Satsuma by shogunal decree. This claim referred to Ashikaga Yoshinori (1394–1441) granting Shimazu Tadakuni "the portal to the Ryukyu islands" in 1441. Another related issue was whether Ryukyu would provide additional gifts. The Ryukyuans agreed in principle, but insisted that Satsuma officials look up and compare the gift list from the previous voyage to verify the alleged disparity. Later, Sesshin privately discussed the matter with the Ryukyuans, who agreed to provide three bars of gold (thirty *ryō*) extra. Subsequently, Yoshihisa declined to accept the gold on the grounds that diplomacy was not about material profit but about future good relations. Ultimately, the two sides worked out their many differences, and the theatrical aspect of the embassy, a formal audience before Yoshihisa followed by a banquet, could proceed. The stress was too much for one of the Ryukyuan envoys, who fell ill and had to be carried to a nearby temple as the banquet started.[15] Relations between Shimazu and the Ryukyuan court had reached a low ebb.

SHŌ EI RESTORES GOOD RELATIONS

Genealogy of Chūzan notes that Ba Seiei joined the Council of Three when Shō Ei was enthroned (sometime in 1573).[16] Ba was Nago Ueekata Ryōin, probable leader of the pro-Shimazu faction at the time.[17] Overall, the official histories have little to say about Shō Ei. There is no mention of policy matters and no hint of the flurry of diplomacy and commerce between the Shimazu domains and Ryukyu that took place during his reign. Instead, the official histories focus on tribute missions and other interactions with China, devoting much space to the placement of the famous "Country of Propriety" (C. Shǒulǐ zhī guó, J. Shurei no kuni) framed inscription (*hengaku*) on the Shurei gate to Shuri castle.[18] The placid surface of the official histories notwithstanding, Shō Ei's court inherited a diplomatic crisis and actively began working to reduce tensions with Shimazu in 1577.

That year, the abbot of Tenkaji sailed to Kagoshima bearing a letter apologizing for Ryukyu's recent past behavior, congratulating Yoshihisa for recently having pacified all of Satsuma, Ōsumi, and Hyūga, and promising that a full embassy would arrive the following year. The 1578 decorated ship arrived in Kagoshima well stocked. Significantly, one item was thirty *ryō* of gold, the precise monetary value of the shortfall in connection with the 1575 embassy. Clearly, Ryukyu's pro-Shimazu faction was trying to make amends. Yoshihisa responded quickly and favorably, sending a ship to Ryukyu bearing news of further Shimazu conquests. Yoshihisa sent the *Kuniyoshi-maru* to Ryukyu in 1579. It was the same ship whose first mate had been beheaded in Naha. An accompanying letter stated that ever since that incident, the *Kuniyoshi-maru* had been prohibited to sail to Ryukyu. Now, however, the prohibition had been lifted and normal commerce could resume. In short, Shimazu restored full diplomatic and trade relations with Ryukyu in 1579. On this voyage was Yamashita Chikugo, dispatched by Shimazu to observe the investiture rites for Shō Ei and to gather intelligence.[19]

Good relations continued during the 1580s, but Shō Ei died in 1588 at the young age of thirty. The official histories list no cause of death. Moreover, as we have seen, Shō Ei had a younger brother, Shō Kyū, who lived well into the seventeenth century. How and why did a king from the Urasoe branch of the royal line come to the throne despite the presence of an obvious candidate from the main line? The official sources are silent, except for the claim found only in 1725 *Genealogy* that Shō Ei adopted Shō Nei. While it is possible that Shō Ei indeed designated Shō Nei as his successor, it is also possible that Shō Nei came to the throne in connection with pressure by anti-Shimazu forces at court unhappy with Shō Ei's policies. Not only would this faction have had many reasons to dislike Shō Ei, Hideyoshi's defeat of Shimazu in 1586 may have emboldened Shimazu's opponents at the Ryukyuan court.

SHŌ NEI'S TROUBLED REGIME

Whatever the circumstances of his enthronement, Shō Nei was never able to unite the royal government. The relatively brief *Kyūyō* account of the Jana family revolt of 1592, examined in chapter 8, provides no details about why it took place. As we will see, the revolt most likely was a violent reaction to heavy taxes imposed to meet demands from Shimazu and Hideyoshi. Significantly, pro-Shimazu official Ba Seiei (Nago Ueekata Ryōin) stepped down from the Council of Three the same year. The next year, Council of Three member Kin Kokki died. Shō Nei's early years on the throne were turbulent, and the unrest continued.[20]

Ō Kishō was appointed to the Council of Three in 1601, but he was dismissed in 1605 and demoted to commoner status, according to *Genealogy*. The reason for the dismissal was that Jana Teidō lodged "accusations" (C. *chánbiǎn*, J. *zanhen*) against Ō. According to household records, those charges were resolved in 1608, and Ō was reappointed. We have no idea about the fine points, but it is clear that Ō and Jana were opponents.[21] Taichū resided in Ryukyu between 1603 and 1606. In *Ryūkyū shintōki*, he wrote that during this time an incident involving an anonymous tract slandering the king and his officials took place. The royal court tried to deduce the culprit or culprits but was unable to do so. Over the course of twenty-seven days, officials prayed at the Benzaiten shrine. The culprits were thereby revealed and exiled to a remote island. Taichū's main point was to illustrate the Okinawan custom of deities revealing criminals, but in this example we can glimpse political fault lines destabilizing Shō Nei's reign.[22]

There is further evidence of internal dissent. A peculiar 1597 letter, ostensibly from the Ryukyuan king, congratulates Shimazu Tadatsune on his return to Kagoshima from Korea. Only someone with close ties to Shimazu would have known this information. Moreover, given the poor state of Ryukyu–Shimazu relations after 1593, it is highly implausible that Shō Nei would have sent such a letter. The "from" line at the end of the letter, the part stamped by the royal seal for authenticity, is irregular. It reads "Ryūkyūkoku" (country of Ryukyu), not the usual "Chūzan ō" (Chūzan king). These points, plus a peculiar self-referential term in the text, strongly suggest that Shō Nei did not send or know of the letter; instead, pro-Shimazu officials within Ryukyu had forged a royal letter.[23]

TOYOTOMI HIDEYOSHI

Between approximately 1585 and 1590 Toyotomi Hideyoshi solidified his power over Japan, including the Shimazu domains. By the end of the decade he had set his sights on conquering vast territory on the Asian continent.

In 1589.1.17, Hideyoshi sent a strongly worded communiqué to Shimazu Yoshihisa chastising him for failing to act on earlier promises. The letter included a veiled threat of the extinction of the Shimazu house and the possibility of Hideyoshi taking direct military action in Ryukyu. It directed Shimazu to serve as an intermediary in restoring the tally (*kangō*) trade with Ming China and order on the seas by suppressing pirate ships headed for China.[24]

Acting quickly, Yoshihisa dispatched the priest Daijiji to Ryukyu, but when he arrived in Naha, politics were in confusion because of the regime change from Shō Ei to Shō Nei. Toward the end of 1589, the situation was stable enough for Ryukyuan envoys Chōan and Adaniya Peechin to travel with Daijiji to Kagoshima. Yoshihisa met them, and the group hurried to Osaka for audiences with Hideyoshi. They spent the rest of the year in the area, and just before they were to return Hideyoshi gave the Ryukyuans two letters to the king dated 1590.2.28. One expressed a desire to make the world into one family, and the other ordered Ryukyu to assist with near-future plans to invade China. Internal military affairs occupied Hideyoshi for several months, but he sent a letter dated 1590.8.21 to Shō Nei via Yoshihisa. It ordered Ryukyu to prepare a decorated ship over the winter and sail to Osaka in the coming spring. Ryukyu's actual dispatch was one year later owing to the difficulties of preparing such an embassy.[25]

In the meantime, Hideyoshi became determined to launch his invasion and set Katō Kiyomasa and other generals to work making preparations. In the midst of this situation, Kamei Korenori (1557–1612), a key general in Hideyoshi's Kyushu campaigns, entered the picture. Kamei apparently used Hideyoshi's military buildup as an opportunity to press a claim to Ryukyu, which Hideyoshi initially granted. Despite Kamei's having assembled a fleet and thirty-five hundred soldiers to invade Ryukyu, or perhaps because of it, Hideyoshi suspended the operation at the last minute and awarded Kamei alternate territory in China. The ostensible reason was that invading Ryukyu would detract from the invasion of the continent. This whole matter appears to have been a way for Hideyoshi to pressure the Shimazu leaders to get their subordinate lords lined up and ready to contribute to the invasion of the continent. In this context, Hideyoshi regarded Ryukyu as functionally equivalent to one of Shimazu's subordinates.[26]

In 1591.10.24, Yoshihisa sent Shō Nei a detailed letter outlining the king's military obligations for the invasion of the continent. The essence of it was that Yoshihisa ordered Ryukyu to provide ten months of food for seven thousand soldiers, to be delivered to Bōnotsu by the second month of next year. It also warned Ryukyu not to tell any other country about the invasion plans.[27] An official notice from Hideyoshi to Shimazu dated 1592.1.19 formally designated Ryukyu as a *"yoriki"* (supporter) of Shimazu. A follow-up letter to the Shimazu leaders a few days later stated that, in light of Hideyoshi's formally attaching Ryukyu to Shimazu and granting alternative territory to Kamei, it was essential that Ryukyu dispatch a decorated ship to Hideyoshi. It appears that sometime between the second and third months of 1592, Shō Nei dispatched the decorated ship to Kagoshima (at this point Hideyoshi was in Kyushu).[28]

However, the sparse and poor-quality gifts that the Ryukyuan envoys brought caused difficulty. In a letter to the Ryukyuan envoy dated 1592.4.8, Yoshihisa complained about the "absurdity" of the "poor gifts." Yoshihisa also rushed to forewarn Ishida Mitsunari, a top official in Hideyoshi's administration, who sent a retainer to Kagoshima to see for himself. Frustrated by what he regarded as Ryukyu's continuing passive resistance, Yoshihisa sent a letter to Shō Nei dated 1592.7.26 ending with a threat that there would be peace only after Ryukyu was incorporated into Japan. These words, and the de facto start of the invasion of Korea, probably caught the attention of Ryukyu's leading officials. Early in 1593, Ryukyu belatedly made the food contribution that Yoshihisa had demanded, but not the full amount. The remainder of the full contribution was not delivered until the summer. This delay contributed to significant food shortages among the Shimazu forces in Korea.[29]

The late provision of the supplies Shimazu had demanded marked the end of even modest Ryukyu cooperation with him. Ryukyu began working against Shimazu and Hideyoshi, mainly by continuing to pass along information about Japan to the Ming court. Uezato Takashi has argued that the probable cause of the Jana revolt of 1592 was the heavy silver tax the royal government imposed on elite households in order to meet its obligations to Shimazu and Hideyoshi.[30] The demand for food supplies alone would have been a massive burden. Whatever the cause of the revolt, Shō Nei clearly came under intense pressure on multiple fronts.

In 1591 Ryukyu sent tribute envoys to China, who reported on Hideyoshi's impending invasion. Their information reached Fujian Grand Coordinator (Fújiàn xúnfǔ) Zhào Cānlǔ. He conveyed the information to the Ministry of War, which sent an official communication to the Korean court.[31] Another route for information about the invasion was a Chinese physician from Fujian, Xǔ Yíhòu, who resided in Satsuma as the personal physician of Yoshihisa. He and another expatriate, Guō Guóān, sent secret messages to China via the Fujian merchant Zhū Jūnwàng. One reason that Xǔ was able to operate so effectively is that Yoshihisa had entrusted him with maintaining contact with Fujian officials. Yoshihisa hoped that in a postwar future he would be able to establish trade ties with the Ming court. Ryukyu was in a position to access a wide range of information in this environment. Ryukyuan envoys conveyed news of the 1597 Keichō no eki (Hideyoshi's second invasion) to the Ming court, and in 1599 they reported Hideyoshi's death.[32]

INVESTITURE DIFFICULTIES

This same information network, however, quickly disseminated the news that Shō Nei had been ordered to provide food supplies to Hideyoshi in connection with the invasion. Shǐ Shìyòng was a Ministry of War official sent to Kyushu in 1593 to gather intelligence. Shĭ reported that Shō Nei had delayed requesting investiture because Ryukyu was too impoverished to bear the costs of hosting an investiture embassy. In that context, he also reported on the matter of Ryukyu providing food supplies to Hideyoshi. Moreover, Ryukyu's provision of food aid later became widely known among Chinese officials in coastal areas.[33]

Poverty was probably sufficient to explain Shō Nei's not requesting investiture promptly. It was also possible that, given Chinese requirements that top Ryukyuan officials certify the legitimacy of kings (technically, crown princes) seeking investiture, Shō Nei might not have been in a position to move forward. Nevertheless, even before the food supplies became a potential issue, the Ming court inevitably conflated Ryukyu's delay with Hideyoshi's military plans. In 1591, the Board of Rites urged tributary envoys not to delay requesting investiture by using strained conditions in Ryukyu as an excuse.[34] Clearly the Ming court wanted to keep Ryukyu in China's orbit and was concerned that it might drift toward Japan.[35] When Ryukyu did request investiture in 1595, however, maritime security problems and related expenses caused Ming officials to hesitate. After several rounds of debate about whether to send a military envoy or to perform the ceremonies in China, in 1596 the emperor ordered that the investiture ceremonies take place in Fujian, with an envoy from Ryukyu standing in for the king.[36]

Given that Shō Nei's legitimacy was precarious within Ryukyu, he pushed back vigorously against any alteration in investiture practices. It was a long process. To summarize briefly, in 1599 Jana Teidō went to China to request investiture, but he did not possess the required verification document from Ryukyu's officials stating that Shō Nei was the legitimate king. As a Kumemura China expert, Jana surely knew this document was required, but perhaps dissent among Ryukyu's officials had prevented his obtaining it. In any case, the emperor intervened and, as a compromise, stated that a military official would travel to Ryukyu to perform the rites. Shō Nei objected again, and he sent Sai Kei to China in 1601. Sai pointed out that dispatching a military official would be widely seen as inauspicious and that Shō Nei's subjects would assume the king was being chastised for committing an offense. The result might even be a revolt, and the Chūzan royal line could become unstable. Shō Nei's having sent food supplies to Hideyoshi lurked in the background of this diplomacy, and the Board of Rites became concerned that Ryukyu would drift out of China's orbit. Therefore, in 1601 it decreed that an ordinary investiture by two civil officials sent to Ryukyu would take place.[37]

The war of 1609 had several causes, but the overwhelmingly important one was Ryukyu's refusal to serve as an intermediary between the Tokugawa *bakufu* and the Ming court. At this point, we have sufficient information to understand the basic reason for what might otherwise seem like an irrational policy. Shō Nei's bending to pressure from Shimazu and Hideyoshi probably prompted an armed revolt in 1592. The Chinese decisions to hold the investiture ceremonies in Fujian and, later, to send a military official might well have been justifiable as wartime expedients. However, from the standpoint of the Ryukyuan court—Shō Nei, his supporters, and his enemies—such measures appeared to be a reprimand for Shō Nei's having supported Hideyoshi's invasion. The year 1593 was a turning point. After that, Shō Nei became determined never again to appear as an agent of any Japanese polity.

The massive Ming resistance to Hideyoshi's invasions of Korea also played a psychological role. From a Ryukyuan perspective, it appeared that the Ming court would go to war for its tributary states. As we will see, leading Ryukyuan officials apparently became convinced that China would back Ryukyu in a military conflict, that Ryukyu was too geographically dispersed and remote for Shimazu successfully to launch an invasion, and that Ryukyu's deity, Benzaiten, would protect the kingdom.

THE REGIONAL GEOPOLITICAL SITUATION AFTER 1598

Control of piracy was an issue of much concern during the late sixteenth century. Hideyoshi, Shimazu, and the council that succeeded Hideyoshi in 1598 issued prohibitions against piracy and demanded active cooperation by Ryukyu in this endeavor. Moreover, very soon after Hideyoshi's death, Shimazu and other powerful lords in Japan sought to establish trade relations with Ming China. Shimazu may have come close to succeeding. The domain enlisted the Bōnotsu merchant Torihara Sōan to head an expedition to repatriate captured Ming general Máo Guókē. According to Satsuma's account, Torihara traveled all the way to Beijing in 1600, and the Chinese court promised to send two ships to Satsuma each year. In 1601, the ships sailed, but pirates attacked and destroyed them in the vicinity of Iōjima in the Satsunan islands. Key details concerning these events are not clear.[38]

For our purposes, the main point is that after Hideyoshi's death leaders of Japan vigorously pursued paths to reestablish good relations with China, and the Shimazau lords understood the importance of this opportunity. Ryukyu's location made it an integral part of the process. From the standpoint of Shimazu or Tokugawa Ieyasu, the ideal option was that

Ryukyu actively cooperate in suppressing piracy and restoring Sino-Japanese trade. The less desirable option was to use coercive force in an attempt to compel such cooperation. Ryukyu's continued resistance to Satsuma and *bakufu* entreaties to assist in restoring relations with Ming China eventually tipped the scales in favor of military action.

SUSPICIOUS RYUKYUANS

Hideyoshi's invasions of the Asian continent exacerbated the previously existing tendency of Ming authorities to regard any vessel with a Japanese crew as a pirate or smuggling ship. The same events also caused the Ming court to place greater value on Ryukyu as a generally friendly state that could provide them with vital information.

One practical problem, however, was that it was difficult to distinguish Ryukyuans from Japanese. Their vessels, clothing, weapons, and other items of material culture were often similar or identical. The interpreters who worked for the Ming authorities, often people of *wakō* background, also experienced actual or claimed difficulty distinguishing Ryukyuan languages from Japanese languages or dialects. For example, one interpreter in connection with a case in 1595 stated: "Japan and Ryukyu are neighbors. Their language and appearance are nearly the same, and it is truly difficult to tell them apart."[39] Even though certain islands in the East China Sea network belonged, at least nominally, to the king of Ryukyu, to the Shimazu lords, or to other rulers, borders in the zone were entirely fluid. The broad cultural similarities along sea routes in the region facilitated mariners of different origins sailing on the same ship. Particularly prominent were mariners from the Tokara islands, technically Japanese, who plied the seas throughout the region. The typical crew of a private ship, which might engage in both legal and illegal activities, consisted of Tokara islanders, people from various Ryukyu islands, and sometimes a few people of Chinese origin.[40]

There are several well-documented cases of suspicious ships being apprehended by Chinese forces, often after deadly fighting. Despite significant indications to the contrary, the crews eventually, often after repeated rounds of interrogation, claimed to be Ryukyuans. Moreover, Ryukyuan officials in China or in Shuri vigorously claimed such crews as Ryukyuan after learning of the relevant incident. Chinese officials tended to err on the side of caution after crews began claiming they were Ryukyuans. Watanabe Miki has studied the cases in detail.[41] Here I briefly summarize only one of them as an example, the Hana incident of 1595.

Hana was part of a group of twenty-eight survivors suspected of being Japanese who were arrested off the Zhèjiāng coast. With them was Zhèng Liángnéng, a Chinese from Fujian who said he had been abducted and brought to Japan in 1577. Others in the group drowned or were killed by soldiers when they were arrested. The group changed their story three times. At first they said they were Ryukyuan tribute envoys, but later they claimed they had come to warn that Japanese who had sought provisions in Ryukyu were planning to invade China. Eventually, the group all claimed to be Ryukyuans, even Zhèng, who said he was a Ryukyuan who had come to Fujian to conduct trade. Wēnzhōu Prefect (*zhīfǔ*) Liú Fāngyù led the initial investigation.

Prefect Liú regarded the group as Japanese, partly because all the items in their possession were from Japan. Moreover, he forcefully criticized the changes in the versions of their story. He pointed out that the previous Ryukyuan tribute envoy was still in Fujian and had not yet returned to Ryukyu, so why would Ryukyu send another one? Moreover, a real embassy would have arrived in a large ship, its crew properly attired. Finally, the group had no documentation that they were merchants. When approached by a government ship, real merchants would lower their sails and enter a dialogue. Instead, this ship had raised its sails, brought up cannons, and the crew brandished swords, shot arrows, and wounded a soldier. Moreover, there was no evidence that their ship carried any of the typical goods that merchants from the Japanese islands would sell, and since there was no Ryukyu marketplace in Fujian, why would Zhèng be leading a group of Ryukyuans there? If they had come to China to issue a warning, Liú added, they would have an official document from Ryukyu. Moreover, they were ignorant about any details, and their story sounded like a variation of what Shǐ Shìyòng had reported in 1593.[42]

Despite Liú's making a very strong case that the crew was engaged in unlawful activities and could not have been Ryukyuans on legitimate business, there were three subsequent investigations by different officials using different interpreters. Zhèng killed himself as the matter dragged on. A fourth inquest reached a hesitant conclusion and remanded the case to the Ryukyuan king for further investigation. When the matter was brought to the attention of Ryukyuan tribute envoy Kin Shireki, he stated that Hana had been sent as a "supplementary tribute envoy." Based on this claim, the Fujian Grand Coordinator (*xúnfǔ*) reported that the tribute envoy hypothesis had indeed been correct, which then caused a debate about whether Hana should travel to the capital. What happened after that is unclear.[43] *Genealogy of Chūzan* states that Hana drifted to

Wēnzhōu and was repatriated to Ryukyu the next year on a Chinese ship.[44] *Rekidai hōan* contains a more detailed version of the same basic story.[45]

The case of Hana and the others, several of which were even more complex, highlight some important points. To summarize some of Watanabe's conclusions, Naha was a mixed port city in which people from various parts of Japan, the Tokara islands, and China lived. Cultural and residential boundaries were often unclear. The early years of Shō Nei's reign were a time of confusion, and it is likely that Shuri did not have tight control over foreign relations and envoys at this time. Therefore, private vessels might plausibly claim to be conducting official business. Moreover, many mariners in the region undoubtedly possessed multiple identities. It is likely that during the course of interrogation, the detainees came to realize that Chinese officials regarded Japan as an enemy country and Ryukyu as a friendly country. They therefore assumed Ryukyuan identity. The Ming interpreters were typically of Japanese origin, often prisoners who had been spared the death penalty and who worked as interpreters to express their gratitude. Such interpreters never had the complete trust of local officials, which is one reason they often erred on the side of caution.[46]

A final point Watanabe makes is that Satsuma's post-1609 cultural policies and the prohibition of Japanese entering Ryukyu helped clearly delineate Ryukyu as a separate entity from Japan. After 1609, Japanese, Koreans, or Chinese living in Okinawa soon all became Ryukyuans. At nearly the same time, foreign travel and residence restrictions in Tokugawa Japan helped delineate Japan as a clearly bounded entity.[47] I revisit this matter in chapter 15.

ATTEMPTS TO RESTORE TIES WITH MING CHINA

In light of Shimazu's 1601 failure to establish relations with China, a new opportunity arose in 1602 when a disabled Ryukyuan ship drifted into Mutsu (Aomori Prefecture) at the northern tip of Honshu. The Ryukyuan crew traveled from there to Edo to Osaka. In Osaka, escorts sent by Shimazu took over the job of repatriating the thirty crew members. *Bakufu* orders specified that if a single Ryukyuan died en route the five escorts would be beheaded.[48] In other words, Ieyasu regarded this incident as an opportunity to forge close relations with Ryukyu. The crew reached Okinawa safely in 1603.

In 1604, an envoy from Shimazu arrived in Ryukyu. He demanded the king send an embassy of thanks to Ieyasu for repatriating the crew.

The envoy further stated that one reason Shō Nei must send an embassy was that Ryukyu had been a subordinate domain of Satsuma since 1441. This claim was a revival of the idea that Ashikaga Yoshinori had given Shimazu control over trade with Ryukyu, but now with a much more aggressive interpretation. While no doubt intended to pressure Ryukyu to act, Shimazu's assertion that Ryukyu had been its territory since 1441 probably backfired. In any case, it put Ryukyu in a bind. Dispatching an envoy of thanks to Ieyasu would have been a de facto endorsement of the claim. Not sending an envoy would frustrate *bakufu* foreign-policy plans.[49] Shō Nei's post-1593 unwillingness to appear in Chinese eyes as an ally of Japan, combined with Shimazu's demand that Ryukyu thank Ieyasu because it had long been Satsuma's territory, explains Shuri's repeated refusals to mediate between Ieyasu and the Ming court.

Even though Shimazu and the *bakufu* were ostensibly working together to open relations with China, their interests were not always congruent. This lack of congruency became clear in 1605, when a Ryukyuan tribute ship drifted into Hirado. The details are complex, but Shimazu insisted that the ship and crew be sent to Kagoshima. Ryukyu sought a direct return, and the *bakufu* intervened, in part because the ship contained desirable cargo items that it ordered shipped to Edo. This incident impressed on Shimazu the urgency of its asserting control over Ryukyu.[50]

In the meantime, in 1604 Ryukyu dispatched a priest to Kagoshima as an envoy. However, the envoy stated that his purpose was not to thank the *bakufu* for the 1602–1603 repatriation but to congratulate Shimazu Iehisa (Tadatsune). From Shimazu's point of view, by 1605, Ryukyu had repeatedly refused to send an embassy of thanks to Ieyasu, had refused to recognize Hideyoshi's bestowal of Ryukyu to Shimazu, had refused to acknowledge Shimazu's role in preventing Kamei from invading Ryukyu, and had undermined Shimazu's interests in the Hirado ship incident.[51]

In 1606, top Shimazu deputies began discussing an invasion to seize Amami-Ōshima. The reason was not simply to settle grievances. Satsuma was in the midst of a serious financial and managerial crisis. For example, by 1606 its revenue levels had fallen approximately 20 percent compared with 1599 levels. Eventually most of the domain leadership agreed to the plan. Moreover, they extended it to encompass an invasion of all of Ryukyu so that they could justify the idea to the *bakufu* as a measure to force Ryukyu to cooperate with Ming trade negotiations. During the sixth month of 1606, Shimazu secured *bakufu* permission to invade. Chinese envoys had arrived in Ryukyu to invest Shō Nei, however, so the *bakufu* ordered the invasion delayed.[52]

While the investiture envoys were in Ryukyu, Shimazu wrote to Shō Nei to urge, yet again, the dispatch of an embassy to Ieyasu. Ominously, he wrote, "if next year this negligence continues, the existence of Ryukyu will be in jeopardy." The letter went on to explain that the shogun sought a restoration of relations with Ming China and that Ryukyu should show its gratitude by facilitating that process. Moreover, facilitating a connection between Japan and China would not only enrich Japan, it would enrich Ryukyu. It ended with an appeal to sympathize with the pressure Iehisa was under from the shogun.[53] Ryukyu's stance did not change, but the invasion did not materialize the next year. *Bakufu* negotiations with Korea in 1607 delayed it again. Shimazu continued to seek Ryukyuan cooperation throughout 1608, but to no avail.

In 1608.9, for example, Jana Teidō, the first Kumemura resident to win appointment to the Council of Three, bluntly rejected the demands of Shimazu envoys Ryūun, Sesshin, and Torihara Sōan. Jana stated that Ryukyu had long been attached to China and that it had no connection to Japan. He disparaged the envoys, and when asked what to send back with them as a ritual gift, he made the bizarre choice of rice, stating that nothing else was available.[54] It is possible that the successful investiture of Shō Nei had emboldened Ryukyu's anti-Shimazu faction.[55] In any case, Ryukyu was rapidly heading for disaster.

The last chance to avoid war came on 1609.2.1. Shimazu sent a letter to Shō Nei listing past grievances and explaining that the invasion was fully operational and imminent. "The self-destruction of Ryukyu is something that you alone have caused," warned the letter. "However, if you correct past failings and serve as an intermediary for trade between China and Japan, I and Satsuma will work fully on your behalf. In that case, you can save your country and achieve peace."[56]

A CHINESE ENVOY'S PERSPECTIVE

Investiture envoy Xià Zǐyáng, who arrived in Ryukyu in 1606, noted that because Ryukyu was an island country, there was a tendency to think that it must be militarily strong. He disagreed. Xià pointed out that Ryukyu was isolated 10,000 *li* out to sea from Fujian and far from other countries. Ryukyu's islands appeared as shapes above the waves, dispersed like the stars in the heavens. Their appearance did not resemble a dragon. Japan was strong and cunning. Sometimes Ryukyu was threatened by Japan, but seemed to take no notice of it. Relying on mountains and sea, the generations succeeded each other calmly.[57] In other words, Ryukyu had existed as a kingdom, not because it was strong, an external indication of which would be islands forming the shape of a dragon, but because it was remote.

Xià was well aware of rumors of an impending invasion, and he found the kingdom's lack of concern about Shimazu perplexing. In his official report, Xià stated that Ryukyu ignored the threat of invasion and made no military preparations. He asked the Council of Three about reports that numerous Japanese ships had been spotted near other Ryukyu islands. Their reply was that such reports had been common for years.[58] Because Ryukyu was under the protection of a powerful deity, there was no need to worry. Xià commented that if Ryukyu were to undertake serious military preparations, including organizing an effective defense, acquiring weapons, and undergoing training, then such a state of preparedness would probably deter an attack. When Xià asked Ryukyuan officials about what they relied upon for defense, their answer was "remoteness and deities."[59]

Because his report was an official record, Xià was relatively restrained in his critique of Ryukyu. After returning to China later in 1606, he spoke more frankly to a colleague, who recorded the conversation. Xià explained that a thousand Japanese armed with swords came to trade and that Ryukyu would soon bow before Japan. He stated that Ryukyu's way of serving the Chinese court was extremely shallow, and that Ryukyuan officials were manipulative, wavering, and sly. He complained that he and his assistant envoy lacked the power to coerce Ryukyu, nor was any law effective for that purpose. The next time envoys crossed over to Ryukyu, he said, the humiliation of the country would be obvious.[60] Xià's frustrations and the Hana incident are reminders of the contrast between official rhetoric praising Ryukyu as a steadfast servant of the Ming court versus the potential for tensions at ground level. Moreover, insofar as any Ryukyuan officials assumed that the Ming court would intervene militarily on their behalf they were engaged in fanciful thinking.

CHAPTER FOURTEEN

The War

The war of 1609 was the pivotal event in Ryukyuan history. It is somewhat odd, therefore, that most survey histories have very little to say about it. Modern survey histories tend to follow the framework of the official histories, which mention the war only briefly. *Kyūyō*, for example, lists only two short items for 1609. One is the establishment of a Shuri-ōyako official in Miyako, thus initiating the "three heads" system of governing Miyako.[1] The other explains that, for over a century, Ryukyu had been sending decorated ships to Satsuma. "Unfortunately, trusting the words of the minister Jana caused the loss of the proper diplomatic propriety." That was the cause of the invasion. Unable to prevail in the fight, the result was the king being taken to Satsuma.[2] The next passage is from two years later, announcing the king's return. Given their purpose of glorifying the royal line and presenting a morally driven version of the past, it should be clear why the official histories pass over the war as quickly and mention it as minimally as possible.

In contrast, this chapter examines the war in some detail. There is a high-quality secondary literature, and for the most part I rely on it here.[3] Occasionally, I highlight passages in primary or early sources or compare different sources.

MAJOR PREMODERN SOURCES

It is beneficial to be aware of the nature of several key early sources for the war. *Kian nikki* (Kian diary) is the only source written from a Ryukyuan perspective. Recall that Kian Nyūdo moved to Okinawa from Sakai in

1600. Although presented in a diary format covering 1609.3 to 1611.10, the work was actually written sometime between 1621 and 1640. Although Kian was a close adviser to the king and was in a good position to observe events, *Kian nikki* reflects some influence of classic war tales such as *Heike monogatari*, *Hōgen monogatari*, and *Heiji monogatari*.

Ryūkyū tokai nichinichi ki (Daily record of crossing to Ryukyu), by Ichiki Magobei, is another diary-style account of the war from the point of view of the invading forces. Its author was a member of the Takayama contingent from the southern part of the Ōsumi Peninsula, an area that came under Shimazu control in the 1570s. The content of *Ryūkyū tokai nichinichi ki* generally accords with that of *Kian nikki*.

Perhaps the most intriguing but also problematic source is *Ryūkyū-iri no ki* (Account of the Ryukyu incursion). It was apparently written by a descendant of the twenty-four Tokara ship captains (*sentō*) who took part in the invasion as part of a two-hundred-and-fifty-man Tokara contingent. It was written approximately a century after the event and seeks to highlight the importance of the Tokara mariners. The identical work is found under the alternate title *Ryūkyū gunki* (Ryukyu military account). *Ryūkyū-iri no ki* tends to include a greater number of concrete details and dramatic episodes than the other sources. For these reasons and its late date of composition, *Ryūkyū-iri no ki* is generally regarded as the least reliable major source.

Finally, *Nanbei kikō* (Accounts of southern missions) is a work in three volumes covering the period 607–1832 by Satsuma historian Ijichi Sueyoshi (also known as Ijichi Sueyasu and Ijichi Kian, 1782–1867). Volume 3 (*ge*) begins with 1609. This work is the only academic history among the major sources. While its own source base is not always clear, *Nanbei kikō* often discusses points not found in other sources. Household records are useful for corroborating or elaborating on items in this and other sources.

MILITARY REGULATIONS AND PREPARATIONS

The invasion force came from Satsuma and other Shimazu territories.[4] In 1608.9.6, domain officials issued detailed military regulations for soldiers making the journey to Ryukyu (*Ryūkyū tokai no gunshū hatto no jōjō*).[5] One interesting feature is that the equipment list includes agricultural tools for reaping crops. Shimazu forces had direct experience in food, or its lack, as a factor in battle. Because of Ryukyu's lateness in sending provisions, the Shimazu army suffered food shortages in Korea and had to rely on scavenging crops to get by. The invasion force was hedging against the possibility that the war would be a protracted one. The regulations also list a breakdown of expenses. Significantly, the vast majority of a silver levy raised ostensibly to fund the invasion was spent, not on military equipment and supplies, but on maintaining Shimazu's hostages in Suruga and on other domain administrative costs. In other words, the invasion of Ryukyu also functioned as a de facto extraction of wealth from the retainers under Shimazu suzerainty (the *kashindan*) to help overcome the financial crisis mentioned in chapter 13.[6]

In 1609.2.26, the domain reissued a revised *Ryūkyū tokai no gunshū hatto no jōjō*, and this time it included the signatures of Shimazu Yoshihisa, Yoshihiro, and Iehisa, all in a row.[7] In other words, the leadership of the domain had become unified behind the invasion. The thirteen main provisions were nearly the same as those of the previous year. For example, they prohibited violence against peasants, the destruction of shrines and temples, the ransacking of sutras and other texts, the killing of innocent people, and the kidnapping of local residents. The extent to which the Shimazu commanders or individual soldiers sought to abide by these regulations is unclear. Some of the actions of the invading army described below seem to have been in violation of the letter or spirit of some of the regulations, as is often the case in warfare.

The reissuing most likely marked the start of mobilization. By 1609.3.1, most of the various contingents had arrived at Yamakawa in Satsuma. They departed on 3.4 (month.day, here and below) with Kabayama Hisataka in command.[8] The day before their departure, Yoshihisa, who had long opposed the invasion, apparently wrote to Iehisa. From Iehisa's reply, we know that Yoshihisa was concerned about reports that soldiers at Yamakawa had adopted a contemptuous attitude toward Ryukyuans. Iehisa hastily issued five additional directives, though almost certainly they came from Yoshihisa: (1) actively engage any peace overtures from the Ryukyuan side; (2) if all goes well, try to finish military operations by the sixth or seventh month; (3) bring along leading officials and local island chiefs as hostages to indicate that, from now onward, administrative authority would be exercised by Satsuma; (4) if the king hunkered down in his castle for a long siege, the extreme measure of burning it down and taking hostages from surrounding areas would be justified; (5) if food ran short, it would be permissible to confiscate it from Ryukyuan peasants.[9] Again we see the Shimazu leadership concerned about a protracted war.

Guided by Tokara mariners, a force of approximately one hundred ships carrying some three thousand well-armed, battle-hardened soldiers sailed out of Yamakawa and into the Ryukyu islands. Its main goals were to seize the northern Ryukyu islands, to subdue Okinawa, and to force the king and his officials to surrender and ultimately sign a peace treaty. Owing in part to the cost of the invasion and to avoid possible political complications, the Shimazu forces were under pressure to achieve a decisive victory rapidly and then bring the king to Japan. Although the soldiers were capable and well-armed, the invasion force had been assembled from different parts of the Shimazu domains. The potential therefore existed for internal dissension should the war become a prolonged conflict or if the force faced serious adversity. Ryukyuan officials, however, were probably unaware of this point or of any other details explained in this section.

AMAMI-ŌSHIMA AND KIKAI SURRENDER

The fleet arrived in Kasari, at the northern tip of Amami-Ōshima, on 3.7 (see fig. 5). They encountered no organized defenses. The Shimazu forces easily took control of Kasari, which was sparsely populated by the time they arrived. Most of the population had fled into the nearby mountains, and the "Naha Taiyaku"—that is, the Shuri-ōyako—surrendered immediately.[10] This Shuri-ōyako was none other than Tamekoro. He was the young lad studying at Enkakuji when his father vanished at sea in 1579, as discussed in chapter 11. Tamekoro did quite well as a result of the invasion. He remained in his post at Kasari, and his salary doubled from ten *koku* to twenty when Shimazu became his overlord.[11] Moreover, Tamekoro traveled with the Shimazu forces to encourage other local rulers to surrender.[12]

The second landing was at Yamatohama (Yakiuchi district), in the middle of the western coast of Amami-Ōshima on 3.12. Household records and all the major sources except *Ryūkyū-iri no ki* report the same course of action as at Kasari. Local officials immediately surrendered without a fight. According to *Ryūkyū-iri no ki,* the local *ōyako* organized several thousand peasants, who had hastily erected barricades. Gunfire from the ships destroyed the barricades, and the erstwhile defenders fled. The teenage son of the *ōyako* fled with his mother to the hills and organized continued resistance.[13] The official in charge of Yakiuchi district was Motetaru, and according to household records, he surrendered immediately.[14] One of his subordinate officials at Yamatohama was Omotarugane (Umitarugane), who was also a young lad studying at Enkakuj in 1579 when his father Inutarugane disappeared at sea. He too surrendered and was rewarded with rice and a five-*koku* salary.[15] Shuri's official in Kikai, Kantarugane, sailed to Amami-Ōshima to surrender that island in advance of any possible military landing.[16] It is possible that some local residents put up a show of resistance to the invaders, perhaps with some support from local officials. However, there is no reliable evidence of any significant defense preparations or resistance on the part of Shuri's officials in Amami-Ōshima.

On 3.16, the fleet arrived in Nishikomi on the southwestern coast of Amami-Ōshima. Part of it departed for Tokunoshima and part of it remained behind owing to poor weather. Shuri had sent Hachimine Peechin to Amami-Ōshima as a scout. He witnessed the quick collapse of Kasari and took a fast boat to Okinawa to report. Word reached Shuri on 3.10. The king immediately sent a priest envoy to Amami-Ōshima in an attempt to negotiate a settlement before Shimazu forces reached Okinawa. Rumors spread fast in Okinawa, and an incorrect report on 3.16 stated that the invaders had landed at Nakijin. The royal government had a messenger network in place to learn about the progress of the war, but there was no mechanism for disseminating information to ordinary people. The spread of rumors fueled confusion and panic.[17]

FIGHTING AT TOKUNOSHIMA

Clearly the royal government had not made effective military preparations. Once it realized the invasion was under way, Shuri pursued a dual strategy of suing for peace while also rushing to assemble defense forces. The apparent military plan was to resist the invaders at Tokunoshima, thus buying time to organize defenses in Okinawa. There is evidence of some advanced preparation. Shuri sent Yonabaru Peechin Chōchi to Tokunoshima, possibly as early as 1608. At the time, Yonabaru was part of the royal government's Hokuzan kanshu office at Nakijin.[18]

When the initial fleet arrived at Kanamasaki (northeast edge of the island) on 3.17, they encountered no resistance. When seven Satsuma ships arrived at Wan'ya on the northwest coast, however, a thousand defenders surrounded them along the shore. On 3.18, the two to three hundred troops aboard the ships went ashore and defeated the defenders, taking some fifty heads in the process. Such heads were probably preserved in brine on the ships to be brought back as evidence of battlefield exploits.[19] The most intense fighting took place on 3.20 in the southeast at Akitoku. Remnants of the Wan'ya defenders and a local militia using mainly homemade weapons such as knives attached to the end of poles attacked the invaders vigorously, led by two brothers who were the local officials. The invaders suffered casualties and were briefly pinned down. However, once the Shimazu forces were able to get in position to fire their muskets effectively, the defense quickly collapsed under a withering fire.[20]

Another battle took place at nearby Kametsu, most likely on 3.21. After the fighting, Ryukyuan officials fled into the nearby mountains, and on 3.22 members of the invasion force "hunted" for them. They captured Yonabaru, who cooperated with the Shimazu forces and later rose through the ranks of the royal government. In some sources, Jana Teidō looms large as a formidable opponent during the war. Perhaps because the resistance at Tokunoshima was so stiff, some sources claim that Yonabaru was Jana's son-in-law, but that is unlikely.[21]

Approximately two to three hundred Ryukyuan soldiers died on Tokunoshima. It is possible that the death toll was substantially higher, because only formal soldiers wearing armor and helmets would have been counted, not the local civilians who mobilized for the battle. The casualty count among the invaders is more difficult to discern.[22] An official's ledger from later in the century notes that even as late as 1682–1683, elderly Tokunoshima survivors of the Akitoku battle got together and talked about it.[23]

The Shimazu force moved on to Okinoerabu, an island surrounded by coral reefs. The main official there was confident that the large ships of the invaders would not be able to enter the harbor safely. However, an unusually high tide permitted some of the force to land near China at the southern end of the island, and the surprised official surrendered without a fight on 3.24.

ARRIVING IN OKINAWA

Bypassing Yoron, on 3.25 the fleet arrived at the small island of Kouri, just across from Unten harbor, the gateway to Nakijin. On 3.27, it occupied Nakijin castle, which had been abandoned. As soon as the fleet arrived in northern Okinawa, the king hurriedly dispatched the priest Kikuin, who had lived in Satsuma for several years and was well connected there, and Council of Three member Nago Ueekata Ryōhō (Ba Ryōhitsu) as peace envoys. However, Kabayama refused to meet with them in Nakijin. Nago Ueekata entered the Satsuma camp as a hostage, and Kikuin rushed back to Shuri. He arrived there just before the invaders did, after a grueling trek. "Blood from his feet stained the sand and turned his white robes crimson" according to *Kian nikki*.[24]

At this point, with Nago Ueekata a prisoner in the Nakijin area and the aged priest Kikuin rushing back to Shuri, let us pause and consider part of a detailed letter Shō Nei sent to the Ming court approximately a month after he had surrendered. Smuggled out of Okinawa, the letter explained the invasion and begged the Ming court's understanding that Ryukyu would not be able to send tribute embassies in the near future. The king stated that, on 3.12, he dispatched Ba Ryōhitsu (Nago Ueekata) to northern Okinawa at the head of an army of a thousand. On 3.26, the invaders landed and began setting fire to homes and buildings. Ba sent scouts to observe the enemy. They reported back that the invaders were actually fewer in number than earlier reports had indicated. Cheered by their report, the Ryukyuan army attacked, but it was a diabolical ruse: Japanese soldiers had been hiding deep in the mountains. They emerged as the Ryukyuans attacked, surrounding the Ryukyuan force and killing half of it. Taken prisoner, Ba denounced the invaders and declared that he would gladly face death. However, the Shimazu commanders were impressed by Ba's courage and patriotism and spared his life.[25]

The manner in which Nago Ueekata ended up as prisoner of Satsuma according to the king's letter is dramatically different from our understanding of events based on other sources. The letter, of course, was intended to portray valiant, proactive resistance by the Ryukyuan forces for Chinese consumption. Shō Nei's account was fanciful, and the invaders found Nakijin castle abandoned. Nevertheless, it is likely that fighting did take place in the vicinity of the castle, perhaps a day later. The reason is that the top Ryukyuan military official in the region, Hokuzan kanshu Shō Kokushi, died at age twenty-eight on 3.28, the day after the occupation of Nakijin castle.[26] Possible resistance by Shō Kokushi's forces, however, did not significantly slow the invaders' progress.

FIGHTING IN NAHA AND SHURI

When the blood-soaked priest arrived at Shuri castle, the king was visibly shaken to learn that Kabayama had rejected peace negotiations at Nakijin and would soon arrive in the capital region with his army. According to *Kian nikki,* young officials in the palace declared that there was nothing left to do but fight and rushed to Naha.[27] If the invasion of the capital region had been as simple as the Shimazu fleet trying to push its way into Naha, the Ryukyuan defenders might have had a chance to delay the outcome and possibly strengthen their negotiating position. Knowing that Naha was well defended, however, on 3.29 the majority of the invasion force landed at Ōwan in Yomitan, near the mouth of the Hija River, and began an overland march south to the capital region. Kabayama sent the Tokara sailors with part of the fleet to try their hand at pushing into Naha harbor.

The *hiki* forces manned their battle stations. Jana Ueekata, the main architect of the disaster that was unfolding, led roughly a thousand soldiers to defend the shore around Naha harbor. Normally Nago Ueekata would have led a second army of a thousand, but because he was in Satsuma's custody, Tomigusuku Ueekata took his place. A third army under Urasoe Ueekata, a close political ally of Jana, assembled to defend Shuri castle. The great chain was in place, blocking Naha harbor, and the artillery pieces in the Yarazamori and Mie fortresses were ready to fire. The invaders arrived, the battle began, and among the invaders, "the dead numbered too many to count" according to the king's letter to the Ming court.[28] Although the bodies were probably well within counting range, all sources agree that the Ryukyuan defenders beat back the attackers decisively.[29]

The Tokara mariners had sought to break through into Naha harbor and were repulsed. According to *Ryūkyū-iri no ki,* their ships suffered damage but there were no human casualties. They made it back to Kabayama's main fleet and were able to get aboard undamaged ships. Kabayama was angry, apparently because of the successful resistance. He faced the Tokara sailors and said that "Jana" (his name written in derogatory characters from this point on in the account) must be brought to Kagoshima and made to kill himself. The Ryukyuan resistance also caused logistical problems with respect to the Tokara sailors and their ships. They ended up joining the march to Naha.[30]

The fighting grew more intense as the invaders approached the capital. While the cannon roared around Naha harbor, the capital region was in a state of confusion as people sought to escape the fighting. Shimazu forces approached the Taihei bridge on the outskirts of Shuri. Goeku Ueekata rushed to defend the bridge with one hundred soldiers. The defenders faced a volley of gunfire "like rain" and scattered after one of their officers was killed.[31] According to the king's letter to China, the "lowly Japanese" approached from the north, burning everything along their path. With the limited resources of a small country, "when we sent our military to the north, we lost in the south; when we attacked south, we lost in the north."[32] Most Ryukyuan defenders retreated to Shuri castle, which was soon surrounded. A group of Shimazu soldiers attempted to force their way into the castle at Iri no Azana (an observation platform), but a Ryukyuan force led by Yamazaki Nikyūshusan, the physician from Echizen, beat them back.[33] On 4.1, the Shimazu fleet successfully entered Naha harbor and land forces captured Urasoe castle. Shuri was completely surrounded at that point. Negotiations began soon thereafter at Naha harbor. *Kian nikki* lists the participants on each side.

Significantly, the names Jana Ueekata, Urasoe Ueekata, Kabayama, and the vice-commander Hirata are missing. In other words, Jana and Urasoe were still fighting.[34] In the meantime, the invaders had set fire to vast areas of the capital region.

One other point that *Kian nikki* reports is that when Kikuin arrived with news of an impending invasion of the capital region, although many of the young officials advocated fighting, Ōzato Aji, Kunigami Aji, Gusukuma Ueekata, Mabuni Ueekata, and several other high-ranking officials immediately fled the castle and hid in the countryside and mountains. They were not present when Shō Nei left the castle, and later they were censured.[35] Uehara Kenzen points out that this flight of top officials exemplifies the weakness of Shō Nei's administration.[36] Incidents of Ryukyuan soldiers taunting Shimazu forces from atop the castle ramparts was another indication. Ryukyuan warfare sometimes featured "cursing battles" prior to actual battles, in which priestesses chanted abusive *omoro* at the opposing side.[37] The king ordered that this unhelpful verbal skirmishing end, but it did not.[38]

ADDITIONAL FIGHTING AND SHŌ NEI'S SURRENDER

What happened to Jana's force defending Naha? Despite variations in the details from source to source, it seems that they withdrew to Kumemura and continued to fight throughout 4.1 and 4.2. According to what is surely an exaggerated account in *Ryūkyū-iri no ki,* Jana held out with his three-thousand-man army for three days and nights in Kumemura. However, the area was not easy to defend, and he tried to escape to Shuri castle on horseback. An eighteen-year-old Shimazu soldier pursued and captured Jana, presenting him to Kabayama.[39] *Nanbei kikō* provides a more plausible account. Jana retreated to Kumemura and fought a battle in which some three hundred of his men were killed or captured. At that point, he tried to flee to Shuri castle and was captured along the way. There is also an account in the Sata household records. Reading *Nanbei kikō* and the Sata account together, we can surmise that (1) Jana led a Kumemura-based force in resisting, and about three hundred of that force were killed or captured; (2) the person who captured him as he fled toward Shuri castle was a Tokara sailor named Komatsu Sukejirō; and (3) Sukejirō did not capture him single-handedly but was assisted by Sata Hisanobu. It is unlikely that Jana led the people of Kumemura to resist, but it is quite likely that the remnants of his army, the one drawn from the southern districts, continued to resist in the vicinity of Kumemura for approximately one day. *Kian nikki* notes on 4.2 that Jana and his ally, Urasoe Ueekata, were in Naha as prisoners.[40]

Shō Nei agreed to surrender on 4.3, but some resistance continued. As the king's luggage was being prepared, twenty retainers escaped the castle by rope, all members of the pro-Jana faction. Soldiers coming around to check on the luggage noticed and gave chase. The Ryukyuans fought back. Taking a composite picture from all the sources, we can conclude that (1) on 4.3, a group of royal retainers fled the castle; (2) their leaders were the three sons of Urasoe Ueekata; (3) the fight with their pursuers at Shikinabaru caused the deaths of the three brothers and the death and injury of several Shimazu soldiers.[41]

The king's decision to surrender created another split among his retainers. At this point, we can identify three specific groups. We might call the first one the cowardly faction, consisting of Ōzato Aji and the others who hid in the mountains. Next were those in favor of surrender, including Prince Gushikami, Council of Three member Nago Ueekata, the priest Kikuin, Ikegusuku Anrai (instrumental in crushing the 1592 Jana revolt), and Tomigusuku Seizoku. The pro-resistance faction included Council of Three members Jana and Urasoe, Urasoe's sons, and the seventeen or so others who had left the castle, most likely to continue the fight.[42] Kian and Yamazaki Nikyūshusan stood by Shō Nei, although we cannot say whether they advocated surrender or continued resistance.

Shuri castle was a powerful fortress, and by the end of the day on 4.1 it was full of well-armed soldiers, many of whom appeared eager to fight. The castle would surely have fallen eventually, but the Ryukyuan defenders could have delayed the process. No doubt Shō Nei realized the severity of the situation and sought to save what was left of the capital and his throne from going up in flames. An important factor in the king's decision to surrender was the fact that intermediaries assured him Satsuma's main territorial goal was to take the northern Ryukyu islands, not to destroy the whole kingdom.[43]

On 4.4, Shō Nei left Shuri castle to reside at Nago Ueekata's mansion. Satsuma forces occupied Shuri castle at that point. They took some valuable items, but strict controls prevented looting on a massive scale. In terms of lives lost, the Shimazu forces suffered approximately two hundred battlefield deaths plus an unspecified number of soldiers wounded. The Ryukyuan death toll was much higher, although records are insufficient even to approximate a figure.[44]

Uezato provides the following overall assessment of why the war turned out as it did:

> According to Shimazu's initial plans, if the war had dragged on for a long time, the Satsuma forces would likely have abandoned their plan to occupy Okinawa and have pulled back. If the war had developed into a siege of Shuri castle or a guerrilla conflict, internal divisions within Shimazu's heterogeneous force had the potential to manifest themselves and cause disintegration.
>
> However, Ryukyu's government lacked unity, consisting of factions of officials who favored military resistance, those who favored peace negotiations, and those who fled. A feud between the Urasoe and Shuri branches of the royal family, which had been under way before the war, probably influenced the internal divisions and confusion. The royal government initially relied on its defense system but in the end sought a solution through peace negotiations. The faction advocating all-out battle did not occupy the dominant position.[45]

If the royal government had possessed good intelligence about Shimazu's intentions and resources, if it had been unified, if it had made better military preparations, and if its officials and soldiers had all fought with resolve, the kingdom might have pushed back or blocked the invasion force and negotiated a better peace treaty.

Each of these points, of course, is a large "if." Moreover, the war itself could have been prevented on several occasions had the royal government decided to cooperate with Shimazu and Tokugawa Ieyasu. Perhaps the best thing Shō Nei could have done would have been quietly to reach out directly to Ieyasu. In any case, what actually happened was nearly the worst possible outcome. It is no wonder that the official histories have little to say about these matters.

CHAPTER FIFTEEN

Aftermath

The immediate Ryukyuan response to the war was what we might call triage. The king and his entourage of officials set out for Japan, while Nago Ueekata took charge of the government in Shuri during their absence. The king and Nago both sent messages to the Ming court. After the king returned in 1611, much uncertainty remained. With Shimazu in direct control of Michinoshima, and given the necessity of creating the appearance of independence for what remained of Shuri's empire, Shō Nei was able passively to continue resisting demands that Ryukyu serve as an intermediary with China. Such resistance was not viable in the long run however, as Shō Nei's successor realized. As Ryukyu and Satsuma began to cooperate in the 1630s in pursuing tribute trade, the Ming dynasty began to falter, ultimately giving way to the Qing and creating more confusion. The changes during the period from approximately 1609 to 1650 were many, and this chapter discusses only a small subset.

TRIAGE VIS-À-VIS CHINA

We have already seen part of Shō Nei's letter to the Ming court, sent just before he departed for Japan. Its major points are (1) a claim that Nago Ueekata fought bravely and aggressively but had to surrender after losing half of his army; (2) a claim that the invaders demanded that Ryukyu provide soldiers to help with an invasion of Taiwan, refused out of Ryukyuan loyalty and love for the Ming court; (3) a claim that Ryukyu was forced to cede Iheya island to the invaders; and (4) an emphasis on Ryukyu looking to China as a source of learning, culture, and civilization.[1] There is no evidence for the first three items, and the fourth appears to be standard flattery.

A follow-up communiqué from Nago Ueekata to the Board of Rites contains similar content, but it stresses that Satsuma has been merciful and that Ryukyu is working hard to restore good relations with Japan. Nago's message also claims that the invaders were persuaded by Ryukyu's remonstrance to suspend their plans to invade Taiwan. Moreover, it states that the threat to Taiwan will abate for the long term if Ryukyu is able to forge peaceful relations with Japan. Nago's communiqué indicates a departure from the policies of Jana and a look forward to the reestablishment of tribute relations.[2] For his part, Jana sent a secret message to the Ming court via Chinese in Nagasaki. Ikegusuku Anrai heard of the matter and had the letter intercepted. If it had not been intercepted, the letter probably would have inflamed Ming antagonism toward Japan and delayed the normalization of tribute relations.[3]

Despite attempts to assure the Ming court that all was well, in 1612.7.7, the Fujian grand coordinator reported that even though the king had returned to Ryukyu, his country was still under Japanese control.[4] Ten days later, the supervising secretary of the Office of Scrutiny for War replied in part: "As for this Chūzan king, why in the world would he, after being spared death and released from captivity, suddenly forget the power of Japan and revere the righteousness of far-away China? . . . It is clear that Japan tells him what to do."[5] The royal government had much work to do if it was to restore some semblance of normal relations with the Ming court. Suspicious of a Japanese-controlled Ryukyu, the Ming court set the tribute frequency to once in ten years in 1612. Repeated entreaties and diplomacy resulted in a change to once in five years in 1622. A return to the prewar frequency of once every two years took place in 1633, soon to be disrupted by the decline and fall of the Ming dynasty.

TRIAGE VIS-À-VIS JAPAN

Shō Nei and Shimazu Iehisa traveled to Sunpu for an interview with Ieyasu. Shō Nei was away from Okinawa for two and a half years, returning in the autumn of 1611. In the meantime, agents of Shimazu conducted a survey of the agricultural productivity of Ryukyu, the first of its kind. This survey highlighted a major change in Ryukyuan society, one that had been under way for decades. As foreign trade decreased, Ryukyu increasingly had to rely on its own resources, especially agriculture. Before

Shō Nei could return to Okinawa, he and his leading ministers were presented with a document of surrender to which they had to affix their signatures and seals. The first of its articles stated that Ryukyu had long been part of Satsuma.[6] Jana refused to sign the document and was immediately taken away and beheaded. In subsequent documents, it became common practice to write "Jana" using Chinese characters with a derogatory meaning.

In 1611, Satsuma issued specific directives to Ryukyu stating the broad outlines of territory, authority, finances, and other matters. For example, Ryukyu's total assessed productivity (kokudaka), measured as units of rice, was 110,304 koku. Of this amount, 89,086 koku stayed in Ryukyu, and, in principle, the other 21,218 koku went to Satsuma as an annual tax. The royal government also paid an annual tax to Satsuma of cloth, cowhide, and other goods.[7] The key point is that, after 1609, Ryukyu faced significant externally imposed constraints. On the other hand, changing world conditions, especially the Ming to Qing transition of the 1620s–1640s, provided Ryukyu with some leverage to create a quasi-autonomous situation for itself.[8]

It is well known that Satsuma used Ryukyu for access to China, especially after Tokugawa Iemitsu (r. 1623–1651) moved to restrict Japan's foreign relations during the 1630s. In 1609, however, Tokugawa Ieyasu was in the middle of a vigorous effort to restore Japan's foreign relations. In other words, there was no way that anyone in 1609 could have predicted the future foreign-policy restrictions, often called sakoku (closed country). The immediate goal of the Shimazu leadership in 1609 was to seize the northern Ryukyu islands. The use of Shuri as a trade and information portal vis-à-vis China was an afterthought, and the process took several decades to reach maturity.

As for Michinoshima, in 1610, Kagoshima's Ōshima daikan replaced Ryukyu's official in Amami-Ōshima and oversaw all of Michinoshima. This official underwent a title change to Ōshima bugyō in 1613. In 1616, the Tokunoshima bugyō was established to administer Tokunoshima, Okinoerabu, and Yoron. New regulations issued in 1623 created a system whereby a Satsuma-appointed bugyō supervised local officials. The older ōyako rank was abolished and yoriki became the highest post that islanders could attain. A 1621 survey of Michinoshima assessed its total productivity at 43,257 koku. Administrative reforms and cultural policies in the 1620s attempted to sever lingering ties with the Ryukyu king. However, in relation to foreign countries, especially China, Michinoshima remained nominally part of the Ryukyu kingdom.[9]

REMNANTS OF THE EMPIRE

For the same reasons that it is appropriate to regard sixteenth-century Ryukyu as an empire (chapter 11), it would also be appropriate to regard early modern Satsuma (the various Shimazu domains) as an empire. Kagoshima was the center, and the northern Ryukyu islands came into its orbit. Shuri also became tied to Kagoshima, albeit less directly. Although ultimately subordinate to Satsuma, Shuri's reduced empire continued to exist. The major peripheral region in the new arrangement was Sakishima. On balance, the living conditions of ordinary Ryukyuans in islands other than Okinawa often worsened during the early modern era.

Conditions after 1609 forced Shuri to rely more heavily on extraction of resources from Sakishima. Let us briefly zoom in on taxation as an example. I start with documents from the head of the Bureau of Revenue from the period 1789–1801, which are similar to the figures found in the only other document of royal revenues we have, *Go-zaisei* (1728).[10] I take the main annual rice-based tax (*shōzei*) for the Yaeyama islands, versus the same tax for Okinawa, and divide by the percentage of Yaeyama's population circa 1800. The total population of the Ryukyu kingdom was about 155,637 in 1800. Yaeyama's population in 1803 was 15,858, which is very close to its population in 1798 (15,957) and 1810 (15,533).[11] Therefore, as of approximately 1800, Yaeyama comprised 10 percent of Ryukyu's population, but it paid 13 percent of the basic rice tax. The real burden on Yaeyama, however, was substantially heavier, because of the way in which taxation was assessed in Sakishima, the relative lack of resources in these islands, and the fact that extra and ad hoc taxes were particularly heavy. During the nineteenth century, the population of Yaeyama decreased in absolute terms and relative to the total population of the kingdom. By 1871, Yaeyama was shouldering a similar 13 percent basic tax burden, but with only 7 percent of Ryukyu's population.[12]

The broader point to this example is that during the early modern era Shuri extracted resources from the outlying areas of what remained of its empire. When Japan's Meiji state moved definitively to annex Ryukyu in 1879, some Ryukyuan elites protested and passively resisted. The annexation, however, engendered no widespread popular opposition, whether in Okinawa or other islands. During the late nineteenth century, there was little popular loyalty to or nostalgia for the kingdom, or what might be better termed the regime in Shuri.[13] As it turned out, life under the Meiji state, initially at least, was not much different or better than it was during the latter years of the kingdom, especially in Sakishima. Nevertheless, only former elites made any effort to maintain or restore institutions from the kingdom.

A POSSIBLE TRAJECTORY FOR RYUKYUAN CULTURE

This book is mainly a political history, not a theory of Ryukyuan culture. Nevertheless, at this point it is possible to make some comments about the big-picture trajectory of Ryukyuan culture.

In 1879 Japan's Meiji state annexed Ryukyu and created Okinawa Prefecture. From then until well into the twentieth century, questions of culture and its relationship with individual and national identity became almost an obsession in journalistic and academic discourse within Okinawa.[14] The assimilation of Okinawa Prefecture into Japan was a protracted process that was economically and psychologically difficult for many Okinawans. At the heart of this difficult transition was a cultural gap, both actual and perceived, between overdetermined "Ryukyuan" and "Japanese" identities.[15] Partly because of social constructions and partly because of historical legacies, Ryukyuan and Japanese cultures often stood in opposition during the modern era, and this opposition caused much suffering. Let us take the early twentieth century as an end point in a big-picture trajectory for the development of Ryukyuan culture.

The Beginning

In chapter 1, following research findings in the fields of archaeology and anthropology, I argue that immigrants from Japan populated the Ryukyu islands fairly rapidly between approximately the eleventh and thirteenth centuries. The Ryukyu islands had been inhabited well before that time, but these Japonic Gusuku-era migrants and their descendants displaced and/or absorbed the sparse populations already present. Specific prehistoric scenarios are inevitably speculative, but it is likely that the Northern Tier, especially Kikai, served as one major crossroads between Japan and Korea and Ryukyu islands to the south. Major political events in Japan, especially the civil wars of the fourteenth century, also generated southward migrations into the Ryukyu islands; however, by then the basic Japonic population was already in place.

The Sakishima islands nicely illustrate the chronology I have outlined. It is well established that Sakishima underwent a fundamental change during the eleventh or twelfth centuries. Prior to the eleventh century, the islands were sparsely populated by non-Japonic, nonagricultural peoples of southern origin. After the eleventh century, agriculture appeared in Sakishima, and the human population came to resemble those of the rest of the Ryukyu islands. Particularly important is the fact that all of the languages of the southern Ryukyu islands are Japonic, even though non-Japonic peoples from places like Taiwan or the Philippines once lived there.[16] In other words, there was a rapid replacement of the population, and it took place around the eleventh century or slightly later.

We can therefore take the eleventh century as the approximate beginning of something we might reasonably call "Ryukyuan culture." Strictly speaking, however, the eleventh century was the start of Ryukyuan culture *within the Ryukyu islands*. The history of Ryukyuan languages is almost certainly older than the eleventh century. Speakers of proto-Ryukyuan would have existed in Japan prior to the southward migrations into Ryukyu. There are different hypotheses for the geographic locus or loci of proto-Ryukyuan, most focusing on Kyushu or Yamaguchi Prefecture.[17] Taking circa the eleventh century as the starting point, some eight or nine centuries elapsed between then and the start of the twentieth century.

Linked-in Ryukyu

Was the development of Ryukyuan culture a steady accretion over the entire span of these centuries? Possibly, but my hypothesis is that the pace at which a distinctly Ryukyuan cluster of cultures developed accelerated after 1609. What I have stressed in this book is that early Ryukyu was not a closed-off political or cultural space until the seventeenth century. Even after the initial migration wave or waves during the eleventh through thirteenth centuries, the Ryukyu islands continued to receive people from other parts of the East China Sea network. Recall also the point, made in chapter 1, that DNA evidence suggests that the Ryukyu islands have not experienced a long period of isolation. Despite its importance, we cannot quantify this flow of people, nor can we know its precise impact on the cultural geography of early Ryukyu.

Migration was the driving force in early Ryukyuan history. The initial king of the first Shō dynasty, Shō Shishō, may have been a first-generation immigrant to Okinawa. Moving ahead to the early seventeenth century, Yamazaki Nikyūshusan, Kian Nyūdō, and Sōmi Nyūdō were examples of first-generation Japanese immigrants to Ryukyu who served Shō Nei. There had been many such people in the past, and there would be a few more in the future. Tōma Jūchin (1591–1676), who was instrumental in currency reform, is another example. He was originally from the Shimazu domain of Ōsumi, where his name was Ijichi Tarōbei. Tōma changed his name and at around age twenty became, in effect, a naturalized Ryukyuan. The process worked in reverse as well. One example is Kunigami Samanokami (1591–1635), of *aji* status. He went to Satsuma in 1614 to serve as an official hostage. There, he adopted his Japanese name (Samanokami) and otherwise became Japanese, serving as a military officer in Shimazu Iehisa's army. Kunigami even participated in the siege of Osaka Castle in 1615. He returned to Ryukyu in 1616 after his term as a hostage ended, later traveling to Satsuma in 1632 as a royal envoy.[18]

Were language barriers significant in the Ryukyu islands or between Ryukyu and Kyushu? Probably, although these barriers are difficult to map from documentary sources. Moreover, sociolinguistic circumstances were probably significant. For example, the two Ryukyuan envoys to Satsuma in 1575 could make themselves understood only with difficulty and therefore had to use interpreters to facilitate negotiations. Those interpreters were sailors.[19] Recall the difficulty that Chinese-employed interpreters experienced during the 1590s distinguishing between Ryukyuan and Japanese sailors on cultural grounds, including language (see chapter 13). It suggests that, at least among seafarers, sharp cultural differences between Japanese and Ryukyuans had yet to emerge. Based on the limited evidence appearing in these pages, there may have been few sharp cultural dividing lines between the Ryukyu islands and maritime regions of Kyushu, even as late as circa 1600. Government officials in Naha and Kagoshima may not have been able to converse freely in 1550, but sailors in the region and Buddhist priests probably would have experienced fewer difficulties. Insofar as cultural barriers remained relatively small across the region through the sixteenth century, the circulation of people must have played a key role.

Closed-off Ryukyu

We know that a significant cultural divide existed between "Ryukyu," however defined, and Japan circa 1900. If my hypothesis that this divide was present but relatively minor around 1600 is correct, then how did a significant cultural divide develop over the relatively short span of approximately three centuries? Stated differently, what accelerated the rate of cultural change in Ryukyu? There were probably three major contributing factors. The most important was the cessation of the flow of people. During the early seventeenth century, Ryukyu became part of the Shimazu territories, and the practical effect of this change was for it to be closed off from the rest of Japan. The diverse *wajin* community or communities in the Naha area faded into the broader society. Satsuma prohibited Japanese from traveling to or residing in Ryukyu except for one Satsuma official and his small staff, who kept a low profile, and occasional ship crews from Satsuma, whose range of motion on shore was restricted.[20]

At approximately the same time that Satsuma severely restricted the flow of people into and out of Ryukyu, the *bakufu* was doing the same thing with respect to Japan as a whole. The boundaries of Japan and of Ryukyu became clearer than they had ever been before, and also distinct from each other.

Cultural Policies

Another contributor to the acceleration of cultural divergence were active de-Japanification policies. Satsuma initiated these policies, but Ryukyuan officials carried them out with vigor because they were connected to the very survival of the kingdom. After the failure of *bakufu* attempts to forge a diplomatic relationship with China in 1615, Satsuma began to fashion Ryukyu into an ostensibly independent country that could serve as a conduit to China. Maintaining the China connection became essential to the continued survival of the Shuri royal court and its officials. In this context, Kumemura, which had been languishing for a century or so, became a magnet for talent throughout the capital area during the latter half of the seventeenth century. Knowledge of Chinese high culture gradually improved among the Ryukyuan elites, some of whom took Chinese names and relocated to Kumemura.[21] The modern notion that Ryukyu was culturally Chinese stems from these early modern circumstances.

Specific de-Japanification policies were intended, not as attempts deeply to transform people's cultural identity, but to ensure a plausible non-Japanese appearance for Ryukyu in Chinese eyes. Regulations forbade Ryukyuans to appear as Japanese with respect to names, clothing, hairstyle, and language. Similarly, Ryukyuan ships no longer received a *-maru* name.[22] After the 1620s, Shuri went to great lengths to mask any ties with Japan when Chinese investiture envoys were in Okinawa or when Okinawans were in China. When a disabled Ryukyuan ship drifted toward the Shāndōng coast in 1673, for example, its crew threw all Japanese items overboard.[23] In Miyako, an overseer from Shuri arrived in 1629, in part to ensure that no Japanese language, songs, clothing, names, or other ties to Yamato would be evident when there was even a remote a possibility of any Miyako resident encountering Chinese (for example, when investiture embassies were at sea). Mainly for this reason, the popularity of adopting Japanese childhood names declined. This point applied especially to Gaara names because of their strong association with both Japan and *wakō*. Shuri's control had limits, of course, and was directed mainly at local elites. As Gaara group names declined sharply among local elites, they became associated with low status and poverty.[24]

Such policies are often cited as the main reason for the acceleration of cultural differences between Ryukyu and Japan during the early modern era. They undoubtedly contributed, but actual isolation from Japan was surely the more important force. Moreover, it is likely that internal social changes during the early modern era, such as the full transition from an economy based on maritime commerce to one based on agriculture, played roles in the process. This realm is a subject for further research.

Different Social Milieu

Finally, we should bear in mind that overall social perceptions had changed markedly between 1600 and 1900. It is quite possible that modern people attributed greater significance to real or perceived cultural differences compared with the premodern era.

A discussion of modern forms of nationalism and national identity is beyond our scope, but in general, cultural and state boundaries tended to become more congruent over the course of the early modern era. Modern ethno-nationalism typically linked national identity and culture. In this context, cultural differences on the part of less powerful social groups could function as social barriers. For example, differences in language that might have been perceived as practical inconveniences in 1600 would have been more likely in 1900 to function as markers of inferior social status, or even different national identities, in addition to causing practical problems. It is worth noting that neither Okinawan nor any of the dialects of Kagoshima would have been understood in Tokyo circa 1900. A migrant to Tokyo from Kagoshima might well have come under pressure to master standard Japanese (*hyōjungo*), but his or her credentials as a member of the Japanese national group would not have come into question. In short, the social environment circa 1900 probably functioned to amplify perceptions of cultural differences in many circumstances.

SHŌ SHŌKEN

Some of the findings of this book help to contextualize early modern reformers. For example, Shō Shōken endeavored to separate the public and private realms of government. He decreed that royal orders would no longer be conveyed by female officials. Recall that Korean castaways observed fifteenth-century kings surrounded by female officials inside the palace; among other functions, they conveyed the king's orders. This seventeenth-century change was one of many examples whereby early modern reformers tried to remake Shuri's political culture.[25]

Shō Shōken was also in a position to understand the consequences of the recent war with Satsuma. His explanation of Ryukyu's relationship with Japan in *Reflections on Chūzan* is subtle. He acknowledges what had become the required official line: Ryukyu had been attached to Satsuma since the Eikyō era (1429–1441). However, Shō Shoken adds that Ryukyu "had been sending tribute to Japan for over one hundred years before this time, but Shō Nei ignored this legacy." Furthermore, the wicked minister Jana "lost sight of whom he truly should serve."[26]

Ōyama Ringorō has argued that this choice of words was significant. The temporally strong connection with Japan as stated in *Reflections* was a reference to the Muromachi *bakufu*. Shō Shōken was painfully aware that Jana and Shō Nei had led the kingdom into virtual slavery under Satsuma's thumb despite a long history of good relations with other powers in Japan.[27] Of course, Shō Shōken had to express such sentiments in carefully measured language, but a close reading of *Reflections* supports Ōyama's interpretation. Shō Shōken strove to make the best of a difficult situation and to push his society to adapt to changed circumstances.

CHAPTER SIXTEEN

Many Ryukyus

Historian Takara Kurayoshi has argued for an expanded vision of Japanese history that situates Japan within East Asia and includes Ryukyu. Focusing on the medieval era, he writes:

> Revising the habit of thought that confines our image of medieval Japanese history to the Japanese islands, we can create a model of medieval Japanese history with a gaze broad enough to include the diverse realities of maritime Asia and the Ryukyu kingdom. This new medieval history not only affords access to the realm of Ryukyuan history. It is a vantage point for accurately grasping the historical variety within the Japanese islands and one that permits us to consider a Japan situated in the dynamic condition of the East Asian world. Our aim is not the Ryukyu kingdom in isolation. Our task is to create a model of medieval Japanese history that engages the manifold realities of East Asia, including the Ryukyu kingdom.[1]

My goal in this book is similar, for I argue for a broader version of Ryukyuan history, one that encompasses Japan and the East China Sea network. I also advocate a more complex version of Ryukyuan history, one that treats the Ryukyu islands not as a self-contained natural political or cultural community but as the abode of diverse maritime groups who often clashed and competed for wealth and the control of resources. There is more work to be done in this realm, and my hope is that this book is a useful step toward enlarging the scope of both Ryukyuan and Japanese history.

Readers familiar with George H. Kerr's *Okinawa: The History of an Island People* will surely have noticed a vastly different Ryukyu—or

Ryukyus—in these pages. I have endeavored to write a history of early Ryukyu without relying on the convenient but often problematic narrative framework provided by the official histories, which I have read comparatively and against the grain wherever possible. More important, I have relied almost entirely on other sources for material prior to the sixteenth century. Therefore, this book is a first attempt in English to write a substantially new history of early Ryukyu. Needless to say, however, the book would not have been possible without the work of the many scholars on whom I have relied. As we have seen, Mitsugu Sakihara used the *Omoro* to supplement the official histories, and scholars such as Murai Shōsuke and Tanaka Takeo have worked extensively on Ryukyu as part of the East China Sea network. Particularly important for this book have been the findings and the methodologies of multidisciplinary scholars such as Ōyama Ringorō, Tanigawa Ken'ichi, Fuku Hiromi, and Yoshinari Naoki. The pioneering and wide-ranging work of Iha Fuyū and Higashionna Kanjun has often constituted a starting point for my analysis or for the analysis of others whose work has informed it. Iha in particular, understood the value of leveraging the *Omoro* to gain alternative perspectives. Even though the history of Ryukyu presented here differs greatly from that of Kerr, had I not more or less randomly pulled his book off a library shelf as an undergraduate, Ryukyu might never have come to my attention.

I hope that interested readers will take up the matters I have discussed, conduct further research, carry forward with new scholarship, and perhaps raise entirely new issues. Should future scholarship revise, supersede, or contradict some or even all of my conclusions, I will be grateful for having helped move the process along. In the sections below, I summarize several of the major arguments of this book by revisiting the basic question of what early Ryukyu was at different times and as seen from different perspectives.

RYUKYU STARTS WITH KIKAI

Using gravity as a metaphor, from around 1500 onward Shuri became a massive center, bending the space around the Ryukyu islands and pulling them all into its orbit. By the time the official histories were written, it was probably inconceivable that early Ryukyuan history could be anything other than centered on Okinawa, especially the Urasoe-Shuri-Naha region. Modern works have almost all followed this pattern, locating the earliest traces of Ryukyuan history in the island of Okinawa. As we have seen, however, the early center of population, economic vigor, advanced material culture, military power, and more within the Ryukyu islands were the three northernmost islands, with Kikai as the administrative center. This Northern Tier was a human and cultural junction between the Japanese islands, the Korean peninsula, probably coastal China, and possibly elsewhere.

The best turbo shells were found in the northern Ryukyu islands. As demand for this product increased, the shell trade expanded southward, setting the stage for the gradual emergence of centers of population and power in and around the harbors of Okinawa. Naha was particularly advantageous because the influx of fresh water into the harbor suppressed the growth of coral. Starting in the thirteenth century and extending into the fourteenth, the Ukishima in Naha harbor gradually displaced the Ukishima that was Kikai. Although we cannot know the details, this displacement was not always a peaceful process. One indication is rounds of warfare circa the 1440s–1460s between Kikai and power centers in the Naha area, and possibly elsewhere in Okinawa.

RYUKYU AS NAHA

At no time were any of the Ryukyu islands the territory of a Chinese dynasty. Nevertheless, the Ming court created Ryukyu as a state for trade purposes in an attempt to control piracy and smuggling. It is important to stress, however, that the "country of Ryukyu" (or Chūzan), headed by a king who appeared on the regional scene in the 1370s, was actually the domain of whichever local ruler controlled the Naha area. Insofar as the term "kingdom" suggests a wide area of contiguous control under bureaucratic government headed by a hereditary monarch, Ryukyu of the fifteenth century was different.

The port of Naha became the center of extensive Chinese-directed and -enabled regional trade. This trade took place under the auspices of a variety of kings and royal relatives. The king of Chūzan resided in Shuri castle from Shō Hashi onward. Where the king of Sanhoku or the complex tangle of kings, crown princes, and royal relatives of Sannan resided we cannot be certain. However, all of their trade went through Naha harbor, and all of it was managed by resident Chinese located in what later would be called Kumemura. Whatever the three principalities may have been, in a real sense they were all centered at Naha.

These principalities vanished circa the 1420s, apparently in connection with new Chinese management and the rise of Shō Hashi in the wake of Bunei's having angered the Ming emperor. From that point onward, the Chūzan king of Ryukyu became the exclusive agent who authorized trade with China, Korea, and the Muromachi *bakufu*. Chinese-made ships with Chinese officers and Ryukyuan sailors aboard traded under the auspices of Okinawan kings. They sailed to China, and from there often onward to Southeast Asia. Naha engaged in trade with Korea, typically mediated by powerful Japanese, at least some of whom were *wakō*. This profitable trade encouraged political instability in Ryukyu. Naha became a prized target, seized not only by Shō Hashi, but also most likely by Shō Taikyū and Shō Toku, as well as Kanemaru (Shō En), and Shō Shin.

Obviously, fifteenth-century Ryukyu was much more than the Shuri-Naha area, as the geographically varied *Omoro* songs attest. However, the lack of internal documents from within the Ryukyu islands tends to divert our attention to the Chinese and Korean sources and thus to the trade centered at Naha. It is clear from archaeological evidence and *Omoro* songs that other power centers flourished during this time, but the absence of documents limits what we can know about them mainly to their material wealth. The kings in Shuri castle or elsewhere almost certainly extended their power to other locations, including places in Michinoshima, by military conquest and cooperative alliances. Nevertheless, it was the Naha-based trade that defined Ryukyu or any of its principalities as formal states in Chinese and Korean eyes.

RYUKYU AS SHURI

Shō Shin's seizure of the throne, his long reign, his likely ambition, and the many challenges he confronted changed Ryukyu fundamentally. Shuri transformed from the site of a castle housing the ruler of the Naha area to the center of a politically united Okinawa and of a sprawling Ryukyu empire. In the sense of ruling over a wide area by means of a centralized bureaucratic government, Shō Shin was Ryukyu's first king and its first emperor. We have seen that household records from the families of local officials in Amami-Ōshima sometimes explicitly referred to the king in Shuri as the emperor, using the same terms that in different contexts might indicate Chinese or Japanese emperors.

A crucial step in Shō Shin's consolidation of power was his making Shuri into the administrative, symbolic, cultural, and religious center of an expanding empire. Shuri castle took on its Chinese look beginning in the 1490s. Enkakuji and other temples reinforced the political, religious, and cultural power of Shuri. Local officials in Amami-Ōshima, for example, sent sons to Shuri to study at Enkakuji and apprentice themselves to powerful officials in Shuri castle. In documents, this apprenticeship, and the periodic journey of island officials to the royal court to receive appointments, were typically a "return to Ryukyu." Writs of appointments always began with "Orders of Shuri." During the sixteenth century, "Shuri" and "Ryukyu" functioned as metonyms of each other. They were interchangeable in the context of the empire Shō Shin created. New parks, groves of trees, monuments, and religious rites enhanced Shuri's gravitas.

RYUKYU AS FRONTIER

The centers of power in Ryukyu and their relationships to each other transformed over the centuries. Until the seventeenth century, the Ryukyu islands existed within what I have called the East China Sea network. It has long been commonplace in studies of early Ryukyu to include "within East Asia" (*Higashi-ajia ni okeru* and similar phrases) in article and book titles. In practice, this qualifying phrase usually means that the Ryukyu kingdom conducted trade with a variety of surrounding countries. One point I have stressed in this book is that, at least until approximately 1500 and to some extent even thereafter, the Ryukyu islands themselves constituted a region of diverse political communities. Moreover, these communities existed within an even larger human, cultural, and economic network created and sustained by sea-lanes. Obviously trade connected Ryukyu with places outside the Ryukyu islands, but I have sought to highlight broader regional human, cultural, and political connections.

Although people moved in every direction across the East China Sea network, of particular importance is a north to south migration over centuries. Studied in isolation, it might seem that distinctive forms of culture developed within Okinawa and spread outward from there to the other Ryukyu islands. More often, however, people migrating southward from as far away as the Korean peninsula, through Tsushima, Iki, western Kyushu, and the Tokara islands, brought their cultures into the Ryukyu islands, where they mixed and developed. Interaction across the network via sea-lanes circulated not only goods but peoples, cultures, and even balances of power.

The Ryukyu islands functioned as a frontier region of places farther north, especially Japan. During the eleventh and twelfth centuries, Kikai dangled just inside or just outside the real or imagined borders of Japan, and the Northern Tier islands prospered as a regional crossroads. During the eleventh through thirteenth centuries, mariners from Japan (and possibly the Northern Tier) migrated farther south and settled into the harbors of the rest of the Ryukyu islands, often displacing or absorbing previous populations. Trade in turbo shells, *kamuiyaki,* talc stoneware (*ishinabe*), and iron goods was a major impetus for this process. During the fourteenth century, the decline of the Southern Court stimulated another wave of southward migration. The groups migrating into the Ryukyu islands from farther north were not genteel literati or other social elites. They were, for the most part, *wakō* bands, defeated warriors, adventurers, and pioneers. Not surprisingly, therefore, warfare and violence were endemic. It went with the territory, as was often the case in premodern frontier regions. Early Ryukyuan history cannot be well understood without considering this violence.

I have stressed that early Ryukyuan rulers—a term encompassing the various kings, *aji,* and local strongmen—were either *wakō* leaders themselves or were closely associated with *wakō* bands. Given their prevalence in the East China Sea network, it would have been remarkable had a location such as the Ryukyu islands not been the abode of *wakō*. As we have seen, the reason the Ming court extended lucrative tribute-trade terms to Ryukyu was not because the early Ming emperors admired the islands or their inhabitants. The Ming creation of Ryukyu as a state for trade purposes was in pursuit of taming piracy and control over smuggling. Moreover, poorly behaving Ryukyuans strained Chinese patience throughout the fifteenth century.

One broad generalization we can make about the Ryukyu islands is that throughout historical times their base culture has been Japonic. One common and erroneous idea held in modern Japan is that the residents of Okinawa Prefecture were more culturally akin to China than to Japan. This notion was largely the result of Ryukyu's post-1609 situation. In recent years, in concert with an increasingly muscular foreign policy, it has become common in China to claim that the Ryukyu islands are properly within China's orbit and are not legitimately Japanese territory.[2] Although claiming historical legitimacy as cover, such assertions reflect the changing economic and military balance of power in today's world, not deep cultural roots or past territorial configurations.

RYUKYU AS EMPIRE

Early in his reign, Shō Shin and his confidantes experienced the wrath of a Ming court fed up with violence and abuses of the system by Ryukyuans in China. Although we cannot reconstruct the precise sequence of events, in general the Ryukyu empire emerged from Shō Shin's struggles to consolidate power, to create a stable, centralized regime, and to restore yearly tribute voyages to China. It is reasonable to call Shō Shin's empire "Ryukyu" because, at least nominally, it encompassed all of the Ryukyu islands. However, "Shuri empire" would be a more precise characterization.

In any case, some readers are likely to wince at the term "empire" applied to the Shuri-based Ryukyu state circa 1500–1879. Modern history and habits of thought play a role in the tendency to avoid seeing premodern Ryukyu as an empire. Annexation of Ryukyu by Japan in 1879 had the potential significantly to improve the general standard of living. Instead, however, Okinawans in that era continued to suffer poverty and encountered severe discrimination for alleged cultural or character flaws. A fearsome toll of death and destruction swept through Okinawa in 1945, and as "The Ryukyus" the territory of Okinawa Prefecture endured U.S. military control until 1972. Today military bases continue to occupy roughly 20 percent of Okinawa's land. This history promotes a tendency, especially in Western-language literature, to portray Okinawa and its people as victims. Insofar as Okinawa's people have indeed been victims, it has been at the hands of the Japanese empire, the de facto empire of the United States, and earlier, what we could reasonably call a Satsuma empire. The habit of regarding the Ryukyu islands and their inhabitants as victims of powerful outside forces can make it difficult to acknowledge that Ryukyu itself existed in the form of a Shuri-centered empire between about 1500 and 1879.

A related problem is the modern tendency to think of national or ethnic identity in essentialist terms. If nothing else, I hope that this book has made it abundantly clear that no stable "Ryukyuan" essence, geopolitical or cultural, has been transmitted through the centuries. Indeed, throughout this book the term "Ryukyu" has functioned as a geographic label of convenience, applied to complex and shifting amalgamations of peoples, cultures, and political communities.

RYUKYU AS THEATRICAL STATE

Late imperial China's conceptions of and approaches to foreign relations is typically called the "tribute system" as a convenient shorthand. Tributary relations are an excellent example of diplomacy and foreign relations as theatrics performed through ritual protocols (J. *rei*, C. *lǐ*). Foreign states sent envoys to China bearing "humble products" from their countries. These envoys literally bowed before the Chinese emperor in ritual displays of cultural subordination. In return for such adulation, the emperor presented the envoys with gifts worth much more than the products they brought and permitted accompanying merchants to conduct private trade. Moreover, the emperor provided formal diplomatic recognition of the tribute state's ruler by investing that person as king via a formal ceremony. Economic exchange flourished under a veneer of ritual enactments and reenactments of an idealized relationship between the Chinese emperor and the various subordinate kings who maintained tributary relationships with him.

All indications are that before 1609, and certainly before Shō Shin's time, Ryukyuans did not always play their theatrical roles with great skill. They could rely on Ming indulgence, albeit sometimes strained, and Kumemura personnel to take care of key administrative details. After coming under Satsuma's control, however, Ryukyu's survival depended on its skill in playing elaborate theatrical roles vis-à-vis Qing China and Japan. As a result, by the nineteenth century, Ryukyu had become a preeminent theatrical state.[3] The creation of official histories was part of this process. These histories constituted the major public relations documents whereby Shuri elites presented Ryukyu to the outside world.

RYUKYU AS AN IMAGINARY

I have worked on Ryukyuan history since the late 1980s, albeit with a ten-year hiatus during which time I worked on earthquakes. Whether in person or, especially via the Web, I have encountered a vast array of differing conceptions of early Ryukyu. The topic of Ryukyu as a contemporary construct deserves a book of its own, and therefore I will not discuss it here at any length. Instead I will comment narrowly only on two points, anachronism and romanticism.

Simply defined, anachronism refers to placing something into a period other than when it actually existed. Specifically, historians have a tendency to project ideas, political systems, and institutions further back into the past than good evidence warrants. We have seen, for example, that Ryukyu's official histories project a centralized kingdom much further back in time than critical interpretation of the evidence allows. One reason the official histories have been so influential in framing modern histories is that they are narrative texts. It is easy to fashion narratives from narratives. To see the broader point, consider the study of medieval Japanese history. Writing in the 1990s, Jeffrey P. Mass points out that the most striking trend in historical scholarship has been "the increasing emphasis on documents rather than narrative materials." As a result:

> The origins and life spans of many key institutions have been pushed forward in time, rather than backward. It is well-known, for example, that the imperial family is not as old as we once thought it was. But the same is true for both the flowering and decline of both the *ritsuryō* and *shōen* systems, the emergence of independent warriors, the ascendency of the re-

tired emperors and the Taira, and the appearance of *shugo, jitō, gokenin,* and a shogunal tradition—to name only a few cases. In other words, we have been misled, and the retrospective narrative sources, traditionally accepted at face value, are to blame. . . . Now, however, skepticism has replaced credulity, and the historicity of traditional depictions is taken much less for granted. This does not mean that traditional sources are being discarded, only that new questions are being posed as scholars consider the full range of materials bearing on different topics. Historians, both Japanese and Western, are becoming more critical.[4]

It is in this spirit that I have attempted to write a critical history of early Ryukyu that does not take official histories at face value.

The result is likely to cause some anxiety, particularly for readers grounded in the English-language literature, which often romanticizes Ryukyu (sometimes spelled Loo Choo or Luchu). Romanticized Ryukyu typically takes the form of a pacifist island paradise. This imaginary Ryukyu is European in origin, and first developed as a reaction to the Napoleonic Wars. Those bloody conflicts created an understandable desire to find proof, even if just a single case, that a state could exist without violence or warfare. Ryukyu emerged as the only apparent example.

The pioneering Japanologist Basal Hall Chamberlain made a brief visit to Ryukyu and published a lengthy article in *The Geography Journal* in 1895. Perpetuating the myth of Ryukyuan pacifism, he wrote: "In some important respects, the country really deserved the title bestowed upon it by a Chinese emperor in 1579 . . . the title of 'The Land of Propriety.' There were no lethal weapons in Luchu, no feudal factions, few if any crimes of violence. . . . Confucius' ideal was carried out—a government purely civil, at once absolute and patriarchal, resting not on any armed force, but on the theory that subjects owe unqualified obedience to their rulers."[5] Despite mentioning the year 1579 and providing a brief narrative of Ryukyuan history elsewhere in the article, Hall is steeped in modern essentialist notions that render Ryukyu timeless: "The most prominent race-characteristic of the Luchuans is not a physical, but a moral one. It is their gentleness of spirit, their yielding and submissive disposition, their hospitality and kindness, their aversion to violence and crime."[6]

Hall's romanticized Ryukyu is very much alive and well today, having been passed along by Kerr and others, and of course, being inherently attractive. As much as I might prefer Hall's Ryukyu, this book presents Ryukyu and its people as being subject to the same forces, motivations, and behaviors as other people around the world. In other words, I argue that Ryukyu's early history was not an exceptional process, unrelated to and of a different character from those of other maritime societies in the region. The narrative I have presented here is more complex than many of its predecessors, but I argue that it is more plausible. It represents my best interpretation at this time, and I hope that it will be useful as a starting point for the work of others.

Notes

Introduction

1. Pearson, *Ancient Ryukyu*, esp. 145–151.
2. Xià, *Shi Ryūkyū roku*, 190.
3. *Reflections on Chūzan*, 3.
4. Sakihara, *A Brief History of Early Okinawa*, 2–3.
5. Yoshinari and Fuku, *Ryūkyū ōkoku to wakō*.
6. Akamine, *The Ryukyu Kingdom*.
7. Iha, *Iha Fuyū zenshū*, 6:217.
8. Fuku, *Kikaijima*, 121.
9. Nelson, "Japan in the Life of Early Ryukyu."
10. Coined by linguist Leon Serafim, "Japonic" refers to a family of related languages spoken from Hokkaidō through the Ryukyu Arc.

Chapter 1: Ryukyu in the East China Sea Network

1. Schottenhammer, *Trade and Transfer across the East Asian "Mediterranean,"* 2.
2. Tanigawa, *Rettō jūdan, chimei shōyō*, 127–129, and Ikeno, *Ryūkyū Yanbarusen*, 28–36. As a biological barrier, the Kuroshio flowing through the Shichitō-nada is commonly known as the Watase Line.
3. Sasamori, *Nantō tanken*, 1:14–15.
4. For an explanation of wind patterns and currents around the Japanese and Ryukyu islands, see Kitami, *Nihon kaijō kōtsūshi no kenkyū*, 117–164. See also Sakihara, *A Brief History of Early Okinawa*, 127.
5. *Omoro sōshi*, nos. 780, 925.
6. Nagayama, "Bunken kara miru Kikaigashima to Gusuku isekigun," 163; Yoshinari, *Ryūkyūshi o toinaosu*; and Batten, *Gateway to Japan*, 95–96.
7. For details on the 1019 Toi Invasion of Tsushima, Iki, and the Hakata area, and raids prior to it, see Batten, *Gateway to Japan*, 81–104.
8. Nagayama, "Bunken kara miru Kikaigashima to Gusuku isekigun," 155–156, and Yoshinari, *Ryūkyūshi o toinaosu*, 23–24.

255

9. Tanaka, "Kodai no Amami, Okinawa shotō to kokusai shakai," 62.
10. Yoshinari, *Ryūkyūshi o toinaosu*, 23.
11. Pearson, *Ancient Ryukyu*, 164–165.
12. Takanashi Osamu has called this unit "the Kikaijima—Amami-Ōshima orbit of power." See Takanashi, *Yakōgai no kōkogaku*, 208–210.
13. Kuroshima, "Kamakura bakufu to minami kyōkai," 126–127; Yoshinari, *Ryūkyūshi o toinaosu*, 25; and Uezato, *Umi no ōkoku, Ryūkyū*, 31–32. For tables listing the many ways Kikai appears in documents, see Nagayama, "Bunken kara miru Kikaigashima to Gusuku isekigun," 158, and Fuku, *Kikaijima*, 6.
14. Fuku, *Kikaijima*, 64–68.
15. Murai, "Chūsei Nihon to Ko-Ryūkyū no hazama," 106.
16. Pearson, *Ancient Ryukyu*, 158, 161, 163–164, and Tanigawa and Orikuchi, *Ryūkyū ōken no genryū*, 12–13.
17. Sumita and Nozaki, "Kikaijima Gusuku isekigun," 156, 160–162, 164–166, and Pearson, *Ancient Ryukyu*, 160–164.
18. Sagawa Shin'ichi, "Gusuku isekigun no chūsei haka," 205–208, 209.
19. Ikehata, "Kikaijima no kodai, chūsei iseki," 252.
20. Yoshinari, *Ryūkyūshi o toinaosu*, 37–38, and Yoshinari and Fuku, *Ryūkyū ōkoku tanjō*, 115.
21. Yoshinari, *Ryūkyūshi o toinaosu*, 39–42, and Pearson, *Ancient Ryukyu*, 160.
22. Fuku, *Kikaijima*, 115–116, 118–119. See also Tanigawa, *Yomigaeru kaijō no michi*, 222–225.
23. Murai, "Chūsei Nihon to Ko-Ryūkyū no hazama," 117–118.
24. Yoshinari, *Ryūkyūshi o toinaosu*, 20, 36, 46–48, and Pearson, *Ancient Ryukyu*, 167.
25. Yoshinari and Fuku, *Ryūkyū ōkoku tanjō*, 291.
26. Ibid., 110–112, and Yoshinari, *Ryūkyūshi o toinaosu*, 64–65.
27. Yoshinari and Fuku, *Ryūkyū ōkoku tanjō*, 116–119, and Yoshinari, *Ryūkyūshi o toinaosu*, 48.
28. Pearson, *Ancient Ryukyu*, 141.
29. Takanashi, *Yakōgai no kōkogaku*, 184, and Yoshinari and Fuku, *Ryūkyū ōkoku tanjō*, 88–89.
30. Yoshinari and Fuku, *Ryūkyū ōkoku tanjō*, 103.
31. Naka, "Okinawa (Ryūkyūkoku) no gusuku (shiro) kenkyū ryakushi," 57–59.
32. *Omoro sōshi*, no. 791, and Yoshinari and Fuku, *Ryūkyū ōkoku tanjō*, 96–97.
33. *Omoro sōshi*, nos. 1134, 1144.
34. Yoshinari and Fuku, *Ryūkyū ōkoku tanjō*, 86–87 (photos 87).
35. *Omoro sōshi*, nos. 759, 760, 791, 1356, and Yoshinari and Fuku, *Ryūkyū ōkoku tanjō*, 92–97.
36. Uezato, "The Formation of the Port City of Naha," 57–77 (conceptual map, 61).
37. *Omoro sōshi*, no. 4. See Yoshinari and Fuku, *Ryūkyū ōkoku tanjō*, 102–103 for analysis.
38. This official was Tameharu. See Kamei, *Amami-Ōshima shoka keifu shū*, 59.
39. *Omoro sōshi*, no. 554. For a similar *omoro* with slightly different places at the end, see no. 868. See also Fuku, *Kikaijima*, 80–83, and Yoshimari and Fuku, *Ryūkyū ōkoku tanjō*, 267–271.
40. Sakita, "Hokuzan bunkaken e no kōsō," 133–146.
41. Ibid., esp. 141–145; Hokama, *Omoro sōshi*, 173–174; and Yoshinari and Fuku, *Ryūkyū ōkoku to wakō*, 82–89.
42. Nagayama, "Bunken kara mita Kikaigashima," 156–159, and Ōta, "Futatsu no 'Ryūkyū,'" 206–207.
43. *Omoro sōshi*, no. 1208, and Yoshinari and Fuku, *Ryūkyū ōkoku tanjō*, 150–153.

44. Nishizato, "Ryūkyū—Okinawashi ni okeru 'minzoku' no mondai," 185. See also Nagoya, *Nantō zatsuwa*, 2:130–131, 178–179, and Matsushita, *Kinsei Amami no shihai to shakai*, 45–46.
45. *Omoro sōshi*, nos. 942, 944, and 947.
46. Shimono, "Noro ishō ron," 103–104, and Yoshinari and Fuku, *Ryūkyū ōkoku tanjō*, 264–267.
47. For a discussion of cultural links between mainland Japan, Ryukyu, and the Tokara islands, see Shimono, *Amami, Tokara no dentō bunka*, 376–378, and elsewhere.
48. According to *Joseon Veritable Royal Records*, entry no. 72 (1453), 19 / 93–94, four castaways arrived in the Gaja (Tokara) islands, which "lie at the border of Ryukyu and Satsuma. Half of them went into the custody of Satsuma, half into the custody of Ryukyu." For an extended discussion of this boundary zone, see Murai, "Chūsei Nihon to Ko-Ryūkyū no hazama," 110–114.
49. Shimono, *Minzokugaku kara gen-Nihon o miru*, 204–205.
50. Fuku, *Omoro sōshi to gun'yū no seiki*, 109–114.
51. For an early discussion and illustration (1939), see Iha, *Iha Fuyū zenshū*, 5:27–29. For other examples, see Yoshinari and Fuku, *Ryūkyū ōkoku to wakō*, 84–88, and Yoshinari and Fuku, *Ryūkyū ōkoku tanjō*, 166–167.
52. Nagoya, *Nantō zatsuwa*, 2:58–59, and Ōbayashi, *Sōsei no kigen*, 143.
53. Ōbayashi, *Sōsei no kigen*, 143–144.
54. Ibid., 145–146.
55. Ibid., 147–149. See also Suzuki, *Nihon bunka to Hachimanjin*, 28–29.
56. Yanagita, *Nihon densetsu meii*, 26, and Ōbayashi, *Sōsei no kigen*, 142.
57. Ōbayashi, *Sōsei no kigen*, 148.
58. Mamiya, *Okinawa kogo no shinsō*, 118–119.
59. Yoshinari and Fuku, *Ryūkyū ōkoku to wakō*, 83–87; Yoshinari and Fuku, *Ryūkyū ōkoku tanjō*, 167–170; and Yoshinari, *Ryūkyūshi o toinaosu*, 155–159.
60. Another cultural marker that substantially overlaps with this burial practice is a type of patrilineal descent group marked in Okinawa by the name -*hara* or -*bara*. Although common today in names of lineage groups in the south of Okinawa, the distribution of -*hara* lineage groups included Okinawa, Amami-Ōshima, Korea, and northern Asian peoples. For details, see Yoshinari, *Ryūkyūshi o toinaosu*, 159–160, and Kanehisa, *Amami ni ikiru Nihon kodai bunka*, 47–59.
61. Tanigawa and Orikuchi, *Ryūkyū ōken no genryū*, 32; Yoshinari and Fuku, *Ryūkyū ōkoku to wakō*, 263–267; and Yoshinari and Fuku, *Ryūkyū ōkoku tanjō*, 188–189.
62. *Reflections on Chūzan*, 13.
63. Iha, *Iha Fuyū zenshū*, 5:29–30. Iha was also struck by the resemblances between Ryukyuan languages and the language of Iki despite their geographical separation. The resemblance was "far greater than that of the languages of Kagoshima and Okinawa, which had been in close and continuous contact since the Keichō era [1596–1615]." Iha, *Iha Fuyū zenshū*, 4:233–276.
64. Tanigawa, "'Ko-Ryūkyū' izen no sekai: Nantō no fūdo to seikatsu bunka," 58–59.
65. Tanigawa, *Yomigaeru kaijō no michi*, 67–71.
66. University of the Ryukyus Repository, http://ir.lib.u-ryukyu.ac.jp/handle/20.500.12000/10213, left side of digital page "Iha-0090-005" regarding his local wife.
67. *Omoro sōshi*, nos. 212 and 512 (the *o* in "Hachiro" is short).
68. Yoshinari, *Ryūkyūshi o toinaosu*, 129.
69. Hashimoto, *Chūsei Nihon no kokusai kankei*, 122–126, and Yoshinari, *Ryūkyūshi o toinaosu*, 114–121.
70. Hashimoto, *Chūsei Nihon no kokusai kankei*, 125–126.
71. My thanks to Leon Serafim for verifying this possibility (personal communication).

72. Tanigawa, *Rettō jūdan, chimei shōyō*, 124–125. Orikuchi Shinobu made this point in the 1930s. For an updated presentation of Orikuchi's argument, see Tanigawa and Orikuchi, *Ryūkyū ōken no genryū*, 48–54. For examples and analysis of *omoro* containing the Yashiro-Yamato pair, see Yoshinari, *Ryūkyūshi o toinaosu*, 126–129. A similar pairing of Kyō (Kyoto) and Kamakura appear in several songs (*Omoro sōshi*, nos. 246, 311, 356, 377, 1058, and 1134). In other words, Yashiro-Yamato (Yatsushiro-Satsuma) and Kyō-Kamakura appear as collocations in the *Omoro*. My thanks to Leon Serafim for these details (personal communication).

73. Inamura, *Wakō shiseki*, 293. My thanks to Leon Serafim for verifying this distinction (personal communication).

74. *Origins of Ryukyu*, 2:529. Also discussed in Tanigawa and Orikuchi, *Ryūkyū ōken no genryū*, 49–50.

75. Makishi, "*Omoro sōshi* ni miru Kumejima shutsuji no kamigami," 216–217, 245.

76. *Omoro sōshi*, no. 685.

77. Ibid., no. 163. See also Makishi, "*Omoro sōshi* ni miru Kumejima shutsuji no kamigami," 226–228.

78. Mishina, "Tsushima no tendō densetsu," 166–170, 181–183, and Nagatome, "Tsushima no minzoku shinkō," 45–56 (altar photo, 53).

79. *Omoro sōshi*, no. 157. See also no. 159.

80. Yoshinari and Fuku, *Ryūkyū ōkoku to wakō*, 101–115, and Yoshinari and Fuku, *Ryūkyū ōkoku tanjō*, 185–188.

81. Yoshinari and Fuku, *Ryūkyū ōkoku tanjō*, 177–178, 188; Yoshinari, *Sake to shaaman*, 59–60; Shimono, *Amami, Tokara no dentō bunka*, 120, 354–355 and elsewhere; and Shimono, *Minzokugaku kara gen-Nihon o miru*, 132–135 and elsewhere.

82. Shimono, "Noro ishō ron," 7.

83. Tanigawa, *Yomigaeru kaijō no michi*, 222–225.

84. Doi, "Okinawa-ken shutsudo no jinkotsu," 584–585, 597, 600–601; Asato, *Ryūkyū no ōken to gusuku*, 97; Takamiya, *Shima no senshigaku*, esp. 182–187; and Fuku, *Omoro sōshi to gun'yū no seiki*, 47–49.

85. Pellard, "The Linguistic Archeology of the Ryukyu Islands," 31.

86. Uehara, "Buki, bugu no yōsō," 319–322, and Fuku, *Omoro sōshi to gun'yū no seiki*, 49–56.

87. Conclusions of Thomas Pellard synthesizing several studies published between 2004 and 2010. See Pellard, "The Linguistic Archeology of the Ryukyu Islands," 28–29.

88. Ibid., 30–31.

89. Sakima Toshikatsu argues at length that the fundamental layer of Ryukyuan religion and culture came from the Kumano cult, centered in the Wakayama area. In my view, he overstates the case, and many of his examples would apply better to the Hachiman cult. Nevertheless, clearly there was an important cultural link between the Kumano shrines and the Ryukyu islands. See Sakima, *Nirai-kanai no genzō*.

90. Uezato, *Umi no ōkoku, Ryūkyū*, 60–61.

91. Fuku, *Omoro sōshi to gun'yū no seiki*, 60–67.

92. Uezato, "Port City of Naha," 58, and Yoshinari, *Ryūkyūshi o toinaosu*, 114–121.

93. Fuku, *Omoro sōshi to gun'yū no seiki*, 58–60.

94. Ibid., 87–88.

Chapter 2: *Wakō* and the Ryukyu Islands

1. Takara, *Ryūkyū ōkokushi no tankyū*, 13–17. See also Okamoto, "Ryūkyū ōkoku ni okeru kōnōsei no tenkai to kōeki," 51–53.

2. Yoshinari Naoki, *Ryūkyūshi o toinaosu*, 56–58.

Notes to Pages 36–44   259

3. Regarding sharply different conceptions of law prevailing in Japan on the one hand, and Korea and China on the other, see Shapinsky, *Lords of the Sea*, esp. 187–228.
4. Tanigawa, *Okinawa, Amami to Yamato*, 11.
5. For summaries, see Batten, *Gateway to Japan*, 81–104, and Tanaka, *Wakō to kangō bōeki*, 19–21.
6. Tanaka, *Wakō to kangō bōeki*, 19.
7. Kim, *A History of Korea*, 169.
8. Conlon, *In Little Need of Divine Intervention*, esp. 71.
9. Hazard, "Japanese Marauding in Medieval Korea," 95.
10. See Shapinsky, *Lords of the Sea*, for nuanced discussions of *wakō* as both brigands and anti-brigand security forces in a Japanese context and the extreme difficulty Chinese or Korean authorities experienced in conceptualizing this fluid situation.
11. Takahashi Kimiaki points out that the terms corresponding to *wajin*, *wazoku*, and *wakō* in Korean records typically indicated borderland peoples, whereas terms specifically indicating Japanese included "inland *wajin*" and "*Nihonjin*." Ōishi, Takara, and Takahashi, *Shūen kara mita chūsei Nihon*, 278.
12. For details, see Murai, *Ajia no naka no chūsei Nihon*, 328–334.
13. Tanaka, *Wakō to kangō bōeki*, 26.
14. Saeki, *Tsushima to kaikyō no chūseishi*, 23.
15. Tanigawa, *Yomigaeru kaijō no michi*, 120–121, and Shapinsky, *Lords of the Sea*, 65–66, 148.
16. Tanigawa, *Yomigaeru kaijō no michi*, 124–125. See also Tanigawa, "'Ko-Ryūkyū' izen no sekai," 59–60.
17. For example, Tanaka, *Wakō to kangō bōeki*, 215–223.
18. *Joseon Veritable Royal Records*, entries no. 35 (1430), no. 59 (1437), 11, 16, 61–62, 81–82; Tanaka, *Wakō: Umi no rekishi*, 92–93; Tanaka, *Higashi Ajia*, 29; and Li, "Jinteki kōryū o tsūjitemiru Chōsen-Ryūkyū kankei," 131–132.
19. *Joseon Veritable Royal Records*, entries nos. 38 (1431), 48 (1432), 50 (1433), 12, 14, 15 / 66–67, 74–76, 77; *Rekidai hōhan*, 2:381, 1–40–10; Tanaka, *Wakō: Umi no rekishi*, 93–94; and Tanaka, *Higashi Ajia*, 29. For a detailed discussion of Rokurōjirō's activities with respect to Ryukyu, see Higashionna, *Higashionna Kanjun zenshū*, 3:44–50.
20. Saeki, *Tsushima*, 17.
21. Tanaka, *Higashi Ajia*, 28–30, quoted passage, 30.
22. Ōta, *Wakō*, 473–479 and elsewhere.
23. Ibid., 485.
24. Bender, "The Hachiman Cult," 125–153.
25. Bender concisely summarizes several hypothesized origins of the Hachiman cult; see "The Hachiman Cult," 127–130. Regarding Jingū and/or Ōjin as Hachinan and Korean immigrants to Japan, see Varley, *A Chronicle of Gods and Sovereigns*, 101–108.
26. Inamura, *Wakō shiseki*, 82–83.
27. Suzuki, *Kan Higashi-shinakai no kodai girei*, 151–160. For a discussion of the many Japan-Korea connections relevant to Hachiman, see Suzuki, *Nihon bunka to Hachimanjin*, 29–49, 73–73–80, 106–105 (*onarigami* resemblance, 105). See also Kim, *Nihon no naka no Chōsen bunka*, 11:249–256.
28. I have condensed many details. See Ōta, *Wakō*, 504–537.
29. For details, see ibid., 527–528, 536–537, n. 35.
30. Yoshinari and Fuku, *Ryūkyū ōkoku to wakō*, 133.
31. Tanigawa, *Yomigaeru kaijō no michi*, 182–190, and Yoshinari and Fuku, *Ryūkyū ōkoku tanjō*, 196–199.
32. Suzuki, *Kan Higashi-shinakai no kodai girei*, 154–155, and Ōta, *Wakō*, 459–571.
33. Regarding the distribution of Hachiman in the Tokara islands, see Shimono, *Amami, Tokara no dentō bunka*, 413–414.

Notes to Pages 45–51

34. *Origins of Ryukyu*, 1:234–235.
35. *Ryūkyū shintōki*, 90–91. *Origins of Ryukyu*, 1:228, repeats the story.
36. For details, see Higashionna, *Higashionna Kanjun zenshū*, 7:393–395.
37. Kamakura, *Okinawa bunka no ihō*, 1:133. See also Yoshinari and Fuku, *Ryūkyū ōkoku tanjō*, 67, and Yoshinari, *Ryūkyūshi o toinaosu*, 136.
38. Suzuki, *Nihonbunka to Hachimanjin*, 88.
39. Tanigawa, *Yomigaeru kaijō no michi*, 143–145.
40. For example, *Omoro sōshi*, no. 5 (Shuri), no. 850 (Okinoerabu), nos. 1289 and 1292 (Sashiki), no. 1308 (Chinen). See also Fuku, *Omoro sōshi to gun'yū no seiki*, 258–267, and Yoshinari and Fuku, *Ryūkyū ōkoku tanjō*, 257–258.
41. *Omoro sōshi*, no. 350, and Fuku, *Omoro sōshi to gun'yū no seiki*, 264–265.
42. *Omoro sōshi*, no. 5. There are several interpretations of this *omoro*, and I thank Leon Serafim for calling them to my attention.
43. Fuku, *Omoro sōshi to gun'yū no seiki*, 265–266.
44. Yoshinari and Fuku, *Ryūkyū ōkoku to wakō*, 122–140.
45. *Omoro sōshi*, no. 683. The Kumejima version of Aoriyae is also associated with the *tomoe* symbol. See Makishi, "*Omoro sōshi* ni miru Kumejima shutsuji no kamigami no henyō to sono rekishiteki haikei," 220–221.
46. Tanaka, *Wakō to kangō bōeki*, 24–36, and Ōta, *Wakō*, 13–20, 289.
47. Inamura, *Wakō shiseki*, 1–13, and Yoshinari, *Ryūkyūshi o toinaosu*, 112–118.
48. Kawazoe, "Japan and East Asia," 423–424.
49. Quoted in Kawazoe, "Japan and East Asia," 427.
50. Miyara, "Yaeyama shotō no Heike densetsu to wakō no kōseki," 266.
51. Murai, *Chūsei Nihon no uchi to soto*, 152–156.
52. For a concise summary of these details, see Tanigawa, *Yomigaeru kaijō no michi*, 130–131.
53. Miyara, "Yaeyama shotō no Heikei densetsu to wakō no kōseki," 266.
54. Inamura, *Wakō shiseki*, 6–16.
55. Tanaka, *Wakō to kangō bōeki*, 42–44.
56. Robinson, "Centering the King of Chosŏn," 110–111.
57. Takara, *Ryūkyū no jidai*, 108–109.
58. *Goryeosa*, in Ikeya, Uchida, and Takase, *Chōsen ōchō jitsuroku Ryūkyū shiryō shūsei*, 1:141–142.
59. Takara, *Ryūkyū no jidai*, 105.
60. Tanaka, *Higahsi Ajia*, 13.
61. *Joseon Veritable Royal Records*, entry no. 72 (1453), 19/94.
62. Murai, "Chūsei Nihon to Ko-Ryūkyū no hazama," 112.
63. Ōyama, "Amami ni okeru jinshin baibai, 168–171.
64. Tanaka, *Higashi Ajia*, 17–19; Tanaka, *Wakō to kangō bōeki*, 34–35; Saeki, *Tsushima*, 7 (headnotes); Takara, *Ryūkyū no jidai*, 105; Yoshinari and Fuku, *Ryūkyū ōkoku to wakō*, 227–229.
65. *Joseon Veritable Royal Records*, entry no. 125 (1462), 32/140, and Higashionna, *Higashionna Kanjun zenshū*, 3:81. See also Tomiyama, "Ryūkyū, Okinawashi no sekai," 44–45, and Yoshinari and Fuku, *Ryūkyū ōkoku tanjō*, 219–221. Regarding the likely location of Ryang's lodging as Tomari, not Naha, see Makishi, "Ryūkyū ōkoku jūgoseiki chūki ikō no kinaiseitekina tokuchō to ōjō girei," 207.
66. *Joseon Veritable Royal Records*, entry no. 125 (1462), 34/143, and Higashionna, *Higashionna Kanjun zenshū*, 3:81, 84.
67. Ikuta, "Ryūkyū Chūzan ōkoku to kaijō bōeki," 288–289.
68. Uezato, "The Formation of the Port City of Naha," 60.
69. *Origins of Ryukyu*, 2:600–601, and Tanigawa, *Yomigaeru kaijō no michi*, 192–194.
70. Tanigawa, *Yomigaeru kaijō no michi*, 191.

71. Ibid., 156–157, and Inamura, *Wakō shiseki*, 317.
72. Tanigawa, *Yomigaeru kaijō no michi*, 194–195.
73. Ibid., 156–158.
74. Nakasone, "Miyako no rekishi to shinkō," 508–510.
75. Inamura, *Wakō shiseki*, 57–72.
76. Ōyama, "Ryūkyū ōchō fukuzoku jidai," 236–242.
77. Sakihara, *A Brief History of Early Okinawa*, 49–50.
78. *Omoro sōshi*, no. 1027.
79. Iha, "Ryūkyū kyūki kaisetsu," 27–28.
80. Sahara, "Okinawa no yoroi to katana," 96–97.
81. For a volume of several early modern compilations, see Inamura, *Miyakojima kyūki*.
82. Pearson, *Ancient Ryukyu*, 167–168.
83. Version of the legend included in Hirara-shi shi hensan iinkai, *Hirara-shi shi*, vol. 1, Tsūshihen 1, 54–55.
84. Discussion here derived from different legends pulled together in Hirara-shi shi hensan iinkai, *Hirara-shi shi*, vol. 1, Tsūshihen 1, 67–75. See also Nakasone, "Sakishima," 99–101, and Iha, *Iha Fuyū zenshū*, 4:493–494.
85. Ikuta, "Ryūkyū Chūzan ōkoku to kaijō bōeki," 289.
86. Nakasone, "Sakishima," 102.
87. Ibid., 99.
88. Inamura, *Wakō shiseki*, 74–88, and Tanigawa, *Yomigaeru kaijō no michi*, 179–180, 190–191.
89. Inamura, *Wakō shiseki*, 89–100.
90. Ibid., 157.
91. Ibid., 157–160, 308, and Miyara, "Yaeyama shotō no Heike densetsu to wakō no kōseki," 277.
92. As a suffix on male names, *-kane* can also mean "dear-" or "beloved-" (Leon Serafim, personal communication).
93. Narrative in these paragraphs is based on Ōshiro, *Ryūkyū no eiketsutachi*, 494–496.
94. See Inamura, *Wakō shiseki*, 322–332, for a full discussion.
95. Ibid., 305–306.
96. Ibid., 343.
97. Ibid., 290–293. In the song, Yamato is paired with "Yasurai no kuni," like the "Yamato-Yashiro" pair in the *Omoro*. Inamura claims that Yasurai corresponds to Yatsushiro on the Higo coast, as does Yashiro in the *Omoro* (see Chap. 1), although he does not provide details. If Inamura's claim is correct, the song is about a Southern Court *wakō* group returning to, or contemplating a return to, their Kyushu homeland.
98. Inamura, *Wakō shiseki*, 294.
99. Higuchi, *Himitsu no Nihonshi*, 45–51, and Inamura, *Wakō shiseki*, 343–344, 361.

Chapter 3: A State for Trade Purposes

1. Ōyama, "Shimazu-shi no Ryūkyū iri to Amami," 275, and Tanaka, *Wakō to kangō bōeki*, 175. The standard narrative is that firearms first arrived in Japan at Tanegashima via Portuguese ships in 1543.
2. von Verschuer, *Across the Perilous Sea*, 110–111.
3. Tan, *The Muslim South and Beyond*, 128–129.
4. For the full text of the letter, see Tanaka, *Wakō: Umi no rekishi*, 66–67.
5. Tanaka, *Wakō: Umi no rekishi*, 67–68, and Tanaka, *Wakō to kangō bōeki*, 55–57.
6. Inamura, *Wakō shiseki*, 14–15.
7. Kawazoe, "Japan and East Asia," 423, 425–426.

8. Ōta, *Wakō*, 297.
9. Andrade, *The Gunpowder Age*, 55.
10. Ōta, *Wakō*, 287–288, 300–302.
11. For details, see ibid., 287–297; Tanaka, *Wakō to kangō bōeki*, 57–58; Inamura, *Wakō no shiseki*, 16; and Kawazoe, "Japan and East Asia," 430–432.
12. Ōta, *Wakō*, 287–293, and Kawazoe, "Japan and East Asia," 431–432.
13. Inamura, *Wakō no shiseki*, 16, 27.
14. Akamine, *The Ryukyu Kingdom*, 22.
15. Ikuta Shigeru has hypothesized that places like Katsuren and Goeku along the east coast of Okinawa were the earliest power centers. The Urasoe-Naha area developed relatively late, after larger ships came into use in trade. It was this region that the Chūzan kings controlled. See Ikuta, "Ryūkyū Chūzan ōkoku to kaijō bōeki," 287–288, and Ikuta, "Ryūkyūkoku no 'Sanzan tōitsu,'" 187–188.
16. Ikuta, "Ryūkyūkoku no 'Sanzan tōitsu,'" 117.
17. *Rekidai hōan*, 1:523, 1–17–07.
18. Akamine, *The Ryukyu Kingdom*, 28–31, Okamoto, "Foreign Policy and Maritime Trade," 88.
19. The term many Japanese scholars use is *ukezara*, literally a vessel for receiving or containing *wakō*. Terrell and Huey translate *ukezara* as "decoy," for *wakō*, which brings out another dimension of its meaning; Akamine, *The Ryukyu Kingdom*, 29–31. See also Yoshinari and Fuku, *Ryūkyū ōkoku to wakō*, 227–230, and Tomiyama, "Minami no Ryūkyū," 195–196, 214.
20. Okamoto, "Foreign Policy and Maritime Trade," 42.
21. According to Yoshinari Naoki: "Considering that when *wakō* activity flourished, Ryukyu received favorable trade terms, and when *wakō* activity decreased, the favorable terms ceased, there is no doubt that the Ming court was clearly aware of the connection between Ryukyu and *wakō*." Yoshinari, *Ryūkyūshi o toinaosu*, 99.
22. Okamoto, "Foreign Policy and Maritime Trade," 42–43.
23. For a detailed study of Ryukyu's trade with Southeast Asia, see Kobata and Matsuda, *Ryukyuan Relations with Korea and South Sea Countries*. See also Hamashita, "The *Lidai Baoan* and the Ryukyu Maritime Tributary Trade Network," 107–129.
24. Akamine, *The Ryukyu Kingdom*, 28–29, 31. These ships were known as *zìhao chuán* (J. *jigōsen*), "character-number ships." Each was named by a single character combined with a number, and the ships were registered at Ming coastal military fortresses. For details and a complete chart, see Okamoto, "Ko Ryūkyūki no Ryūkyū ōkoku ni okeru 'kaisen' o meguru shosō," 223–224, 235, and Tomiyama, "Minami no Ryūkyū," 197–209.
25. Tomiyama, "Minami no Ryūkyū," 201–202 (based on research by Wáng Liánmào), and Okamoto, "Ko Ryūkyūki no Ryūkyū ōkoku ni okeru 'kaisen' o meguru shosō," 224. See also *Ming Veritable Records*, 1:29 (no. 62, Xuāndé 6.10.5), in which the envoy appears as Guō Zǔměi, and *Rekidai hōan*, 1:515, 1–16–24, for mention of the ship.
26. Akamine, *Daikōkai jidai no Ryūkyū*, 21–22, 24. It was not until 1584 that the first Ryukyuan, Kanematsu, appears as captain of a tribute ship in official records. See also Tomiyama, "Minami no Ryūkyū," 209.
27. Yoshinari, *Ryūkyūshi o toinaosu*, 89; Tomiyama, "Tōitsu ōkoku keiseiki no taigai kankei," 143–150; and Ikuta, "Ryūkyū Chūzan ōkoku to kaijō bōeki," 289.
28. Tomiyama, "Minami no Ryūkyū," 212–213.
29. Ibid., 209–210, 214–125.
30. *Ming Veritable Records*, 1:23 (no. 75, Yǒnglè 13.11.16).
31. Ibid., 2:14 (no. 20, Zhèngtǒng 4.8.15); Tomiyama, "Tōitsu ōkoku keiseiki no taigai kankei," 160–161; and Tomiyama, "Ryūkyū, Okinawashi no sekai," 45–46.
32. *Ming Veritable Records*, 2:55 (no. 20, Chénghuà 8.4.21); Tomiyama, "Tōitsu ōkoku keiseiki no taigai kankei," 161–162; and Tomiyama, "Ryūkyū, Okinawashi no sekai," 46.

Notes to Pages 67–73   263

33. *Rekidai hōan*, 2:349, 1-39-08.
34. *Ming Veritable Records*, 2:24 (no. 30, Chénghuà 14.3.26), about an incident from 1475, and Tomiyama, "Ryūkyū, Okinawashi no sekai," 47. The details of what transpired are unclear.
35. *Ming Veritable Records*, 1:28 (no. 48, Xuāndé 5.8.25). See also Uezato, *Ryū-Nichi sensō 1609*, 29.
36. *Ming Veritable Records*, 2:49 (no. 64, Jǐngtài 3.6.20).
37. My summary here is based on several quantitative studies. See Okamoto, "Ryūkyū ōkoku ni okeru kōnōsei no tenkai to kōeki," esp. 54–55. For the same data in English, see Okamoto, "Foreign Policy and Maritime Trade," 37–41. For a different arrangement of this data, see Asato, *Kōkogaku kara mita Ryūkyūshi, jō* [vol. 1], 162–165. Another quantitative study of early Ryukyuan trade is Ikuta Shigeru, "Taigai kankei kara mita Ryūkyū kodaishi," 94–125.
38. The quantities extracted from Iōtorishima, located west of Tokunohsima, were typically 20,000 *jīn* per year throughout the early modern era. Kadena, "Iōgura" and "Iōtorishima," 147.
39. Ikuta, "Taigai kankei," 98–102.
40. This unit was variable, but it became standardized at nearly 600 grams throughout most of East Asia in the modern era. It is sometimes called a "catty."
41. Modified version of Table 3 in Ikuta, "Taigai kankei kara mita Ryūkyū kodaishi," 99.
42. *Ming Veritable Records*, 2:23 (no. 24/Chénghuà 11.4.10); Okamoto, "Foreign Policy and Maritime Trade," 51; and Akamine, *The Ryukyu Kingdom*, 46–48.
43. Zhang, "Ancient Chinese Sulfur Manufacturing Processes," 491.
44. Ōta, *Wakō*, 343.
45. Yoshinari, *Ryūkyūshi o toinaosu*, 120, 197.
46. Yoshinari and Fuku, *Ryūkyū ōkoku tanjō*, 51–54; Yoshinari, *Ryūkyūshi o toinaosu*, 103–106; Murai, *Ajia no naka no chūsei Nihon*, 329; and Nagahama, "Miyako uma no rūtsu o saguru," 13.
47. Nagahama, "Miyako uma no rūtsu o saguru," 12–13.
48. Ibid., 15 (table 9).
49. Yoshinari and Fuku, *Ryūkyū ōkoku tanjō*, 51–53.
50. *Omoro sōshi*, no. 936. For analysis, see Yoshinari and Fuku, *Ryūkyū ōkoku tanjō*, 54–55.
51. *Omoro sōshi*, no. 860; Tanigawa, *Rettō jūdan, chimei shōyō*, 138–139; and Yoshinari and Fuku, *Ryūkyū ōkoku tanjō*, 60–61.
52. Akamine, *Daikōkai jidai no Ryūkyū*, 21–22. Mamoru Akamine points out that "the ships granted to the Ryukyuans ostensibly to carry their tribute legations were in fact naval ships attached to coastal defense installations." See Akamine, *The Ryukyu Kingdom*, 31.
53. *Joseon Veritable Royal Records*, entry no. 85 (1458), 23/106–107.
54. Takara, *Ryūkyū no jidai*, 104–105, 108.
55. Tanaka, *Wakō*, 88–89, and Son, "Chō-Ryū kōrin taisei," 33.
56. Robinson, "Centering the King of Chosŏn," 114.
57. Tanaka, *Wakō*, 85, and Son, "Chō-Ryū kōrin taisei," 33.
58. Son, "Chō-Ryū kōrin taisei," 33–34.
59. *Joseon Veritable Royal Records*, entries nos. 168–174 (1479), 54–56 / 215–220.
60. Robinson, "The Jiubian and Ezogachishima Embassies to Chosŏn, 1478–1482," 62–63. See also Robinson, "Centering the King of Chosŏn," 112–122.
61. For a detailed discussion, see Robinson, "Centering the King of Chosŏn," 116–122.
62. *Joseon Veritable Royal Records*, entry nos. 181–187 (1479), 67–70/250–259. For a detailed account of these matters, see Kobata and Matsuda, *Ryukyuan Relations with Korea and South Sea Countries*, 21.
63. Saeki, *Tsushima*, 9, 83–84.

64. In this context, Peter D. Shapinsky calls these *wakō* bands "sea lords." See Shapinsky, *Lords of the Sea*.
65. For a detailed analysis of childhood names in Sakishima, see Inamura, *Wakō shiseki*, 244–283.
66. *Omoro sōshi*, no. 637.
67. For an analysis of correspondence between Ryukyuan rulers and the Muromachi shoguns, see Tanaka, *Taigai kankei to bunka kōryū*, 106–130.
68. Uehara, *Ryū-nichi sensō 1609*, 59–64.
69. Akamine, *Daikōkai jidai no Ryūkyū*, 21–22.
70. For the full text of the inscription an analysis, see Higashionna, *Higashionna Kanjun zenshū*, 3:8–15. For a recent essay, see McNally, "A King's Legitimacy and a Kingdom's Exceptionality," 87–103.
71. Yano, *Ko-Ryūkyūki Shuri ōfu no kenkyū*, 45.
72. McNally, "A King's Legitimacy and a Kingdom's Exceptionality," 87.
73. Akamine, *Daikōkai jidai no Ryūkyū*.
74. Ōta, *Isetsu Okinawa shi*," 8–117.
75. Irei, "Maboroshi no Ryūkyū ōkoku," 104–111 (quotation on 111).

Chapter 4: The Enigma of the Three Principalities

1. Uezato, *Umi no ōkoku, Ryūkyū*, 77–84.
2. *Ming Veritable Records*, 1:13 (no. 25/Hóngwǔ 21.1.1). See also Sun, *Chūgoku kara mita Ko-Ryūkyū no sekai*, 53–57.
3. For his final tribute shipment, see *Ming Veritable Records*, 1:16 (no. 605/Hóngwǔ 29.4.20).
4. Sun, *Chūgoku kara mita Ko-Ryūkyū no sekai*, 58–60.
5. Bunei's name was the same as that of King Muryeong of Baekje (r. 462–523). Muryeong had legendary roots connecting him with Kakara Island near Iki and claiming Jingū as his mother. See Tanigawa, *Yomigaeru kaijō no michi*, 116–118.
6. *Ming Veritable Records*, 1:20 (no. 26/Yǒnglè 4.3.2).
7. Ibid. (no. 30/Yǒnglè 5.4.11).
8. Ibid., 2:22–23 (no. 13–19/Chénghuà 7–8 years).
9. *Reflections on Chūzan*, 41–42.
10. Ikuta, "Ryūkkūkoku no 'Sanzan tōitsu,'" 184–185.
11. *Ryukyu Record*, 61.
12. Ibid., 64.
13. Higashionna, *Higashionna Kanjun zenshū*, Vol. 3, 26.
14. Ibid., 27–29. In Chinese transliteration, the name of this envoy was Wèicí Bóyě. Ryukyuan pronunciation of his name is unknown.
15. Compare *Ming Veritable Records*, 1:25 (no. 3/Yǒnglè 22.10.17), with *Ming Veritable Records*, 1:27 (no. 20/Xuāndé 2.4.18). The former envoy would be Ān dān nī jié zhì, sounded out in Chinese. The latter envoy would be Ān dān jié zhì in Chinese—clearly the same person but with the middle character dropped. It would have been either a clerical error or a slightly different transliteration. Ryukyuan pronunciation of the envoy's name is not clear.
16. Wada, *Ryūkyū ōkoku no keisei*, 30–31. See also Uezato, *Umi no ōkoku, Ryūkyū*, 77.
17. Wada, *Ryūkyū ōkoku no keisei*. For the basic argument, see 1–40; for an extended argument, 41–55.
18. Ikuta, "Ryūkyūkoku no 'Sanzan tōitsu,'" esp. 117.
19. Ikuta, "Ryūkyū Chūzan ōkoku to kaijō bōeki," 285–286, and Ikuta, "Ryūkyūkoku no 'Sanzan tōitsu,'" 185–186. Ikuta's positing of Unten as "Sanhoku" derives mainly from his analysis of the oldest extant map of Ryukyu.
20. Ikuta, "Ryūkyūkoku no 'Sanzan tōitsu,'" 181–182.

Notes to Pages 81–91   265

21. Ibid., 187.
22. Ikuta, "Ryūkyū Chūzan ōkoku to kaijō bōeki," 286.
23. *Omoro sōshi*, no. 47. For analysis, see Yoshinari, *Ryūkyūshi o toinaosu*, 164–165.
24. *Joseon Veritable Royal Records*, entry no. 5 (1394), 5/31–32.
25. *Ming Veritable Records*, 1:15 (no. 49/Hóngwǔ 27.1.25).
26. Even a summary of the various explanations would be lengthy. See Ikeya, Uchida, and Takase, *Chōsen ōchō jitsuroku Ryūkyū shiryō shūsei, yakuchū hen*, 32 (note 3) for summaries of several proposals with citations.
27. Ikuta, "Ryūkyū Chūzan ōkoku to kaijō bōeki," 286, and Ikuta, "Ryūkyūkoku no 'Sanzan tōitsu,'" 178–180.
28. Ikuta "Ryūkyūkoku no 'Sanzan tōitsu,'" 179.
29. Sun, *Chūgoku kara mita Ko-Ryūkyū no sekai*, 41–47.
30. Yoshinari and Fuku, *Ryūkyū ōkoku tanjō*, 28–29; and Yoshinari, *Ryūkyūshi o toinaosu*, 142–144.
31. *Ming Veritable Records*, 1:14 (no. 39/Hóngwǔ 25.11.17).
32. According to *Genealogy of Chūzan*, 24: "The lord of Nakijin was called King of Sanhoku." Taking this claim literally, Sun Wei posits two kings during this period, Nakijin and Haniji. The former was a "phantom" (*maboroshi*), who does not appear in Ming records and about whom we have no biographical information. Sun, *Chūgoku kara mita Ko-Ryūkyū no sekai*, esp. 110–111, 133–139.
33. Kadena, "Bin," 333.
34. *Ming Veritable Records*, 1:12 (no. 15/Hóngwǔ 16.1.3).
35. Okinawa kenritsu hakubutsukan, *Kizamareta rekishi*, 16, 82, and Gregory Smits, "Making Destiny in the Kingdom of Ryukyu," 114.
36. For the details, see Asato, *Kōkogaku kara mita Ryūkyūshi, jō* [vol. 1], 149–181. See 182–190 for additional archaeological evidence and details about the *gusuku* bases of the local lords.
37. In addition to Ikuta Shigeru, cited above, see Yoshinari and Fuku, *Ryūkyū ōkoku to wakō*, 215–231, and several of their subsequent books.
38. Dumézil, *L'idéologie tripartie des Indo-Européens*.
39. Ōbayashi, *Higashi Ajia no ōken shinwa*, 426–439.
40. *Omoro sōshi*, no. 1295. For analysis, see Ōbayashi, *Higashi Ajia no ōken shinwa*, 434–435.
41. Torigoe, *Okinawa no shinwa to minzoku*, 222.
42. Ōbayashi, *Higashi Ajia no ōken shinwa*, 427–430.
43. *Kyūyō*, no. 84, and Ōbayashi, *Higashi Ajia no ōken shinwa*, 431–432.
44. Ōbayashi, *Higashi Ajia no ōken shinwa*, 433–434.
45. Ikuta, "Ryūkyūkoku no 'Sanzan tōitsu,'" 203–204.
46. *Genealogy of Chūzan*, 20–21.
47. Ibid., 24.
48. Asato has argued that the excavation of the Urasoe yōdore tomb complex, near Urasoe castle, indicates that the official histories were correct in asserting that Eiso ruled all of Okinawa as king from his base at Urasoe during the late thirteenth century. See Asato, *Ryūkyū no ōken to gusuku*, esp. chapters 4–6. For a rebuttal of this claim, see Yoshinari, *Ryūkyūshi o toinaosu*, 76–80.
49. Fuku, *Omoro sōshi to gun'yū no seiki*, 160–161.

Chapter 5: Geographies of Power

1. For an illustrated summary of military items, see Uehara, "Gusuku jidai," 316–322.
2. *Omoro sōshi*, no. 546 and partially repeated in no. 866. For analysis, see Yoshinari and Fuku, *Ryūkyūkoku tanjō*, 39–42.

3. For a detailed analysis of this lord of the south, see Fuku, *Omoro sōshi to Gun'yū no seiki*, 105–162.
4. *Omoro sōshi*, no. 446, and Yoshinari and Fuku, *Ryūkyū ōkoku tanjō*, 44–45.
5. Asato, *Gusuku*, 25, 31–34.
6. Higashionna, *Higashionna Kanjun zenshū*, 3:69–70, and Asato, *Gusuku*, 16.
7. Takara, *Ryūkyū ōkokushi no tankyū*, 22–23.
8. Higashionna, *Higashionna Kanjun zenshū*, 3:81–85; *Joseon Veritable Royal Records*, entry no. 125 (1462), 32/140–143; Takara, *Ryūkyū ōkokushi no tankyū*, 32; and Makishi, "Ryūkyū ōkoku jūgoseiki chūki ikō no kinaiseitekina tokuchō to ōjō girei," 162.
9. *Joseon Veritable Royal Records*, entry no. 126 (1462), 38/154, and Makishi, "Ryūkyū ōkoku jūgoseiki chūki ikō no kinaiseitekina tokuchō to ōjō girei," 163.
10. Higashionna, *Higashionna Kanjun zenshū*, 3:85–86; *Joseon Veritable Royal Records*, entry no. 125 (1462), 35/144; and Takara, *Ryūkyū ōkokushi no tankyū*, 33–34.
11. Higashionna, *Higashionna Kanjun zenshū*, 3:88, and *Joseon Veritable Royal Records*, entry no. 126 (1462), 36/153.
12. Pearson, *Ancient Ryukyu*, 255.
13. Ibid., 256.
14. Kubota, *Tetsu kara yomu Nihon no rekishi*, 127–140.
15. Pearson, *Ancient Ryukyu*, 256.
16. *Ming Veritable Records*, 1:12 (no. 8/Hóngwǔ 9.4.1).
17. In addition to Han'anchi's former sword and Teganemaru/Tsukushi-chara, there is a short sword, Chatan-nakiri. For a photo of all three, see Uezato, "Bunken shiryō kara mita Ko-Ryūkyū no kinkōhin," 226.
18. For a summary of the story, see Takara, *Ryūkyū no jidai*, 71–72. Takara is well aware that this account reads like dramatic fiction and that what actually happened "is entirely unclear." See also Sun, *Chūgoku kara mita Ko-Ryūkyū no sekai*, 128–132, including photos of Chiyoganemaru.
19. Kanesaki, *Kōko to kodai*, 23–24, and Ōbayashi, *Higashi Ajia no ōken shinwa*, 432–433. See also Yoshinari and Fuku, *Ryūkyū ōkoku to wakō*, 92–93.
20. *Omoro sōshi*, no. 1185.
21. Ibid., no. 1186. For analysis, see Fuku, *Omoro sōshi to gun'yū no seiki*, 78–79.
22. *Omoro sōshi*, no. 164. For analysis, see Yoshinari and Fuku, *Ryūkyū ōkoku to wakō*, 66–67.
23. See headnote "Kanahiyabu" in Hokama and Saigō, *Omoro sōshi*, 72 (referring to song no. 163).
24. For a detailed discussion of Nakijin as template, see Yoshinari and Fuku, *Ryūkyū ōkoku to wakō*, 52–57.
25. *Omoro sōshi*, no. 829.
26. Yoshinari and Fuku, *Ryūkyū ōkoku to wakō*, 64–82.
27. Ibid., 78–82, 102–103.
28. Shimono, *Amami, Tokara no dentō bunka*, 362–363 (photo 361).
29. The term for this type of deity is *kinmamun* (or *kimimamono*). For details, see Iha, *Iha Fuyū zenshū*, 5:322–328.
30. Makishi, "*Omorosōshi* ni miru Kumejima shutsuji no kamigami no henyō to sono rekishiteki haikei," 233.
31. Iha argues that their names essentially mean the same, both referring to an umbrella that could block the wind. Iha, *Iha Fuyū zenshū*, 5:324.
32. For example, *Omoro sōshi*, no. 174.
33. They are the 1522 Madama minato himon (monument G, chapter 8) and the Yarazamori gusuku inscription. For the latter, see *Reflections on Ryukyu*, 78. See also Makishi, "*Omoro sōshi* ni miru Kumejima shutsuji no kamigami no henyō to sono rekishiteki haikei," 233.

34. Shimono, *Amami, Tokara no dentō bunka*, 362.
35. See, for example, *Omoro sōshi*, no. 479.
36. *Omoro sōshi*, nos. 1287, 1289.
37. Sasaki, "Nantō chūseiteki inasaku gijutsu," 46–47. See also Asato, *Gusuku, kyōdōtai, mura*, 59–60, and Fuku, *Omoro sōshi to gun'yū no seiki*, 215–217.
38. Higashionna, *Higashionna Kanjun zenshū*, 3:84; *Joseon Veritable Royal Records*, entry no. 125 (1462), 34/143; and Sasaki, "Nantō chūseiteki inasaku gijutsu," 33–34, 46–47.
39. *Origins of Ryukyu*, 19.
40. Tanigawa Ken'ichi, *Yomigaeru kaijō no michi*, 154.
41. Sakima, *Nirai-kanai no genzō*, 263–264.
42. It is common to find Teganemaru glossed as "Jiganemaru" to accord with the first Chinese character used to write it.
43. *Omoro sōshi*, no. 1356; one line is split and two reversed to fit English syntax. See also Yoshinari, *Ryūkyūshi o toinaosu*, 110–111, and Yoshinari and Fuku, *Ryūkyū ōkoku tanjō*, 96.
44. Yoshinari and Fuku, *Ryūkyū ōkoku tanjō*, 98–99, and Yoshinari, *Ryūkyūshi o toinaosu*, 108–112.
45. Quoted in Kerr, *Okinawa*, 127.
46. Uezato, "Bunken shiryō kara mita Ko-Ryūkyū no kinkōhin," 236–237.
47. *Omoro sōshi*, no. 597; two lines were reversed to fit English syntax. See also Yoshinari and Fuku, *Ryūkyū ōkoku tanjō*, 46–47.
48. *Omoro sōshi*, no. 606, repeated in no. 1426; and Fuku, *Omoro sōshi to gun'yū no seiki*, 159–160.
49. Topographic map of Okinawa island. http://en-us.topographic-map.com/places/Okinawa-Island-9353902.
50. For a somewhat disorganized account of these details, see Inamura, *Wakō shiseki*, 356–361.
51. Ibid., 351.
52. Ibid., 355–357.
53. Ibid., 357–358, 360.
54. *Omoro sōshi*, nos. 583–586, 1473. See also Sakima *Nirai-kanai no genzō*, 35–50, 202–206.
55. Sakima, *Nirai-kanai no genzō*, 35–45.
56. Iha, *Iha Fuyū zenshū*, 6:551.
57. Yoshinari and Fuku, *Ryūkyū ōkoku tanjō*, 170–177, 302–304.
58. Tanigawa, *Yomigaeru kaijō no michi*, 176, and Tanigawa, *Okinawa, Amami to Yamato*, 16.
59. Sakita, "Hokuzan bunkaken e no kōsō," 140.
60. Iha, *Iha Fuyū zenshū*, 4:498–500.
61. Yoshinari and Fuku, *Ryūkyū ōkoku tanjō*, 61–62.
62. Ōyama, "Ryūkyū ōchō fukuzoku jidai," 223–226.
63. Takahashi, *Unabara no Heike denshō*, 145–146, 230–239 (quote on 238).
64. Yoshioka, "Nantō no chūsei sueki," 429, and Yoshinari and Fuku, *Ryūkyū ōkoku tanjō*, 78–80, 257.
65. Inamura, *Wakō shiseki*, 244–247.
66. Iha, *Iha Fuyū zenshū*, 4:495–496, 501.
67. Inamura, *Wakō shiseki*, 308–311, 351.
68. Tanigawa Ken'ichi states that the name Kawara in northern Kyushu indicated places and a deity associated with immigrants from Silla, who came to extract copper from Mount Kawara. I have omitted many details for the sake of brevity. See Tanigawa, *Rettō jūdan, chimei shōyō*, 100–101.
69. Mamiya Atsushi proposes the Japanese *omoto* (place where a person of noble status is) as the origin of *obotsu*; see Mamiya, *Okinawa kogo no shinsō*, 123–125. My thanks to Leon Serafim for this reference.

70. Inamura, *Wakō shiseki*, 351–361, and Yoshinari and Fuku, *Ryūkyū ōkoku tanjō*, 83–84, 174–177.

Chapter 6: The First Shō Dynasty

1. Tanigawa, *Yomigaeru kaijō no michi*, 70–71.
2. Kumamoto chūseishi kenkyūkai, *Yatsushiro nikki*.
3. There is also a Jashiki in northern Okinawa, pronounced locally as Jajichi or Jaichi.
4. For the full analysis, see Orikuchi-hakase kinen kodai kenkyūjo, *Orikuchi Shinobu zenshū*, 16:14–68, and Tanigawa and Orikuchi, *Ryūkyū ōken no genryū*.
5. Yoshinari, *Ryūkyūshi o toinaosu*, 132–134; Yoshinari and Fuku, 305–306; Tanigawa, *Yomigaeru kaijō no michi*, 177–178; and Tanigawa, *Rettō jūdan, chimei shōyō*, 124–126.
6. Tanigawa, *Rettō jūdan, chimei shōyō*, 124–126.
7. Tanigawa, *Yomigaeru kaijō no michi*, 130–139, 150–153, 156–158, and Yoshinari, *Ryūkyūshi o toinaosu*, 133–134.
8. Mikami, *Tōji bōekishi*, 1:223.
9. Tanaka, *Higashi Ajia tsūkōken to kokusai ninshiki*, 148–170, and Fuku, *Omoro sōshi to gun'yū no seiki*, 213–214.
10. Recall also that Okinoerabu was a major *wakō* base and served as a pasture for horses. The official histories provide biographies of Shō Hashi, all legendary. One detail is that, while in Sashiki, he trained war horses; see *Kyūyō*, no. 74.
11. Hokama, *Koten o yomu Omoro sōshi*, 173–174.
12. Yoshinari and Fuku, *Ryūkyū ōkoku tanjō*, 255–256.
13. *Origins of Ryukyu*, 2:320, and Tanigawa and Orikuchi, *Ryūkyū ōken no genryū*, 32–36.
14. Yoshinari and Fuku, *Ryūkyū ōkoku tanjō*, 137.
15. There is a Katsuren lineage in Kikai, but we cannot be certain whether it was connected with Katsuren in Okinawa. See Fuku, *Kikaijima*, 75–80.
16. *Record of East Sea Countries*, 233.
17. *Joseon Veritable Royal Records*, entry no. 23 (1418), 8–9/48.
18. For a detailed analysis, see Ikuta, "Ryūkyūkoku no 'Sanzan tōitsu,'" 183–184. Ikuta proposes that Katsuren-gusuku and Shō Hashi were relatives who struggled for power while Shō Shishō was on the throne.
19. Based on the name Kimishi in *Omoro sōshi* no. 985 referring to Shō Kinpuku's deity name, and on Mashi-Furi in nos. 938 and 939 as referring to Furi. See Ōyama, "Ryūkyū ōchō fukuzoku jidai," 250, 253–254. According to *Okinawa kogo daijiten*, Kimishi in no. 985 indicates a lord other than the king (p. 231, "Kimishi"), but that would not necessarily exclude Shō Kinpuku if he was associated with Katsuren before becoming king. Similarly, this source defines Mashi-Furi as "a Katsuren person" (p. 606, "Mashifuri").
20. *Kyūyō*, no. 66.
21. *Ming Veritable Records*, 1:20 (no. 25, Yŏnglè 4.1.11).
22. Ibid. (no. 30, Yŏnglè 5.4.11).
23. *Origins of Ryukyu*, 1:56.
24. *Genealogy of Chūzan*, 45.
25. Ibid., 49, and *Ming Veritable Records*, 1:21 (no. 45, Yŏnglè 9.4.3).
26. *Ming Veritable Records*, 1:21 (no. 45, Yŏnglè 9.4.3), and *Genealogy of Chūzan*, 55, 63, 65, 67.
27. Higashionna, *Higashionna Kanjun zenshū*, 7:189.
28. Ibid., 190.
29. For a detailed record of Kaiki's activities with respect to overseas trade and diplomacy, see *Rekidai hōan*, 2:453–467, 1–43–04 through 1–43–23. See also Tomiyama, "Tōitsu ōkoku keiseiki no taigai kankei," 143–149, and Ikuta, "Ryūkyū Chūzan ōkoku to kaijō bōeki."

30. Tomiyama, "Minami no Ryūkyū," 218.
31. Harada, *Ryūkyū to Chūgoku*, 22–26; Uezato, *Ryū-Nichi sensō 1609*, 19–20; and Ōta, *Isetsu Okinawa shi*, 33–36.
32. Yano, *Ko-Ryūkyūki Shuri ōfu no kenkyū*, 31–32, 44–45.
33. *Genealogy of Chūzan*, 68–69, and Pearson, *Ancient Ryukyu*, 236, 251.
34. Pearson, *Ancient Ryukyu*, 236, 244, 251.
35. *Ming Veritable Records*, 2:19 (no. 70/Jǐngtài 5.2.18).
36. Sakihara, *A Brief History of Early Okinawa*, 159–160.
37. Takahashi, "Ryūkyū ōkoku," 311. See also Yoshinari, *Ryūkyūshi o toinaosu*, 170–175.
38. *Reflections on Chūzan*, 47.
39. Higashionna, *Higashionna Kanjun zenshū*, 3:11, 13.
40. *Ming Veritable Records*, 2:19 (no.70/Jǐngtài 5.2.18). See also pp. 92–93, n. 239, for many more details.
41. *Genealogy of Chūzan*, 68.
42. *Omoro sōshi*, no. 78. For analysis, see Yoshinari, *Ryūkyūshi o toinaosu*, 172.
43. Higashionna, *Higashionna Kanjun zenshū*, 3:589.
44. See, for example, *Kyūyō*, nos. 106 and 107.
45. Yamauchi, *Sengo Okinawa tsūka hensenshi*, 62, 64–65.
46. Ibid., 65.
47. Uehara, *Shimazu-shi no Ryūkyū shinryaku*, 20.
48. Tanigawa, *Yomigaeru kaijō no michi*, 144, and Tanigawa and Orikuchi, *Ryūkyū ōken no genryū*, 44.
49. *Genealogy of Chūzan*, 72 and *Kyūyō*, no. 111. The second divine title is Setaka-ō (Acclaimed King).
50. Makise, *Nihonshi no genten, Okinawashi*, 202, and Yoshinari and Fuku, *Ryūkyū ōkoku tanjō*, 67.
51. *Kyūyō*, no. 115; *Genealogy of Chūzan*, 73–74; and *Origins of Ryūkyū*, 235.
52. Kamakura, *Okinawa bunka no ihō*, 1:133, and Fuku, *Kikaijima*, 72–74.
53. Yoshinari, *Ryūkyūshi o toinaosu*, 137. See also Yoshinari and Fuku, *Ryūkyū ōkoku tanjō*, 67–68.
54. Higashionna, *Higashionna Kanjun zenshū*, 3:69.
55. *Ryūkyū shintōki*, 100–101.
56. Higashionna, *Higashionna Kanjun zenshū*, 3:85, and *Joseon Veritable Royal Records*, entry no. 125 (1463), 34–35/144.
57. Higashionna, *Higashionna Kanjun zenshū*, 7:765.
58. Kamei, *Amami-Ōshima shoka keifu shū*, 180.
59. Ishigami, "Ryūkyū no Amami shotō tōchi no shodankai," 6–8, and Hamada, *Amami no rekishi*, 31–33.
60. Iha, *Iha Fuyū zenshū*, 6:546–585.
61. *Omoro sōshi*, no. 53.
62. *Omoro sōshi*, nos. 938, 939. See also Yoshinari and Fuku, *Ryūkyū ōkoku to wakō*, 124–125.
63. Shapinsky, *Lords of the Sea*.

Chapter 7: Seizures, Erasures, and Resurgences

1. *Reflections on Chūzan*, 49.
2. Ibid., 54.
3. Ibid., 55.
4. *Genealogy of Chūzan*, 96.
5. *Origins of Ryukyu*, 2:298.
6. Ibid., 299. See *Kyūyō*, no. 122, for a more thorough explanation.

270   Notes to Pages 123–133

7. *Origins of Ryukyu*, 2:321.
8. *Kyūyō*, no. 844.
9. Ibid., no. 815.
10. For details, see Yoshinari and Fuku, *Ryūkyū ōkoku to wakō*, 190–194.
11. *Kyūyō*, nos. 121, 122.
12. Tanigawa, "'Ko-Ryūkyū' izen no sekai," 57–58.
13. For a detailed analysis, see Sakima, *Nirai-kanai no genzō*, 119–158.
14. *Omoro sōshi*, nos. 467, 538, 1204, and 1348.
15. Ibid., no. 74.
16. Sakima, *Nirai-Kanai no genzō*, 158–164, and Yoshinari and Fuku, *Ryūkyū ōkoku tanjō*, 229–233.
17. I have condensed a very complex topic. For the full analysis, see Yoshinari and Fuku, *Ryūkyū ōkoku tanjō*, 224–261, esp. 260–261 for the conclusion.
18. *Omoro sōshi*, nos. 1025–1028, and Yoshinari and Fuku, *Ryūkyū ōkoku to wakō*, 51–63.
19. Yoshinari and Fuku, *Ryūkyū ōkoku to wakō*, 51–64, 71–82, 259, 272–273.
20. Ibid., 65–66.
21. *Omoro sōshi*, nos. 74, 75, 76.
22. Fuku, *Omoro sōshi to gun'yū no seiki*, 188–189.
23. *Omoro sōshi*, no. 1202.
24. Ibid., no. 716, repeated as no. 1203.
25. Yoshinari and Fuku, *Ryūkyū ōkoku tanjō*, 71–76.
26. Kerr, *Okinawa*, chap. 3, "The Great Days of Chuzan (1398–1573)," 83–150.
27. Sai Taku, *Sai Taku bon Chūzan seifu*, 123–127.
28. *Reflections on Chūzan*, 56.
29. *Omoro sōshi*, no. 1554 and part of no. 662. Both *omoro* refer to the dancing of Shō En's daughter, so the point of the song in the context of this passage in *Reflections* is unclear. See headnotes, Hokama and Saigō, *Omoro sōshi*, 241, 492.
30. *Reflections on Chūzan*, 56.
31. Takara, *Ryūkyū no jidai*, 187.
32. *Reflections on Chūzan*, 57.
33. Yano, *Ko-Ryūkyūki Shuri ōfu no kenkyū*, 31–33.
34. *Genealogy of Chūzan*, 83.
35. For details, see Tanigawa, *Yomigaeru kaijō no michi*, 143–146, and Tanigawa and Orikuchi, *Ryūkyū ōken no genryū*, 44–46.
36. *Omoro sōshi*, no. 862.
37. *Origins of Ryukyu*, 2:318–320; Tanigawa and Orikuchi, *Ryūkyū ōken no genryū*, 34–35, 37; and Okinawa kogo daijiten henshū iinkai, ed., *Okinawa kogo daijiten*, 545.
38. China, *Ryūkyū Bukkyōshi*, 95–105.
39. *Kyūyō*, no. 167.
40. *Origins of Ryukyu*, 1:191–192.
41. *Kyūyō*, no. 267, *Genealogy of Chūzan*, 89.
42. *Ryukyu Record*, 50.
43. *Joseon Veritable Royal Records*, entry no. 240 (1500) 93–94/325–327, and China, *Ryūkyū Bukkyōshi*, 109–111.
44. *Ryukyu Record*, 19, 153–155. Chén Kǎn elaborated on the matter by making reference to succession intrigues and warfare from the Spring and Autumn period (ca. 771–476 BCE) and the Eastern Jin dynasty (317–420); see p. 20, notes 4 and 5.
45. *Reflections on Chūzan*, 58.

Chapter 8: The Second Shō Dynasty's Challenges

1. Uehara, *Shimazu-shi no Ryūkyū shinryaku*, 6–7.
2. *Ming Veritable Records*, 2:23 (no. 24/Chénghuà 11.4.10). See also p. 102, n. 78.
3. *Rekidai hōan*, 1:427–429 (1–12–21). For details, see Tomiyama, "Tōitsu ōkoku keiseiki no taigai kankei," 159.
4. *Ming Veritable Records*, 2:24 (no. 33/Chénghuà 14.4.18).
5. *Rekidai hōan*, 1:28 (1–01–25), and Tomiyama, "Tōitsu ōkoku keiseiki no taigai kankei," 160.
6. *Ming Veritable Records*, 2:23 (no. 15/Chénghuà 7.3.25).
7. Tomiyama, "Tōitsu ōkoku keiseiki no taigai kankei," 160. A message from the emperor to Shō En reporting this matter is dated Chénghuà 7.4.8. See *Rekidai hōan*, 1:21 (1–01–17), and Akamine, *The Ryukyu Kingdom*, 45–46.
8. *Genealogy of Chūzan*, 85, *Kyūyō*, no. 195, and Harada, *Ryūkyū o shugosuru kami*, 33–37.
9. As historian of medieval Japan, Jeffrey P. Mass cautions in this context, "phenomena assumed to be old and potentially older sometimes turn out to be just the opposite." Mass, *Antiquity and Anachronism in Japanese History*, 45.
10. *Ryukyu Monument Inscriptions*, 69–70.
11. Ibid., 65–68.
12. Ibid., 71–73.
13. Ibid., 75–76.
14. Ibid., 78–79.
15. Ibid., 81–83. For an English translation, see Mitsugu Sakihara, *A Brief History of Early Okinawa*, 164–166.
16. *Ryukyu Monument Inscriptions*, 83.
17. Ibid., 88–89.
18. *Genealogy of Chūzan*, 85.
19. *Ryukyu Monument Inscriptions*, 86–87.
20. *Kyūyō*, no. 183.
21. China, *Ryūkyū Bukkyōshi no kenkyū*, 29–47.
22. Ibid., 47–57.
23. Ibid., 73–94.
24. Ibid., 138. See also 78–81.
25. Quoted in ibid., 140.
26. For example, *Ryukyu Monument Inscriptions*, 89 (Monument G above).
27. Based on *Ryūkyū Shintōki*. See China, *Ryūkyū Bukkyōshi no kenkyū*, 148–149, for a chart and detailed breakdown. China regards Enkakuji as having been established before Shō Shin's reign began.
28. *Genealogy of Chūzan*, 98–99.
29. Ibid., 100.
30. One other official associated with Kunigami, Tomoyose Chokunō, was exiled to Kikai at the same time. For details see Dana, "Kunigami Keimei," 961.
31. Ishigami, *Amami shotō hennen shiryō: Ko-Ryūkyū ki hen*, 178–188.
32. *Geneaology of Chūzan*, 106.
33. Sai Taku, *Sai Taku bon Chūzan seifu*, 143.
34. *Geneaology of Chūzan*, 107, and Sai Taku, *Sai Taku bon Chūzan seifu*, 143.
35. *Kyūyō*, no. 238.
36. For a concise summary, see Yoshinari, *Ryūkyūshi o toinaosu*, 183–187.
37. Many scholars have discussed this matter, and I engage some of their work in later chapters. For a concise analysis of the relevant geopolitics and symbolism, see Kuroshima, *Ryūkyū ōkoku to sengoku daimyō*, esp. 53–63.

38. The pro-Satsuma official was probably Nago Ueekata Ryōin (Dōrin). See Kuroshima, *Ryūkyū ōkoku to sengoku daimyō*, 66.
39. Ibid., 64–65.
40. Only three ships reached Taiwan and were easily repulsed. Murayama's apparent plan was to use Taiwan as a base for trading with China. See Tomiyama, *Ryūkyū ōkoku no gaikō to ōken*, 155–157, and *Ming Veritable Records*, 3:20 (no. 71, Wànlì 44.6.16).
41. Tomiyama, *Ryūkyū ōkoku no gaikō to ōken*, 176–177.

Chapter 9: Assembling a Royal Line

1. *Ryukyu Monument Inscriptions*, 89, and Dana, "Ryūkyū ōken no keifu," 182–183.
2. *Ryukyu Monument Inscriptions*, 96, and Dana, "Ryūkyū ōken no keifu," 183.
3. Dana, "Ryūkyū ōken no keifu," 183, and Yano, *Ko-Ryūkyūki Shuri ōfu no kenkyū*, 206–207.
4. Dana, "Ryūkyū ōken no keifu," 183–188.
5. For example, *Reflections on Chūzan*, 29–36.
6. *Reflections on Chūzan*, 36. The reference to sensual pleasure and hunting is from the "Wǔzǐ zhī gē" chapter of the Chinese classic *Shūjīng* (Classic of documents), a song that purports to encapsulate the teachings of the legendary sage king Yǔ. See Nomura, *Shokyō*, 77.
7. Yoshinari and Fuku, *Ryūkyū ōkoku to wakō*, 51, 58–59, 76–78.
8. *Reflections on Chūzan*, 51.
9. Sai Taku, *Sai Taku bon Chūzan seifu*, 111.
10. *Reflections on Chūzan*, 76.
11. Sai Taku, *Sai Taku bon Chūzan seifu*, 83.
12. *Genealogy of Chūzan*, 47.
13. *Origins of Ryukyu*, 2:341.
14. Yano, *Ko-Ryūkyūki Shuri ōfu no kenkyū*, 209. See also Dana, "Ryūkyū ōken no keifu," 189–191.
15. Tameharu, for example, is listed as the founder of the Kasari lineage, and the names of his successors all begin with *tame* of Tametomo. See Kamei, *Amami-Ōshima shoka keifu shū*, 78–82.
16. Ibid., 171–172.
17. Tanigawa, *Yomigaeru kaijō no michi*, 67–70.
18. *Omoro sōshi*, no. 212.
19. For a more detailed analysis, see Yoshinari and Fuku, *Ryūkyū ōkoku to wakō*, 28–36.
20. *Omoro sōshi*, no. 512.
21. Ibid., 281.
22. Ibid., 1041.
23. Nanpo Bunshi, *Nanpo bunshū*, 3:59–60.
24. For a thorough discussion of this mater, see Ōyama, "Shimazu-shi no Ryūkyū iri to Amami," 267–270.
25. For a psychological and literary analysis, see Yoshinari and Fuku, *Ryūkyū ōkoku to wakō*, 77–78, 309–320, and Fuku, *Kikaijima*, 39–47, 110–111.

Chapter 10: Centering Shuri and Forging an Empire

1. Takahashi, *Umi no "Kyōto."*
2. *Kyūyō*, no. 155 (1492).
3. For more details, see Makishi, "Ryūkyū ōkoku jūgoseiki chūki ikō no kinaiseitekina tokuchō to ōjō girei," 168–169.

Notes to Pages 163–174   273

4. *Omoro sōshi*, no. 218. See the other songs in volume 5 for more examples of this and similar messages about Shuri.
5. Hokama and Saigō, *Omoro sōshi*, 89.
6. For a thorough study of male and female officials during Shō Shin's reign and slightly before, see Makishi, "Ryūkyū ōkoku jūgoseiki chūki ikō no kinaiseitekina tokuchō to ōjō girei," 155–245.
7. *Ryukyu Record*, 67.
8. *Ryukyu Monument Inscriptions*, 113–117.
9. For more details, see Higashionna, *Higashionna Kanjun zenshū*, 10:308–314.
10. *Ryukyu Record*, 65. See also Makishi, "Ryūkyū ōkoku jūgoseiki chūki ikō no kinaiseitekina tokuchō to ōjō girei," 169–170.
11. Makishi, "Ryūkyū ōkoku jūgoseiki chūki ikō no kinaiseitekina tokuchō to ōjō girei," 176–177.
12. Ibid., 181–182. See also discussion of Sashikasa/Sasukasa in chapter 5.
13. *Origins of Ryūkyū*, 2:594–595.
14. *Kyūyō*, no. 172.
15. Makishi, "*Omoro sōshi* ni miru Kumejima shutsuji no kamigami no henyō to sono rekishiteki haikei," 213–214.
16. *Kyūyō*, no. 163.
17. Yoshinari and Fuku, *Ryūkyū ōkoku tanjō*, 83–84.
18. For a summary of some of this warfare, see ibid., 82.
19. *Genealogy of Chūzan*, 89.
20. Sai Taku version of *Genealogy of Chūzan*, quoted in Ōhama, *Oyake Akahachi*, 45.
21. Ōhama, *Oyake Akahachi*, 46–49.
22. *Kyūyō*, nos. 159, 160, and 161. In no. 160, the lead Shuri general is Ōzato.
23. Tabatake household of the Kasari lineage inserted into the Gushiken household records. See Kamei, *Amami-Ōshima shoka keifu shū*, 59.
24. A 1522 *Kyūyō* entry reports on Nakasone traveling to Shuri to give his prized sword to Shō Shin. It refers to him as Miyako's "Shark ancestor." The passage explains that on the return voyage to Miyako, Nakasone's ship sank but a giant shark rescued him. (The type of fish is *saba*, which means shark, not mackerel, in local speech.) The next entry explains, after a very long story, that "Shark ancestor Nakasone Toyomiya" was the seventh-generation descendant of someone who was also rescued by a shark, which is why the story is included here. *Kyūyō*, nos. 181 and 182.
25. *Kyūyō*, no. 162.
26. *Genealogy of Chūzan*, 91, and *Ming Veritable Records*, 2:32 (no. 2/Jiājìng 1.5.23).
27. Okamoto, "Ko-Ryūkyūki no Ryūkyū ōkoku ni okeru 'kaisen' o meguru shosō," 228.
28. Ibid., 222–228.
29. The main reason was severe budget limitations owing to Ming military expenditures. See Akamine, *The Ryukyu Kingdom*, 48.
30. Tomiyama, "Minami no Ryūkyū," 296–297.
31. Akamine, *The Ryukyu Kingdom*, 48.
32. Tomiyama, "Minami no Ryūkyū," 298–299.
33. Kishaba, "Ayabune," 113.
34. *Omoro sōshi*, no. 790.
35. Tanigawa, *Yomigaeru kaijō no michi*, 200–201.
36. Inamura, *Wakō shiseki*, 66–72, and Kitami, *Nihon kaijō kōtsūshi*, 554–555.
37. Pearson, *Ancient Ryukyu*, 168.
38. *Omoro sōshi*, no. 760, repeated as no. 1549.
39. Ibid., no. 901. See also no. 908 for a similar relationship between priestess, ship, and carpenter/shipwright.

40. Tanigawa, *Yomigaeru kaijō no michi*, 211–212.
41. The case of Yūfu Tatsu and his ship, taken into custody at Wēnzhōu in 1601, is one example. See Watanabe, *Kinsei Ryūkyū to Chū-Nichi kankei*, 35–36.
42. Yoshinari Naoki points out that the Ming court's goal was to "emasculate" the *wakō* state in Ryukyu via the tribute system. Yoshinari, *Ryūkyūshi o toinaosu*, 99.
43. Uezato, *Ryū-Nichi sensō 1609*, 190–193.
44. Tomiyama, "Minami no Ryūkyū," 299.
45. *Omoro sōshi*, no. 279. My thanks to Leon Serafim for his analysis of this song.
46. Hokama and Saigo, *Omoro sōshi*, 104. "Kane no shima" can also refer to Tokunoshima.
47. *Omoro sōshi*, no. 95, *Origins of Ryukyu*, 1:53–54, and Takara, *Ryūkyū ōkoku no kōzō*, 106–116.
48. Takara, *Ryūkyū ōkoku no kōzō*, 166–119. Monument G (Madama minato himon, 1522) also explains some of these details.
49. *Kyūyō*, nos. 186 and 187; "Yaeyama utaki yuraiki," 706; Makishi, "*Omoro sōshi* ni miru Kumejima shutsuji no kamigami no henyō to sono rekishiteki haikei," 215; and Yano, *Ko-Ryūkyūki Shuri ōfu no kenkyū*, 171–172. According to local lore, a man named Nishitō also came to Okinoerabu from Okinawa to build the tomb for that island's local rulers, one of whom had been Guraru Magohachi; see Nagayoshi, *Erabu no koshūzoku*, 92. It is possible that "Nishitō" was a generic name.
50. Ishigami, *Amami shotō hennen shiryō: Ko-Ryūkyū ki hen*, 98–102; *Kyūyō*, no. 202; and Makishi, "*Omoro sōshi* ni miru Kumejima shutsuji no kamigami no henyō to sono rekishiteki haikei," 215–216.
51. Yano, *Ko-Ryūkyūki Shuri ōfu no kenkyū*, 173–174.
52. Makishi, "*Omoro sōshi* ni miru Kumejima shutsuji no kamigami no henyō to sono rekishiteki haikei," 205–258, and Makishi, "Ryūkyū ōkoku jūgoseiki chūki ikō no kinaiseitekina tokuchō to ōjō girei," 182–183; 186; 235, n. 56.

Chapter 11: The Ryukyu Empire

1. Uezato, *Ryū-Nichi sensō 1609*, 12.
2. For a chart of *jiresho*, see Takara, *Ryūkyū ōkokushi no tankyū*, 56–57. For an analysis of *jiresisho*, see Takara, *Ryūkyū ōkoku no kōzō*, esp. 33–79, and Ōishi, Takara, and Takahashi, *Shūen kara mita chūsei Nihon*, 225–241.
3. *Kyūyō*, nos. 160, 169.
4. *Omoro sōshi*, no. 4.
5. Kamei, *Amami-Ōshima shoka keifu shū*, 59 and 78.
6. Ibid., 86.
7. Ibid., 35.
8. Ishigami, *Amami shotō hennen shiryō: Ko-Ryūkyū ki hen*, 77–82.
9. Kamei, *Amami-Ōshima shoka keifu shū*, 492. For a flow chart of ranks, see Matsushita, *Kinsei Amami-Ōshima no shihai to shakai*, 31.
10. For the *jiresisho*, see Kamei, *Amami-Ōshima shoka keifu shū*, 78. The original document is not extant.
11. Ibid., 59, 78.
12. Ibid., 78.
13. Ibid., 59–60, 78–79.
14. Composite of three different records in the Ushuku-ōya collection; Kamei, ibid., 86, 89, 92.
15. Tameyoshi returning from Shuri, ibid., 59; Inutarugane sailing to Shuri, ibid., 92.
16. Ibid., 171–172.

17. Ishigami, *Amami shotō hennen shiryō: Ko-Ryūkyū ki hen*, 191–198, 203–214.
18. *Joseon Veritable Royal Records*, entry no. 215 (1493), 78/282–283.
19. *Kyūyō*, no. 160.
20. *Ryukyu Record*, 78, 217–218.
21. *Ming Veritable Records*, 2:35 (no. 36/Jiājìng, 37.1.26), referring to a previous year.
22. *Rekidai hōan*, 1:68–69, 1–02–05.
23. *Ming Veritable Records*, 2:49 (no. 64/Jǐngtài 3.6.20).
24. Uezato, *Ryū-Nichi sensō 1609*, 37–40.
25. Uehara, *Shimazu-shi no Ryūkyū shinryaku*, 35–36.
26. Dana, *Okinawa kinseishi no shosō*, 19–21.
27. *Kyūyō*, no. 202.
28. *Genealogy of Chūzan*, 95–96.
29. *Reflections on Chūzan*, 67–68. According to a biography based on household records, Kunigami Seiin (Ba Shiryō, d. 1537) was a descendant of the Okuma blacksmith. This blacksmith saved Kanemaru's life, according to the legendary biography of Shō En. Okuma is in northern Okinawa (Kunigami). See Miyazato, *Okinawa monchū daijiten*, 275.
30. Kanehisa, *Amami ni ikiru Nihon kodai bunka*, esp. 57–58. For a similar account from household records, see Ishigami, *Amami shotō hennen shiryō: Ko-Ryūkyū ki hen*, 108–109.
31. Kamei, *Amami-Ōshima shoka keifu shū*, 171–172.
32. *Genealogy of Chūzan*, 102–103, and *Kyūyō*, nos. 224 and 226.
33. Supplementary materials appended to *Kyūyō* include the story of a Council of Three member banished to Kunigami because Shō Sei accused him of killing peasants during the 1537 war. See Ishigami, *Amami shotō hennen shiryō: Ko-Ryūkyū ki hen*, 104–105.
34. Kuroshima, *Ryūkyū ōkoku to sengoku daimyō*, 40–44.
35. Ishigami, *Amami shotō hennen shiryō: Ko-Ryūkyū ki hen*, 262–263.
36. Ibid., 191–198, and Ōishi, Takara, and Takahashi, *Shūen kara mita chūsei Nihon*, 231–241.
37. Doyle, *Empires*, 45.
38. Burbank and Cooper, *Empires in World History*.
39. For an analysis of the *hiki*, see Takara, *Ryūkyū ōkoku no kōzō*, 103–119. See also Uezato, "Ko-Ryūkyū no guntai," 112, 118–119.
40. Makishi, "Ryūkyū ōkoku jūgoseiki chūki ikō no kinaiseitekina tokuchō to ōjō girei," 171.
41. Uezato, "Ko-Ryūkyū no guntai," 113; Uezato, "Ryūkyū no kaki ni tsuite," 78; Uezato, *Ryū-Nichi sensō 1609*, 34–37; and Uehara, *Shimazu-shi no Ryūkyū shinryaku*, 7–9.
42. Uezato, "Ko-Ryūkyū no guntai," 117–119, and Uezato, "Ryūkyū no kaki," 82–87.
43. Uezato, "Ko-Ryūkyū no guntai," 124, and Uezato, "Ryūkyū no kaki," 82–83.
44. Uezato, "Ko-Ryūkyū no guntai," 123. For illustrated archaeological summaries of weapons in early Ryukyu, see Uehara, "Buki, bugu no yōsō," 315–322, and Yamamoto and Uezato, "Shuri gusuku shutsudo no bugu shiryō no ichikōsatsu."
45. Uezato, "Ko-Ryūkyū no guntai," 120–121, and Uezato, "Ryūkyū no kaki," 84.
46. Uezato, "Ko-Ryūkyū no guntai," 115–116, 121–124; Uezato, "Ryūkyū no kaki," 82–88; and Uezato, *Ryū-Nichi sensō 1609*, 232–234.
47. Xià, *Shi Ryūkyū roku*, 193.
48. Uezato, *Ryū-Nichi sensō 1609*, 231–237.

Chapter 12: Politics and Religion

1. China, *Ryūkyū Bukkyōshi no kenkyū*, 150–151.
2. The seminal work for this point is Yoshinari and Fuku, *Ryūkyū ōkoku to wakō*.
3. Nakamura, "Ryūkyū ōkoku keisei no shisō," 69–73, and Higa, *Ko-Ryūkyū no shisō*, 97–110.

4. China, "Okinawa no Taiyō shinkō to ōken," 101–122; Sakima, *Nirai-Kanai no genzō*; and Sakima, *Omoro shisō*.
5. Smits, "Ambiguous Boundaries," esp. 95–106.
6. Regarding this last point, see Yoshinari, "Ryūkyū rettō ni okeru 'josei no reiteki yūi' no bunkashiteki ichi," 129–182.
7. Regarding Bishōmon, see Fuku, *Kikaijima*, 91–93.
8. Yoshinari and Fuku, *Ryūkyū ōkoku tanjō*, 206–20, and Fuku, *Kikaijima*, 98–102.
9. Quoted in Yoshinari and Fuku, *Ryūkyū ōkoku tanjō*, 207.
10. Kishaba, *Tōtei zuihitsu*, 105–106.
11. During the sixteenth century in the area around Lake Biwa, Benzaiten played a role in the supernatural geography protecting Kyoto. Later, the Tokugawa shoguns attempted to replicate this geography, in part by building a shrine to Benzaiten in an artificial island in Shinobazu pond. See Smits, "Conduits of Power," 41–65, esp. 49–51, 56–57.
12. For more on this triad, see Harada, *Ryūkyū o shugosuru kami*, 200–203, and Iyanaga, *Daikokuten hensō*, esp. 600–617.
13. For details about Kangiten, Dakini, demon deity rites, and Go-Daigo, see Fujimaki, "Onryō to Nanbokuchō," 98–103.
14. I have left out many details. For the full story, see Harada, *Ryūkyū o shugosuru kami*, 152–154.
15. For a full analysis, see Harada, *Ryūkyū o shugosuru kami*, 172.
16. Ibid., 155–157.
17. Quoted in ibid., 155–156.
18. *Ryukyu Record*, 69, 207.
19. Harada, *Ryūkyū o shugosuru kami*, 173–182.
20. *Ryūkyū shintōki*, 139.
21. Makishi, "Ryūkyū ōkoku jūgoseiki chūki ikō no kinaiseitekina tokuchō to ōjō girei," 180–181.
22. *Ryukyu Record*, 68–69, 206–208.

Chapter 13: A Changing World and the Road to War

1. For details see Yano, *Ko-Ryūkyūki Shuri ōfu no kenkyū*, 187–196.
2. Uezato, *Ryū-Nichi sensō 1609*, 26–27, 41–52. For a chart of all known voyages of Ryukyuan ships to Southeast Asia, see Takeshi Hamashita, "The *Lidai Baoan* and the Ryukyu Maritime Tributary Trade Network with China and Southeast Asia," 110–112. The classic and most detailed study of Ryukyu's trade with Southeast Asia is Kobata and Matsuda, *Ryukyuan Relations with Korea and South Sea Countries*, 53–197.
3. Hamashita, "The *Lidai Baoan* and the Ryukyu Maritime Tributary Trade Network with China and Southeast Asia," 123–124.
4. Ibid., 124–125.
5. Uezato, *Ryū-Nichi sensō 1609*, 78–79. See also, "Kumejima tsumugi," Okinawa kenritsu toshokan (Okinawa Prefectural Library) website, http://archive.library.pref.okinawa.jp/?page_id=346.
6. Uezato, *Ryū-Nichi sensō 1609*, 78–79, and Uehara, *Shimazu-shi no Ryūkyū shinryaku*, 20–21.
7. Uehara, *Shimazu-shi no Ryūkyū shinryaku*, 37–38.
8. Letter quoted in Kuroshima, *Ryūkyū ōkoku to sengoku daimyō*, 22–23. See also Uezato, *Ryū-Nichi sensō 1609*, 72–75.
9. The term is *yoribune*. See Kuroshima, *Ryūkyū ōkoku to sengoku daimyō*, 50.
10. Uehara, *Shimazu-shi no Ryūkyū shinryaku*, 17–19.
11. Kuroshima, *Ryūkyū ōkoku to sengoku daimyō*, 53–63.

12. For lists of the specific complaints, see Uezato, *Ryū-Nichi sensō 1609*, 82–83; Kuroshima, *Ryūkyū ōkoku to sengoku daimyō*, 47; and Uehara, *Shimazu-shi no Ryūkyū shinryaku*, 24.
13. Kuroshima, *Ryūkyū ōkoku to sengoku daimyō*, 48–50, and Uehara, *Shimazu-shi no Ryūkyū shinryaku*, 25–28.
14. Regarding the different diplomatic styles as expressed in correspondence, see Fuku, *Omoro sōshi to gun'yū no seiki*, 11–17.
15. Uehara, *Shimazu-shi no Ryūkyū shinryaku*, 28–33.
16. *Genealogy of Chūzan*, 104.
17. Based on analysis of a 1573 letter from Nago to *rōjū* Ijūin Tadamune. See Kuroshima, *Ryūkyū ōkoku to sengoku daimyō*, 66.
18. *Genealogy of Chūzan*, 104–106, and *Kyūyō*, nos. 229–236.
19. Uehara, *Shimazu-shi no Ryūkyū shinryaku*, 33–36.
20. Ibid., 93–94.
21. *Genealogy of Chūzan*, 109, and Uehara, *Shimazu-shi no Ryūkyū shinryaku*, 94–95.
22. *Ryūkyū shintōki*, 142, 225. See also Uehara, *Shimazu-shi no Ryūkyū shinryaku*, 94–95, and Uezato, *Ryū-Nichi sensō 1609*, 142.
23. For the original text and analysis, see Kuroshima, *Ryūkyū ōkoku to sengoku daimyō*, 147–149.
24. Uehara, *Shimazu-shi no Ryūkyū shinryaku*, 47–50, and Uezato, *Ryū-Nichi sensō 1609*, 104–105.
25. Uehara, *Shimazu-shi no Ryūkyū shinryaku*, 51–57, and Uezato, *Ryū-Nichi sensō 1609*, 110–114.
26. Uehara, *Shimazu-shi no Ryūkyū shinryaku*, 58–60, and Uezato, *Ryū-Nichi sensō 1609*, 117–123.
27. Uehara, *Shimazu-shi no Ryūkyū shinryaku*, 61–62.
28. Ibid., 64, and Uezato, *Ryū-Nichi sensō 1609*, 123–126.
29. Uehara, *Shimazu-shi no Ryūkyū shinryaku*, 64–65, 120–121, and Uezato, *Ryū-Nichi sensō 1609*, 126–127.
30. Uezato, *Ryū-Nichi sensō 1609*, 141–142.
31. *Ming Veritable Records*, 3:13–14 (nos. 25 and 26, Wànlì 19.7.20 and 19.8.11).
32. *Rekidai hōan*, 2:203–204, 1–31–31; 2:207–209, 1–32–05, and 1–32–06; 1:244–245, 1–07–06; Uehara, *Shimazu-shi no Ryūkyū shinryaku*, 66–67; and Uezato, *Ryū-Nichi sensō 1609*, 128–131.
33. *Rekidai hōan*, 1:230–232, 1–07–02; 1:233–243, 1–07–04; and Watanabe, *Kinsei Ryūkyū to Chū-Nichi kankei*, 30–31.
34. *Ming Veritable Records*, 3:14 (no. 28, Wànlì 19.11.29).
35. Uehara, *Shimazu-shi no Ryūkyū shinryaku*, 69.
36. *Rekidai hōan*, 1:233–243, 1–07–04; *Ming Veritable Records*, 3:14 (nos. 32, 34, 35, 36, Wànlì 23.4.24, 24.5.3, 24.5.4, 24.5.6); and Uehara, *Shimazu-shi no Ryūkyū shinryaku*, 69.
37. *Rekidai hōan*, 1:144–155, 1–04–04; 2:64–66, 1–26–10, 1–26–11; 2:209–211, 1–32–07, 1–32–09; *Ming Veritable Records*, 3:15 (nos. 40–43, Wànlì 28.2.3, 29.7.21, 29.9.15, 29.11.15); and Uehara, *Shimazu-shi no Ryūkyū shinryaku*, 69–71.
38. See Watanabe, "An International Maritime Trader Torihara Sōan," 169–176, and Uezato, *Ryū-Nichi sensō 1609*, 186–189.
39. Quoted in Watanabe, *Kinsei Ryūkyū to Chū-Nichi kankei*, 32.
40. Uezato, *Ryū-Nichi sensō*, 195–196.
41. Watanabe, *Kinsei Ryūkyū to Chū-Nichi kankei*, 24–56.
42. Ibid., 29–31.
43. Ibid., 31–33.
44. *Genealogy of Chūzan*, 107–108.
45. *Rekidai hōan*, 2:207, 1–32–04.
46. Watanabe, *Kinsei Ryūkyū to Chū-Nichi kankei*, 47–55.

47. Ibid., 55–56.
48. Uezato, *Ryū-Nichi sensō 1609*, 197, and Kamiya, "Satsuma no Ryūkyū shinnyū," 43.
49. Kamiya, "Satsuma no Ryūkyū shinnyū," 44.
50. Uehara, *Shimazu-shi no Ryūkyū shinryaku*, 99–100, and Uezato, *Ryū-Nichi sensō 1609*, 197–201.
51. Uehara, *Shimazu-shi no Ryūkyū shinryaku*, 96–99.
52. Yuge, "Satsuma ni yoru chokkatsu shihai to sakuhō taiseika no Amami shotō," 17; Uehara, *Shimazu-shi no Ryūkyū shinryaku*, 99–108; and Ishigami, *Amami shotō hennen shiryō: Ko-Ryūkyū ki hen*, 265–273.
53. Uehara, *Shimazu-shi no Ryūkyū shinryaku*, 109–110.
54. Uezato, *Ryū-Nichi sensō 1609*, 226–227.
55. Uehara, *Shimazu-shi no Ryūkyū shinryaku*, 129–130.
56. Quoted in Uezato, *Ryū-Nichi sensō 1609*, 225.
57. Xià, *Shi Ryūkyū roku*, 192–194.
58. This reply may have been conditioned by past rumors of an impending Shimazu invasion that circulated in 1593 and again in 1598. In both cases, they caused Shō Nei to dispatch So Kenri to inspect the northern Ryukyu islands. See Ishigami, *Amami shotō hennen shiryō: Ko-Ryūkyū ki hen*, 238–243, 253–254.
59. Xià, *Shi Ryūkyū roku*, 193–194. See also Harada, *Ryūkyū o shugosuru kami*, 175–176.
60. Harada, *Ryūkyū o shugosuru kami*, 176.

Chapter 14: The War

1. *Kyūyō*, no. 248.
2. Ibid., no. 249.
3. The most thorough studies of the fighting are Uehara, *Shimazu-shi no Ryūkyū shinryaku*, and Uezato, *Ryū-Nichi sensō 1609*. See also Kamiya, "Satsuma no Ryūkyū shinnyū," 33–72; Matsushita, *Kinsei Amami no shihai to shakai*, 20–33; and Ryūkyū shinpōsha and Nankai nichinichi shinbunsha, *Satsuma shinkō 400-nen mirai e no rashinban*, esp. 35–83.
4. See Uehara, *Shimazu-shi no Ryūkyū shinryaku*, 136–138, for a detailed table of the composition of the force.
5. Ishigami, *Amami shotō hennen shiryō: Ko-Ryūkyū ki hen*, 297–300.
6. Uehara, *Shimazu-shi no Ryūkyū shinryaku*, 120–124.
7. Ishigami, *Amami shotō hennen shiryō: Ko-Ryūkyū ki hen*, 302–304.
8. Uehara, *Shimazu-shi no Ryūkyū shinryaku*, 132–133.
9. Ishigami, *Amami shotō hennen shiryō: Ko-Ryūkyū ki hen*, 332, and Uehara, *Shimazu-shi no Ryūkyū shinryaku*, 133–135.
10. Uehara, *Shimazu-shi no Ryūkyū shinryaku*, 139–140, and Uezato, *Ryū-Nichi sensō 1609*, 241–242.
11. Tabatake household of the Kasari lineage, inserted into the Gushiken household record. See Kamei, *Amami-Ōshima shoka keifu shū*, 60.
12. Uezato, *Ryū-Nichi sensō 1609*, 242.
13. Yamashita, *Ryūkyū gunki, Satsu-Ryū gundan*, 18; Uezato, *Ryū-Nichi sensō 1609*, 242–243; and Uehara, *Shimazu-shi no Ryūkyū shinryaku*, 141.
14. Kamei, *Amami-Ōshima shoka keifu shū*, 99.
15. Ibid., 86.
16. Ibid., 180.
17. Uehara, *Shimazu-shi no Ryūkyū shinryaku*, 151–152, and Uezato, *Ryū-Nichi sensō 1609*, 244.
18. Kamiya, "Satsuma no Ryūkyū shinnyū," 58, and Uezato, *Ryū-Nichi sensō 1609*, 251–252.

19. Uezato, *Ryū-Nichi sensō 1609*, 245–246.
20. Ibid., 247–250; Uehara, *Shimazu-shi no Ryūkyū shinryaku*, 144; and Matsushita, *Kinsei Amami no shihai to shakai*, 29–30.
21. Uehara, *Shimazu-shi no Ryūkyū shinryaku*, 145–146.
22. Uezato, *Ryū-Nichi sensō 1609*, 247–249, and Ishigami, *Amami shotō hennen shiryō: Ko-Ryūkyū ki hen*, 375–376.
23. Ishigami, *Amami shotō hennen shiryō*, 382.
24. Ikemiya, *Kian nikki*, 256–260.
25. *Rekidai hōan*, 1:539–544, 1–18–03. See p. 539 regarding Ba Ryōhitsu. See also Harada, *Ryūkyū o shugosuru kami*, 26.
26. Uezato, *Ryū-Nichi sensō 1609*, 262–263.
27. Ikemiya, *Kian nikki*, 25.
28. *Rekidai hōan*, 1:539, and Harada, *Ryūkyū o shugosuru kami*, 26.
29. Uezato, *Ryū-Nichi sensō 1609*, 265–272.
30. Yamashita, *Ryūkyū gunki, Satsu-Ryū gundan*, 19–20. At this point, perhaps to underscore the anger of the Tokara mariners at having been repulsed, *Ryūkyū-iri no ki* describes a scene of gratuitous murder of civilians. Along the road to the capital, peasants working in their fields saw the army and hid in fear. Kabayama ordered a Tokara mariner named Hikosaku (or Hikosako) to flush them out and kill them. Hikosaku did so, and reported that, because he used his personal sword, a famous blade made in Bizen, the twelve or thirteen peasants he cut down did not appear to suffer any pain (*Ryūkyū gunki, Satsu-Ryū gundan*, 20). No other sources mention this event.
31. Ikemiya, *Kian nikki*, 26.
32. *Rekidai hōan*, 1:539–540, and Harada, *Ryūkyū o shugosuru kami*, 27.
33. Ryūkyū shinpōsha and Nankai nichinichi shinbunsha, *Satsuma shinkō 400-nen mirai e no rashinban*, 63
34. Ikemiya, *Kian nikki*, 26, and Uehara, *Shimazu-shi no Ryūkyū shinryaku*, 155.
35. Ikemiya, *Kian nikki*, 30.
36. Uehara, *Shimazu-shi no Ryūkyū shinryaku*, 155–156.
37. Leon Serafim, personal communication.
38. Uehara, *Shimazu-shi no Ryūkyū shinryaku*, 155–156.
39. Yamashita, *Ryūkyū gunki*, 20.
40. Uehara, *Shimazu-shi no Ryūkyū shinryaku*, 156–158, and Ikemiya, *Kian nikki*, 27.
41. Uehara, *Shimazu-shi no Ryūkyū shinryaku*, 158–161, and Ikemiya, *Kian nikki*, 27. The three brothers' names were Mayamato, Momochiyo (or Hyakuchiyo), and Mamakaru. See also Ryūkyū shinpōsha and Nankai Nichinichi shinbunsha, *Satsuma shinkō 400-nen*, and Kamiya, "Satsuma no Ryūkyū shinnyū," 59.
42. Uehara, *Shimazu-shi no Ryūkyū shinryaku*, 161.
43. Ryūkyū shinpōsha and Nankai nichinichi shinbunsha, *Satsuma shinkō 400-nen*, 65–66.
44. Uezato, *Ryū-Nichi sensō 1609*, 285–287.
45. Ibid., 289–290.

Chapter 15: Aftermath

1. *Rekidai hōan*, 1:539–543, 1–18–03, and Uehara, *Shimazu-shi no Ryūkyū shinryaku*, 178–181.
2. *Rekidai hōan*, 1:543–545, 1–18–04.
3. Uehara, *Shimazu-shi no Ryūkyū shinryaku*, 177, 181–183.
4. *Ming Veritable Records*, 3:18 (no. 62, Wànlì 40.7.7).
5. Ibid. (no. 63, Wànlì 40.7.17).

6. The text of the surrender articles can be found in Kerr, *Okinawa*, 162–163.
7. Kamiya, "Satsuma no Ryūkyū shinnyū," 63–64.
8. Akamine, *The Ryukyu Kingdom*, and Smits, *Visions of Ryukyu*.
9. For a comprehensive study of the development of Satsuma control over and governance of the northern Ryukyu islands, see Matsushita, *Kinsei Amami no shihai to shakai*.
10. For a tabular compilation of the figures in *Go-zaisei*, see Naha-shi shiminbunka-bu rekishi shiryōshitsu, *Naha-shi shi*, shiryōhen, pt. 1, vol. 12 (kinsei shiryō hoi, zassan), front matter ("kaidai").
11. For population data, see Dana, "Shizoku, machikata mondai to Sai On," 52–53, and Takara, "Kinsei makki no Yaeyama tōji to jinkō mondai," 23 (Table 2).
12. Ōhama, *Yaeyama no nintōzei*, 26–37, esp. 26 (Table 1).
13. Smits, "New Cultures, New Identities."
14. Ibid.
15. Christy, "The Making of Imperial Subjects in Okinawa."
16. Pearson, *Ancient Ryukyu*, 77–81, 167–170; Pellard, "The Linguistic Archeology of the Ryukyu Islands," esp. 29, 30; and Yoshinari, *Ryūkyūshi o toinaosu*, 126–130.
17. Leon Serafim, personal communication. See also Serafim, "Linguistically, What Is Ryukyuan?"
18. Dana, "Kunigami Samanokami," 961.
19. Uehara, *Shimazu-shi no Ryūkyū shinryaku*, 27.
20. As late as 1638 some Japanese from outside of the Shimazu domains could be found in Naha. However, by the 1640s Satsuma had succeeded in preventing Japanese from other domains from traveling to Ryukyu. Some Ryukyuan elites traveled to Satsuma, and an even smaller number sometimes went as far as Edo. These embassies to Edo were carefully controlled. The days of Ryukyuans freely traveling to "Yamato" ended by the middle of the seventeenth century. For more details, see Uezato, "The Formation of the Port City of Naha in Ryukyu and the World of Maritime Asia," 71–74.
21. This process is discussed in detail in Akamine, *The Ryukyu Kingdom*, and Smits, *Visions of Ryukyu*.
22. Ikeno, *Ryūkyū Yanbarusen*, 96–97.
23. For examples of emergency measures whereby personnel on ships with mixed Ryukyuan-Japanese crews drifting into China quickly changed their national identities, see Watanabe, "Nihonjin ni narisumasu Ryūkyūjin," 111–121.
24. Inamura, *Wakō shiseki*, 255–279. One example is the modern derogatory label *binbō gaara*.
25. For a discussion of Shō Shōken's policies and reforms, see Smits, *Visions of Ryukyu*, 51–62.
26. *Reflections on Chūzan*, 12.
27. Ōyama, "Shimazu-shi no Ryūkyū-iri to Amami," 282.

Chapter 16: Many Ryukyus

1. Ōishi, Takara, and Takahashi, *Shūen kara mita chūsei Nihon*, 44.
2. For example, see McCurry, "China Lays Claim to Okinawa as Territory Dispute with Japan Escalates," and Ryall, "Japan Angered by China's Claim to All of Okinawa."
3. See Smits, "Making a Good Impression: Cultural Drama in the Ryukyu-China Relationship."
4. Mass, *Antiquity and Anachronism in Japanese History*, 129.
5. Chamberlain, "The Luchu Islands and Their Inhabitants," 310–311.
6. Ibid., 318–319.

Bibliography

WORKS CITED

The place of publication for Japanese books is Tokyo unless otherwise specified.

Akamine, Mamoru. *The Ryukyu Kingdom: Cornerstone of East Asia.* Translated by Lina Terrell. Edited by Robert Huey. Honolulu: University of Hawai'i Press, 2017.

Akamine Seiki 赤嶺誠紀. *Daikōkai jidai no Ryūkyū* 大航海時代の琉球. Naha, Japan: Okinawa taimususha, 1988.

Andrade, Tonio. *The Gunpowder Age: China, Military Innovation, and the Rise of the West in World History.* Princeton, NJ: Princeton University Press, 2016.

Asato Susumu 安里進. *Gusuku, kyōdōtai, mura* グスク・共同体・村. Ginowan, Japan: Yōju shorin, 1998.

———. *Kōkogaku kara mita Ryūkyūshi* 考古学から見た琉球史. Vol. 1 (*jō*). Naha, Japan: Hirugisha, 1990, 1993.

———. *Ryūkyū ōken to gusuku* 琉球王権とグスク. Yamakawa shuppansha, 2006, 2010.

Asato Susumu 安里進 and Doi Naomi 土肥直美. *Okinawajin wa doko kara kita ka: Ryūkyū-Okinawajin no kigen to seiritsu* 沖縄人はどこから来たか:琉球=沖縄人の起源と成立. Revised edition. Naha, Japan: Bōdaainku, 2011.

Batten, Bruce L. *Gateway to Japan: Hakata in War and Peace, 500–1300.* Honolulu: University of Hawai'i Press, 2006.

———. *To the Ends of Japan: Premodern Frontiers, Boundaries, and Interactions.* Honolulu: University of Hawai'i Press, 2003.

Bender, Ross. "The Hachiman Cult and the Dōkyō Incident." *Monumenta Nipponica* 34, no. 2 (Summer 1979): 125–153.

Chamberlain, Basil Hall. "The Luchu Islands and Their Inhabitants: I. Introductory Remarks." *The Geographical Journal* 5, no. 4 (April 1895): 289–319.

Chén Kǎn 陳侃. *Shi-Ryūkyū roku* 使琉球錄. Translated by Harada Nobuo. Ginowan, Japan: Yōjusha, 1995.

China Teikan 知名定寛. "Okinawa no Taiyōshinkō to ōken: 'Tedako' shisō no keisei katei ni tsuite" 沖縄の太陽信仰と王権「てだこ」思想の形成過程について. In Kubo

Noritada sensei Okinawa chōsa kinen ronbunshū kankō iinkai, ed., 101–122. *Okinawa no shūkyō to minzoku*. Daiichi shobō, 1988.

———. *Ryūkyū Bukkyōshi no kenkyū* 琉球仏教史の研究. Ginowan, Japan: Yōju shorin, 2008.

Christy, Alan. "The Making of Imperial Subjects in Okinawa." *Positions: East Asia Cultures Critique* 1, no. 3 (Winter 1993): 607–639.

Conlon, Thomas D. *In Little Need of Divine Intervention: Takezaki Suenaga's Scrolls of the Mongol Invasions of Japan*. Ithaca, NY: Cornell East Asia Series, 2001.

Dana Masayuki 田名真之. "Kunigami Keimei" 国頭景明. In Okinawa daihyakka jiten kankō jimukyoku, ed., *Okinawa daihyakka jiten*, 1: 961. Naha, Japan: Okinawa taimusu sha, 1983.

———. "Kunigami Samanokami" 国頭佐馬頭. In Okinawa daihyakka jiten kankō jimukyoku, ed., *Okinawa daihyakka jiten*, 1: 961. Naha, Japan: Okinawa taimusu sha, 1983.

———. *Okinawa kinseishi no shosō* 沖縄近世史の諸相. Naha, Japan: Hirugisha, 1992.

———. "Ryūkyū ōken no keifu ishiki to Minamoto Tametomo torai denshō" 琉球王権の系譜意識と源為朝渡来伝承. In Kyūshū shigaku kenkyūkai, ed., 181–195. *Kyōkai no aidentitii*. Iwata shoin, 2008.

———. "Shizoku, machikata mondai to Sai On" 士族・町方問題と蔡温. In *Sai On to Sono jidai: kinseishi no shomondai shiriizu 1*, 49–59. Naha, Japan: Riuchūsha, 1984.

Doi Naomi 土肥直美. "Okinawa-ken shutsudo no jinkotsu, tokuron ni: Jinkotsu kara mita Okinawa no rekishi" 沖縄県出土の人骨、特論2:人骨から見た沖縄の歴史. In Okinawa-ken bunka shinkōkai kōbunsho kanribu shiryō henshūshitsu, ed., *Okinawa kenshi, kakuronhen*, 2 (kōko): 574–610. Naha, Japan: Okinawa-ken kyōiku iinkai, 2003.

Doyle, Micheal W. *Empires*. Ithaca, NY: Cornell University Press, 1986.

Dumézil, Georges. *L'idéologie tripartie des Indo-Européens*. Brussels: Latomus, 1958.

Fujimaki Kazuho 藤巻一保. "Onryō to Nanbokuchō" 怨霊と南北朝. In Masuda Hidemitsu, ed. *Tennō no hon: Nihon no reiteki kongen to fūin no hisshi o saguru*, 79–110. Gakken, 1998.

Fuku Hiromi 福寛美. *Kikaijima, oni no kaiiki: Kikaigashima kō* 喜界島・鬼の海域:キカイガシマ考. Shintensha, 2008.

———. *Omoro sōshi to gun'yū no seiki: Sanzan jidai no ōtachi* 「おもろさうし」と群雄の世紀:三山時代の王たち. Shinwasha, 2013.

Ginoza Shigō 宜野座嗣剛, ed. and trans. *Zen'yaku Ryūkyū shintōki* 全訳琉球神道記. Tōyō tosho shuppan, 1988.

Hamada Keisuke 浜田敬助. *Amami no rekishi* 奄美の歴史. Umeda insatsu, 1987.

Hamashita, Takeshi. "The *Lidai Baoan* and the Ryukyu Maritime Tributary Trade Network with China and Southeast Asia, the Fourteenth to Seventeenth Centuries." In Eric Tagliacozzo and Wen-Chin Chang, eds., *Chinese Circulations: Capital, Commodities, and Networks in Southeast Asia*, 107–129. Durham, NC: Duke University Press, 2011.

Harada Nobuo 原田禹雄. *Ryūkyū o shugosuru kami* 琉球を守護する神. Ginowan, Japan: Yōju shorin, 2003.

———. *Ryūkyū to Chūgoku: Wasurerareta sakuhōshi* 琉球と中国:忘れられた冊封使. Yoshikawa kōbunkan, 2003.

Hashimoto Yū 橋本雄. *Chūsei Nihon no kokusai kankei: Higashi-Ajia tsūkōken to gishi mondai* 中世日本の国際関係:東アジア通交圏と偽使問題. Yoshikawa kōbunkan, 2005.

Bibliography

Hazard, Benjamin Harrison, Jr. "Japanese Marauding in Medieval Korea: The *Wakō* Impact on Late Koryŏ." PhD diss., University of California, Berkeley, 1967.
Higa Minoru 比嘉実. *Ko-Ryūkyū no shisō* 古琉球の思想. Naha, Japan: Okinawa taimusu sha, 1991.
Higashionna Kanjun 東恩納寛惇. *Higashionna Kanjun zenshū* 東恩納寛惇全集. Edited by Ryūkyū shinpōsha. 10 vols. Dai'ichi shobō, 1978–1982.
Higuchi Kiyoyuki 樋口清之. *Himitsu no Nihonshi* 秘密の日本史. Yōdensha, 1988.
Hirara-shi shi hensan iinkai 平良市史編纂委員会, ed. *Hirara-shi shi* 平良市史. 8 vols. Tsūshihen 1. Hirara [Miyakojima City], Japan: Hirara shiyakusho, 1976–1988.
Hisaoka Manabu 久岡学. "Uta ga tsutaeta waboku kōshō" 唄が伝えた和睦交渉. In Ryūkyū shinpōsha and Nankai nichinichi shinbunsha, eds., *Satsuma shinkō 400-nen mirai e no rashinban*, 47–52. Naha, Japan: Ryūkyū shinpōsha, 2011.
Hokama Shuzen 外間守善. *Omoro sōshi* おもろさうし. Kadokawa shoten, 1993.
Hokama Shuzen 外間守善 and Saigō Nobutsuna 西郷信綱. *Omoro sōshi* おもろさうし (Nihon shisō taikei 18). Iwanami shoten, 1972.
Hucker, Charles O. *A Dictionary of Official Titles in Imperial China*. Stanford, CA: Stanford University Press, 1985.
Iha Fuyū 伊波普猷. *Iha Fuyū zenshū* 伊波普猷全集. Edited by Hattori Shirō, Nakasone Seizen, and Hokama Shuzen. 11 vols. Heibonsha, 1974–1976.
———. "Ryūkyū kyūki kaisetsu" 琉球旧記解説. In Yokoyama Shigeru, ed., *Ryūkyū shiryō sōsho*, 3: 3–38 (at end following p. 288). Hōbun shokan, 1940, 1988.
"Iheyajima kyūki shū" 伊平屋島旧記集. In Shintō Taikei hensankai, ed., *Shintō taikei, jinja hen 52: Okinawa*, 501–518. Seikōsha, 1982.
Ijichi Sueyoshi [Sueyasu; Kian] 伊地知季安. *Nanbei kikō* 南聘紀考, *ge* (vol. 3). http://ir.lib.u-ryukyu.ac.jp/handle/20.500.12000/10219.
Ikehata Kōichi 池畑耕一. "Kikaijima no kodai, chūsei iseki" 喜界島の古代・中世遺跡. In Ikeda Yoshifumi, ed., *Kodai chūsei no ryōkai: Kikaigashima no sekai*, 235–256. Kōshi shoin, 2008.
Ikemiya Masaharu 池宮正治, ed. *Kian nikki* 喜安日記. Ginowan, Japan: Yōju shorin, 2009.
Ikeno Shigeru 池野茂. *Ryūkyū Yanbarusen: Suiun no tenkai* 琉球山原船:水運の展開. Ginowan, Japan: Roman shobō honten, 1994.
Ikeya Machiko 池谷望子, Uchida Akiko 内田晶子, and Takase Kyōko 高瀬恭子, eds. and trans. *Chōsen ōchō jitsuroku Ryūkyū shiryō shūsei* 朝鮮王朝実録琉球史料集成. 2 vols. Ginowan, Japan: Yōju shorin, 2005.
Ikuta Shigeru 生田滋. "Ryūkyū Chūzan ōkoku to kaijō bōeki" 琉球中山王国と海上貿易. In Tanigawa Ken'ichi et al., ed., *Ryūkyū-ko no sekai*, 265–296. Shōgakkan, 1992.
———. "Ryūkyūkoku no 'Sanzan tōitsu'" 琉球国の「三山統一」. *Tōhō gakuhō* 65, nos. 3–4 (1984): 175–206.
———. "Taigai kankei kara mita Ryūkyū kodaishi: Nantō inasakushi no rikai no tame ni" 対外関係からみた琉球古代史:南島稲作史の理解のために. In Watanabe Tadayo and Ikuta Shigeru, eds., *Nantō inasaku bunka: Yonagunijima o chūshin ni*, 94–125. Hōsei daigaku shuppankyoku, 1984.
Inamura Kenpu 稲村賢敷. *Miyakojima kyūki narabini shika shūkai* 宮古島旧記並史歌集解. Shigensha, 1977.
———. *Ryūkyū shotō ni okeru wakō shiseki no kenkyū* 琉球諸島における倭寇史跡の研究. Yoshikawa kōbunkan, 1957.

Irei Takashi いれいたかし. "Maboroshi no Ryūkyū ōkoku" まぼろしの琉球王国. *Shin Okinawa bungaku*, no. 85 (Autumn 1990): 104–111.
Ishigami Eiichi 石上英一, ed. *Amami shotō hennen shiryō: Ko-Ryūkyū ki hen (jō)* 奄美諸島編年史料:古琉球期編（上). Yoshikawa kōbunkan, 2014.
———. "Ryūkyū no Amami shotō tōchi no shodankai" 琉球の奄美諸島統治の諸段階. *Rekishi hyōron*, no. 603 (2000): 2–15.
Iyanaga Nobumi 彌永信美. *Daikokuten hensō: Bukkyō shinwagaku* 大黒天変相:仏教神話学. Kyoto, Japan: Hōzōkan, 2002, 2015.
Kadena Sōtoku 嘉手納宗徳. "Bin" 珉. In Okinawa daihyakkajiten kankō jimukyoku, ed., *Okinawa Daihyakka jiten*, 3:333. Naha, Japan: Okinawa taimusu sha, 1983.
———. "Iōgura" 硫黄蔵 and "Iōtorishima" 硫黄鳥島. In Okinawa daihyakkajiten kankō jimukyoku, ed., *Okinawa Daihyakka jiten*, 1:147. Naha, Japan: Okinawa taimusu sha, 1983.
Kamakura Yoshitarō 鎌倉芳太郎. *Okinawa bunka no ihō* 沖縄文化の遺宝. 2 vols. Iwanami shoten, 1982.
Kamei Katsunobu 亀井勝信, ed. *Amami-Ōshima shoka keifu shū* 奄美大島諸家系譜集. Kokusho kankōkai, 1980.
Kamiya Nobuyuki 紙屋敦之. "Satsuma no Ryūkyū shinnyū" 薩摩の琉球侵入. In Ryūkyū shinpōsha, ed., 33–72. *Shin Ryūkyūshi, kinsei hen*. Naha, Japan: Ryūkyū shinpōsha, 1989.
Kanehisa Tadashi 金久正. *Amami ni ikiru Nihon kodai bunka* 奄美に生きる日本古代文化. Rev. ed. Shigensha, 1978.
Kawazoe Shōji. "Japan and East Asia." Translated by G. Cameron Hurst III. In Kozo Yamamura, ed., *The Cambridge History of Japan, Volume 3: Medieval Japan*, 396–446. New York: Cambridge University Press, 1990.
Kerr, George H. *Okinawa: The History of an Island People*. Rev. ed. Rutland, VT: Tuttle Publishing, 2000.
Kim Dalsu 金達寿. *Nihon no naka no Chōsen bunka* 日本の中の朝鮮文化. Vol. 11. Kōdansha, 1989.
Kim, Jinwung. *A History of Korea: From "Land of the Morning Calm" to States in Conflict*. Bloomington: Indiana University Press, 2012.
Kishaba Chōken 喜舎場朝賢. *Tōtei zuihitsu* 東汀随筆. Edited by Naka Shōhachirō and Gabe Masao, Perikansha, 1980.
Kishaba Kazutaka 喜舎場一隆. "Ayabune" 紋船. In Okinawa daihyakka jiten kankō jimukyoku, ed., *Okinawa daihyakka jiten*, 1:113. Naha, Japan: Okinawa taimusu sha, 1983.
Kitami Toshio 北見俊夫. *Nihon kaijō kōtsūshi no kenkyū: Minzoku bunkashiteki kōsatsu* 日本海上交通史の研究:民族文化史的考察. Hōsei daigaku shuppankyoku, 1986.
Kobata, Atsushi, and Mitsugu Matsuda. *Ryukyuan Relations with Korea and South Sea Countries: An Annotated Translation of Documents from the* Rekidai Hōan. Kyoto, Japan: Kawakita Printing Co., 1969.
Kubota Kurao 窪田蔵郎. *Tetsu kara yomu Nihon no rekishi* 鉄から読む日本の歴史. Kōdansha, 2003, 2016.
Kumamoto chūseishi kenkyūkai 熊本中世史研究会, ed. *Yatsushiro nikki* 八代日記. Kumamoto City, Japan: Seichōsha, 1980.
"Kumejima tsumugi" 久米島紬. *Okinawa kenritsu toshokan* website. http://archive.library.pref.okinawa.jp/?page_id=346.
Kuroshima Satoru 黒嶋敏. "Kamakura bakufu no minami kyōkai" 鎌倉幕府の南境界. In Fujiwara Yoshiaki, ed., *Chūseijin no kiseki o aruku*, 113–130. Kōshi shoin, 2014.

———. *Ryūkyū ōkoku to sengoku daimyō: Shimazu shinnyū made no han-seiki* 琉球王国と戦国大名:島津侵入までの半世紀. Yoshikawa kōbunkan, 2016.
Lebra, William P. *Okinawan Religion: Belief, Ritual, and Social Structure.* Honolulu: University of Hawai'i Press, 1966, 1985.
Li Xun 李薫. "Jinteki kōryū o tsūjitemiru Chōsen-Ryūkyū kankei: Hiryonin, hyōchakumin o chūshin ni" 人的交流を通じてみる朝鮮・琉球関係:被虜人・漂着民を中心に. In Ha Ubong et al., *Chōsen to Ryūkyū: Rekishi no shin'en o saguru*, ed. Akamine Mamoru, 115–159. Ginowan, Japan: Yōju shorin, 2011.
Makise Tsuneji 牧瀬恒二. *Nihonshi no genten, Okinawashi* 日本史の原点:沖縄史. Honpō shoseki, 1984, 1989.
Makishi Yōko 真喜志瑤子. "*Omoro sōshi* ni miru Kumejima shutsuji no kamigami no hen'yō to sono rekishiteki haikei: Aoriyae hoka to 'hiki' seido no kakawari" 『おもろさうし』にみる久米島出自の神々の変容とその歴史的背景:アオリヤヘほかと「ヒキ」制度のかかわり. *Okinawa bunka kenkyū*, no. 28 (2002): 205–258.
———. "Ryūkyū ōkoku jūgoseiki chūki ikō no kinaiseiteki na tokuchō to ōjō girei: Kan'nin soshiki to ōjō girei no hensen" 琉球王国一五世紀中期以降の畿内制的な特徴と王城儀礼:官人組織と王城儀礼の変遷. *Okinawa bunka kenkyū*, no. 38 (2012): 155–245.
Mamiya Atsushi 間宮厚司. *Okinawa kogo no shinsō: Omorogo no tankyū* 沖縄古語の深層:オモロ語の探究. Rev. ed. Shinwasha, 2014.
Mass, Jeffrey P. *Antiquity and Anachronism in Japanese History.* Stanford, CA: Stanford University Press, 1992.
Matsushita Shirō 松下志朗. *Kinsei Amami no shihai to shakai* 近世奄美の支配と社会. Daiichi shobō, 1983.
McCurry, Justin. "China Lays Claim to Okinawa as Territory Dispute with Japan Escalates." *The Guardian,* May 15, 2013. https://www.theguardian.com/world/2013/may/15/china-okinawa-dispute-japan-ryukyu.
McNally, Mark T. "A King's Legitimacy and a Kingdom's Exceptionality: Ryūkyū's Bankoku Shinryō no Kane of 1458." *International Journal of Okinawan Studies* 6 (December 2015): 87–102.
Mikami Tsugio 三上次男. *Tōji bōekishi kenkyū* 陶磁貿易史研究. 3 vols. Chūō kōron bijutsu shuppan, 1987–1988.
Mishina Shōei 三品彰英. "Tsushima no tendō densetsu" 対馬の天童伝説. In Tanigawa Ken'ichi, ed., *Mori no kami no minzokushi,* Nihon minzoku bunka shiryō shūsei, 21:162–187. San'ichi shobō, 1995.
Miyara Angen 宮良安彦. "Yaeyama shotō no Heike densetsu to wakō no kōseki" 八重山諸島の平家伝説と倭寇の行跡. *Okinawa bunka kenkyū*, no. 28 (2002): 259–289.
Miyazato Chōkō 宮里朝光, ed. *Okinawa monchū daijiten* 沖縄門中大辞典. Haebaru-chō, Japan: Naha shuppansha, 2001.
Murai Shōsuke 村井章介. *Ajia no naka no chūsei Nihon* アジアの中の中世日本. Kōsō shobō, 1988.
———. "Chūsei Nihon to Ko-Ryūkyū no hazama" 中世日本と古琉球の狭間. In Ikeda Yoshifumi, ed., *Kodai chūsei no ryōkai: Kikaigashima no sekai,* 97–122. Kōshi shoin, 2008.
———. *Zōho, Chūsei Nihon no uchi to soto* 増補, 中世日本の内と外. Chikuma gakugei bunko, 2013.
Nagahama Yukio 長濱幸男. "Miyako uma no rūtsu o saguru" 宮古馬のルーツを探る. *Miyakojimashi sōgō hakubutsukan kiyō*, no. 16 (2012): 1–25.

Nagatome Hisae 永留久恵. "Tsushima no Minzoku shinkō" 対馬の民族信仰. In Tanigawa Ken'ichi, ed., *Nihon no kamigami*, 1: 45–59. Jinja to seichi. Hakusuisha, 1984.

Nagayama Shūichi 永山修一. "Bunken kara miru Kikaigashima to Gusuku isekigun" 文献から見るキカイガシマと城久遺跡群. *Higashi Ajia kodai bunka*, no. 130 (2007): 153–167.

Nagayoshi Takeshi 永吉毅. *Erabu no koshūzoku* えらぶの古習俗. Kagoshima City, Japan: Michinoshima sha, 1981.

———, comp. *Okinoerabujima kyōdoshi shiryō* 沖永良部島郷土史資料, 177–180. Wadomari-chō, Japan: Wadomari chōyakuba, 1968.

Nagoya Sagenta 名越左源太. *Nantō zatsuwa: Bakumatusu Amami minzokushi* 南島雑話:幕末奄美民俗誌. Edited by Kokubu Naoichi and Era Hiroshi. 2 vols. Heibonsha, 1984.

Naha-shi shiminbunka-bu rekishi shiryōshitsu 那覇市市民文化部歴史資料室, ed. *Naha-shi shi, shiryōhen* 那覇市史資料篇, pt. 1, vol. 12, *Go-zaisei* table in front matter. Kinsei shiryō hoi, zassan. Naha, Japan: Kokusai insatsu, 2004.

Nakamura Akira 中村哲. "Ryūkyū ōkoku keisei no shisō: Seiji shisōshi no ikku to shite" 琉球王国形成の思想:政治思想史の一齣として. *Okinawa bunka kenkyū*, no. 1 (1974): 1–78.

Naka Shōhachirō 名嘉正八郎. "Okinawa (Ryūkyūkoku) no gusuku (shiro) kenkyū ryakushi" 沖縄(琉球国)のグスク(城)研究略史. In Nakijin kyōiku iinkai, eds., *Gusuku bunka o kangaeru: Sekai isan kokusai shinpojiumu "Higashi Ajia no jōkaku o hikakushite" no kiroku*, 53–64. Naha, Japan: Okinawa kōsoku insatsu kabushikigaisha, 2004.

Nakasone Masaji 仲宗根將二. "Miyako no rekishi to shinkō" 宮古の歴史と信仰. In Tanigawa Ken'ichi et al., ed., 503–531. *Ryūkyū-ko no sekai*. Shōgakkan, 1992.

———. "Sakishima ni okeru shūken katei kara mita ōken" 先島における集権過程からみた王権. *Okinawa bungaku*, no. 85 (Autumn 1990): 97–103.

Nanpo Bunshi 南浦文之. *Nanpo bunshū* 南浦文集. 3 vols. Edo [Tokyo], Japan: Nakano Michitomo [compiler and publisher], 1649.

Nelson, Thomas. "Japan in the Life of Early Ryukyu." *The Journal of Japanese Studies* 32, no. 2 (Summer 2006): 367–392.

Nishizato Kikō 西里喜行. "Ryūkyū—Okinawashi ni okeru 'minzoku' no mondai: Ryūkyū ishiki no keisei, kakudai, jizoku ni tsuite" 琉球=沖縄史における「民族」の問題:琉球意識の形成・拡大・持続について. In Takara Kurayoshi, Tomiyama Kazuyuki, and Maehira Fusaaki, eds., *Atarashii Ryūkyū shizō: Araki Moriaki sensei tsuitō ronshū*. Ginowan, Japan: Yōjusha, 1996.

Nomura Shigeo 野村茂夫. *Shokyō* 書経. Meitoku shuppansha, 1975, 1986.

Ōbayashi Taryō 大林太良. *Higashi Ajia no ōken shinwa: Nihon, Chōsen, Ryūkyū* 東アジアの王権神話:日本・朝鮮・琉球. Kōbundō, 1984.

———. *Sōsei no kigen* 葬制の起源. Kadokawa shoten, 1977.

Ōhama Eisen 大濱永亘. *Oyake Akahachi, Honkawara no ran to San'yō-sei ichimon no hitobito* オヤケアカハチ・ホンカワラの乱と山陽姓一門の人々. Ishigaki, Japan: Sakishima bunka kenkyūjo, 2005.

Ōhama Shinken 大浜信賢. *Yaeyama no nintōzei* 八重山の人頭税. San'ichi shobō, 1971.

Ōishi Naomasa 大石直正, Takara Kurayoshi 高良倉吉, and Takahashi Kimiaki 高橋公明. *Shūen kara mita chūsei Nihon* 周縁から見た中世日本. Kōdansha, 2009.

Okamoto Hiromichi. "Foreign Policy and Maritime Trade in the Early Ming Period: Focusing on the Ryukyu Kingdom." *Acta Asiatica*, no. 95 (2008): 35–55.

Okamoto Hiromichi 岡本弘道. "Ko-Ryūkyūki no Ryūkyū ōkoku ni okeru 'kaisen' o meguru shosō" 古琉球の琉球王国における「海船」をめぐる諸相. In *Higashi-Ajia bunka kōshō kenkyū* (premier issue, 2008), 221–248.

———. "Ryūkyū ōkoku ni okeru kōnōsei no tenkai to kōeki: 'Ryūkyūko' ikinai tōgō to kōeki shisutemu" 琉球王国における貢納制の展開と交易:「琉球弧」域内統合と交易システム. In Katō Yūzō, Ōnishi Hiroyuki, and Sasaki Shirō, eds., *Higashi Ajia naikai sekai no kōryūshi*, 42–62. Jimbun [Jinbun] shoin, 2008.

Okinawa kenritsu hakubutsukan 沖縄県立博物館, ed. *Kizamareta rekishi: Okinawa no sekihi to takuhon* 刻まれた歴史:沖縄の石碑と拓本. Naha, Japan: Okinawa kenritsu hakubutsukan tomo no kai, 1993.

Okinawa kogo daijiten henshū iinkai 沖縄古語大辞典編集委員会, ed. *Okinawa kogo daijiten* 沖縄古語大辞典. Kadokawa shoten, 1995.

Orikuchi-hakase kinen kodai kenkyūjo 折口博士記念古代研究所, ed. *Orikuchi Shinobu zenshū* 折口信夫全集. Vol. 16. Chūō kōronsha, 1976.

Ōshiro Tatsuhiro 大城立裕. *Ryūkyū no eiketsutachi* 琉球の英傑たち. Purejidento sha, 1992, 1993.

Ōta Kōki 太田弘毅. *Wakō: Shōgyō, gunji shiteki kenkyū* 倭寇:商業・軍事史的研究. Yokohama, Japan: Shunpūsha, 2002.

Ōta Ryōhaku 太田良博. *Isetsu, Okinawa shi: Kage no ōkoku "Naha Shumeifu"* 異説・沖縄史: 陰の王国「那覇朱明府」. Naha, Japan: Gekkan Okinawasha, 1980.

Ōta Yukio 大田由紀夫. "Futatsu no "Ryūkyū": 13, 14 seiki no Higashi-Ajia ni okeru "Ryūkyū" ninshiki" ふたつの「琉球」:13・14世紀の東アジアにおける「琉球」認識. In Kinoshita Naoko, ed., *13–14 seiki kaijō bōeki kara mita Ryūkyūkoku seiritsu yōin no jisshōteki kenkyū: Chūgoku Fukken o chūshin ni*, 201–218. Kumamoto, Japan: Kumamoto University Repository, 2009. http://reposit.lib.kumamoto-u.ac.jp/handle/2298/16119.

Ōyama Ringorō 大山麟五郎. "Amami ni okeru jinshin baibai, yanchu no kenkyū" 奄美における人身売買・ヤンチュの研究. *Okinawa bunka kenkyū*, no. 7 (1980): 159–178.

———. "Ryūkyū ōchō fukuzoku jidai" 琉球王朝服属時代. In Kaitei Naze-shi shi hensan iinkai, ed., *Kaitei Naze-shi shi 1 kan: Rekishi hen*, 234–261. Naze [Amami City], Japan: Naze shiyakusho, 1996.

———. "Shimazu-shi no Ryūkyū iri to Amami" 島津氏の琉球入りと奄美. In Kaitei Naze-shi shi hensan iinkai, ed., *Kaitei Naze-shi shi 1 kan: Rekishi hen*, 265–289. Naze [Amami City], Japan: Naze shiyakusho, 1996.

Pearson, Richard. *Ancient Ryukyu: An Archaeological Study of Island Communities*. Honolulu: University of Hawai'i Press, 2013.

Pellard, Thomas. "The Linguistic Archaeology of the Ryukyu Islands." In Patrick Heinrich, Shinso Miyara, and Michinori Shimoji, eds., *Handbook of the Ryukyuan Languages*, 13–37. Berlin: Walter de Gruyter, 2015.

Robinson, Kenneth R. "Centering the King of Chosŏn: Aspects of Korean Maritime Diplomacy, 1392–1592." *The Journal of Asian Studies* 59, no. 1 (February 2000): 109–125.

———. "The Jiubian and Ezogachishima Embassies to Chosŏn, 1478–1482." Chōsenshi kenkyūkai, eds., *Chōsenshi kenkyūkai ronbunshū*, no. 35 (October 1997): 56–86.

Ryall, Julian. "Japan Angered by China's Claim to All of Okinawa." *Deutsche Welle*, October 5, 2013. http://www.dw.com/en/japan-angered-by-chinas-claim-to-all-of-okinawa/a-16803117.

Bibliography

Saeki Kōji 佐伯弘次. *Tsushima to kaikyō no chūseishi* 対馬と海峡の中世史. Yamakawa shuppansha, 2008, 2012.

Sagawa Shin'ichi 佐川真 . "Gusuku isekigun no chūsei haka" 城久遺跡群の中世墓. In Ikeda Yoshifumi, ed., *Kodai chūsei no ryōkai: Kikaigashima no sekai*, 199–212. Koshi [Kōshi] shoin, 2008.

Sahara Makoto 佐原真. "Okinawa no yoroi to katana" 沖縄のよろいと刀. In Kanesaki Hiroshi and Harunari Hideji, eds., *Sensō no kōkogaku: Sahara Makoto no shigoto 4*, 96–99. Iwanami shoten, 2005.

Sai Taku 蔡鐸. *Sai Taku bon Chūzan seifu: Gendaigo yaku* 蔡鐸本中山世譜:現代語訳. Translated by Harada Nobuo. Ginowan, Japan: Yōju shorin, 1998.

Sakihara, Mitsugu. *A Brief History of Early Okinawa Based on the Omoro Sōshi*. Tokyo: Honpō shoseki, 1987.

Sakima Toshikatsu 崎間敏勝. *Nirai-kanai no genzō* ニライ・カナイの原像. Yonabaru-chō, Japan: Ryūkyū bunka rekishi kenkyūjo, 1989.

———. *Omoro no shisō* 「おもろ」の思想. Yonabaru-chō, Japan: Ryūkyū bunka rekishi kenkyūjo, 1991.

Sakita Mitsunobu 先田光演. "Hokuzan bunkaken e no kōsō" 北山文化圏への構想. In Nakijin kyōiku iinkai, eds., *Gusuku bunka o kangaeru: Sekai isan kokusai shinpojiumu "Higashi Ajia no jōkaku o hikakushite" no kiroku*, 133–146. Naha, Japan: Okinawa kōsoku insatsu kabushiki kaisha, 2004.

Samekawa-ōnushi yuraiki 佐銘川大ぬし由来記. University of the Ryukyus Repository. http://ir.lib.u-ryukyu.ac.jp/handle/20.500.12000/10213.

Sasaki Kōji 佐々木孝二. *Nihon bunka to Hachimanjin* 日本文化と八幡神. Hachiman shoten, 1989.

Sasaki Kōmei 佐々木高明. "Nantō no dentōteki inasaku nōkō gijutsu" 南島の伝統的稲作農耕技術. In Watabe Tadayo and Ikuta Shigeru, eds., *Nantō no inasaku bunka*, 29–66. Hōsei daigaku shuppankyoku, 1984.

Sasamori Gisuke 笹森儀助. *Nantō tanken* 南嶋探検. Vol. 1, ed. Azuma Yoshimochi 東喜望. Daiichi shobō, 1982.

Schottenhammer, Angela, ed. *Trade and Transfer across the East Asian "Mediterranean."* Wiesbaden: Harrassowitz Verlag, 2005.

Serafim, Leon A. "Linguistically, What Is Ryukyuan? Synchronic and Diachronic Perspectives." Paper given at ISRS Symposium II: "Re-Constructing Ryukyu," Harvard University, Cambridge, MA, 1994.

Shapinsky, Peter D. *Lords of the Sea: Pirates, Violence, and Commerce in Late Medieval Japan*. Ann Arbor: Center for Japanese Studies, University of Michigan, 2014.

Shimono Toshimi 下野敏見. *Amami, Tokara no dentō bunka: Matsuri to noro, seikatsu* 奄美・吐噶喇の伝統文化:祭りとノロ、生活. Kagoshima, Japan: Nanpō shinsha, 2005.

———. *Amami shotō no minzoku bunkashi* 奄美諸島の民族文化誌. Kagoshima, Japan: Nanpō shinsha, 2013.

———. *Minzokugaku kara gen-Nihon o miru* 民俗学から原日本を見る. Yoshikawa kōbunkan, 1999.

———. "Noro ishō ron" ノロ衣装論. *Okinawa bunka kenkyū*, no. 28 (2003): 1–112.

Smits, Gregory. "Ambiguous Boundaries: Redefining Royal Authority in the Kingdom of Ryukyu." *Harvard Journal of Asiatic Studies* 60, no. 1 (June 2000): 89–123.

———. "Conduits of Power: What the Origins of Japan's Earthquake Catfish Reveal about Religious Geography." *Japan Review* 24 (2012): 41–65.

———. "The Intersection of Politics and Thought in Ryukyuan Confucianism: Sai On's Uses of *Quan*." *Harvard Journal of Asiatic Studies* 56, no. 2 (December 1996): 443–477.

———. "Making a Good Impression: Cultural Drama in the Ryukyu-China Relationship." International symposium, "Interpreting Parades and Processions of Edo Japan: History, Culture, and Foreign Relations," University of Hawai'i at Manoa, Honolulu, February 11, 2013. http://scholarspace.manoa.hawaii.edu/handle/10125/26740.

———. "Making Destiny in the Kingdom of Ryukyu." In Chun-chieh Huang and John Allen Tucker, eds., *Dao Companion to Japanese Confucian Philosophy*, 109–140. New York: Springer, 2014.

———. "New Cultures, New Identities: Becoming Okinawan and Japanese in Nineteenth-Century Ryukyu." In Peter Nosco, James E. Ketelaar, and Yasunori Kojima, eds., *Values, Identity, and Equality in Eighteenth- and Nineteenth-Century Japan*, 159–178. Leiden: Brill, 2015.

———. *Visions of Ryukyu: Identity and Ideology in Early-Modern Thought and Politics*. University of Hawai'i Press, 1999.

Son Seungcheol 孫承喆. "Chō-Ryū kōrin taisei no kōzō to tokuchō" 朝琉交隣体制の構造と特徴. In Ha Ubong et al., *Chōsen to Ryūkyū: Rekishi no shin'en o saguru*, ed. Akamine Mamoru, 19–48. Ginowan, Japan: Yōju shorin, 2011.

Sumita Naotoshi and Nozaki Takushi 澄田直敏・野崎拓司. "Kikaijima Gusuku isekigun" 喜界島城久遺跡群. In Ikeda Yoshifumi, ed., *Kodai chūsei no ryōkai: Kikaigashima no sekai*, 153–170. Koshi [Kōshi] shoin, 2008.

Sun Wei 孫薇. *Chūgoku kara mita Ko-Ryūkyū no sekai* 中国から見た古琉球の世界. Naha, Japan: Ryūkyū shinpōsha, 2016.

Suzuki Mitsuo 鈴木満男. *Kan Higashi-shinakai no kodai girei: Kyoju tōkai jōdo, soshite mizu no rei to no seikon* 環東シナ海の古代儀礼:巨樹、東海浄土、そして水の霊との聖婚. Daiichi shobō, 1994.

Tagliacozzo, Eric, and Wen-Chin Chang, eds. *Chinese Circulations: Capital, Commodities, and Networks in Southeast Asia*. Durham, NC: Duke University Press, 2011.

Takahashi Ichirō 高橋一郎. *Unabara no Heike denshō: Amami setsuwa no genzō* 海原の平家伝承:奄美説話の原像. Miyai shoten, 1998.

Takahashi Kimiaki 高橋公明. "Ryūkyū ōkoku" 琉球王国. In Asao Naohiro et al., eds., Iwanami kōza Nihon tsūshi, 10: 301–317. Iwanami shoten, 1994.

Takahashi Yasuo 高橋康夫. *Umi no "Kyōto:" Nihon Ryūkyū toshi-shi kenkyū* 海の「京都」:日本琉球都市史研究. Kyoto, Japan: Kyōto Daigaku gakujutsu shuppankai, 2015.

Takamiya Hiroto 高宮広土. *Shima no senshigaku: Paradaisu de wa nakatta Okinawa shotō no senshigaku* 島の先史学:パラダイスではなかった沖縄諸島の先史学. Naha, Japan: Bōdaainku, 2005.

Takanashi Osamu 高梨修. *Yakōgai no kōkogaku* ヤコウガイの考古学. Dōseisha, 2005.

Takara Kurayoshi 高良倉吉. "Kinsei makki no Yaeyama tōji to jinkō mondai: Onaga ueekata shioki to sono haikei" 近世末期の八重山統治と人口問題:翁長親方仕置とその背景. In *Okinawa shiryō henshūjo kiyō*, no. 7 (1982), 1–45.

———. "Ōfu soshiki no tenbō" 王府組織の展望. In Ryūkyū shinpōsha, ed., *Shin Ryūkyūshi, Ko-Ryūkyū hen*, 163–184. Naha, Japan: Ryūkyū shinpōsha, 1991.

———. *Ryūkyū no jidai: Ōinaru rekishizō o motomete* 琉球の時代:大いなる歴史像を求めて. Rev. ed. Naha, Japan: Hirugisha, 1989.

———. *Ryūkyū ōkoku no kōzō* 琉球王国の構造. Yoshikawa kōbunkan, 1987.

———. *Ryūkyū ōkokushi no tankyū* 琉球王国史の探求. Ginowan, Japan: Yōju shorin, 2011.
Tan, Samuel K. *The Muslim South and Beyond*. Quezon City: University of the Philippines Press, 2011.
Tanaka Fumio 田中史男. "Kodai no Amami, Okinawa shotō to kokusai shakai" 古代の奄美・沖縄諸島と国際社会. In Ikeda Yoshifumi, ed., *Kodai chūsei no ryōkai: Kikaigashima no sekai*, 49–70. Kōshi shoin, 2008.
Tanaka Takeo 田中健夫. *Higashi Ajia tsūkōken to kokusai ninshiki* 東アジア通交圏と国際認識. Yoshikawa kōbunkan, 1997.
———, ed. and trans. *Kaitō shokokuki: Chōsenjin no mita chūsei no Nihon to Ryūkyū* 海東諸國紀:朝鮮人の見た中世の日本と琉球. Iwanami shoten, 1991.
———. *Taigai kankei to bunka kōryū* 対外関係と文化交流. Kyoto, Japan: Shibunkaku shuppan, 1982.
———. *Wakō: Umi no rekishi* 倭寇:海の歴史. Kōdansha gakujutsu bunko, 2012, 2015.
———. *Wakō to kangō bōeki* 倭寇と勘合貿易. Expanded edition, ed. Murai Shōsuke. Chikuma gakugei bunko, 2012.
Tanigawa Ken'ichi 谷川健一. "'Ko-Ryūkyū' izen no sekai: Nantō no fūdo to seikatsu bunka" 「古琉球」以前の世界:南島の風土と生活文化. In Tanigawa Ken'ichi et al., eds. *Ryūkyū-ko no sekai*, 9–66. Shōgakkan, 1992.
———. *Nihon no kamigami* 日本の神々. Iwanami Shoten, 1999.
———. *Rettō jūdan, chimei shōyō* 列島縦断地名逍遥. Fuzanbō intaanashonaru, 2010.
———. *Yomigaeru kaijō no michi, Nihon to Ryūkyū* 甦る海上の道・日本と琉球. Bungei shunjū, 2007.
Tanigawa Ken'ichi 谷川健一 and Orikuchi Shinobu 折口信夫. *Ryūkyū ōken no genryū* 琉球王権の源流. Ginowan, Japan: Yōju shorin, 2012.
Tanigawa Ken'ichi 谷川健一, Ōyama Ringorō 大山麟五郎, and Takara Kurayoshi 高良倉吉. *Okinawa, Amami to Yamato* 沖縄・奄美と日本. Dōseisha, 1986.
Tomiyama Kazuyuki 豊見山和行. "Minami no Ryūkyū" 南の琉球. In Irumada Nobuo and Tomiyama Kazuyoki, *Kita no Hiraizumi, Minami no Ryūkyū*, 165–308. Chūō kōronsha, 2002.
———. "Ryūkyū, Okinawashi no sekai 琉球・沖縄史の世界. In Tomiyama Kazuyuki, ed., *Ryūkyū, Okinawashi no sekai Nihon no jidaishi 18*, 7-83. Yoshikawa kōbunkan, 2003
———. *Ryūkyū ōkoku no gaikō to ōken* 琉球王国の外交と王権. Yoshikawa kōbunkan, 2004.
———. "Tōitsu ōkoku keiseiki no taigai kankei" 統一王国形成期の対外関係. In Ryūkyū shinpōsha, ed., *Shin Ryūkyūshi, Ko-Ryūkyū hen*, 141–162. Naha, Japan: Ryūkyū shinpōsha, 1991.
Topographic map of Okinawa island. http://en-us.topographic-map.com/places/Okinawa-Island-9353902.
Torigoe Kenzaburō 鳥越憲三郎. *Okinawa no shinwa to minzoku: Omorosōshi no furusato kō* 沖縄の神話と民俗:「おもろさうし」のふるさと考. Taihei shuppansha, 1970, 1971.
Uehara Kenzen 上原兼善. *Shimazu-shi no Ryūkyū shinryaku: Mō hitotsu no keichō no eki* 島津氏の琉球侵略:もう一つの慶長の役. Ginowan, Japan: Yōju shorin, 2009.
Uehara Shizuka 上原静. "Buki, bugu no yōsō" 武器・武具の様相 (dai-yon shō, gusuku jidai). In Okinawa-ken bunka shinkōkai kōbunsho kanribu shiryō henshūshitsu, ed., *Okinawa kenshi, kakuronhen*, vol. 2 (kōko), 315–323. Naha, Japan: Okinawa-ken kyōiku iinkai, 2003.
Uezato Takashi 上里隆史. "Bunken shiryō kara mita Ko-Ryūkyū no kinkōhin: Buki, bugu no bunseki o chūshin ni" 文献史料からみた古琉球の金工品:武器・武具の分析

を中心に. In Kubo Tomoyasu, ed. *Higashi-Ajia o meguru kinzoku kōgei: Chūsei, kokusai kōryū no shin-shiten,* 224–255. Bensei shuppan, 2010.

———. "The Formation of the Port City of Naha in Ryukyu and the World of Maritime Asia: From the Perspective of a Japanese Network." *Acta Asiatica,* no. 95 (*Studies of Medieval Ryukyu within Asia's Maritime Network,* 2008): 57–77.

———. "Ko-Ryūkyū no guntai to sono rekishiteki tenkai" 古琉球の軍隊とその歴史的展開. *Ryūkyū Ajia shakai bunka kenkyūkai kiyō,* no. 5 (October 2002): 105–162.

———. *Ryū-Nichi sensō 1609: Shimazu-shi no Ryūkyū shinkō* 琉日戦争一六〇九:島津氏の琉球侵攻. Naha, Japan: Bōdaainku, 2009.

———. "Ryūkyū no kaki ni tsuite" 琉球の火器について. *Okinawa bunka* 36, no. 91 (2000): 73–92.

———. *Umi no ōkoku, Ryūkyū: "Kaiiki Ajia" kusshi no kōeki kokka no jitsuzō* 海の王国・琉球:「海域アジア」屈指の交易国家の実像. Yōsensha, 2012.

Varley, H. Paul, trans. *A Chronicle of Gods and Sovereigns: Jinnō Shōtōki of Kitabatake Chikafusa.* New York: Columbia University Press, 1980.

von Verschuer, Charlotte. *Across the Perilous Sea: Japanese Trade with China and Korea from the Seventh to the Sixteenth Centuries.* Translated by Kristen Lee Hunter. Ithaca, NY: East Asia Program, Cornell University, 2006.

Wada Hisanori 和田久徳, ed. and trans. *Rekidai hōan yakuchūbon* 歴代宝案訳注本. 8 vols. (1–3, 5, 7, 9, 11–13). Naha, Japan: Okinawa-ken kyōiku iinkai, 1994–2016.

———. *Ryūkyū ōkoku no keisei: Sanzan tōitsu to sono zengo* 琉球王国の形成:三山統一とその前後. Ginowan, Japan: Yōju shorin, 2006.

Wada Hisanori, Ikeya Machiko 池谷望子, Uchida Akiko 内田晶子, and Takase Kyōko 高瀬恭子, eds. and trans. *"Min jitsuroku" no Ryūkyū shiryō* 「明実録」の琉球史料. 3 vols. Haebaru-chō, Japan: Okinawa-ken bunka shinkōkai, kōbunsho kanribu, shiryō henshūshitsu, 2001 (Vol. 1), 2003 (Vol. 2), 2006 (Vol. 3).

Watanabe Miki 渡辺美季. "An International Maritime Trader Torihara Sōan: The Agent for Tokugawa Ieyasu's First Negotiations with Ming China, 1600." In Angela Schottenhammer, ed., *The East Asian Mediterranean: Maritime Crossroads of Culture, Commerce and Human Migration.* Wiesbaden: Harrassowitz-Verlag, 2008, 169–178.

———. *Kinsei Ryūkyū to Chū-Nichi kankei* 近世琉球と中日関係. Yoshikawa kōbunkan, 2012.

———. "Nihonjin ni narisumasu Ryūkyūjin: Shin ni taisuru Ryū-Nichi kankei no inpei to hyōryū, hyōchaku" 日本人になりすます琉球人:清に対する琉日関係の隠蔽と漂流・漂着. In Ryūkyū shinpōsha and Nankai nichinichi shinbunsha, eds. *Satsuma shinkō 400-nen: mirai e no rashinban,* 111–121. Naha, Japan: Ryūkyū shinpōsha, 2011.

Xià Zǐyáng 夏子陽. *Shi Ryūkyū roku* 使琉球錄. Translated by Harada Nobuo. Ginowan, Japan: Yōju shorin, 2001.

"Yaeyama utaki yuraiki" 八重山御嶽由来記. In Shintō taikei hensankai, ed., *Shintō taikei, jinja hen 52: Okinawa,* 690–716. Seikōsha, 1982.

Yamamoto Masaaki 山本正昭 and Uezato Takashi 上里隆史. "Shuri gusuku shutsudo no bugu shiryō no ichikōsatsu" 首里グスク出土の武具史料の一考察. *Kiyō Okinawa ribun kenkyū,* no. 2 (2004): 43–64.

Yamamura, Kozo, ed. *The Cambridge History of Japan, Volume 3: Medieval Japan.* New York: Cambridge University Press, 1990.

Yamashita Fumitake 山下文武, ed. *Ryūkyū gunki, Satsu-Ryū gundan* 琉球軍記・薩琉軍談. Kagoshima City, Japan: Nanpō shinsha, 2007.

Yamauchi Masanao 山内昌尚, *Sengo Okinawa tsūka hensenshi: Beigun tōchi jidai o chūshin ni* 戦後沖縄通貨変遷史:米軍統治時代を中心に. Naha, Japan: Ryūkyū shinpōsha, 2004.

Yamazato Eikichi 山里永吉. *Okinawashi no hakkutsu* 沖縄史の発掘. Ushio shuppansha, 1971.

Yanagita Kunio 柳田国男, comp. *Nihon densetsu meii* 日本伝説名彙. Nihon hōsō shuppan kyōkai, 1950, 1971.

Yano Misako 矢野美沙子. *Ko-Ryūkyūki Shuri ōfu no kenkyū* 古琉球期首里王府の研究. Kōsō shobō, 2014.

Yokoyama Shigeru 横山重, ed. *Ryūkyū shiryō sōsho* 琉球史料叢書. 5 vols. Hōbun shokan, 1940, 1988.

"Yononushi [-kanashi] yuisho sho" 世乃主[かなし]由緒書. In Nagayoshi Takeshi, comp., *Okinoerabujima kyōdoshi shiryō*, 177–180. Wadomari-chō, Japan: Wadomari chōyakuba, 1968.

Yoshinari Naoki 吉成直樹. "Ryūkyū rettō ni okeru 'josei no reiteki yūi' no bunkashi-teki ichi" 琉球列島における「女性の霊的優位」の文化史的位置. *Okinawa bunka kenkyū*, no. 27 (2001): 129–182

———. *Sake to shaaman:* Omoro sōshi *o yomu* 酒とシャーマン:「おもろさうし」を読む. Shintensha, 2008.

Yoshinari Naoki 吉成直樹 and Fuku Hiromi 福寛美. *Ryūkyū ōkoku to wakō: Omoro no kataru rekishi* 琉球王国と倭寇:おもろの語る歴史. Shinwasha, 2006.

———. *Ryūkyū ōkoku tanjō: Amami shotōshi kara* 琉球王国誕生:奄美諸島史から. Shinwasha, 2007.

Yoshinari Naoki 吉成直樹, with Takanashi Osamu 高梨修 and Ikeda Yoshifumi 池田栄史. *Ryūkyūshi o toinaosu: Ko-Ryūkyū jidai ron* 琉球史を問い直す:古琉球時代論. Shinwasha, 2015.

Yoshioka Yasunobu 吉岡康暢. "Nantō no chūsei sueki: Chūsei shoki kan-Higashi-ajia kaiiki no tōgei kōryū" 南島の中世須恵器:中世初期環東アジア海域の陶芸交流. *Kokuritsu rekishi minzoku hakubutsukan kenkyū hōkoku*, no. 49 (March 2002): 409–439.

Yuge Masami 弓削政己. "Satsuma ni yoru chokkatsu shihai to sakuhō taiseika no Amami shotō" 薩摩による直轄支配と冊封体制下の奄美諸島. In Okinawa daigaku chiiki kenkyūjo, ed., *Satsuma-han no Amami Ryūkyū shinkō yonhyakunen saikō*, 14–37. Fuyō shobō shuppan, 2011.

Zhang Yunming. "Ancient Chinese Sulfur Manufacturing Processes." *History of Science Society* 77, no. 3 (September 1986): 487–497.

Index

Page numbers in **boldface** type refer to illustrations.

A Ranpō (Yà Lánpáo) 亜蘭匏, 112
Agarinarikane 東なりかね, 56
Akahachi アカハチ (赤蜂), 55, 57–58, 101–103, 167, 169, 176, 182, 188
Akeshino priestess あけしののろ, 53, 126, 165
Akitoku 秋徳 battle, **19**, 228–229
Amami islands. *See* Michinoshima
Amamiku (Amamikyo) あまみく, 15, 29, 97–98, 109, 124–126, 152, 154
Amami-Ōshima 奄美大島, **7**, 9, 17–20, 22, 24, 26, 28, 49, 87, 102–103, 120, 173–174, 178, 256n12; 1537 invasion of, 24, 177, 184–185, 186; 1571 invasion of, 24, 142, 184, 185–186; 1609 invasion of, 221, 227–228; assessed productivity, 237; local officials, 153, 170, 179–182, 194, 248; taxation of, 182, 185, 187–188
Amarifua kankanushi あまりふあ鍛工主 (Heavenly Blacksmith Lord), 55
Amawari 阿麻和利, 4, 23, 110, 116, 120–123
Anjibe 按司部, 165
anti-Satsuma (anti-Shimazu) faction, 146–147, 205, 212, 222
Aoriyae 煽りやへ (阿応理屋恵), 22, 32–33, 46, 96–98, 165–166, 200–201, 260n45
Aragusuku Anki 新城安基 (Mō Ryūgin 毛龍吟), 142
Asakura Yoshikage 朝倉義景, 145, 208
Ashikaga 足利 shoguns, 38, 63, 73–75, 144–145, 205, 208, 211; as kings of Japan, 73, 144, 205; and Ryukyuan kings, 74–75, 208, 211; Yoshiaki 義昭, 145, 208; Yoshinori 義教 and Shimazu control over Ryukyu, 211, 221
assessed agricultural productivity of post-1609 Ryukyu (*kokudaka* 石高), 237
Asumori grove 安須森御嶽, 24, 151–152

Ba Juntoku 馬順徳 (Kunigami Ueekata Seikaku 国頭植親方正格), 186
Ba Ryōhitsu 馬良弼. *See* Nago Ueekata Ryōhō
Ba Seiei 馬世栄. *See* Nago Ueekaga Ryōin
Bāngjī 邦畿. *See* three core districts
Barley Ear Festival (Mugi no ho matsuri 麦の穂祭), 166
Baten 馬天 (place and priestess), 110, **116**, 130, 152–153, 164
Benzai grove 弁財御嶽, 168, 198–199
Benzaiten 弁財天, 11, 131, 164–168, 193, 196–201, **197**, 213, 217, 276n11
Bin 珉, 83
blacksmiths, 43–44, 51, 56, 99, 124, 275n29; and Bōnotomari 坊泊, 51; as deities, 43–44, 51–52, 55, 58, 124, 199–200
bone rank system (K. *golpumjedo* 骨品制度), 124
bones and rain, 29, 123–124, 130
Buddhism, 140–142, 154–155, 193–194, 196–197, 201; and diplomacy, 193–194, 229;

293

Index

and politics, 127, 130–131, 140–142, 201; and technology, 74, 94. *See also* Enkakuji
Bunei 武寧, 78–80, 83, 93, 111–112, **150**, 151, 189, 247, 264n5; eunuch incident, 111, 151, 247

Chén Èrguān 陳二官[観] incident, 69, 135. *See also* problematic behavior of Ryukyuan envoys
Chén Kǎn 陳侃, xii, 5, 79, 131, 165, 182, 199–200, 270n44
Chinese-sponsored coup, 85, 111–113. *See also* eunuch incident
Chinzei Hachirō 鎮西八郎. *See* Minamoto Tametomo
Chiyoganemaru (sword) 千代金丸, 95, 266n18
Chūzan 中山, 9–10, 34, 54, 110, 119, 127, 149–150, 155, 167, 170, 179, 200, 211, 213, 216, 236; as principality, 9, 65, 66, 77–87, 111–112, 114; as Ryukyu, 10, 66, 179, 247
control of wind, water, and storms, 32, 38, 43–44, 53–55, 98, 116, 123–125, 200. *See also* bones and rain; Hachiman
Council of Three, 113, 142, 161, 164–165, 176, 177, 189, 209, 210, 211–212, 222–223

Dakini (Dakiniten) 荼枳尼 (荼枳尼天), 195, 198–201
Dazaifu 大宰府, 18–19, 21, 37, 48
de-Japanification policies, 26, 220, 237, 242–243
Demon Deity (Ryukyu) 鬼神, 193, 195–196, 198, 200–201
distinguishing Ryukyuan and Japanese sailors, difficulty of, 218–220, 241
districts (*magiri* 間切), 162–164, **163**; in Michinoshima, **19**, 179, 180–182, 185, 187. *See also* three core districts
divination manuals (*sōshi* 双紙), 53, 55–57
DNA, 34, 240
Dōan 道安, 27, 42, 50, 72
drum symbolizing power to rule, 85–86, 126

East China Sea network, 15–16, **16**, 22, 25, 27, 29, 33–35, 37, 44, 49, 51, 76, 157, 174, 207, 218, 240, 245–246, 249–250
Echizen 越前, 117, 145, **206**, 207–208, 231
Eiso 英祖, 87–88, 140–141, 149, 150–151, **150**, 265n48

empire, definitions of, 9, 187–189
Enkakuji 円覚寺, 1, 130–131, 138, 139, 141, 149, 181, 194, 227, 248
Enkaku Zenji ki 円覚禅寺記, 138, 162
Enochi 命, 126

Fukudi-gima 福地儀間, 100, 168
funeral rites and practices, 20–21, 27–29, 102

Gaara 甲螺 group names, 101–103, 121, 125–126, 168, 185, 242, 280n24
Gaja 我謝 (Gajajiima), **7**, 27, 49, 257n48. *See also* Tokara islands
Gerae akukabe げらへあくかべ (家来赤頭), 165
Gihon 義本, 87, 148, 150–153, **150**
Goeku 越来, 92, 101–102, 113, 115–116, **116**, 118, 121, 125–126, 128–130, 262n15
golden age of Ryukyu, 75–76, 127, 134
gora ゴラ. *See* Gaara group names
Gores, 99–100
Gosamaru 護佐丸, 4, 116, 120–121
Gotō islands 五島列島, **30**, 62, 70
Gozan 五山 priests and temples, 153–154, 193
gunpowder, 64, 70
Guraru Magohachi 後蘭孫八, **23**, 45, 71, 102, 274n49
Guriya family ぐりやばら (具良原[腹]), 185
Gushikawa gusuku 具志川グスク, 101, 167
gusuku グスク (城), 1, 34–36, 88, 92–93, 94, 96, 110, 125–126, 137, 190
Gusuku Site Group 城久遺跡群, **19**, 20–21
Gusukuma Shūshin 城間秀信, 142

Hachiman 八幡, 32–33, 38, 42–46, 71, 102, 108–109, 118–119, 123, 153, 196, 200–201; and blacksmiths, 43–44, 199; Daibu Hachiman Shrine 大分八幡宮, 43; flags, 37, 42; and Korea, 42–43; ships, 42; shrine in Okinawa, 44–45, 118–119, 200–201; and the *tomoe* emblem, 44, 46; Usa Hachiman Shrine 宇佐神宮 (宇佐八幡宮), **30**, 43, 103, 168, 199. *See also* Aoriyae; Halmang; Shō Toku; Tsukishiro; *wakō*
Haebaru district 南風原間切, 86, 140, 162, **163**. *See also* three core districts
Hakata 博多, 18, 21, 27, **30**, 31, 35, 41–42, 50, 72–73, 134
Halmang, 43. *See also* Hachiman; Yeongdeung

Index 295

Hana 哈那 incident, 218–220, 223. *See also* Zhèng Liángnéng
Han'anchi 攀安知, 83, 95
Haniji 怕尼芝, 83, 265n32
Harimizu 漲水 deities, 199
Hateruma 波照間, **8**, 57, 169
head envoy (*chōshi* 長史), 111–112
Hedo 辺戸, **23**, 87, 98, 109, 148, 151–152, 166
Hideyoshi. *See* Toyotomi Hideyoshi
high priestess. *See* Kikoe-ōgimi
Higo 肥後 (Kumamoto 熊本), 18, 22, 29–32, **30**, 45, 47–48, 52, 58, 70, 101, 107–109, 261n97
hiki 引, 101, 137, 161, 164, 166, 175–177, 189, **190**, 191, 231. *See also* watch
Hirakubo Kana 平久保加那, 57
hiyaa 火矢 (firearms). *See* weapons in Ryukyu
Hokuzan. *See* Sanhoku
Hokuzan kanshu 北山監守, 97, 228, 230
Hóngwǔ 洪武 emperor, 39, 47, 60, 62–65, 70–71, 79, 88, 113, 167
honji-suijaku 本地垂迹, 198–199
Honkawara ホンカワラ, 101–103, 167–168, 170. *See also* Kawara
horses, 39–40, 45, 51, 63–64, 70–72, 94, 191, 268n10
Hōshi 法司. *See* Council of Three
human trafficking, 5, 49–50
Hú Wéiyōng 胡惟庸, 64

Ichiki Magobei 市來孫兵衛, 225
idea of a royal line, 149–150
Iheya island 伊平屋島, 8, 10, **23**, 27, 30–31, 95, 107–109, 142, 148, 152–153, 235
Ijichi Tarōbei 伊地知太郎兵衛. *See* Tōma Jūchin
Iki 壱岐, 15, 16, 18, 20, 22, 29, **30**, 33, 38, 44, 47, 70, 249, 257n63, 264n5
illegal clothing incident, 135–136. *See also* problematic behavior of Ryukyuan envoys
Imagawa Ryōshun 今川了俊, 47
Inutarugane 犬樽金, 181, 227, 274n15
Iō gusuku 硫黄グスク, 191
Iōtorishima 硫黄鳥島, 10, 68, 70, 78, 148, 263n38
Iriomote 西表, **8**, 57–58
iron, 20, 55, 82, 94, 99, 125, 151, 249; and Kumejima, 101, 168, 176; in legendary biographies, 51–52, 55, 58, 99, 151; sand, 20, 101; and shell trade, 22, 249; and *wakō*, 55, 58
Ishiki'nawa 伊敷索, 101
Ishinabe 石鍋. *See* talc stoneware
Izena island 伊是名島, 8, **23**, 27, 30, 95, 97, 115, 125–126, 148, 152

Jana revolt of 1592 謝名一族謀叛, 144, 215, 233
Jana Teidō 謝名鄭迵 (Jana Rizan 謝名利山; Jana Ueekata 謝名親方), 155, 212–213, 216, 222, 224, 229, 231–233, 236–237, 244. *See also* anti-Satsuma faction
Japonic languages and culture, 8, 156–157, 239–240, 250
Jeju island 濟州島, **16**, 40, 43, 70
Jiganemaru (sword). *See* Teganemaru
Jingū 神功, 32, 43–44, 46, 200, 259n25, 264n5
Jiǔbiān 久邊, 73
junshi 殉死. *See* suicide after death of ruler

Kabayama Hisataka 樺山久高, 226, 229–232, 279n30
Kadeshi Spring 嘉手志川, 86
Kagō 華后, 132, **132**
Kaiin 芥隠, 141, 194
Kaiki 懷機 (C. Huái Jī), 84, 93, 112–113, 162
Kakuō 鶴翁, 154, 194
Kamakura 鎌倉, city of, 23, 38, 74
Kamei Korenori 亀井茲矩, 214, 221
Kametoku 亀徳. *See* Akitoku
Kametsu 亀津, **19**, 229
kamuiyaki カムイ焼き, **19**, 21–23, 249; and Korean technology, 22
Kanahiyabu (Kanahyan) 金比屋武, 25, 95–97, 125, 201. *See also* Sonohiyabu
Kanamaru 金丸. *See* Shō En
Kanamori 金盛 (Toyomiya 豊見親), 170
Kanasome hachimaki 金染鉢巻, 165–166
Kanemaru 金丸. *See* Shō En
Kaneshigawa Toyomiya 金志川豊見親, 170
Kaneyoshi, Prince 懐良親王 (J. Ryōkai, C. Liánghuái 懷良), 46–59, 60, 63–64
Kangiten 歓喜天, 198–201
Kanidono 金殿, 51
Kanshōrei ki 官松嶺記, 138
Kantarugane 勘樽金, 119, 227–228
Kasari 笠利, **19**, 20, 22, 24, 49, 178–181, 227
Kasari lineage 笠利氏, 180, 272n15, 273n23, 278n11
Kasasu lord かさす若てだ, 100

296   Index

Kashiigū 香椎宮, 28
Katsu Kashō 葛可昌. *See* Gusukuma Shūshin
Katsuren 勝連, 22–23, **23**, 35, 74, 87, 92, 108, 110, 116, **116**, 120–121, 262n15
Katsuren-gusuku 賀通連寓鎮 (probably Shō Hashi), 110
Keraikedagusuku Yōcho 慶来慶田城用緒, 57
Kerama gap 慶良間ギャップ, **xiv**, 17, 174
Kerr, George H., 127, 246, 253
Kian nikki 喜安日記, 224–225, 229, 230, 231–233
Kian Nyūdo 喜安入道, 208, 224–225, 233
Kikai island 喜界島, 7, 9, 17–22, **19**, 24, 25, 71, 178, 187, 227, 239, 246–247; as administrative center, 20–22, 247; as border with Japan, 8, 19–21, 156, 249; invasions of, 24, 44, 117–120, 247; as Ukishima, 24, 247
kikoe 聞得 (resounding), 22, 32, 45, 46, 82, 100, 175
Kikoe-ōgimi 聞得大君 (high priestess), 11, 24, 32, 46, 94, 98, 130, 161, 164–166, 175–177, 193, 195–196, 199
Kikuin 菊隠, 194, 229, 232–233
Kim Wonjin. *See* Kin Genchin
Kimihae 君南風 (priestess), 101, 165, 167–168, 174, 198–199
Kimitezuri 君手摩, 128, 166
Kin Genchin 金原珍, 41
Kin Ōshō 金応照 (Mabuni Peechin Ankō 摩文仁親雲上安恒), 144
kinai 畿内. *See* three core districts
king (*wáng* 王): Chinese concept of, 62
Kishaba Chōken 喜舎場朝賢, 196
Kishitō-Ueekata 喜志統親方 lineage, 179–180
Kokuō shōtoku hi 国王頌徳碑 (1498), 138
Kokuō shōtoku hi 国王頌徳碑 (1522), 140, 149, 168
Konkōkenshū 混効験集, 199
Kōntofushi-kawara 幸本フシカワラ, 101
Korea: attacks on, 39–40, 45, 46–50, 61–62; *bakufu* negotiations with, 222; embassies to and trade with, 72–73, 74, 110, 182, 248; and Hachiman, 43–44, 259n25, 259n27; and Higo, 31; immigrants to Ryukyu from 8, 33, 39, 50–51, 75, 220; as part of East China Sea network, **16**, 20, 27–29, 31, 42, 95, 156, 195, 239, 247, 249, 257n60;

pirates from, 18–19; political upheavals in, 37–39; Shimazu (Satsuma) military forces in, 213, 215, 225; spurious embassies to, 72–73, 134, 144; sutras from 130–131; technology from, 22, 110. *See also* repatriation of Koreans
Korean: ideas about bones, 124; maps of Ryukyu, 35; records, 3, 5, 41, 49, 55, 77–78, 80, 82–83, 90, 96, 119, 259n11; sojourners in Ryukyu, 2, 5, 27, 41–42, 49–50, 92–94, 96, 119, 243; *wakō*, 40. *See also* Dōan; Kin Genchin; Sōda Rokurōjirō
Kubamoto 幸本御嶽 (or Kōnto) grove, 103
Kudakajima 久高島, **12**, 98–99, **116**, 129, 130, 163–164, 166
Kumano gongen 熊野権現, 34, 45, 258n89
Kume Nakagusuku 久米仲城. *See* Shō Shin
Kumejima 久米島, 11, 22–23, **23**, 33, 35, 50, 52, 58, 88, 90, 98, 100–101, 103, 137, 165, 174, 187, 188, 198–199, 208; and Aoriyae (Aoriyae-sasukasa) deity, 32, 98, 166–167, 201; and the *hiki* system, 175–177; and Kawara/omoto lineage, 103, 198–199; Shuri conquest of, 24, 100–101, 136, 167–170, 174, 176–177
Kumemura 久米村 (Kuninda), 50, 78, 112–113, 135–136, 150, 165, 173, **190**, 194, 216, 222, 232–233, 242, 247, 252
Kumenri 久面里. *See* Kumemura
Kundagusuku クンダグスク, 123–124. *See also* bones and rain; Madama grove
Kunigami Keimei 国頭景明 (Wa Ibi 和為美), 142
Kunigami Samanokami 国頭左馬頭, 240–241
Kuniyoshi-maru 国吉丸, 210, 212
Kuroshio 黒潮, 17, 174, 255n2
Kyojin 居仁, 132, **132**, 144
Kyokutei (Takizawa) Bakin 曲亭 (滝沢) 馬琴, 107
Kyūshū tandai 九州探題. *See* Imagawa Ryōshun

Latter Southern Court (Gonanchō 後南朝), 59
Liánghuái. *See* Kaneyoshi
Liáng Mín 梁珉, 71, 84
Lín Xián 林賢, 64
Liú Fāngyù 劉芳誉, 219

Index

Madama grove (Madama-mori 真珠杜), 122–124, 163, 175. *See also* Kundagusuku
Madama minato himon 真珠湊碑文, 140, 266n33
Madama road 真珠道, 140, 190–191, **190**
Madan bridge (Madanbashi) 真珠橋, 86, 140
Makarigane 真刈金 (真刈金 in *Kyūyō*), 170
Mansairei ki 万歳嶺記, 138
Máo Guókē 茅国科, 217
Maritime Prohibitions (*hǎijìn* 海禁), 61, 66, 74–75, 145, 173, 207
Masaku 真佐久. *See* Yonaha-sedo Toyomiya
Matsunoto site マツノト遺跡, 22
Mawashi district 真和志間切, 162, **163**. *See also* three core districts
Mayamato toki no shu まやまと時の主, 55
Meguromori 目黒盛, 54
Michinoshima 道之島, 7, **7**, 26–27, 33, 52, 95, 102, 120–121, 182, 184, 235, 248; governance of after 1609, 237; relations with Okinawa after 1609, 26, 235, 237
Mie gusuku 三重城, 190–191, **190**
Minamoto Tametomo 源為朝, 27, 29–31, 45, 53, 58, 86–87, 98–99, 108, 149, 153–157, 272n15. *See also* Teda Hachiro
Ming naval vessels. *See* ships and shipbuilding
Ministry of Justice (Xíngbù 刑部), 1452 order from, 68, 183
Miusuku Shishikadun 明宇底獅子嘉殿, 57–58, 169
Mō Hōgi 毛鳳儀 (Ikegusuku Peechin Anrai 池城親雲上安頼), 144
Mō Ryūgin. *See* Aragusuku Anki
Momoto-fumiagari 百度踏揚, 116
Momourasoe rankan no mei 百浦添欄干之銘, 139–140, 141, 170
Mongol incursions, 38, 44
Monument to the Garden that Benefits the Country (Ankoku zanju kaboku no kihi 安国山樹華木之記碑), 84, 93, 138
Mottaimatsu site 持躰松遺跡群, 21
Mount Negami and (generic) Negamiyama 根神山, 33, 97
Mount Omoto 於茂登岳 (in Ishigaki), **8**, 100–101, 103, 168, 198–199
Mount Omoto 御許山 (in Usa, Kyushu), **30**, 103, 168, 198–199
Mount Ōtake 大岳, 100–101
Mount Yuwan 湯湾岳 (Mount Obotsu), 103
Murayama Tōan 村山等安, 146, 272n40

Muromachi *bakufu* 室町幕府, 12, 34, 38, 47–49, 74, 145, 244, 248. *See also* Ashikaga shoguns
Muryeong 武寧, 264n5. *See also* Bunei

Naata Ufushu 長田大翁主, 58
Nagara Hachimaru 名柄八丸, 185
Nago Ueekata Ryōhō 名護親方良豊 (Ba Ryōhitsu), 229–231, 233, 235; message to Board of Rites, 236
Nago Ueekata Ryōin 名護親方良員 (Ba Seiei), 211–212, 272n38
Naha, defense of, 189–191, **190**, 230–233; as multi-ethnic port city, 220, 241; as new Ukishima, 23–25, 247; as regional center of human trafficking, 49–51, 188; as "Ryukyu," 247–248; as shipping terminal, 60, 65–66, 72, 74–75, 81, 84, 85
Nakagusuku 中城, 82, 92, 116, **116**, 120
Nakama Mitsukeima Eikyoku 仲間満慶間英極, 57–58, 154
Nakasone Toyomiya 中宗根豊見親, 55, 57–58, 140, 167–170, 177, 179, 188, 273n24
Nakijin 今帰仁, **23**, 24–26, 30, 32, 35, 53, 81, 82, 86, 88, 92, 94–99, 108, 125–126, 137, 148, 163–166, 201, 228–230, 265n32
Nanbei kikō 南聘紀考, 225, 232
Nangumori family なんぐもりばら (難具母里原[腹]), 185
Nanpo Bunshi 南浦文之, 155, 194
Nantō zatsuwa 南島雑話, 28
Nanzan. *See* Sannnan
navigation know-how, 7, 17, 56, 174
Nebara Kanidono 根原金殿, 51
negami 根神, 33
Negami yaemori sashikasa-no-goze 根神八重盛左志笠乃御前, 97
Negamiyama 根神山. *See* Mount Negami
Nirai ニライ (Nirai-kanai ニライカナイ), 199
Nishihara district 西原間切, 114–115, 122–123, 125–126, **163**; *gaara* names in, 101–102. *See also* three core districts; Uchima
Nishikomi 西古見, **19**, 228
Nishitō 西塘, 176–177, 274n49
noro のろ (priestesses), 25–26, 29, 165, 185
Northern Court (Hokuchō 北朝), 38, 47–48
Northern Tier Cultural Zone and islands, 18–28, **19**, **25**, 31, 87, 88, 90, 94, 101, 103, 239, 247, 249
Nyoyō 如瑶, 64

Ō Kishō 翁寄松, 212–213
Ōamu 大阿母, 161, 164, 166
obotsu オボツ (*obotsu-kagura* オボツカグラ), 27–29, 103, 168, 195–196, 198–199, 267n69
Ōei no Gaikō 応永の外寇, 43
official histories (*seishi* 正史), 1–5, 11, 15, 24, 37, 44, 76, 78, 80, 85–87, 90–91, 93–95, 97, 107, 110–115, 118–119, 121, 124, 129–130, 136–137, 140–141, 144, 148–154, 167, 169, 179, 184–186, 211–212, 224, 234, 246, 252–253, 265n48, 268n10
Ogyaka おぎやか, 138
Okinoerabu 沖永良部, 7, 24, 26–27, 40, 45–46, 71, 102, 109, **109**, 120–121, 229, 237, 268n10, 274n49
Ōmo (Wáng Mào) 王茂, 112
Omoigwabe 思子部, 165
O-mono gusuku 御物グスク, 92–93, **190**
Omoro sōshi おもろさうし, xii, 2–3, 137, 194
Omotarugane (Umitarugane) 思樽金, 181, 195
onarigami おなり神, 43
oni (as prefix) 鬼, 95, 195
Oni-Ōgusuku 鬼大城, 116–117, 121, 130
Onisanko おにさんこ. *See* Shō En
Onitora (Unitura) 鬼虎, 168, 170, 188
Ōōso 汪応祖, 78, 80–81
Origins of Lord Samekawa, 31
Orikuchi Shinobu, 108, 258n72
Ōuchi 大内, 74, 193, 205
Oyake Akahachi オヤケ・アカハチ (遠弥計赤蜂). *See* Akahachi
Ō-Yamato 大大和. *See* Yamato
Ōzato 大里 (place), 31, 80, 82, 86, 88, 92, 98–99, **116**, 123, 140

Philippines, the, 62, **206**, 207, 240
plausible procreation zone, 151–153
Portugal, 134, 206
prime minister (*ōsō* 王相 or *kokusō* 国相), 111–112, 194
Prince Ie 伊江王子, 142
problematic behavior of Ryukyuan envoys, 60–61, 67–69, 134–136
pro-Satsuma (pro-Shimazu) faction, 146–147, 182, 211–213, 272n38

rain prayers (*amagoi* 雨乞い), 123
repatriation of Koreans, 41, 49–50, 257n48
repatriation of Ryukyuan ships: from Hirado (1605), 221; from Kaseda (1568), 209–210; from Mutsu (1602), 220–221
rice cultivation in Ryukyu, 45, 98–99, 102, 125
Rice Ear Festival (Ine no ho matsuri 稲の穂祭), 166
Rinkei (Lín Huì) 林恵, 67
royal ancestral tablets. *See* Sōgenji
royal bones. *See* bones and rain
Ryang Seong 梁成, 50, 93–94, 96, 98, 119, 260n65
Ryōkai. *See* Kaneyoshi
Ryukyu 琉球: as de facto shipping company, 60, 66, 74, 80; definitions of, 7–10, **7**, **8**, 246–254; as an empire, 9–11, 76, 96, 127, 161–164, 168–171, 178–189, 238–239; as an imaginary/romanticized place, 252–254; and Japonic culture, 8, 156–157, 239–240, 250; as a maritime frontier, 6, 8, 63, 76, 156, 249–250; as a receptacle for *wakō*, 64–66, 68, 136, 250; as a theatrical state, 251–252;
Ryukyu embassy to Shimazu (1575), 186, 210–211
Ryūkyū gunki 琉球軍記. *See* *Ryūkyū-iri no ki*
Ryūkyū tokai nichinichi ki 琉球渡海日々紀, 225
Ryūkyū tokai no gunshū hatto no jōjō 琉球渡海之軍衆法度之条々, 225–226
Ryūkyū-iri no ki 琉球入の記, 225, 227, 231–232, 379n30

Sado 使道 (K.). *See* Satto, as generic name
Sai On 蔡温, 3, 80, 115, 123–124, 137, 150, 152, 175
Sai Taku 蔡鐸, 3, 150
Sakai merchants (Sakai *shōnin* 堺商人), 34, 74–75, 134, 211
Sakamoto Fuki 坂本普基. *See* Sōmi Nyūdō
Sakibaru grove 崎原御嶽, 51
Sakishima 先島, 8, **8**, 17, 20, 26, 28, 33, 36, 51–52, 101, 103, 136, 168, 170–174, 238, 239; early history of, 53–55, 57–58; Southern Court immigrants to, 58–59. *See also* Akahachi; Honkawara
Samekawa 鮫川 (also 佐銘川), 29, 30–31, **30**, 45, 52, 79, 86, 98, 107–110, **109**, 130, 148–149, 152–154, 200
Samekawa-ōnushi yuraiki 佐銘川大ぬし由来記. *See* *Origins of Lord Samekawa*

Sanban no ōyakumoi 三番の大やくもい, 165
Sanhoku 山北, 9, 65, 77–87, 94, 247, 264n19, 265n32
Sannan 山南, 9, 77–87, 247
Sanshikan 三司官. *See* Council of Three
Sanzan 三山. *See* Three Principalities
Sappanwood, 206–207
Sasamori Gisuke 笹森儀助, 17
Sashikaeshi matsuo no himon サシカヘシ松尾之碑文, 139
Sashikasa 左志笠 (Tokara islands deity), 97–98. *See also* Sasukasa
Sashiki 佐敷 (in Kyushu), 30, **30**, 45, 48, 86, 107–108, 154
Sashiki 佐敷 (in Okinawa), **23**, 29, 30–31, 45, 52–53, 78, 80, 85–86, 88, 92, 98, 108–111, 117, 129–130, 137, 152–153, 164, 268n10
Sashiki grove 佐敷[の]森, **116**, 117, 168
Sasukasa 差す笠 (Kumejima and Okinawan deity), 97–98, 165–167, 200
Sata Ufuhito 佐多大人, 54
Sato 查都 (C. Zhādōu), as alternative for King Satto, 83
Satokan 察度官, 165
satonushi 里主, 83, 164–165
Satonushibe 里主部, 165
Satsuma 薩摩 (province and shorthand for Shimazu territories), 6, 9, 12, 18, 26–28, **30**, 32, 41, 49, 51, 53, 73, 108, 131, 134, 143–147, 155, 181–183, 186, 194, 206, 210–211, 215, 217–218, 220–222. *See also* anti-Satsuma; pro-Satsuma; Shimazu; Shimazu-Ryukyu war
Satto 察度, King, 39, 54–55, 65, 74, 78, 80, 82–84, 125, 140, 149–151; as generic name, 83
Satto (Sato) 察都 (C. Chádōu), as envoy to China from King Satto, 83
screen (*byōbu* 屏風) symbolizing economic wealth, 86, 99
Sea Bridge to the Many Countries Bell. *See* temple bells
sedo 勢頭, 164
Seifaa grove 斎場御嶽, **116**, 129, 164
Seii 西威, 150, **150**
Seiseifu 征西府, 42, 47–48, 56, 63–64
Serikaku priestess 勢理客ののろ, 53, 125, 165
Sesshin 雪岑, 210–211, 222
Shichitō 七島. *See* Tokara islands
Shichitō-nada 七島灘, **xiv**, 17, 174, 255n2

Shidama lineage 師玉家, 153, 181, 185
shigechi シゲ地. *See shike*
shike しけ, 32–33, 44
Shikema River 志慶真川, 95
Shikinabaru 識名原, fighting at, 233
Shimasoe-Ōzato gusuku 島添大里グスク, 80, 86, **116**, 140
Shima-watari no umui 島渡のうむい, 109
Shimazu 島津, 9, 41, 49, 208–213, 218, 236–238, 241–243; attempts to control shipping, 73, 134, 145–146, 208, 210; attempts to trade with China, 63, 145, 213, 217, 220–221; Iehisa 家久 (Tadatsune 忠恒), 213, 221, 226; plans to invade Ryukyu, 221–222; and subordinate lords (*kashindan* 家臣団), 208, 214, 226; Tadaharu 忠治, 145; Tadakuni 忠国, 211; Takahisa 貴久, 209; territorial claims to Ryukyu, 155, 211, 220–221, 244; Yoshihiro 義弘, 209, 226; Yoshihisa 義久, 208–210, 213–215, 226
Shimazu-Ryukyu war, 12, 41; in Amami-Ōshima, 227–228; battle for Naha harbor, 231; Chinese perceptions of, 236; composition of forces, 225–227, 234; Jana Teidō's letter to China, 236; Jana Teidō's resistance, 232–233, 236–237; in northern Okinawa, 229–230; Ryukyuan complacency, 192, 217, 223; Ryukyuan factions, 232–234; Shō Nei's letter to China, 230–231, 235–236; Shō Nei's surrender, 233; in the Shuri area, 230–232; sources, 224–225; in Tokunoshima, 228–229; and Tokara mariners, 225–226, 231; warnings by Shimazu, 220–223; warnings by Xià Zǐyáng, 191–192, 222–223. *See also Ryūkyū tokai no gunshū hatto no jōjō*; weapons in Ryukyu
shinkoku 神国 (land of deities), 192, 199
ships and shipbuilding, 66, 171–176; in Akune, **30**, 174; decorated ships (*ayabune* 綾船), 173, 209–211, 214, 224; disabled Ryukyuan ships, 175, 182, 209, 220, 242; dugout vessels, 173–174; naming conventions, 66, 172, 242, 262n24; in *Omoro sōshi*, 91, 173–174; shipwrights, 174; and timber, 175; Uruka ships, 174–175
Shǐ Shìyòng 史世用, 215, 219
Shō Chū 尚忠, 114, **114**, 117

Shō Ei 尚永, 142–144, **143**, 146, 181–182, 186, 210–212
Shō En 尚円 (Kanemaru), 11, 30, 44, 67, 69, 79, 96–97, 102, 115, 117, 122, 125–131, **132**, 134–135, 138, 141, **143**, 148, 150, **150**, 152, 168, 176, 248, 275n29
Shō Furi (Furi) 尚布里, 110, 113
Shō Gen 尚元, 24, 142–144, **143**, 146–147, 179–183, 185–186, 210
Shō Hashi 尚巴志, 42, 45, 52–53, 59, 74, 78–81, 84–88, 93, 95, 97–99, 107–108, 110–117, **114**, 121, 130, 151–152, 161–162, 164, 189, 200, 247–248, 268n10. *See also* Chinese-sponsored coup; Samekawa
Shō Hō 尚豊, 131, 143, **143**, 146–147
Shō Ikō 尚維衡, 132–133, **132**, 139, 142–144
Shō Kinpuku 尚金福, 110, 112–114, **114**, 268n19
Shō Kyū 尚久, 143–144, **143**, 212
Shō Nei 尚寧, 107, 127, **132**, 143–144, **143**, 220–222, 229–230, 232–237, 240, 278n58; and factionalism, 144, 146, 212–213, 232–233; and Toyotomi Hideyoshi, 213–215; and men from Japan, 208; investiture difficulties, 215–217. *See also* Jana revolt of 1592
Shō Sei 尚清, 5, 11, 127, 129, 132–133, **132**, 137, 142, 146, 149, 165–166, 172, 177–178, 194–196, 275n33; invasion of Amami-Ōshima, 177, 179, 184–185; and military infrastructure, 166, 190–191
Shō Sen'i 尚宣威, 113, 127–130, 132, **132**, 139, 142, 144, 166, 168
Shō Shin 尚真, 11, 69, 76, 84, 135–136, 144–146, 149, 154, 178, 248–249; conquest of other islands, 24, 55, 59, 100–101, 167–171, 199, 201, 250; as de facto first king of a centralized state, 86–88, 248; legitimacy problems, 127–129, 132–133, **132**; and military infrastructure, 176–177, 189–191; missing in *Reflections*, 127; monuments, 6, 138–140; religious infrastructure, 94, 96–97, 130–131, 140–142, 164–166, 193–196, 199–201; seizure and consolidation of power 128–131, 136–137, 161–162, 164–167, 178, 250
Shō Shiro (Shiro) 尚志魯, 113–114
Shō Shishō 尚思紹, 30, 78, 86, 108, 110–113, 117, 149, **150**, 152–153, 189, 240
Shō Shitatsu 尚思達, 112, 114, **114**, 117

Shō Shōken 向象賢 (Prince Haneji 羽地王子), xii, 1, 3, 87, 129, 150, 243–244
Shō Shoku 尚稷, **143**, 152
Shō Tai 尚泰, **143**, 196, 198
Shō Taikyū 尚泰久, 11, 74–75, 102, 113–121, **114**, 125, 128, 130, 138, 141, 168, 200, 248. *See also* Goeku
Shō Toku 尚徳, 4, 11, 21, 44–45, 73, 113, **114**, 115, 117–120, 122–124, 130–131, 149–150, 168, 200. *See also* bones and rain; Hachiman, shrine in Okinawa
Shōsatto 承察度, 78, 82–83
Shōten 聖天. *See* Kangiten
Shunten 舜天, 29, 87, 99, 140, 148–151, **150**, 153–154
Shureimon gate 守礼門, 96, 131, 211
Shuri 首里, **23**, 24, 35, 45, 68, 71, 74, 78, 82, 86, 96–97, 100–101, 116, **116**, 189–199, 237–238; castle, 27, 81, 87, 92–94, 191, 230–234, 250–251; king as "Shuri emperor," 180, 248; local officials and apprentice system for their sons, 179–182, 224, 248–249; as strong center of an empire, 6, 9–11, 86, 127, 136–137, 161–164, **162**, 178, 187–189, 199–201, 246, 248–249
Shuri-mori 首里杜 (sacred grove), 25, 46, 98, 109, 112–113, 117, 119–120, 124, 163–164, 175–176
Shuri-ōyako 首里大屋子, 170, 180, 227
silver, 12, 183, 207, 215, 226; from the Americas, 207; exchange ratios to gold, 207; mines in Japan, 207–208
skeletal analysis, 33–34
slavery. *See* human trafficking
smuggling, 35, 60–61, 63–64, 66, 70, 75, 136, 218, 250
Sōda Rokurōjirō 宗田六郎次郎, 42
Sōda Saemontarō 宗田左衛門太郎, 42
Sōgenji 崇元寺, 149, 240
Sōmi Nyūdō 宗味入道, 208
Song of Eagle Island (*Washi no shima uta* 鷲の島唄), 58
Sonohiyabu (Sonohyan) 園比屋武, 96–97, 131, 163, 177, 199, 201. *See also* Kanahiyabu
Sonton 尊敦. *See* Shunten
Southeast Asia, trade with, 5, 18, 48, 61, 66, 69, 72, 74–75, 134, 145, 173, 174, 206–207, **206**, 248, 276n2
Southern Court (Nanchō 南朝), 11, 31, 34, 38–39, 42, 46–49, 53–54, 56–59, 63–64, 107–108, 157, 200, 250, 261n97

Index 301

Spain, 206–207
suicide after death of ruler (*junshi* 殉死), 140, 149, 168
Suku period スク時代, 54
sulfur, 21, 39, 51, 63–64, 68–72, 78, 94, 263n38
Sulu, sultanate of, 62
Sunagawa 砂川. *See* Uruka
Sutras, 130–131, 141, 164, 170, 226

Taichū 袋中, xii, 5, 119–120, 187, 208, 213
Taihei bridge 太平橋 battle, 231
Taisei (Ōyo) 大世 copper coins, 117
Taiwan, 7, 17, 34, 146, 235–236, 240, 272n40
Takase-Fujian 高瀬-福建 route, 31, 35, 70
Taketomi (island) 竹富島, 8, 51, 58, 101, 103, 176–177
talc stoneware, 21, 249
Tamagusuku 玉城, 53, 92, 98, **116**, 118
Tamaodon no hi no mon たまおどんのひのもん, 139
Tamaudun 玉陵, 139
Tameaki 為明, 180
Tameharu 為春, 170, 179–180, 256n38, 272n15
Tamekoro 為轉, 181, 227
Tamemitsu 為充, 180
Tametomo shrine 為朝神社, 30, **30**, 154. *See also* Minamoto Tametomo
Tameyoshi 為吉, 180–182, 274n15
Tanegashima 種子島, 7, 27, 44, 70, 208, 261n1
Tarama island 多良間島, **8**, 52, 170
Tarumi (Taromai) 他魯毎, 80–81, 86
taxation: by Satsuma, 237; by Shuri, 50–51, 185–188, 215, 238
Teda てだ, 31, 154, 195
Teda Hachiro てだはちろ, 31, 154. *See also* Minamoto Tametomo
tedako shisō てだこ思想, 137, 195
Tedashiro てだしろ, 130
Teganemaru 治金丸 (sword), 99, 140, 266n17. *See also* Tsukushi-chara
Teichō (Zhèng Zhǎng) 鄭長, 67
Teifuku (Chéng Fù) 程復, 112
temple bells, 6; casting in Okinawa, 94, 115; floating on the sea, 45, 118–119; Sea Bridge to the Many Countries Bell (Bankoku shinryō no kane 万国津梁の鐘), 75–76, 114, 117, 138
Tenpi. *See* Tiānfēi

Teruhi 照日 (O-Hideri お日照), 32–33. *See also shike*
Thailand, 35, 134, 206, **206**
Thirty-three Kimi, 165, 196
three core districts, 138, 162, 164
three-in-one deity, 164, 196, 198–201. *See also* Benzaiten
three principalities (Sanzan 三山), 11; Chén Kǎn's conjecture about, 79; as de facto dummy corporations, 77, 84–85; as different brands, 80; disappearance of, 78–79, 111–112; as later constructions, 86–87; no mention in the *Omoro*, 77, 82; royal lines connected with, 78; royal names connected with, 83–84, 247; skepticism regarding existence as territorial states, 78–85, 247; as symbols, 85–87, 161–162
three sister priestesses, 11, 167, 193. *See also* Benzaiten
three sisters deities, 198–199. *See also* Benzaiten
Tokara Cultural Zone, 25, **25**, 27, 32–33, 94, 97
Tokara islands トカラ (吐噶喇) 列島, **7**, 8, 16–17, 27, 33, 43, 49, 97–98, 166–167, 174, 195, 249
Tokara mariners, 174, 218, 220, 225–226, 231, 279n30
Tokugawa Ieyasu 徳川家康, 206, 217, 220–222, 234, 236–237
Tokunoshima 徳之島, 10, 18, **19**, 21–22, 24, 26, 58, 102, 109, 120, 182, 228–229, 237
Tōma Jūchin 当間重陳, 240
Tomari 泊 (near Naha), 24, 50, 81, 93, **190**, 260n65
Tomé Pires, 99
Tomigusuku gusuku 豊見城グスク, **190**, 191
Tomigusuku Ueekata 豊見城親方, 231, 233
tomoe 巴 symbol, 44, 46, 125, 260n45. *See also* Hachiman; *wakō*
tonchi 殿地 (and *tonjū* 殿住), 27. *See also* Tokara Cultural Zone
Torihara Sōan 鳥原宋安, 217, 222
Toyotomi Hideyoshi 豊臣秀吉, Chinese agents seeking information about, 215; defeat of Shimazu in Kyushu, 145, 208–209, 212; demands on Ryukyu, 212, 214–217, pressure on Shimazu to influence Ryukyu, 213–214; information from Ryukyu to China about, 215; and Ryukyu as *yoriki* (supporter) of Shimazu, 214
tribute to Shuri. *See* taxation

tribute trade: as catalyst for power centers in Okinawa, 23, 55; as catalyst for warfare, 88, 121, 136; commodities, 50–51, 70–72; decline of, 69–70, 134, 171–173; frequency and volume, 68–70, 84–85, 88, 171–173; as piracy and smuggling control measure, 60–67, 77–78; restrictions on other countries, 61–62; restrictions on Ryukyu, 69, 135, 171; Ryukyuan abuses of, 60, 67–69, 134–136, 250
Tsukishiro 月代, 45–46, 71, 109, 130, 200–201
Tsukushi-chara (sword) 筑紫ちゃら, 22, 99, 266n17. See also Teganemaru
Tsunagi 津奈木. See Sashiki (in Kyushu)
Tsushima 対馬, 15–16, **16**, 18, 20, 22, 30, **30**, 32–33, 38, 40, 42–44, 47, 49, 61, 70, 72, 134, 195, 200, 249
turbo shells (*yakōgai* 夜光貝), 21–22, 34, 36, 87, 247, 249

Uchima 内間, 115, **116**, 122, 125–126. *See also* Nishihara district
Ufudōmō no himon 大道毛之碑文. *See* Sashikaeshi matsuo no himon
Ugajin 宇賀神, 196
Ukishima 浮島 (in Naha harbor), 23–25, 50–51, 81, **190**, 247
Umi-Kyōtaru 思京樽, 181–182
Ungusuku grove 運城御嶽, 52
Unitora. *See* Onitora
Unten 運天 harbor, **23**, 30, 53, 81, 229, 264n19
Urasoe castle 浦添城, 81, 112, **116**, 129, 141, 231
Urasoe gusuku no mae no hi 浦添城の前の碑, 165
Urasoe line (Urasoe branch) 浦添家, 132–133, **132**, 143, 212, 234. *See also* Shō Ikō; Shō Nei
Urasoe Ueekata 浦添親方, 231–233
Uruka 砂川 (Sunagawa), **8**, 52, 55–56, 174–175
Uruka Ōtono 砂川大殿, 52
Ushuku-ōya lineage 宇宿大親家, 181

Verses and Preface on the Chastisement of Ryukyu (C. Tǎo Liúqiú shī bìng xù 討琉球詩并序), 155

Wa Ibi. *See* Kunigami Keimei
wajin 倭人 (Japanese or quasi-Japanese), 51, 241, 259n11
wakateda shisō 若てだ思想, 195

wakō 倭寇, 6, 174–175; armed merchants in Naha, 183–184; attack of 1556, 183; attacks on Korea, 39, 47–49; Chinese attempts to control, 61–66, 68, 70, 74–75, 136, 247, 250; diverse roles and composition of, 11, 39–41; and early Ryukyuan rulers, 37, 90–92, 107–109, 120–121, 250; and Hachiman, 42–46, 200–201; as intermediaries between Ryukyu and Korea, 41–42, 72–73, 248; and Kumejima, 100–101; latter-period (second-wave), 41, 183; names, 101–103, 242–243; in the *Omoro*, 91–92, 100; in Sakishima, 55–59, 167–168, 174; Shō Taikyū and Shō Toku as, 115, 118–120; and the Southern Court, 46–49, 58–59, 157, 249–250; and sulfur and horses, 40–41, 45–46, 70–72; symbols, 42, 44; and trade in captives at Naha, 49–51
watch (*ban* 番), 161, 169, 176, 189, **190**. *See also hiki*
weapons in Ryukyu, 41, 43, 93–94, 118, 137, 189, 191–192, 218; assessed by Chinese envoys, 182, 191–192; excavated, 34, 90, 102; modern claims that they did not exist, 253–254; in the *Omoro*, 34, 82
wind patterns, 17–18, 39

Xià Zǐyáng 夏子陽: assessment of Ryukyuan geography, 222–223; assessment of Ryukyuan literary culture, 1, 5; assessment of Ryukyuan weapons, 191–192; criticism of Ryukyu, 1, 222–223
Xiè Jié 謝杰, 183

yabusa 藪房 (*yabosa* 矢保佐), 27, 29–30, 33, 44. *See also* Hachiman; Minamoto Tametomo
Yabusatsu grove 藪薩御嶽, **23**, 29–30. *See also* Amamiku; *yabusa*
Yaeyama 八重山, 8, **8**, 53, 55, 57–59, 175, 187; close ties with Kumejima, 101, 167–170, 198–199; early-modern resource extraction by Shuri, 238–239; invasion of (1500), 26, 55, 136, 139, 167–171, 179, 182, 198–199; Kawara and Mt. Omoto, 102–103, 167–171; and Nishitō, 176–177
Yafusa-san. *See* Minamoto Tametomo
Yakushima 屋久島, 7, 27, **30**, 51, 58, 70, 208
Yamashita Chikugo 山下筑後, 183, 212
Yamato ヤマト, 23, 51–53, 55, 73–74, 95–96, 100, 102–103, 242; versus Ō-Yamato, 31; as

Yamato-in 山戸院 or Satsuma, 31–32, 51–53, 73, 108, 258n72, 261n97
Yamatohama 大和浜, **19**, 227
Yamato no ikusa taishō 大和の戦大将 (Great Yamato general), 102
Yamazaki Nikyūshusan 山崎二休守三, 208, 231, 233, 240
Yáng Zài 楊載, 62, 64–65, 74
Yarazamori gusuku 屋良座森グスク, 190–191, **190**, 231, 266n33
Yashiro やしろ (in the *Omoro*), 31–32, 53, 73–74, 108, 258n72. *See also* Yatsushiro
Yatsushiro 八代, 30–32, **30**, 48, 53, 58, 73, 108, **109**, 258n72
Yeongdeung, 43–44. *See also* Hachiman; Halmang
Yoasutabe 世司部. *See* Council of Three

Yomitan 読谷, **23**, 25, 117, 129, 168, 230. *See also* Sashiki grove
Yonabaru 与那原 family, 54
Yonabaru Peechin Chōchi 与那原親雲上朝智, 228
Yonaguni 与那国, 7, **8**, 9–10, 17, 51, 178; invasion of, 136, 168, 170. *See also* Onitora
Yonaha-sedo Toyomiya 与那覇せど豊見親, 54
Yoron island 与論島, 7, 9, **23**, 24, 27, 109, 180, 237
Yuwan 湯湾, 103, 177, 184–186

Zhào Zhì 趙秩, 63
Zhèng Liángnéng 鄭良能, 219. *See also* Hana incident
Zhū Yuánzhāng 朱元璋. *See* Hóngwǔ

About the Author

Gregory Smits is professor of history and Asian studies at Pennsylvania State University. He is the author of *Visions of Ryukyu: Identity and Ideology in Early-Modern Thought and Politics; Seismic Japan: The Long History and Continuing Legacy of the Ansei Edo Earthquake;* and *When the Earth Roars: Lessons from the History of Earthquakes in Japan.*